Praise for
Letters to Poets:
Conversations about Poetics, Politics, and Community

The dialogists of *Letters to Poets* pry open contemporary poetics to expose the social and relational spine of our current world(s) of words. From important emerging writers to America's poetry icons, *Letters to Poets* sizzles into public purview the exchange-values that underpin the contemporary culture of verse.

—Mark Nowak

These correspondences are lengthy treatises on poetry and poetic theory, grief, racial and gender conflicts, teaching, and the minutia of life. These letters are moving, contentious, philosophical, and illuminating. Ultimately riveting, they give you wildly diverse blueprints on what it means "to survive as a poet."

—Cathy Park Hong

In this extraordinary collection, I found a letter written on the day my son was conceived. His moment to choose earth, ours to choose heaven. In the travel between dialogues, between the lessons in these letters, maybe our past gets revealed as students floating in the other's eye.

—Edwin Torres

Reconstructing the mentorship model, *Letters to Poets* revels in literary relationships and discovers new learning systems through the timely pen strokes of 28 poets, offering solid breaths of inspiration, fun, and lessons learned. Within these brave pages are the guiding elements every writer needs in her repertoire.

—Amy King

Letters to Poets is a collection of wildly diverse, thoughtful dispatches that place poets as lineage holders and gatekeepers of cultural memory. These poets' letters bid us to hold what is dear and gift what is known; in this sense, they are all, at their best, love letters.

—Akilah Oliver

Letters to Poets:

Conversations about Poetics, Politics, and Community

saturnalia books

Photo of Alfred Arteaga by Alfred Arteaga
Photo of Jennifer Firestone by Jonathan Morrill
Photo of Eileen Myles by anonymous
Photo of Karen Weiser by Anselm Berrigan
Photo of Anne Waldman by Matt Valentine
Photo of Jill Magi by Jonny Farrow
Photo of Cecilia Vicuña by James O'Hern
Photo of Rosamond S. King by Swati Khurana
Photo of Jayne Cortez by Mel Edwards
Photo of Judith Goldman by Judith Goldman
Photo of Leslie Scalapino by Thomas J. White
Photo of Traci Gourdine by Bryce Marck
Photo of Quincy Troupe by Jerry Jack
Photo of Brenda Iijima by Brenda Iijima
Photo of Joan Retallack by K. Callater
Photo of Dana Teen Lomax by Sweet Angelmouth
Photo of Claire Braz-Valentine by Paulette Fox
Photo of Albert Flynn DeSilver by Mallory Cremin
Photo of Paul Hoover by Paul Hoover

We would like to thank the fourteen poet-pairs who spent several years working on *Letters to Poets*. Their generosity and eagerness to undertake this project made it possible. We also greatly appreciate the editors of *Dusie*, *How2*, *Jacket*, *Poets & Witers Magazine*, *listenlight*, and *Poetry Flash* who published sections of the letters and recognized the project's value early on. We are grateful to everyone at Saturnalia Books, particularly Mishael Devlin for her thorough proofing and fact checking, and Henry Israeli for his enthusiasm and support. Special thanks to Laurie Brooks, Molly Dorozenski, Sarah Rosenthal, Joanna Sondheim and Brenda Tucker for their invaluable insights, and to our interns Lindsey Boldt, Saskia Everts, Ariella Goldberg, Caitlin McGinn, and Roxane Perez for their dedication and skill. Finally, our deepest thanks to Steve Emrick and Jonathan Morrill whose contributions to the project have been immeasurable.

IN MEMORIAM

Alfred Arteaga
May 5, 1950-July 4, 2008

When we asked Alfred Arteaga to be part of the *Letters* project, he agreed imme-
diately. But he had one condition. He wanted to have coffee and find out more
about who we were and our vision for the book. He asked us, "Why are you
selecting me, what is it about my writing that interests you?" He was genuine and
joyful and demanded human connection. This desire to connect on more than a
superficial level, to reach out beyond the project, beyond the page, was Alfred's
gift. His final letter to Hajera Ghori underscores this:

"So while you might hum yourself to individuation on a bus of strangers, I,
instead, consider the dark matter surrounding the both of us that is cancelled
when we see each other, when we speak words, write letters, smile, touch."

We were fortunate to have the opportunity to work with him. He will be
deeply missed.

Contents

To our children
Ava, Judah, & Una

Introduction

Letters to Poets developed from an interest in how we could redefine, renegotiate, and extend the concept of collaboration. For this project, fourteen poet-pairs from various regions, races, class backgrounds, sexual preferences, and aesthetics came together and wrote letters during approximately a one-year period. From the start, the *Letters to Poets* project has been experimental in nature. Having provided no strict formal or thematic guidelines, we had little idea what the poets in this collection would choose to write about. We thought that if poets had the opportunity to correspond with each other over the course of a year, important and intriguing conversations would emerge, prompting further discourse among poets and people in other disciplines. Letters have proven powerful texts. (Consider the correspondences between Dickinson and Higginson, Hughes and Bontemps, Zukofsky and Niedecker, Levertov and Duncan, Celan and Sachs, Silko and Wright, and so on.) We believed the epistolary format would create a sense of intimacy, allowing readers to feel privy to "inside" information about poets' ideas and experiences.

Perhaps the paradigmatic example of poets' correspondence is Rainer Maria Rilke's *Letters to a Young Poet*. The centennial anniversary of this book's publication seemed a timely occasion to commemorate and markedly deviate from our predecessor's "master work." As two feminists from Northern California, we were eager to challenge the approach of *Letters to a Young Poet*. While generally taken as a formidable "how to" on poetry, from many vantages this beloved book of letters may also be seen as flawed and exclusionary, entirely omitting Franz Kappus' voice, and in so doing, marginalizing the questions and real preoccupations of the aspiring poet. Further, Rilke's advice and ideas, while perhaps inspired, are also, in a certain light, questionable. For example, he writes:

> Nobody can counsel and help you, nobody. There is only one single way. Go into yourself. Search for the reason that bids you write; find out whether it is spreading out its roots in the deepest places of your heart, acknowledge to yourself whether you would have to die if it were denied you to write. This above all—ask yourself in the stillest hour of your night: *must* I write?

While it may be sound advice, there are many valid alternative views to this "write or die" paradigm. Flannery O'Connor offers quite a different kind of claim, stating simply, "I am a writer because writing is the thing I do best." And artists from other disciplines describe their relationship to their art somewhat more organically as well; Georgia O'Keeffe once said, "Singing has always seemed to me the most perfect means of expression. It is so spontaneous. And after singing, I think the violin. Since I cannot sing, I paint." There is no pretense of death without their work for these artists; you create what you can when you can because you can.

Moreover, Rilke's tone is that of an accomplished master or what one literary critic calls "absolute authority," which imbues the conversation with a hierarchical dimension, one that keeps the correspondents in their places. Interestingly, Franz X. Kappus himself affirmed this hierarchy: in his introduction to *Letters to a Young Poet*, which he compiled and helped publish after Rilke's death, Kappus claims, "And where a great and unique man speaks, small men should keep silence." We, as the editors of *Letters to Poets*, wanted to allow and encourage nonhierarchical models in this anthology. While we recognized the undeniable power of mentorship, we felt conflicted at the project's outset about using the labels of "established" and "emerging" poets (terms we eventually chose because poets from different periods of their writing lives would be writing to each other), and wanted ways to challenge, skirt, and re-imagine them, which is precisely what many of the participating writers were able to do. Some of the poets address the notion of mentorship head on by either intentionally inverting the prototypical mentor/apprentice line of questioning ("established" poets Leslie Scalapino and Anne Waldman initiate their conversations with Judith Goldman and Karen Weiser, asking them many questions and addressing them as peers and colleagues rather than students or apprentices) or by using their letters to address their discomfort with a mentoring relationship. In his letter to Paul Hoover, Albert Flynn DeSilver asks, "And so, am I supposed to ask a question of the wise elder? Pine for acceptance, praise your genius, or just be with the words and write a letter as it comes in direct correspondence from the void, in the moment?" Paul Hoover responds in turn, "I too feel uneasy with the elder/younger frame of this project. The young poet asks Horace a question and Horace goes on for hours."

Yet our main intent was not to counter or respond to *Letters to a Young Poet*. Instead, we hoped to develop a project that wasn't altogether familiar to readers, that wasn't another anthology of poetry or poetics. Most importantly, we wanted to provide poets with an open forum in which to exchange ideas and discuss their genuine concerns.

Over the course of these correspondences, shared ideas and concerns became apparent. Despite the fact that the participating poets were given no thematic guidelines, the exchanges exhibit a repetition, perhaps an anxiety, regarding certain issues. For instance, the question of the poet's relationship to academia gets scrutinized and argued in various lights, often in surprising ways. When Eileen Myles writes, "I think you have to care less about teaching and wowing them [students] and spend more time going to the movies, and reading and writing and hanging out with your friends. Give less!" she asserts a feminist challenge to young female teachers' overzealous work habits and opens new doors for re-envisioning the teaching artist's role. Similarly, Kathleen Fraser confronts the academy's influence on current poetic practice, questioning the hyper-intellectualization of poetry by proposing "to divert or subvert the poet's riveted attention *away* from the worship of any stylish cookie-cutter vocabulary or self-important drone that seems, too often of late, to precede or diminish a certain spirit of investigatory delight in doing what we do best." Both Fraser and Myles insistently protect the poet's lived experience and warn against various forms of institutional constraints.

Karen Weiser further interrogates academic institutions by pointing out many poets' economic dependence on them, writing that "dropping out isn't a possibility for poets today, as far as I can tell, and definitely not in New York City. Every poet I know has a job, whether it is in academia or not, and struggles with how to balance making money and making art."

Another area of recurrent discussion is the issue of race. In 1903, the same year that Rilke crafted his first letters to Franz X. Kappus, W. E. B. Du Bois published his famous, prescient book, *The Souls Of Black Folk*, in which he examined the nature and complexities of racism. Not surprisingly, the letters in *Letters to Poets* reflect the fact that the "problem of the color line" persists into the 21st century, and analyze the specific and all too real ways that racism and conservatism still remain part of the American experience. Truong Tran describes being asked by a publisher to submit "work that was more traditionally lineated and work that was more Vietnamese in flavor." For Truong, this request reveals what he calls "a society that still insists on filing individuals into a neat rolodex system of race, gender, and sexual orientation." Wanda Coleman responds, "This insidious means of confounding and trivializing the literary excellence of we so-called minorities has been used against virtually every member of every ethnic group American society has produced." Similarly, Rosamond King addresses society's "rolodex system" by challenging the existence of a prescribed order regarding race and art. She writes, "Still, everything tends to fall outside of the lines others have drawn: writing and movement which are too 'weird' (read 'experimental') to be 'Black,' work that is too 'Black' to be included in 'experimental' events or publications (as opposed to Special People of Color Editions). . . ." Jill Magi questions the poetry community itself: "For a long time I have been thinking about how the avant-garde or experimental poetry scene appears to me to be racially segregated, and perhaps also segregated in terms of class. This kind of poetry is so very firmly rooted in the expansion of consciousness, the open reader, open listener. But why are so many participants and audience white?" In turn, Joan Retallack suggests how poets might change (among other things) racist constructs: "I think poets should be offering intelligent (if not always intelligible) and inventive alternative visions for human society. Linguistically enacted thought experiments of various kinds. Alternatives to entrenched language usage that perpetuates current power asymmetries and unwarranted assumptions are always a good start."

These are just a few examples of the many concerns the poets in *Letters to Poets* attend to, and in the process, this anthology forms its own kind of "relational aesthetics." In coining the term "relational aesthetics" in the 1990s, Nicolas Bourriaud claimed, "the role of artworks is no longer to form imaginary and utopian realities, but to actually be ways of living and models of action within the existing real, whatever scale chosen by the artist." Leslie Scalapino implicitly speaks to these "models of action" when she writes, "It seems that now 'the difficulty' (the necessity) of writing is both to be and to apprehend utter transformation of reality, by everyone at once, at every instant of the writing." Hers is a tall order, to make art that changes how we understand and act in the world, and to write from within this action of change, to become it. One of the ways these letters enact this is through the relationships they foster. Ultimately the letters in *Letters to Poets* are neither escapist nor decorative; rather, the core of the project is simply about human connection. As Victor Hernández Cruz writes to Brenda Coultas, "We could be worlds apart but I know we have a lot in common."

*

Letters to Poets developed from a sequence of events that began in the late 1990s, a few years after we met in the San Francisco State University MFA poetry program. The SFSU climate was exciting, driven, and at times alienating; San

Francisco was still buzzing with the vibrations of the language poets, and if a writer wasn't a language poet per se, he or she was most likely discarding/reframing imagistic or narrative tendencies and toying with the concept of being an "experimental" writer.

Though a genuine camaraderie existed as we participated in local readings, exchanged books and ideas, and began our own smaller writing groups at each other's apartments, there was a gap between our ongoing dialogues with each other and our interactions with our professors and with the "established" poets living within the community. Other disconnects existed within our own peer groups. Some classmates were receiving prizes, winning contests, getting published, giving readings. News of these accomplishments would leak into the classroom and create a certain awe and distance around the recognized peers. How did they do it? Did they have connections? Some of these questions exposed our naiveté about what being a poet *should* mean, and some perhaps stemmed from the usual competition and tension that pervade the culture of graduate school. Yet on a larger level, these questions of *how* and *what* these social recognitions meant to the working poet, to her art, were never completely demystified or addressed.

The idea for *Letters to Poets* began to take shape in 2004. Dana was teaching at San Francisco State University and Napa State Hospital and living at San Quentin. Jennifer was living in Brooklyn and teaching at Hunter College and Eugene Lang College at the New School for Liberal Arts. We had many conversations about community, collaboration, and mentorship. Were these words just abstractions? Ideals? We saw how in the places we lived, writers promoted each other by writing blurbs for each other's books, arranging readings together, etc. This mutual support network seemed like a good idea in that it encouraged peers whose aesthetics and politics were appreciated and respected. With this in mind, we wanted to develop a larger collaborative community for ourselves while also bringing together writers of different generations, thereby giving "emerging" writers a chance to ask questions and engage with a series of older, "established" writers whose work they valued.

We set up the project's parameters as follows. We decided that the letters should be written over the course of one year, which seemed enough time for a substantial dialogue to evolve, but not so much time as to dilute the immediacy of the project. We suggested three letter exchanges within the year's span and that each letter should be approximately two to four pages long. We did not require the poets to address any particular theme; the only guideline we offered was that the letters should include the poets' most pressing concerns about poetics, politics, and community.

We ultimately decided to include fourteen established poets whose work we admired and who seemed to be seriously invested in their communities. We primarily selected poets who were located in our immediate areas (New York and San Francisco) so that we could have direct, personal contact with them. However, sometimes this wasn't achievable as poets' jobs or projects forced them to frequently shift their geographical locations.

We began by inviting each "established" poet to select a younger (in writing life, at any rate), "emerging" poet with whom he or she would like to begin an epistolary exchange. We liked the idea of the "established" poets expressing interest in the "emerging" poets' work rather than the more traditional model of the "emerging" poet trying to curry favor with an "established" poet. We also gave each "established" poet the option of having us select the corresponding "emerging" poet.

Selecting and soliciting participants was a learning process. We spent months coming up with what we hoped would be an inclusive list of various poets who were of diverse backgrounds and aesthetics. Yet as the list developed, we began to realize that the very nature of editing an anthology means that in the selection process many fine writers would be excluded. Shortly after the invitations were sent out, rejections began rolling in. For some poets, it was a time issue. Others expressed doubts about the project, believing it to be too self-conscious. Wouldn't poets put their best face forward as they wrote each word? Or as one poet who emphatically declined to participate asked, wasn't the original book, *Letters to a Young Poet*, successful because it was Rilke who wrote it?

Yet those who did accept our invitation were able to avoid such perceived shortcomings. Perhaps it is the personal nature of letter writing, the opening "Dear X," the intimate quality of this project that accounts for its success. In fact, one aspect of *Letters to Poets* that is especially interesting is the nearly universal apprehension and/or discomfort the participating poets initially felt about how to approach their exchanges. Yet the intimacy of the letter form drove people to be more candid than they might otherwise have been. The epistolary model seemed to build in an element of risk and vulnerability. You can't edit out what another writer has written to you.

The initial deadline for the first set of letters was January 2005. Most poets used e-mail to send their letters because of the ease and efficiency. Some poets dropped out of the project for various reasons and others joined as opportunities presented themselves. The project continued to develop over time and several of the dialogues it incited are ongoing, perpetuated by the ideas and controversy they stimulate.

It is also interesting to note the many developments that have taken place since the inception of this project. Some of the poets who began *Letters to Poets* without a published book have gone on to see their first collection in print. Recent conversations with several of the writers in this anthology have revealed their new perspectives on issues discussed in their letters, and a few of them have wished that they could strike parts or even whole sections from their correspondences. But that is the nature of letters: they mark a specific time and understanding that (thankfully) evolves.

—Jennifer Firestone and Dana Teen Lomax

Anselm Berrigan & John Yau

Anselm Berrigan is the author of three books of poetry from Edge Books: *Some Notes on My Programming* (2006), *Zero Star Hotel* (2002), and *Integrity & Dramatic Life* (1999). A CD (poetry, no music), *Pictures for Private Devotion*, is available through Narrow House Records (2003). With his mother Alice Notley and brother Edmund Berrigan, he co-edited *The Collected Poems of Ted Berrigan*, published in 2005 by the University of California Press. From 2003-2007 he was the Artistic Director of the Poetry Project at St. Mark's Church. He has received grants from the Fund for Poetry and the New York Foundation of the Arts, and is core faculty at Bard College's summer MFA program.

John Yau has published more than two dozen books of poetry, fiction, and art criticism. His most recent books include *Paradiso Diaspora* (Penguin, 2006), *The Passionate Spectator: Essay on Poetry and Art* (University of Michigan, 2006), and *Ing Grish*, with drawings by Thomas Nozkowski (Saturnalia Books, 2005), which won Small Press Traffic's Book of the Year. He currently is the Art Editor of the *Brooklyn Rail*, a free monthly maga-zine. He has received awards and grants from the John Simon Guggenheim Memorial Foundation,

NEA, New York Foundation of the Arts, Ingram Merrill Foundation, Peter S. Reed Foundation, and the Foundation for Contemporary Performance Arts. In 2002, the French Ministry of Culture named him a Chevalier in the Order of Arts and Letters. He is an Associate Professor at Mason Gross School of the Arts (Rutgers University) and lives with his family in New York.

Dear John,

I'm staring at a picture of myself holding a fake tommy gun in one of those black and white boardwalk "throwback photos" and remembering how the photographer, a girl of about 16, wouldn't let me pose with the gun pointing up at my chin. She was right to be dismayed, of course, but it was supposed to be a fake photo, and I was supposed to be dressed as some kind of Capone-era gangster, so I figured the gesture of aiming the gun at myself could be included as part of this phony reproduction – if everything else in it was fake, why couldn't the gesture of self-inflicted harm remain? I am enclosing a copy of the photo for you to admire, and wondering what it would be like to have all memory of my life obliterated in the future save this small piece of demented nostalgia.

Part of the reason this has come up for me in the space of this letter to you is the fact that I've wondered recently if early on when I was starting to write (not just poems but record reviews and small pieces of fiction beginning around 18), I wasn't (in part, mind you) using the space of writing as a place to act out self-destructive tendencies that I mostly avoided engaging in for real (except for one incident with a knife and several dozen instances of hopping on the backs of buses and trucks when I was younger). An interviewer asked recently about the relationship between the body and the text in my poems, and beyond the fact that the word "text" drives me completely crazy when referring to poems and makes me feel like a fucking clown (as my brother might say), I could only think of this kind of transferal of harm from body to page.

At this point, fourteen years after starting to write poems, I'm not terribly concerned about the rote psychology of this jag, but instead am interested in the fact that poetry has the capacity to handle the darker aspects of one's imagination (and behavior) while making said aspects be part of the deal (part of the work) rather than taking over and enforcing a standard narrative-as-reproduction-of reality. I mean, I don't think I am capable of slitting anyone's throat, but I've used a poem to really ask myself if I could, and I still wanted the poem to work as a piece of art in the sense of being shapely and sonically alive. One is exposed to so much real and imagined violence in our culture and simultaneously – if you don't do your own research – kept in the dark when it comes to recognizing the totality of suffering taking place in lands where we are at war and doling out death (Iraq) or standing by while masses of people are starved and executed on genocidal levels (Darfur). I feel like my poems have been full of explosions for the last three or four years, and one formal by-product of that is an increased erosion of the boundaries between thoughts as they occur on the surface of the work. I can't tell the difference at any given time between my imagination acting and being acted upon as I write, or at least I feel that way at times. Information comes streaming in at all points of time and space, and I've lately felt like what my poems do for me is regurgitate a lot of that information on my own terms. All that said, I'm still really attracted to humor and weirdness and technical aspects of poetry that, for me, are capable of producing great moments of music and beauty. But I think all of those things have been internalized to some extent so I appreciate them without ever thinking about them anymore, or at least without thinking about producing them.

I realize that I'm not exactly asking you questions, but I think you can get the gist of where I'm coming from enough to respond. Feel free to add or change the terms of anything. It's not a case where I'm asking "what is the role of art, etc.," since I think artists and poets act that out in large numbers every day and the question, a common question in some quarters, is any cultural arbiter's method of actually avoiding the work that's being done altogether, but I am wondering if you can talk to me about writing poems in terms of all the horrific input we receive, are subject to, instigate, live through. What do you think Rilke's poems would have been like if World War I was on 24-hr cable news? I've been trying off and on to figure out a way to get back to writing poems addressed to one person I care for in the last year or so, but it ain't happening. And when I put it in terms of "getting back" I realize it can't happen, and I don't want it to happen. Someone recently asked me about the division between notions of text-based poetry and voice-based poetry, and I mainly thought "ack" . . . I will do what I have to do according to no one's dogma about what a poem should be like, and my life will always be in there somewhere, since it is difficult, I imagine, to write poems when you are dead (though it doesn't seem as difficult to get published).

The funny thing is, finally, that I don't think about poems when I'm writing them. I do think about emotion and information, but it's more like they're passing through than sticking around for analysis of the degradable-type.

I'm going to head off to the latest, greatest institutional space for visual art in New York City, the refurbished MOMA, when I finish this letter. Is there any new work there, or am I to just be impressed by a different space filled with the same art (or maybe some stuff from their big basement)? Have you seen it yet? Has Cerise helped you write any of your poems yet?

Love,
Anselm

New York, New York

January 13, 2005

Dear Anselm,

There are so many people who are convinced that they have the right answers that I am wondering if we haven't started losing sight of what the questions might be. Or, worse, there are rote answers to what have become rote questions. If one were to take a test, how could one not be the perfect student? The dance steps have been laid out on the floor, and one need only follow in the appropriate manner. In this way, the new story mirrors many of the old stories. Once, at a dinner in Marseilles, during a large gathering of poets after a reading, I asked the person sitting next to me where she was from. It was a clumsy attempt at small talk. The person across from me, a French poet who has translated many American poets, interrupted me and said this was a typically stupid American question. She pointed out that in France it wasn't interesting or even necessary to ask such a question because one's family most likely would have stayed in a town or region for many generations. I was dumbfounded because I thought this person had made, and had felt comfortable making, a number of presumptions. I did not tell this person that my mother-in-law is French and Jewish and had to hide in France in World War II, that she went to Israel after the war. In my experience, this person's finger-wagging lecture is not atypical. She made a gesture, and wanted to make sure I understood how right that gesture was. It was not a gesture to be answered, because that person spoke from the position of absolute authority. It was a way of being clear that no dialogue would take place.

The question I think you are asking, and the one I am trying to answer, is how do any two people begin talking to each other. I don't think I began writing poetry out of a desire to talk to someone, to send (one could say) a love poem to either a specific or general you, but out of the recognition that there was no one to talk to. I don't mean this as a dramatic fact, but as a fundamental one. I suspect that Rilke wouldn't have felt different if World War I was on 24-hour cable news. I have been wondering about this division you seem to imply in your letter. Does one write poems addressed to a general you or to a specific you? Does one speak for some, many, all, any, one or none? Perhaps this is the wrong order. A few years ago I read a number of books on Multiple Personality Disorder, language acquisition, and recovered memory. And during this time, I considered (as I did before and still do, which is not to say "conclude") that one might no longer be writing a poem addressed to one person (Rilke's angel) out there. Rather, it might be that one is trying to write a poem addressed to all the voices (manifestations) one hears in one's head. Or maybe, and here I am thinking of Jack Spicer, one is trying to register their different tonal registers, the range of sounds they make, the inchoate emotions. In a taped conversation of Stan and Jane Brakhage and Hollis Frampton, Frampton says this about the well-known image of St. George slaying the dragon: "The dragon has often been emblematic of what is unwarranted and surprising, and thus undesirable, in perception and imagination." Stan's response speaks, I think, to the question you've raised. He proposes that Sergei Eisenstein made the "mass of people" into "the hero," and that until then they existed in history as a "pretty ugly apparition." Baudelaire would agree. The other dilemma the artist faces is "to find a way to make manifest to the general air [one's] own socially unacceptable particularities."

Where I think things have changed since Brakhage made these observations is in one's sense of place. The bustling, terrifying crowds that Baudelaire encountered in the streets of Paris shared the same physical space but did not, as the poet made evident, experience it in the same way. But what is the physical space we share today? If you happen to live in New York (as we do), is it MOMA? Is it "reality TV?" Is it the spaces that are offered to us in carefully edited glimpses (the so-called news)? Is it the spaces we see in the photographs of Robert Frank and Garry Winogrand, but which are now gone? Is it the megalopolis we inhabit, built on the ruins of hundreds of civilizations, and containing neighborhoods we will never visit or perhaps even know about. For this megalopolis is both lateral and vertical.

A few years ago, Paul Theroux published a piece about a dominatrix in the *New Yorker*. At that moment something in the general air changed. As you know, one of things Theroux publishes is called travel writing. In this piece, Theroux meets the dominatrix on a safari, and the writing that appears in the *New Yorker* could be called a "profile." The reader learns various facts about her and her clients. She likes to eat sushi for breakfast, because it has a lot of protein. She was on the safari with one of her clients. Twenty years ago (was it more or less?), Raymond Carver published his fiction in the *New Yorker*. They were stories about people living in trailer parks, about people who did not read the *New Yorker*. And, to come at it from another perspective, these characters lived in places that people who read the *New Yorker* don't generally inhabit or visit. With Theroux's piece, the terrain shifted a little (a tiny temblor, you might say), if only for the time of that article (a week). So the news of different neighborhoods and cultures is filtered through the *New Yorker* and other strainers, and made palpable to the taste of the audience. With Carver and Theroux, the reader becomes a voyeur. But we also know that that audience consists of people for whom Theroux's piece is not news. How can the erosion you mention not be inevitable?

The poetry world isn't divided between those who believe in (insert whatever word you wish) and those who believe in (insert whatever oppositional word you wish). It is adrift and breaking apart and reforming itself. It is difficult to get a larger perspective. We can't rise above this thing we are on (and in) to get a sense of where it is going, and what it is becoming. There are those who believe they can and should steer this raft, and are angry because not enough people listen to them. Or perhaps this raft is really made up of many smaller versions, each with its own constituency. Or perhaps the point is not to climb aboard any of the ones you encounter. Ack, I am getting allegorical.

One thing you wrote that sticks in my mind, which is that you don't think about poems when you are writing them. We live inside language. How to think in it and write at the same time? I don't think I can talk to you about writing poems in terms of all the horrific input that comes at us everyday. The person in Marseilles could tell us, but that is not who I want to listen to. I think you make art in spite of everything, and that maybe instead of teaching others, you learn something from this thing that we do.

Love,
John

Brenda Coultas & Victor Hernández Cruz

Brenda Coultas is the author of *The Marvelous Bones of Time* (Coffee House Press, 2007), *Early Films* (Rodent Press, 1996), and *A Handmade Museum* (Coffee House Press, 2003), which won the Norma Farber First Book Award from The Poetry Society of America and a Greenwald grant from The Academy of American Poets. She was a New York Foundation for the Arts Fellow in 2005. Her poetry has been published in the *Brooklyn Rail*, *Encyclopedia*, *Conjunctions*, and in many other journals. Brenda Coultas lives in the East Village in Manhattan.

Victor Hernández Cruz completed his first collection of verses, *Papa Got His Gun, and Other Poems* (Calle Once Publications, 1966), in his teens and published *Snaps* (Random House, 1969) at age 20. His other works include *Mainland* (Random House, 1973), *Tropicalizations* (Reed, Cannon & Johnson, 1976), *By Lingual Wholes* (Momo's Press, 1982), *Rhythm, Content, and Flavor: New and Selected Poems* (Arte Publico Press, 1989), *Red Beans: Poems* (Coffee House Press, 1991), and *Panoramas* (Coffee House Press, 1997). He lectured at the University of California, Berkeley and taught at San Francisco State University. Among his numerous awards are the Guggenheim Fellowship and the New York Poetry Foundation Award. Born in Puerto Rico, he writes in English and Spanish, and moved with his family to New York City in 1954.

Dear Mr. Cruz,

It is difficult to write a letter to someone you mostly know on the page. I have
heard you read at the Poetry Project at St. Mark's Church on the Bowery, and I
know that you won the title of "Heavyweight Poetry Champion of the World,"
which is further evidence that you are a master of the oral tradition and a fierce
competitor. On the surface, we are an unlikely pair of correspondents, but there
are some things we share. We are both poets of lower Manhattan, respectively, the
East Village and Loisaida, and we are poets of the countryside: Indiana and
Puerto Rico.

In your essay "Writing Migrations," you state "Forget about history textbooks;
poems are the best way to study and teach history. Poems are testaments of the
actual experience of living through a personal and public event; they are the
closest thing to the truth." I see that in your work, the documenting of place,
people, events, and languages. Your poems serve as maps of the physical as well as
maps of the emotional life of a community.

Also I am not a young poet, I guess the term is "emerging poet." I'm a slow poet.
An underachiever. About ten years ago when I was a "young poet," some of my
peers were invited to appear in a major women's magazine as poets who repre-
sented the glamorous side of poetry; however, I was rejected by the editors
because of my age. I nearly died laughing, so much for women's rights! Too old
and too unglamorous!

A late bloomer, I started my serious writing at 27. I had tried to write a novel
when I was about 10 but I couldn't figure out how to move a character from one
place to another without describing every step and every thought. I couldn't get
someone out of a room in less than a page.

On the serious side, sometimes in the dark, I wonder if I have wasted my life.
Maybe the price has been too high? I remember a line from an Allen Ginsberg
poem written in his later years, "If had a soul I sold it for pretty words." Sometimes

I wonder if I have only one book in me. Those are the dark days when my writing is suffering or I feel overwhelmed by other commitments. And I know that they will come again when I have been away from my writing for too long, then I have to fight past the garbage and noise in order to find my voice and subject. It's a painful and long process, sometimes taking a week or more of sitting and staring before anything promising emerges. Do you have this difficulty? These demons?

I write in a railroad tenement with my husband, our desks side by side, in this city where the average apartment sells for half a million dollars. I have a desktop of my own, that's the best one can hope for. What I lack is the open time needed for language, images, and ideas to develop, for the mind to quiet. In the apartment, there are distractions, the dishes, the phone, the gritty floors (the air is dirty). Do you believe that there is a generation of poets missing in action because they are working three or four jobs to pay the rent?

I think my writing is too full of objects. I'm too full of sentences and that comes from teaching composition, my bread and butter. Teaching fills my head with other people's sentences. Sometimes I can't hear my own thoughts. I fear losing my voice, my rhythms. (The truth be told is I'd rather not have a job, but that's another letter.) Plus I had a prose leaning from the get-go, but all of these sentences and objects make it hard to fly. I am afraid of developing a lead foot. A tin ear. And my word choices—I prefer to believe that I am writing in the "plain speech" mode of W.C. Williams whereas some reviewers think my language is simply dull. I'm earthbound, whereas you are able to fly.

It is still difficult to steal time for writing; there will always be the temptation to squander energy elsewhere for more immediate gratification.

After writing about the Bowery for the past few years, I have returned to the Southern Indiana landscape to write about folklore, the north-south border, and the boyhood home of Abe Lincoln, which is my home county. I worry that I am too specific. How can I know if my interests will interest others? Have you ever been afraid of losing your audience? Although I know better than to write for love (of the audience), I think poets want to be heard.

Best,
Brenda Coultas

Brenda,

Good to hear from you, up there in the north. Thanks for those prose poetics containing so much detail of the Lower Manhattan streets. I was once an adolescent through those streets and emerged out of there on the wings of poetry, which after thirty-five years is still a hobby of mine. Well that's what my father once told me . . . "You don't have a profession or a job, you have a hobby." And within this hobby one seems always to be an emerging poet especially in the United States where books of poetry circulate so poorly or rather so it seems, but the shine of poetry is the center of reality, especially in antiquity, but even now we must see the reality occulted by so much mush and kitsch culture. As poetry documents human life when it is within fresh and original winds of observation, away from repetitions and cliché, that we might see the color, texture and emotional experience of our lives within our lives happening, outside of the textbooks and the newspaper, the most accurate temperature of the times.

Poetry in the sense of making something belongs to everyone and is everywhere and happens everyday outside of language as well, dance is very poetic, or contemplating a tropical landscape under a blue sky is a poem. You mentioned William Carlos Williams and I am so glad because I too have learned much from him. He said something to the effect that people suffer from not knowing what is within poems. Even if they could live their lives without ever giving poetry as much as a glance or an ear. But if you take a bird's eye view of history and cultures you will see how poetry takes again and again center stage. And for that we should keep faithful to our wordsmith hobby, productive and observant.

You mentioned the importance of place, you're wavering between Lower Manhattan and Indiana and I for years have had a pendulum swing between the urban and the rural tropical. I also use my Caribbean geography as a point of departure. Here in the Caribbean we are a racial stew, many geographies come together here . . . the Andalusian culture of Spain which came here upon boats to find the native Taino yucayeyes and the aroma of tobacco. The Spanish brought the African, our San Juan architecture is Andalusian. Many of the southern Spanish cities were built up during the Muslim occupation. Walking around seeing the melting of the races is always a narration, a poetics of migration and the appropriation of other parts of the world. It is an endless study and mission within my poems; the poem to me is more and more a place where I think and where I have doubts. I like that quality when one feels the poet breathing, analyzing openly as one goes forward, in the writing. When I write poems, I almost never look back. It's like the poem happens within a now that is shifting to a future; I never look back as I do when I am writing prose narrative. Maybe that's why poets and poetry stay within an eternal emergence. Poetry is fresh and stimulating, it also comes like a nervous charge to me; I'm sure it raises the blood pressure. It's nomadic and unsettled, maybe that's why prose narrative is coming to me now after so much jumping around. I heard a writer say once that she began writing novels when she calmed herself down, became tranquil. You have lived more and have observed. Which is not to say that fine narration does not come out of the blue to someone very young, this happens too. Your little stories are poetic; I have trouble with my prose, writing is a very painful (torturous) process, I don't know but it doesn't come naturally to me. When I have worked on long narration it takes a sitting just to do three pages. Prose I always write by hand first, with pencil on a legal pad, then into the computer rewriting as I go along. And no matter what I write I am always insecure about it, insecurity is something like the other side of the coin of writing.

We could be worlds apart but I know we have a lot in common. I have lived in Puerto Rico for fifteen years and seven years ago I traveled to Morocco and met there my wife, and now the last seven years I live between Puerto Rico and Morocco. In Puerto Rico, I am surrounded by Spanish, in Morocco, by Arabic, my literary language is English and sometimes Spanish but mostly English so I am always somewhat at odds with the local phonetics of where I happen to be. Actually it makes me focus, it isolates and separates me. Yet so much comes to me not through language but through gestures, grimaces, climatology, smells. So much of a poem is not words but an environment, physical and emotional, created within us. Let me know if you feel what I am saying, I am full of contradictions in the same way as I am full of races and rhythms and landscapes. Precisely that is what I like in a poem, when it breathes gardens of ideas and is not concerned with making polemical or logical sense all the time. Or something called accuracy. Poetry is not an encyclopedic entry. It does not have to be true. Reality is a chaos, approximating it is always beautiful. Poems are just glimpses, evidence which no science can dismiss. Let me know what you are writing of late and what you are reading. Stay warm up north. I almost feel guilty, we are getting some cool breezes down here, they call them las breezas de navidad, but it's just a coolness never encourages snow, snow, I miss it sometimes.

Victor Hernández Cruz

New York, New York
April 11, 2005

Dear Victor,

I'm writing this morning from Canal St., just below Chinatown where I have an office share for the time being ('till May). I've been without a room of my own for over 2 years. Today is a Friday, the building is quiet. I turn off the radio and begin to focus.

We are still absorbing the news that our great friend, Robert Creeley, is gone. Last night I went to a reading of French poetry, good to be among poets in times of grieving. I heard that he had been traveling as a visiting poet and became sick in a damp, drafty house. And this information led to a discussion of whether or not poetry cost him his life, that he should have been home, near family, taking it easy. Some people might think poetry killed him, but I think poetry most likely gave him extra years of life. I think of Herbert Huncke, Gregory Corso, poets whose addictions should have led to an early grave; however, they lived to become old men. I put it down to poetry, the love and pleasures, even the pains, or those things which Williams writes of, or "the hobby," as your father calls it, of poetry. Maybe it's worth sticking around for. When I write "we," I'm speaking of the community of poets whose lives are centered around The Poetry Project, but that is not accurate, not even close; there is Buffalo, San Francisco, Boulder, Providence, Chicago, Austin, Minneapolis, those are some of the places where kindred spirits live. I consider you a member of my community although miles separate us and we've never formally met. It's an idea that makes us one. A utopian impulse, not a geographic location. Victor, how do you define community? In the last two years, there have been many losses: Kenneth Koch, Larry Rivers, Jackson Mac Low,

Pedro Pietri, John Fiske, the sound engineer, not a poet, yet a member. You might have known him or seen him with his long beard, beer in hand, behind the DAT recorder, when you last read there. After his death, we went to his apartment on the sixth floor of a tenement building, to help carry boxes down. In one room were recordings dating back to the 70's. Handwritten on one reel-to-reel tape, "Reznikoff, Koch, Berrigan." Boxes of tapes, some of which are probably the originals and only copies. Although I had known him well for ten years, I never knew that he had regularly traveled to Brooklyn College every Friday to record Allen Ginsberg's class. This one person, a non-poet, gave up his real time for poetry.

I am thinking today of the price we pay to be poets. At age 30, I gave everything up to move to Boulder, Colorado to study with Anne Waldman, Bobbie Louise Hawkins and Allen Ginsberg. I left a horrible, but steady job with health insurance and ten years of seniority. Some people thought I was crazy to go; in fact, I could have retired by now. I had a large and cheap apartment with two fireplaces. My family was there. I ran a reading series and found some satisfaction in that. It took me years to discover my calling and the courage to say yes to it. Was it worth it? I ended up with a livelihood (teaching) and a community. It would have been easier to stay, very comfortable; however, I would never have challenged myself, and I could have easily ended up in a factory ready to shoot my brains out. (Speaking of that, Indiana has a serious crystal meth problem. People are cooking it up at home or in the back of a moving vehicle, have to keep it cool. My brother says you can tell who's on it because their lights are on all night. People are snorting their brains out).

You asked what I'm reading, my officemate has a large collection of French poetry (in translation), so I raid her bookcase when I'm here. I'm reading *Intimate Journal* by Nicole Brossard, a Quebec poet. Eleni Sikelianos' memoir of her dream-struck father, *The Book of Jon*. And *The California Poem*, a long epic history of that state. I'm reading documents from the Indiana historic society on the underground railroad in southern Indiana. I began this exploration after reading a Naropa University summer catalog about crossing borders and how this might include crossing over lines of gender, race, or language. I had never considered the border I grew up on before, between the free and the slave states. Was there an underground railroad? What were the attitudes of the whites towards blacks? How was it possible for Lincoln to have come from my county? I'm reading *Tales of Beatnik Glory*, 4 volumes by Ed Sanders, over 750 pages, for a review on a website. It's set in the East Village in the 60's and I recognize the places, like the Catholic Worker, that are still here. It's partly a romance, labor rights tract, and civil disobedience primer. Reading it from the dystopia of this century, it seems like a fairytale with its talk of cheap rent, love, awesome orgies, and an anarchy. Just bought Bob Dylan's *Chronicles*, which I like for the history of the 60's folk scene. I should note that this list is incomplete and subject to change. Meanwhile, there are books stacked in a holding pattern, waiting their turn to land.

Sincerely,
Brenda

Sale, Morocco
July 7, 2005

Brenda,

I write to you from Morocco from the medina of Sale—centuries back the Moors of this population were the ones that made up the people of Al-Andalus, the name of southern Spain during the Islamic period, really there are some Moroccan families here with last names like Perez and Torres. Traveling here I always venture via Spain staying in hotels either in Madrid or Sevilla to rest a day before I cross the Strait of Gibraltar into North Africa. I have friends in Andalucia and stay there for periods as well, so when you ask me what is my definition of community I have to include the styles and music and sensibilities of Andalucia and that of my second homeland, Morocco. Spanish stretches and spices with accents of North Africa, the Arab language Berber and African culture, the Caribbean is connected through southern Spain, so my sense of community is never local, but a weaving of connections, historical and present. It's exciting that I don't always understand what is being said yet I don't feel threatened, I don't need exactitude, on the contrary it plays into my poetic Improvisations, I observe gestures and I am amazed at how much human communication is without the language of words. Moroccans for instance have a whole system of hand and facial gestures; they can express many specific states by the use of fingers, they can communicate in front of you without you being aware of it, they immediately know when someone is a foreigner, even someone like me who could pass for a native. This reminds me of the language of the hand fan developed in Spain and also used in Puerto Rico especially at the turn of the century. It is a women's language, a secret code, doing certain movements with their fans, opening and closing them, depending if with the right or left hand, if they open them half way, if they make a circle in the air, if they tap their left or right shoulder, hold it in the hand in a certain way, women reputedly communicated with their lovers right in the presence of their husbands. Thus gestures and feelings, intuitions are signs that I constantly look for when I cross borders, enter living rooms, sleep in chambers as a guest. What is my poetry about if not the construction and the reinforcement of bridges visible and occulted that unite people through many geographies.

Last year here in Morocco I read Henry James' *Portrait of a Lady*, talk about contradictions: living in the North African culture and reading about all those anal retentive Euro-Americans and Europeans feeling the sharp splendor of the language; focused in on the English as the sound of Arabic inundates my ears, it privatizes the language for me, makes it all the more special, to feel, observe, the intricate architecture, the floors, chambers that this fine American novelist constructs right through you. Right now I am reading *Madame Bovary* by Gustave Flaubert, an edition of Penguin Popular Classics, it is truly a delight, Flaubert is such a painter, a landscape artist.

". . . his pupils vanishing into the white of his eyes like blue flowers in milk."

Ah when I read such lines I put the book down, such power of description like a definition of writing, in Spanish it's escribir, so close to describir (description) so I long more to exhaust the observations I make in words, what does the physicality of place suggest, what you see should mix with what you imagine. This all should get better with experience. In writing I suppose there are things (strength) that only time will reveal. Reading for me is based upon moves I am either there with the book or I can't penetrate it, we move in the direction closer to grasp like slowing down the jet flow of the motion thought-river, sometimes slowing it such that when it is read it feels so brisk quick, like have you read *On The Road* by Jack Kerouac, the prose in that book, the movement of the scenes, feel like cartoons to me, constantly defying logic yet so accurate to the matter being transferred. Writing makes such everyday things so fresh, those poems you write about the Lower East Side, those walks through the Bowery, the things you observe there are so memorable in the color and odor, have you, you must have read Williams' poems, he has a great eye for shape and color, that poem of his where perhaps he took a break from his duties as an Intern at the French Hospital in Hell's Kitchen and went up on the roof and he sees this broken green bottle; we see with him the pieces of broken green transparency as well. Lorca is also great like this, using colors sometimes mentioning them twice to give more emphasis like when he declares "la leche blanca" white milk as if milk would be anything other than white, yet he had to have it whiter. Look at what I am going to tell you, Latinos sometimes say as if to emphasize the visual quality of the words you are about to hear.

I have fond memories of Robert Creeley, we once went on a four-city tour together and I got to know him better, it was way over a decade ago, something set up by Deborah Oat the then director of the very active Just Buffalo Literary Program. We read in Buffalo, Detroit, Milwaukee and San Francisco. He was a poet that had such a grasp on the exactitude of what he was doing. May he rest in rhythm.

Well I think this is all for now, next week my wife Amina, my son Mohammed Amine and I will go south and spend a week in Marrakech. I have been there before, it is one of my favorite cities.

Salam Aleukum,
Victor Hernández Cruz

New York, New York
September 21, 2005

Dear Victor,

I had been struggling to write a political poem, not just a rant, but also something lyrical and original if possible, but like always, I found myself saying the obvious "fill in blank sucks!" along with a list of grievances. This spring I attended a lecture by the poet Sapphire who said that the current administration left her speechless. That is how I have felt too, speechless: unable to respond to the enormity of the crimes and shocked by the lies and ineptitude.

There are times when I'm going to a march or a benefit and I want to write a poem that will move people to action, that harnesses the power of language. Instead I blank and end up borrowing a slogan or someone else's sign or scrounging my papers for something I can adapt to the cause. Likewise, writing a poem for an occasion, the poem sometimes arrives years late, on its own time. I don't know if there is a way to force a poem (when I force a poem into the world it shows) or a key to instant inspiration, a bottled muse I can open. I suspect that the problem is in my definition of a political poem; I tend to look for the obvious, the direct address rather than the occult.

This summer I tried allegory, using my background of growing up on the border between a free and a slave state on the Ohio River Valley. I grew up a few miles from Abe Lincoln's boyhood home so that enters the poem too. I thought I might find the metaphors, the language there. I've been reading abolitionist writings and slave narratives, researching the Underground Railroad that ran between Kentucky and Indiana. I bought a rare book, a memoir written by the son of a conductor on the railroad and self-published. I thought that by examining this old conflict and divide that I could comment on the current division of this country. At the same time it is difficult to manage the research, there are so many angles and tons of materials to draw upon. So I try to stay narrow in order to create depth. At the moment it's a shapeless mess, and still resting on the surface.

I think of you as a political writer, as original and graceful. Do you think of yourself as a political poet? Or do you even believe in the term? Some poets find it too limiting of a label. How do politics and language influence each other? Do you believe that all writing is political? Is border crossing a political act?

Victor, I want to thank you for your patience, generosity and willingness to share your wisdom and worlds. Perhaps we will meet in person one day on this island called Manhattan.

Yours,
Brenda

Brenda,

I know how your mind is asking questions, it comes down to the event of how is it that we poets can become more effective. For me all observation is a political act, it all leads to an awareness of the human social condition. As we know, aesthetic poetry is off to a margin, but of late, performance poetry, or what is called spoken word, rap, hip hop are all making massive awareness as to the power of poetic evocation. Perhaps here is where Bob Dylan and Agustín Lara (Mexican composer) come in, none of these two songwriters sang too well. In the U.S. the landscape is inundated with language, records, media, print. If you self-publish you just about can say anything you want, the authorities know this, they also know the limit of your reach, the circle of your audience, it's poets of like minds talking to each other, giving each other the exhilaration that they are free to say what the fuck, making them think that this is democracy. The system has lots of censorship when they know your material is tough and crisp and uncompromising. Someone like Amiri Baraka should know about this.

I for one don't care about George Bush, we shouldn't be disturbed by dogs, or low caste people and the power they have, they are average minds with a lot of power and attention, but for me they are just farts who don't know the true history of how cultures and science weave. They are always into themselves, personas of ill-manners and zero imagination, they cannot perceive other people or the pain that they are causing them. Obviously you can't reach them through language.

In my poetry I try to follow the natural flow of culture, music and song, how Arabic musical forms and cantico have survived in certain Puerto Rican and Venezuelan popular forms. This way I spread out geographically, crossing borders, making dialogue with other folks, following this string of a voice that trembles in flamenco, in North African forms and in Caribbean bolero. This is a high task that poets and artists have to their charge, politicians cannot perceive the connections. They run on the mistake of supporting singular interests, they live off antagonisms and public funds, thus they are the last of the welfare recipients. We poets, artists, cultural workers have a larger drama, we are the tempo of the voices of people and the radiation of geologic earth, describers of how ether sits upon earth's face and the drama of lives pushed and pressed against forces almost always unfair. Life is a struggle, life is making a living, life is commerce. Transaction.

Federico García Lorca comes to mind because he got killed due to a series of freak determinations, he is a poet who is not political in his work, for instance. So he was not killed by the Spanish fascist forces because of his politics. Read his poetry. Feel how ingrained he was in the psyche of his people, in the spirit of the eye, the way it looks at sex and color, love and jealousy. The Spanish people saw themselves when they read his poetry, they saw aspects of themselves, the mestizo of themselves when they read his gypsy poems and his Arab-inspired poems. Even if Gypsy and Arab were just themes for him, they were realities entangled in his Andalucia. People who know themselves are difficult to control. But even that I don't think explains his death.

Is it that the Latino Arabic mode is affected more by words? In Latin American countries poets are either tortured, Victor Jara in Chile, or made ambassadors, Octavio Paz in Mexico. But most world regions have this same sense of language penetration. Maybe the matter is in contemporary American culture, inundated by videos, pornography, books, Barnes and Noble, Borders, television, CDs, DVDs, movies, inundated to the point of being ineffectual. Look what happened to Salman Rushdie with a book that is not his best, looking at his work I would say *Midnight's Children* was a stronger work. But it shows the power of language and how it affected a fundamentalist Khomeini, not the whole of the Iranian people, (a survey taken at the time revealed that 80% of Iranians were against this dictate, which is also against Islamic law, for no one can be sentenced without a trial). None of this information came out in the Western media.

It all comes down to the truth that words are effective, that poets combine feeling/thought in fresh combinations. Maybe our poems will move no one to action as you suggest, but the revelations will become part of the slow churning, the slow changing center of populations. Populations are basically conservative, rural people even more so, maybe when the countryside finishes emptying out into the urban centers there will be change in leaps, by that time there will be freaky ecological factors to deal with as well. The rural has always been a warehouse of songs and wisdom, home remedies, that's why your exploration of the Ohio River Valley, highlighting the Underground Railroad between Kentucky and

Indiana, has so much voice, so much pain that can be revealed, so much private embarrassment that it will expose that some people might just repent.

Now I'm down here in the colony and I feel the weight as such. Just recently we were invaded by FBI agents, in other words, the Federal government, and they assassinated Filiberto Ojeda Rios, the leader of the Macheteros, the People's Army for Liberation. They found him after hunting for fifteen years; they shot up his house with high powered guns from the ground and from helicopters, shot him, left him inside wounded to bleed to death, motherfuckers. This is the same way the Israelis kill HAMAS militants in the Middle East—political assassination. Filiberto Ojeda Rios was also a fine Salsa musician who played first trumpet with the Sonora Ponceña and other groups. He was also a 72-year-old man with heart problems; he had a pacer helping his heart tick. His house was filled with music, paintings and books. A bunch of dogs came down here just to assassinate him. And mind you the problem is not Bush, Bush is a lump of shit [1] that will be flushed by history, the problem is the American people who have a wounded psyche, a fear downgrading the potential of what that great culture has produced: Ralph Waldo Emerson, Walt Whitman, what Nathaniel Hawthorne described by revelation in *The Scarlet Letter*. That fine tradition of jazz and blues, that center of fusion, which is New Orleans, ironically now almost destroyed (Hurricane Katrina days). Poets must help, and I agree with you when I feel your inquiry, to heal and lift the wounded psyche of the people, to bring them to more creative ground. To have them feel words thoughts through mind that filter through heart.

My sister up north I am full of hurt down here, we have been reminded of our powerlessness, we have been invaded once again, and like Sapphire I too am speechless but I am also sharpening my pencil because these wounds should always lead to poems, poems that reveal. Poetry is the height of awareness; it is at the margins always threatening the false stability and decor of the center.

Victor Hernández Cruz

---

[1] Don't think that those metaphors are harsh. It is what the devil brings out of us. To say Bush is a lump of shit is an insult to the substance and I would rather the line read that he is a beast that will be caged by history. Overall that's the danger of giving the false power structure so much creative attention, all these figures justifying the killing are the big dance of fear. Look at Donald Rumsfeld, how when he is asked questions in his press conferences, answering back he has this style like he is

searching his profound intelligence, scrutiny-like, his gold-rimmed glasses blasting the venom of the dragon's eyes. His answers always exhibit this molestation, as if he is bothered by the inquiry, his great intellect has been intruded on by the plebian reporters, he answers it as doing a favor. Have you ever seen him, heard him, I mean have you truly seen him. It's as if all the questions are stupid. The dodo really performs. Once again the problem with his performance theater is that the American audience buys it up.

The way Bush sits gives him away, always spreads legs and slams his elbows against his knees. Cowpoke. This is the level of criticism that poets should maintain, making physical and psychological observations. Reveal. Does not have to be direct as anger will make you waver, but keep distance, that beautiful American word 'cool' sharp ice, I've never written about 9-11, no 9-11 poems from me, rather I was thinking of Hiroshima and the instant burning of 150,000 people and think about how the Japanese recuperated and are these Americans going to let go of this bone. Because the lack of imagination does not let you see the pain/damage you have caused others, when the ball bounces back and hits you in the face you jump like a child with a tantrum. So the tight security of the American space is the act of hiding and not facing the force that moved the original charge of the ball, there is a saying down here,

"has bien y no mires por quien,
has mal y escondete."

do good and don't look for who,
do evil and hide yourself.

That's what the United States is doing, hiding itself, rather than to change and be just; it decided to take these Draconian measures.

So we are writing poems under this umbrella of pressure. And your poems about walking around the Bowery, about the streets of New York, that's when a world opens up to us, seeing things, connecting things, these episodes, objects of the real world unfolding is documentation that escapes the censors. Ah, that's what I think poetry should do, escape the censors, it is the most free of the arts, for we negotiate with ourselves and our angels and demons, we do not need museums and clubs or theaters, just the possibility of air through which the sound of our words could travel. Thus we make fewer compromises with the powers that be, our visions are uncontrollable, thus extremely dangerous to the tax collectors and well-behaved. This ultimate is what Plato said, this is why he called for the "banishment of poetry." Ah, and he that was a poet knew the potency, its ability of wild fire, its condition of wild berry. Caña brava. The rural communities resisting the cities. Runaway Taino communities in the mountains, runaway African slaves. Cimmarron culture. Places of improvisation. What the Arabs did to develop the Persian laud, what the Spaniards did to develop the guitar in the street taverns, what the Caribbean has developed, improvisation in music and songs of resistance, holding up the African and Taino elements that society was trying to eliminate, where true poetry is made somewhere between the book and the street. I think that's where we should be at. Going against the grain, which is another way of seeing Williams' In The American Grain. Planting language, watering the language, custodians of language, growing language flowers.

Truong Tran & Wanda Coleman

Truong Tran is a poet and visual artist. His publications include *The Book of Perceptions* (Kearny Street Workshop, 1999, finalist in The Kiriyama Book Prize), *placing the accents* (Apogee Press, 1999, finalist in the Western States Book Prize for Poetry), *dust and conscience* (Apogee Press, 2000, awarded the San Francisco Poetry Center Book Prize), *within the margin* (Apogee Press, 2004) and *Four Letter Words* (Apogee Press, 2008). Truong lives in San Francisco where he is currently teaching poetry at San Francisco State University and Mills College.

"To rehumanize the dehumanized," is a significant part of **Wanda Coleman**'s aesthetic raison d'état as "unofficial poet laureate" of Los Angeles and "L.A. Blueswoman." Born in the community of Watts, she was raised in South Central. Her work has appeared in over 80 anthologies, including Terry McMillan's *Breaking Ice* (Penguin, 1990), *The Norton Anthology of African-American Literature* (W. W. Norton, 2003), *Best American Poetry* (Collier Books, 1988, Scribner, 1996), and Camille Paglia's *Break, Blow, Burn* (Pantheon, 2005). Her fellowships include the N. E. A., Guggenheim, and the California Arts Council (poetry and fiction). She was the Los Angeles Department of Cultural Affairs' first literary fellow, and a finalist for the California Poet Laureate position in 2005. Her books include: *Bathwater Wine* (Black Sparrow Books, 1998; the Lenore Marshall Poetry Prize, 1999), *Mercurochrome* (Black Sparrow Books, 2001; bronze-metal finalist, National Book Awards, 2001), *Ostinato Vamps* (University of Pittsburgh Press, 2003; Pitt Poetry Series) and *Jazz and Twelve O'Clock Tales* (Black Sparrow Books, 2008). She resides in California with her family and husband of 26 years, artist and poet Austin Straus.

San Francisco, California
December 23, 2004

Dear Ms. Coleman,

I do not know how to begin. I do not know where to begin. Perhaps here is as good a place as any. I begin with a confession. The task of writing a letter in the context of this project is completely foreign to me. I can blame this partly on technology and the invention of the cursed email, but ultimately it lies entirely upon my shoulders. Letter writing is an art form that is lost to me. In recent times, it has only served as a tool when looking for a job, writing a recommendation for a student, or writing an appeal to the masses in support of the arts, but it has not, in recent memory, served the purpose of intimate correspondence. The fact that I am writing this letter with the knowledge of it being a part of a project meant for publication makes it that much more difficult. In preparing for this journey, I've revisited your work and the text of *Letters to a Young Poet*. I am at once inspired and in awe. I want to thank you, Ms. Coleman, for this opportunity of exchange. I consider it to be both an honor and a privilege to be in conversation with you on these urgent matters of poetics, politics, life. I also find myself saddened perhaps by the notion that a correspondence similar to Rilke's cannot exist in our times. I began writing this letter in the days following our election questioning my voice and its validity and authenticity as a person living in and as a part of this society. It is now December 26th and I am still trying to find the words to begin a conversation on poetry and life. Perhaps I can begin by addressing the obvious. *Letters to a Young Poet* existed in a world entirely different from the one we live in. It is a correspondence between two white men and in all honesty, in the context of today's world, it is a conversation that is at once innocent and removed. I wonder if poetry can in fact still embody that sense of innocence. I want to share with you a recent experience. When it first happened, I was deeply offended by the turn of events. It is now nothing more than a humorous anecdote. I was asked to submit some poetry to a well-known academic journal for a special issue of literature pertaining to Vietnam, the Vietnam War and the Vietnamese American experience. I sent them a manuscript of my latest book with the knowledge that publication would be unlikely due to the fact that the book layout was rather unorthodox. To my surprise, the editors decided to publish an excerpt from the manuscript. Shortly after this acceptance, another letter came in the mail. The managing editor of this journal essentially asked for the following:

work that was more traditionally lineated and
work that was more Vietnamese in flavor.

I am prepared to accept the thinking of the first request. It is the second request that leaves me at a loss for words. It is a request that reaches far beyond the boundaries of my poetry and is a reflection of life as it exists now in this society. It is a society that still insists on filing individuals into a neat rolodex system of race, gender, and sexual orientation. Every word of every line of every poem I've ever written is an embodiment of who I am as a writer, a gay man, a person of color, a writer. I can retell this story anecdotally for the reason that I am very clear on where I stand. I am a writer first, foremost and last. Ms. Coleman, I look forward to our conversations and reading your views on the state of poetry and the poetic life. It is that existence between the space of perceptions and the perceived that I find my own existence. It is in that space that I will initiate our discourse.

Yours truly,
Truong

P.S. Even at the conclusion of this letter, I still feel foreign to the concept. If you are ever in San Francisco, please allow me the opportunity of inviting you over for a home cooked meal. I would like to meet you face to face, shake your hand and thank you for your work. I would like for us to engage beyond the threshold of the page.

Los Angeles, California
Sunday, January 23, 2005—8:18 AM (#1)

Good morning, Truong Tran. You'll find this letter is now a combination of four. When I was in my mid-twenties, my most important formative years, I hungered for a correspondence like this—for a guidance I never quite received. What I did manage to acquire seemed tainted by the issues of the day, that world in which I was regarded literally as a suspect, born snatching purses, holding up liquor stores, selling sex while still in diapers. Anyway, I'm going to finish this now and mail it in the morning. My apologies for being late.

(#2) Dear Truong,

The Wanda Coleman you meet at this late date is not the optimistic word warrior of previous works. I am the exhausted, "failed" warrior of a terrible present. My dreams reflect this unfortunate turn—as two nights ago I witnessed the glorious moment of destruction as our moon tremored on its axis, left orbit, hurtled toward Earth in brilliant golds, mauves, silver-whites and magenta coronae and plumes, splitting and cracking the cold-perfect blue sky above Southern California, much as I have longed to split and crack the biases and bigotries that bind me to oblivion. I knelt before the roaring winds, embraced my three children (adults, returned to pre-pubescence) and in my final words uttered: "Don't be afraid, I will always love you and we will always be together."

The dream shocked me awake, as I am shocked from sleep quite often these mornings. Grateful to discover I'm still in the fray.

I suppose indifference is the word I'm searching for, Truong. It came to me overnight and wove itself through my subconscious missive to you.

(#3) Dear Truong—Your letter lances many wounds, old and fresh, I don't know where to begin.

I'm old enough to remember this city's last gas-lit street lamps, and the lamp-lighter who came around on his truck, with ladder, to light them—that street Santa Barbara has been renamed Martin Luther King, Jr. Blvd., all the old landmarks, and my great Aunt and Uncle's home, are vanished. Their old neighborhood is not far from Magic Johnson's Shopping Center and Theatre Complex, and many Black and Latino immigrants are displacing the Afro-American population that replaced the Whites who fled after the Baldwin Hills Dam burst, back in 1963. The year I graduated High School, 1964, I took a bus ride into that chic neighborhood. Mr. Newsom, my White English teacher and debate coach lived off Stocker, one of its classier avenues. It was a clean, well-kept neighborhood, then, but notorious for racial and officer involved incidents. I was 17-years-old, big at 5'9" and 200 pounds, but I was terrified that something might happen to me. Mr.

Newsom had invited a handful of his best speech-and-debate students to hang out that afternoon. My nervousness about the trip was so great it has blotted out the visit, leaving only the residue of fear. I was so anxious to get back to my neighborhood, I left the leather-bound caddy I was carrying on the bus stop bench. In it were five plays that I had painstakingly written by hand, under the spell of Eugene O'Neill and Arthur Miller. They were my only copies.

Loss. Your letter underscores the losses that drive me. Lost moments, lost possibilities, all that's been lost on the many gone. The loss of dreams . . .

Truong, I wake each morning in a fury. Each night I descend into fury.

What can I tell you?

No, what can I save you from?

I can tell you to expect nothing from the world of American Letters, so that when something happens you might enjoy it. I can tell you to stop wasting your time on poetry and write a simpering novel or fake self-help book, or some preposterous tome telling morons-of-any-stripe how they can find undying love. Make it as cliché-ridden and banal, as politically correct (or incorrect, since neither matters) as possible, dripping with sentiment. Do it and make the TV talk-show rounds. Make the goo-gobs of money that you will need to buy quality time, time free of dolor, time to write at leisure. Then you can side-step the supercilious fools one often finds on grantsmanship panels and philanthropic committees.

No. Fuck that. The cynic in me grabs the pen. Let me stop this madness and back up. I will address your letter directly. I will use it as ballast to bring me back to the Earth of myself!

(#4) 10:44:44 AM—I'm going to stop now, take a break, and then comment on the critical point you raise in your letter.

1:39:06 PM—Item #1 refers to your form. Let's address item #2, the phrase that has put you at a loss: "work that was more Vietnamese in flavor." This is a variation on the old "you're not Black enough" ploy that, ironically, even when valid, is a convenient repudiation that conceals racist bias (although it may be adamantly claimed otherwise). It is frequently used to demoralize anyone of color. *It refers to the content of the work.*

The critic, editor or publisher or reader who makes this statement is usually a White male or female who presumes to be an expert on "Blackness," or at minimum, to have an appreciative knowledge of Black/ethnic expression, or popular contemporary representation(s) of the Black experience, a.k.a. stereotypes. Depending upon this person's aesthetic criteria, they may want work that's "stronger," that is, work that is militant or decries racism, and/or is urban in tone, subject and point-of-view. Or (as I have encountered in the pitch dens of Hollywood) they may want work that is idyllic, rural, lyrical or "positive" (non-threatening). W*hatever* they think they want, this thoughtless manner of requesting it has bedeviled African-Americans (I'll stick to poets) since the days of Phillis Wheatley (1753-1784), particularly Paul Laurence Dunbar (1872-1906) and Melvin B. Tolson (1900-1966). This insidious means of confounding and trivializing the literary excellence of we so-called minorities has been used against virtually every member of every ethnic group American society has produced. Unless the individual who rejected you was Vietnamese, him or herself, how dare they presume to know what comprises or doesn't comprise "Vietnamese flavor?" In your case this translates as not being Vietnamese enough. Are they referring to a form of pidgin English, a certain regional dialect, issue-oriented content? All of that? If they, themselves, are Vietnamese, other factors may be at work: as aesthetic taste, editorial slant, any subsumed innergroup conflict (as when lighter-skinned Blacks reject darker-skinned Blacks or vice versa), differences in national identity.

On the other hand, it is up to each individual writer to decide how they want to handle this root issue of "otherness." As I have described in some of my writings about writing, the constant re-examination of what is African and what is American in my work has been a ceaseless process. You have two options: 1) to ignore this question, if you can, or 2) devise an answer with which you, and only you, are satisfied, if not permanently, then for the interim, so that it doesn't "fuck with your head" or impede your creative process.

How have I done that?

I was raised by parents who did not allow identifiable idiomatic speech, Black slang or "foul language" into their home. First I memorized the King's English and his grammar. I learned the rules so that I could break them with artistry as opposed to chance. Simultaneously, I then began to "collect" all the language I was not allowed to use, along with various other cants and jargons. I have developed a mental list of stylistic and/or linguistic "signals" or "stops" that tell the initiated and/or sensitive reader that there is "something else" going on underneath my language, something that is out-of-the ordinary. These are widely ranging rhetorical devices by which I _encode_ my blackness (the way 50s scriptwriters encoded sex), using everything from nonsensical "niggerisms," to literary allusions, mock and variant spellings, period slang, song lines and titles, musical notation, etcetera. I've also cultivated an occasionally "skewed" approach to subjects that may be over-worked in the culture at any given moment. I've worked extremely hard to "individuate" my language as opposed to individuating my style, although I think either method is equally valid. (The poems of Timothy Seibles provide a delightful example of how "skewed" points-of-view individuate language.)

[As you might notice, if you read enough contemporary African-American poets, and contemporary poets of other origins under their influence (this touches on the acculturation process), most, with about a half-dozen exceptions, have settled on pouring their "Blackness" or "otherness" into conventional forms, so that the only thing "Black" or "other" about their work is the content. (This, unfortunately, becomes tiresome when one sits through a long evening of Slam poetry.)]

Perhaps it is time for you to examine the work of other Vietnamese poets, and/or those influences at work on your psyche, to attempt to "objectify" them, as much as that's possible, and then apply or test what you garner.

Otherwise, do as I have done with rejections calculated to harm me: forget them.

Hmm. Before I close, I want to tell you a story I often relate that may further illustrate the issue you raise in item #2, summarized in one word: Authenticity.

In 1994, I was invited to be a peer-review panelist for the National Endowment for the Arts. The staff had taken pains to insure the fairness of the panel. Around the table the demographics were covered, some nine panelists encompassing two or three categories including two Latinos, two Black women, at least two identifiable homosexuals (male and female), and one lay person or non-poet, two Californians, two Chicagoans, one D.C. resident, several academics, at least three politicos, etc. I was the least formally educated of the group, having pulled myself up "by my own bootstraps." It is the usual nature of such grant-selection processes that conflicts arise and alliances shift in the name of literary craft excellence, but in two striking instances it came down to one panelist going against the apparent aesthetic values of the other eight. Each time that one panelist was yours truly.

I quickly realized that I was the only one at the table who had read every single bloody application, word for-word. Instead of regarding me as having remarkable integrity, my peers thought me an idiot and fool. I had even taken the pains of jotting down my evaluations on green 5x8 cards in order to present them succinctly and not waste my fellow panelists' precious time. They found this amusing.

In the first of the two conflicts, I was advocating for one of the strongest manuscripts of the hundreds I had read (each panelist read an overlapping 2/3rds of the nine to twelve-hundred manuscripts submitted). Not only was the writing topnotch, it was one of the rare manuscripts that addressed the complexities of human sexuality. When my peers remained unconvinced, I took it upon myself to read one of the misread or unread poems aloud. *I wanted my peers to hear what I heard*. It was titled "Prayer" and it had a litany, a repetition of the words "Gay men." It was obvious to me that the author intended the poem to be read so that "Gay men" sounded like "A-men." I then read the poem in that fashion. My peers immediately changed their votes and supported that particular poet; however, from that point forward they banned me from reading any more poems aloud.

The second instance is more complex, and the more significant. During the initial weeding-out process, we were allowed to select only a small number of semifinalists from the hundreds of manuscripts read. I ended up with four manuscripts of equal merit. But could only select one. I asked my husband, Austin Straus, also a poet and English teacher, to help me out by evaluating the four. The one he selected was a collection of exquisitely painful, excellently written poems. They spun the horrific narrative of a Vietnamese woman who, along with her brother, mother and maternal aunt, had escaped during the evacuation at the end of the war as "boat people." Her tale involved capture by pirates, brutal rape and the separation of herself and her brother from the mother and aunt. The children miraculously ended up in America, the mother and aunt in France, the story ending with a poignant reunion following the untimely death of the mother.

"Wanda," he said, blowing into Kleenex, "these are great poems. She's a great writer. You've got to let her go through the process."

I looked at him quizzically. We had had hundreds of complex discussions, even arguments, on the literary works of others over the years—thirteen at that point. "Austin," I snapped, "those poems weren't written by a woman, they were written by a man—a White one at that."

"You're kidding."

"No, I'm not." I took the MS and explained my reasoning. First, the *traditional* line breaks were perfect and highly sophisticated. Second, the (implied) sentence structure was perfect. The character (if she were also the writer) had not been in the U.S. long enough to develop that much syntactical sophistication. Thirdly, the sexual content was written in a male tone, with a confidence few women writers assume—even feminists. Fourth, the dialogue was perfect, minimal, without a wasted word, and moved the narrative forward in a fashion that told me the writer was an accomplished scriptwriter as well as a poet. Fifth, there was a laid-back or understated polished lyricism to the language that told me this was "someone in our neck of the woods—someone who lives on the West Coast."

"No, no!" Austin vehemently insisted. "Suppose you're wrong? Then you're denying a great woman writer an opportunity. You wouldn't want anyone to do that to you!"

That decided me. I was certain that I was right. But I had had exactly that kind of thing happen to me, and I couldn't do it to anyone else, regardless.

Now it was up for consideration by we nine NEA peer panelists. By chance, the person sitting to my left was the first to present their case for or against the manuscript. That meant I would be last to present my opinion. One by one, each person, regardless of demographics, ranked the manuscript the highest rank possible, a score of 10 points. To a person, each panelist raved about the "Vietnamese woman" who had written these incredible poems, their eyes actually tearing.

My turn came.

"These poems raise the issue of authenticity," I opened. "Ordinarily, I would rank these poems a one or zero because these poems were not written by a woman. They were written by a man." There was a collective gasp. "And a White man at that." All spines went rigid.

One by one, I laid out my criteria, as I had for Austin. My peers were livid with disbelief, so I slammed it to them out loud.

"If he's that good, *good enough to fool all of you*," I smirked, "Let-The-Man-Have-His-Money!"

I gave the manuscript a ten as well.

We were adjourned for lunch without further discussion. Since that was the last manuscript to undergo scrutiny, and finalists had been chosen, it was only a matter of arranging them according to numerical rank, (all ties had been broken) and re-assembling the panel for closing comments and any input regarding the peer-review process. This now controversial manuscript was the highest ranking manuscript, the only one to receive nine straight tens.

Usually, at the end of these processes, everyone is watching the clock, and it is considered a coup when travel-weary panelists can get away early, with extra time to make planes or deepen new alliances. I had been given the impression that it would take at least three hours or more to wrap up everything. During our one-hour lunch I went on a walking tour of the Vietnam memorial, discovering the name of one of my high school classmates.

Unbeknownst to me, I had caused such a hubbub among everyone, the staffers and the peer panel chairperson had decided to forego lunch and complete the final tally, speeding up the process in order to prove me wrong! They thought it intolerable to make everyone go back to their lives with the controversy unresolved, having to wait four-to-six weeks for the bureaucracy to spit out formal letters naming all finalists selected by our panel. Under NEA rules, the only way the identities of the finalists could be revealed was *after* the completion of the final tally, when the grants to the poets were effectively made. Once that was done, they could, in effect, legally "take off the blinders" and reveal the names of the award-winners.

Of course, they were only interested in discovering the name of the Vietnamese woman poet.

I returned from lunch slightly early and as I entered the room, someone screamed.

"Wanda was right!"

As it turned out, the writer of the poems was a highly educated White male, a Californian, a professor at one of the nation's top ten universities, who was also a Hollywood television scriptwriter, the type of poet who usually culls his poems not from the stuff of his life, but from events in the lives of others. Apparently, unlike you, he did manage to write poems that had the proper "Vietnamese flavor."

While it might be unfair, and certainly incorrect, to characterize all my peers as racists, *the complexities of racism did create the subtext for their ignoring or being indifferent to the information I brought to the process. In this democratic republic, these social differences were nevertheless, grounds for the dismissal of my observations, which were not given full weight or importance until they could be absolutely proven true. They were indifferent to my assessment.* (This harks back to the days when Black witnesses were not allowed to testify in court against Whites accused of crimes. Black testimony was held "suspect," unless sanctioned by White authority. Metaphorically, this mechanism is still at work in America.)

This is a textbook example of what you've identified. This society files "individuals into a neat Rolodex system of race, gender and sexual orientation." Instead of an open society, fostering racial harmony and parity, the racists-of-all stripes have seen to it that post-Civil Rights "affirmative-action" America has devolved into a concatenation of socioeconomic elites that is parasitic on the diverse majority of citizens collectively regarded as inferior. It is automatically understood that the representatives of these elites limit their "business" to or feed-on their same ilk only; therefore, as in our 1994 panel, the gays were there to offer expertise on gays, the women on women, the Blacks on Blacks, the Latinos on Latinos, and so on. If the true criterion were literary excellence, and if our society were a true democracy, then *who* sat on that panel would not have mattered.

Truong, I doubt that I was the only one of my so-called peers for whom literary excellence was the only criterion; however, I was the only one able to pierce the fictive narrative and detect the true nature of the poet beneath. In so saying, it doesn't mean that I can't be fooled, it merely indicates that I wasn't fooled on that occasion, and, although largely self-educated, I know my craft extremely well. This incident did not win me any friends I didn't already have, and I have not been invited to sit on a peer panel out-of-state since.

Wanda Coleman

P.S. You may call me Wanda.

San Francisco, California
April 23, 2005

Dear Wanda,

I have been reading and rereading your letter time and time again. I see it as a manual of sorts . . . How to survive as a poet. I will leave it at that. Thank you so much for your thoughtful and thought-provoking response to my own words. I've not responded to you because I have been engaging with your words as they relate to my current state of existence as a writer. I made the decision this past year Wanda, to devote more time to the act of teaching. I teach creative writing at both the college and high school levels. The fear you speak of when you went into your teacher's neighborhood at the age of 17 is the fear I face at the beginning of each semester, each day. I cannot help but wonder if this is in fact the right path, if I possess the capacity to teach a room full of students, most of them white, the construction of words, poetic language, the abstract nature of it. In those moments I tend to revert back to the young man who would begin his readings of poetry with the disclaimer, "I write in a borrowed language." And yet Wanda, it is the only language I truly know. I was recently part of a panel at a local university under the umbrella of "Literature of the Pacific Rims." The title alone should give me cause for concern when it applies to my own struggles as a writer. Nonetheless, I agreed to be a part of this discussion. In the weeks that lead up to the panel itself, I was informed that a fancy brochure was being produced and being sent out to a mailing list of 3,000 strong. I was horrified to find out that they had opted to use my children's book cover as opposed to my new book of poems to represent me. Keep in mind that the other writers involved were all being represented as serious poets and writers. What I am trying to say, Wanda, is that no matter how hard I try to define myself as a writer, the world around me continues to systematically categorize me based on the color of my skin. It is that surface layer that seems impenetrable, as though nothing beneath the surface can and will ever be applied to one's identity. I insisted that they change the brochure or take my name off the panel. Suffice it to say, they changed the brochure. I would have normally let mishaps of this nature slide as I am often guilty of living up to the stereotype of the docile Asian who does not want to rock the boat. On this occasion however, I received notice of their intentions with the brochure right on the heels of your letter. There was no way that I could turn a blind eye. I have you to thank for that. Wanda, your words have already guided me in many ways.

Your story about the NEA panel was enlightening to say the least. I read about it years ago in a lit journal whose name escapes me at the moment. I did not appreciate the depiction of the situation as told by the other writer. Thank you for shedding light on the situation. It brings me back to our ongoing discourse on this notion of the authentic voice. I realized when sitting on a recent panel (different from the above) that what is expected of me is not a truly authentic voice but rather a voice that is representational and written in a familiar language that is often mistaken as original language. It is the language of the immigrant, the survivor of war, the language of those relegated to the space of the margin. By no means is this an indictment of the predominant culture . . . well actually it is but it is also a crime often perpetrated by those in our own community. It is the crime of expectation that so often squelches the writer's strive towards an authentic voice. While on this panel, very little was being asked of my explorations as a writer. The questions were instead directed towards my experiences as an immigrant. Perhaps I, as a gay writer of color, am not supposed to have abstract thought, let alone claim to work within the abstract form of poetry. How did you deal with this? How do you continue to deal with this?

I am going to shift gears again and delve into another subject that has been on my mind as of late. I recently spoke with a fellow colleague about this notion of insider/outsider writing. In countries like Vietnam, these lines are very clearly drawn and are driven by political alignment. Although the lines are far less defined in our own country and society, I cannot help but think that there too exists this division of the insider/outsider when it comes to the poetic landscape of our world. I want to ask you Wanda as a veteran of this poetry world, what do you make of the situation? I fear that we are heading in the same direction as say, Vietnam. I fear that I will write what is expected of me.

I am going to end on this note for now. I will write again as I wrap my head around these issues. School is coming to an end soon and with that a much needed vacation. Perhaps we could meet over the summer.

Austin is definitely invited to dinner. My mother just gave me the recipe for an amazing roasted catfish that I hope to share with you. I look forward to the day when we will meet in person.

Your friend,
Truong Tran

P.S. I am enclosing a copy of my latest book. One of my students said that she was mad that I had used so many pages and so few words. Then it occurred to her that she could always use it as a notebook and in that case, it was fairly affordable.

Los Angeles, California
Sunday, January 23, 2005—11:16 AM[1]

Good morning, Truong,

Excited by our letter-writing process, I began a second letter to you while on the road from Kirkland, Washington, two weeks ago. But I'm too pooped-out at this time to search through my stuff to look for it. Ironically, during my first letter to you I discovered a copy of Rilke's *Letters to a Young Poet* among my deceased son's belongings. Rilke raised several points I thought it might be advantageous to address, since my take on them differ from his, or the manner in which I concur may cast his notion in a different light. But except for one, these thoughts will have to wait until the next letter.

---

[1] During their correspondence, Wanda Coleman continuously wrote to Truong. For this reason, many of her correspondences predate Truong Tran's initial letters.

At one point, Rilke cautions his youthful reader to "rejoice in your growth, in which you naturally can take no one with you, and be kind to those who remain behind, and be sure and calm before them, and do not torment them with your doubts and do not frighten them with your confidence or joy."

I wish, Truong, that someone had spoken that latter phrase to me when I was coming along

"and do not frighten them with your confidence or joy."

However, they would have had to have framed it within another context. They would have had to have taken the pains to explain the complex and bitchy nature of literary jealousy American-style. And in so doing, as discussed in my first/last letter, they would have to have been broad enough in character to appreciate and acknowledge the complex dynamics of racism within these borders.

By showing my *potential* literary competitors (peers—even a couple of people who pretended to be mentors—regardless of race, and a few others, who would go on to become fellow poets, writers, literary critics and/or social critics—the cultural gatekeepers, goal tenders and foremen who are the eternal bane to true Black militancy) my *confidence* in my future abilities as a writer, and sharing with them my anticipated *joy*, I unwittingly made myself vulnerable to their "sabotage."

Am running late. Best. . . .

February 22, 2005-10:13

Re: When Being is Meaning

Dear T.T., I am reading Rilke's *Letters to a Young Poet*. Here is a passage written as though Rilke were addressing us Truong, those of us yet to be born:

. . . be patient toward all that is unsolved in your heart and try to love *the questions themselves* like locked rooms and like books that are written in a very foreign tongue. Do not now seek the answers, which cannot be given you because you would not be able to live them. And the point is to live everything. Live the questions now. . .

Hmm. Locked rooms? I debate that, Truong. I was locked out of completing my education. I was locked out of making a decent living as a Single Mom. Mine has been a life of lonely corridors and locked doors. They have never opened. So this image fails me, at first. On rereading, and accepting Rilke on his own terms, I do understand. Yes. I have many answers. Yet I have learned the difficulty of imparting what I know to others who would rather not have that information, but who would prefer to (the chance to) discover their own versions of those answers at any risk, even death: my children and grandchildren particularly. Thus, I am able to offer my knowledge to strangers more readily; preferably certain, sensitive strangers who are not necessarily confused, hurt or offended by what I present.

> . . . Sex is difficult; yes . . . but . . . almost everything serious is difficult, and everything is serious. If you only recognize this and manage out of yourself, out of your own nature and ways, out of your own experience and childhood and strength to achieve a relation to sex wholly your own (not influenced by convention and custom), then you need no longer be afraid of losing yourself and becoming unworthy of your best possession.

I would revise and modernize his paragraph to read in part: Sex is at the core of creativity. Sex is driven by desire. In America, desire is complicated by racism and too often driven by image, and image driven by wealth or the absence of it. These actualities complicate creativity and matters of desire and make them difficult; yes . . . but . . .

I would also revise it this way: Writing within the margins of society is difficult; yes . . . but in this context . . . almost everything worth writing about is difficult and serious. If you recognize this **otherness** and manage out of yourself, out of your emarginated nature and ways, out of the confluence of circumstances that affect your own experience and childhood, and (through close attention to craft) mitigate the creative drive to achieve a style of writing wholly your own and not deadened by fear of convention or custom), then you need no longer be afraid of losing your particular identity and becoming inauthentic (if not necessarily a great writer or artist).

Received: *within the margin* by Truong Tran, Apogee Press (2004)

Thoughts after reading it: *Envy*. *Why doesn't someone waste a few trees on me (hahaha)*. I enjoy the marriage of your aesthetic essay to your familiar "obsessive" visual idea of the continued or "worried" line (Jeffers was known for his long rambling Germanic or Kantian lines in manuscript; see *Double Axe*), the numberless pages (I had imagined my novel *Mambo Hips* published without page numbers, a running dialogue with The Reader, the use of juxtaposition in building toward a telling yet thinly toned, if poignant, narrative; however, in your use of "unclaimed" spareness (of word choice) lies the danger of stale or overworked language [the ideal is to go for density in meaning, like Southern California poet Bert Meyers (or Picasso as the visual counterpart to this phenomenon; and/or failing that, to achieve the meditative), which is as authentically close to haiku as westerners generally get without visual grounding; to go for *essence* within a given form or word choice]; too, the danger in repeating lines/ideas others have voiced more deeply, more richly, in fictional and non-fictional forms as well poetic forms ("the poet's **gift**/is the poet's **curse**" is a phrase containing two words that are juxtaposed and often used when summarizing the tribulations of the creative entity. I've done it myself. If I were to "diddle" with your phrase and refresh (modify) it, I would say something like "the nigger poet's gift/is the African-American poet's curse" hahaha, thus making a nasty joke or word play of the whole thing, having fun by messing with the minds of people who not only detest the word "nigger" but to whom the idea/condensed essay contained in the wordplay is an affront)—but also rendering it original.

Truong, your present and greatest risk as a writer (poet) is in not knowing or identifying *when* your language becomes stale or unoriginal, and/or who made it so, therefore, you are unable to refresh it, to give it renewed life, or linguistic rebirth. (It is possible that your critical student felt this way about your poems. More on her below. It is also possible that the person who critiqued your work as "not Vietnamese enough" also felt that way, but was reluctant to say so at the risk of wounding your aesthetic ego, was afraid to edify you, and clumsily said something even more stupid than intended.) The additional risk is that some sophisticated readers may find some of what you write uninteresting, while others may be intrigued. I assume you are well aware of *this craft difficulty*; hence, some of our discussion. Remedies for this are 1) vocabulary building by studying various lexicons of interest; 2) extensive casual reading of poets and writers at the top of the American canon, and at the top of the anti-canon, and keep some of their books and write study notes in the margins and on the end pages for periodic rereading and reconsideration; 3) by keeping a lexicon of dead metaphors and overused expressions handy; 4) developing linguistic signatures that individuate your language and imbue it with your beliefs, personality, will, philosophy, etc.

Remember (and excuse the mini lectures): by origin, and by nature, American English is an extremely fluid and rebellious language, more democratic than the democratic republic it flaunts but seldom explains. It is in a constant state of flux, driven by popular art forms, the mass media, and eruptions from *the margins*, those subcultures of *we others* who leak their tongues into the socioeconomic air. And it has the quirky habit of recycling its slang and appropriating the slangs of others in the name of pursuing the immortal dollar bill; although, sometimes, as in the case of "my bad," Americans exhibit their best humanistic trait, that of normalizing what was denigrated as abnormal, or righting what they perceive as a wrong. But public outrage must occur first. If you don't know the story, purportedly a young Black female student used that expression in a classroom and was unfairly penalized (embarrassed) for it. (I witnessed such incidents when I was in high school, White teachers embarrassing Black students for using Southernisms.) Other students took up her idiomatic expression in revolt, and when the story made the newspaper it became a national *cause celebre*. Two days ago, I heard a celebrity use the phrase on a game show when he made a mistake—a White male no less.

Back to your work: Two excellent and striking lines that immediately aroused in me thought, delicious argument, and emotion: 1) "notion of the line as it relates to the body saying I love you" and 2) "art that is viable can only exist in a world that is marginalized."

Thank you for *within the margin*. I'll nest it with our letters and keep it near for rereading. I recommend you read all the work by Reginald Shepherd you can find. I think he will deepen any discussion on otherness. I doubt if you can find anything decent by poet F.A. Nettelbeck, but if you can find a copy of his *Bug Death*, buy it and consider it. I also recommend that you attempt Arno Schmidt (Green Integer Press) at some time in the future, if only out of curiosity; but, be warned, his writing reflects (I believe, when I read him back in the late 60s, early 70s) a private pathology at the core of his language.

*

Dear Truong, to continue: Thank you for the copy of your beautiful book. You must be very proud.

The key points raised in your last letter are: 1) So many pages, so few words. 2) The path of teaching. 3) Receiving recognition for your experiences as an immigrant of color, and as one who has also vaulted the borders of heterosexuality; yet ignored as an intellectual being capable of abstract thought, or of having something of value to contribute other than neatly classified issues. 4) Insider/outsider.

1) I've put your last point first. I have always envied writers lucky enough to find publishers who not only appreciate their work, but who can afford to print them in any *visual* fashion desired. Other than the obvious insult, you student is expressing her distaste for anything outside the conventional narrative. She wants to walk in your shoes and be passively connected with you in the traditional/usual way, and resents being made an active participant in the reading process. *She does not want to think about or argue with the material she's trying to grasp*. Perhaps she wants an epiphany, or to be uplifted, and that didn't happen in the way she had imagined. Other than possibly being a manifestation of the fact that each person goes to poetry for their own specific need; this is the flip side of stereotyping. This happens when you become an archetype or romantic ideal. (As is often made of the American Indian in contemporary Hollywood films, such as Oliver Stone's *The Doors*.) And if you dare exhibit the kind of dignity and bearing of one who has an independent mind (as opposed to one who is proud under demeaning circumstances), unburdened by the definitions of others, within their limitations, then your punishments for what they regard as "arrogance," are insults, dismissals, and the ultimate: being ignored. This directly relates to items 3) and 4). Here's a story that might illuminate this unfortunate process:

About eight years ago, I was browsing in a boutique in Taos, New Mexico, looking for a gift for my granddaughter. There were two tribeswomen present, either owners or workers, silently waiting and watching. As I mused, two White women entered. All of us were roughly in the same age range, save one of the White women, well into forty and pushing fifty. As they quickly selected their items and went to the counter, the White women gave off a nervous energy, a mix of excitement and expectancy, as if wanting something to happen—a reaching out for some unknown intangible. They did not draw me into it, so I kept on with my browsing, unable to tune out their broadcast as they awkwardly engaged the tribeswomen in small talk, one finally asking one of the women her name. She gave it.

"Oh," they said, "does that have a meaning?"

"Yeah," she said, and gave it.

"Oh," said the women, sincerely, "that is quite lovely," they nodded to one another, approving. And one added, writing it down, "When I have my daughter, I'm going to name her that!"

As they huddled together over the notepad, the eldest beaming at the younger, I realized the younger woman was expecting a child, and the older woman was either the mother or mother-in-law.

"Yes, that's quite lovely," they repeated, nodding to one another then taking deep sighs of satisfaction, as if some secret mission had been accomplished. I shook my head and kept browsing.

"Thank you," said the tribeswoman. "I'm told it is very ancient."

They nodded blissfully and stared.

"Oh!" said the disconcerted tribeswoman, as she quickly bagged their purchases and handed them over the counter.

I had found something. A bracelet.

Another moment of smiles-all-around awkwardly passed, after which the two White women took their bags and left.

"What in-heck was thaaaat about!?" piped the second tribeswoman as she returned a dress to a rack. The one at the counter shook with laughter.

"I mean, who in the world would want to name their child after a stranger? Somebody they don't even know!"

As I approached check-out, the tribeswomen drew me into their circle.

"White women!" the name-giver shouted. "Isn't that the craziest thing you ever heard of?"

They looked directly at me. I smiled, nodded in agreement, and handed over the bracelet.

"Yeah," her partner took over the register and rang me up. "Don't make one damn bit of sense."

Rather than give them the explanation, which they would have found insulting and racist, I simply took my purchase and left the shop, thinking about that incident over the hours to come: How I was actually moved by the pathetic attempt of the White women to connect with something they thought magical. How devoid contemporary life is of spirituality; so devoid, that people seek it in the wrong ways in the wrong places, invariably going unfulfilled and mystified as to why. And yet, few, if any, suspect that this great void in their lives is a major portion of the price they are paying for the racism that taints everything American—every aspiration, dream and religious credo.

As for letter items 3) and 4) we are overlapping in artistic choices, temperaments, and circumstances. In item 1), we are not so much opposites, as correlations, moving along at different points in time. My letters to you underscore that I-have-so-much-to-tell-you point. As for item 2) we meet depart meet and depart again:

I suspect that your homosexuality may eventually prove less an issue than being Vietnamese, given how many Americans, across demographics, feel about the Vietnam war. No matter what you do, you are attached *by your flesh* to the painful memory of a war that America lost (just as I am attached *by my skin* to The Civil War and Slavery), yet many Americans are still fighting, as exhibited in our last presidential election. As you are repeatedly learning, Americans do not handle their losses or shames with grace, but with a smoldering rage and a subsumed simmering, as they spoil for revenge and reversal. And they will act on and express it loudly, at the first opportunity, as in the national response to the verdict of guilty in the *civil* trial of O.J. Simpson.

When America demands it, guilt by association and/or implication carry physical weight, even when there is no concrete evidence of crime. When "they" like you, they will overlook your homosexuality and embrace you as one of the good Vietnamese who fought gallantly on our side, even if you were too young to be in the war. That is the irrational nature of such thinking. You will be rewarded, eventually. If they don't like you, there is nothing you can do, not even achieving greatness, that will put a dent in their distaste, and anything you do or say will be (as the police say) used against you.

My feelings about teaching as a profession are colored by my great contempt for the institutionalized and calcified racism that continues to reside in too many of post Civil Rights America's grade schools, colleges and universities. The majority of them have not fully divested themselves of it; in fact, they are often centers in which it is housed and perpetuated. Otherwise, I think teaching itself, is as honorable a profession as any, if not more so.

But: Unless one is blessed with phenomenal luck, wealth or cunning, or a second gift in one of the white-collar professions, the path of teaching is virtually the only path available to the creative intellectual in present day America. Institutions provide protection from the ferocity of American life, and a poorly educated citizenry that is under siege by every corporate crook who has a scheme, and every politician in corporate pockets—not to mention the rules and regulations of four levels of government. There are few other institutions that would openly welcome (or at least pretend to welcome) the artist and/or effete. How well one does depends on the quality of the institution into which one is hired; its history, its current faculty, and to what extent the institution (or particular department within it) is mired in the filth of intellectual dishonesty, such as grade inflation, and squeezing students for the Holy Buck. The "academy" will eagerly, and frequently pleasantly, embrace and drain or mute, what it can't contain and homogenize. On the other hand, fortunately, it is not universally that way. A healthy learning environment and openness to change, yet respect for tradition—is difficult to achieve and maintain. There are those institutions that have succeeded marvelously in doing so, but positions at them are highly sought after and the competition intense in a world that is making fewer permanent hires, and using more adjuncts and TAs.

For the poet/writer there are numerous perks and benefits, and the possibility of on-going intellectual dialogue with colleagues in like institutions globally—if one is so inclined; to obtain stimuli from quarters that cannot be reached from the desert or the streets. One may rise within such institutions to operate at the top of American and, perhaps, World culture. The potential for that mitigates any negatives perceived, depending on what the teacher wants. To date, I have had very little long-term success with these institutions, although my short-term successes (as visiting writer or guest lecturer) are numerous. I attribute this disparity primarily to "what Wanda-the-teacher once wanted and still wants." Truong-the-teacher has many more options and should take them and enjoy them—given his wants.

Too: for my particular psyche, teaching taps into the same wellspring from which the writing flows, and exhausts it without replenishing it.

Saturday, June 4, 2005

Dear Truong,

Western Myth: Abstract thought, discourse, is a sign of superior intelligence.

It may also be a sign of ignorance, an inability to organize one's thoughts clearly, and symptomatic of disease process and/or depression.

I'm going to backtrack and comment on the abstract in language/thought and density: *a private pathology at the core of language*. Over the years, I have noticed a tendency in certain types of men-of-color, particularly ill-educated Black men and/or ex-convicts, to speak in abstractions and metaphors as if unable to get their tongues around the concrete. As a child, my father irritated me endlessly by speaking in stories, similes and metaphors. "Can't you tell it to me straight, in plain English?" I'd demand, not understanding that he probably couldn't. His brain simply wasn't wired that way; to the extent that he had once had that ability, it had most likely been impaired by repeated blows to his head in the boxing ring. I have also encountered women like this, but most of them African-Americans or in menopause. Recently, I have noticed this *tendency toward abstractions* in myself. (In recent years, pertinent points in conversations evaporate on my tongue, I make incomplete sentences during discussions, and get lost in unnecessary convolutions.) And not only that, but a sudden inability to put things in order of importance (incredibly frustrating to someone who has prided herself on being an organizer); even to execute simple tasks, such as reading a novel.

About three weeks ago, I sat down to read a novel written in colonial English and an islander patois. I was stunned that I was simply unable to read it. It was as if I were climbing a hill with an elephant on my back. I felt crushed in the effort. I put the book aside. A few days later, I returned to it and zipped through it within a matter of hours. This was a first for me.

What had happened?

Well, the complicating factors of age and hypertensive disease (high blood pressure). But beyond that, I've looked to the brain, one of my casual areas of study over the decades. My latest hero is Nancy C. Andreasen, M.D., Ph.D. I often recommend her book *Brave New Brain*, her first, because the title is easy to recall. But the book I should be recommending is *The Broken Brain*. In it she puts forth some intriguing analyses and discussions of the language center of the brain, confirming what I have always suspected/observed, that there is some physiological aspect to writing, and that how well one writes may be largely determined by how healthy and how strong one's language center happens to be. The desire to write may not be sufficient. And then there is that unknown quantity, that comes in degrees, creativity.

Thus to admire what is abstract, or to use abstraction as a criteria or measurement for anything may net the deceptive.

Points 2), 3) and 4) comprise the endless circle in which you will travel again and again as a poet within the margins of American society. To the extent that you obtain satisfaction, or ever escape those margins, will depend . . . on your inner resources . . . on future changes in the global social fabric and America's intellectual climate.

A style of writing wholly your own: This is the most difficult challenge facing the creative writer who desires to be an original, and to have a uniquely original voice, to say things previously unuttered, and, perhaps, to think thoughts that are new. Antonin Artaud tried drugs in his pursuit of The Muse (Erato), as have many others. The poets and writers who flourished mid-twentieth century were devastated by alcohol and alcohol combined with drugs (a narcotic ingredient found in the cough syrups of the day, and heroin, among others), and not just The Beatniks (aka The Beats). These questionable means proved destructive not only to the creative processes but to the creators themselves.

Whatever *creative genius* is, it is not something that can be obtained by drugs, study, or attending a workshop, or attending a university. All the college degrees and all the awards philanthropy offers cannot make a dent or a difference in it, nor can they determine it. Educators and so-called intellectual elitists might, by chance, recognize it, and if so moved, foster it. *It is, by Nature, an organic part of being—the potential occasionally evident at birth.* Not everyone possesses it, and that is not a crime. Unfortunately, in the name of money, American education and its conservative swamp of pseudo intellectuals has sold the public the notion that genius is a commodity, like God, Jesus and sneakers, and that it can be certified. But for a few gallant art-and-word warriors, trying to "work within the system," this cruelly ludicrous mindset governs all our arts, depending on the region, often to the detriment of the very kinds of genius it purports to support.

Now wed that notion to race and ethnic origin, Truong, and you have the endless circle that must be traveled in until that true paradigm shift takes place.

What will dominate our writing courses in the future will not be the literary, it will be the commercial (the salable)—people who want or need to make money as scriptwriters, genre writers and writers of so-called humor or the inspirationally inane. That is happening now, especially among Black writers in the margins, where a science fiction or mystery writer is equated to a poet, where a filmmaker is equated to a philosopher, because anyone of any accomplishment at all is, by simply *having accomplished something noted*, anointed spokesperson for the group or race. This has not been so among dominant culture writers, but I predict, that if the pseudo-intellectuals (such as TV and radio gab show personalities) continue to dominate our discourse, this is going to change, most likely irrevocably. This will have an impact, eventually, on those who want to teach the excellent in writing. Keeping in mind, that teaching is often an art unto itself.

Factor in the internet, unless some "genius" figures out how to return books to prominence, and another "genius" figures out how to stop the assault on public education and reverse the last 30 years of damage done by organized racists and religious bigots. America's yahoos, in their ceaseless conspiracy to undo, or render moot, the so-called progress of the Civil Rights era, continue to mount *a silent assault* that keeps the majority of African Americans segregated and denied full access to the Halls of Knowledge. They have done this by developing sophisticated and complex bureaucratic (and legislative) "mindfields," that have virtually destroyed urban centers and their attendant public schools. This has been accompanied by a systematic *underfunding*.

In sum: Answer to 3) Whether or not you receive recognition for your experiences as an immigrant of color, depends on luck and your ability to persist. Even if you succeed, expect that you will continue to be ignored as an intellectual capable of abstract thought, unless you publish something in the future that resoundingly demonstrates otherwise. Having something of value to contribute other than neatly classifiable issues, may be impossible to surmount for the present, Truong. Therefore, focus on your craft issues, writing and publishing as much of quality as possible.

Answer to 4) As for being an Insider, I would ask "Inside what?" A literary priesthood comprised largely of racists, co-opted or cowed Blacks, and immigrant writers allowed *inside* as long as they don't rock the ideological boat? An elitist Hollywood that largely relegates Blacks to selling out other Blacks and insists on perpetuating new and hi-tech variations on old stereotypes? An arrogant academe that severely restricts tenure and salaries to women and teachers-of-color? A dwindling and cowardly fourth estate that ignores the greatest issues of our times, perpetuates the myth of objectivity, and prostitutes celebrities to sell newspapers and magazines? On the occasions that I found myself "Inside," I detested the company I was forced to keep. However, being on the *outside* has had some terrible consequences; but, being *outside* has also left me free to develop my own voice and writing style. *That was important to me*. I may have paid an unfair price, but I have paid it nevertheless. And I am still paying.

Truong, perhaps for your generation an alternative ground is emerging from the oceans of change like a new island from the Pacific—one in which those who grapple with the coming together of Being and Meaning can flourish undiminished. What we are grappling with, each in our own time, is a notion beyond Rilke's comprehension, and beyond the comprehension of most. We reside in a space that cannot be easily visited through simple terms like "inside" and "outside." Our mental, physical and spiritual states of being have become synonymous with our social states of being, and there is no immediate way to disentangle the resulting mess. One must simply cope with the bullshit however one can.

Your friend and correspondent,
Wanda

San Francisco, California
September 26, 2005

Dear Wanda,

A whisper she handed me as a keepsake of existence wrapped in a black scarf between two bricks of rice for when you get hungry when craving the bland

A whisper not a shout finds its way through time into a book through the eyes a whisper not a shout finds its way to the lips stop look listen he is saying something he is undressing in the window

A whisper of the words made ugly offer them shelter in your pockets build them a house within a book hide them from those who would use them as a weapon let them go when the time is right

A whisper she says says I love you and I hate just the same

Dear Wanda,

That I've been thinking about a way to write this letter, to respond to this time, to salvage some semblance of a lost lyrical language that my student comes to me and says, I want to do the work but someone was shot on my street just last night and right now Gertrude Stein is just plain stupid that she says it and she means it that I am at a loss for words that in another class I tell my students that as writers we are conscious of the world and our words of what is beneath that brick of a poem that even as it is being hurled through a window the glass shattering the child crying the mother sweeping shards into a neat pile of fragments that when lifting up this brick to discard it from the memory she finds meaning hidden on the one side laid flat pressed to the floor that as an adult I saw myself as the kid on the outside unwrapping this brick from a black wool scarf that I was the one who threw it through a window that as an adult I can still feel my heart beat in that moment in the past running laughing thinking of the power I had found in the breaking of things

Dear Wanda,

That I've gone about this I've gone about this all wrong that wrong is a word defined as not right that right is a matter of opinion perceptions that perception is a perspective one of many among the many she was arrested for looting that to some looting is the equivalent of looking for food that food is a condition of neither famine nor feast that feast is determined by the organic privilege that privilege is to self as other is to refugee that refugee was a word used out of context

Dear Wanda,

That I've been trying to find the words to write to read to speak between the lines of authentic language that shards and fragments are shaping my way that the sentence complete yields incomplete thoughts that writing is about taking reading about breaking that I've taken from language this half eaten fruit that even in its rotting state it was so sweet so cold to the touch

Dear Wanda,

This is not about the broken window the words of war the war of there of here this is not of what of what of words this is not about a time a place this is not about the act of writing this is not an act about poetry and the self the conscious self conscious about documentation dated and referred to it is not about the need to transcend it is not about art the beauty of words the ugliness of language the line nor the silence this is not about the nature of things of human beings being human this is not about needs nor necessities the 10-year-old orphan my mother or yours this is not about the poor the poet he carries his poems in a metallic red box this is not about a box red black white or grey this is not about gestures of refusal acceptance the questioning of one's place this is not about one's place in the world the preceding statement a cliché or not this is not about what is natural and what is man made this is about a condition it is not a condition a statement it is not a statement this is not about a contradiction this is a contradiction this is not about numbers contained in the night this is not about this night or the next this is not about meaning or making sense this is not I repeat this is not a poem

Truong

Los Angeles, California
Tuesday, September 20, 2005

Dear Truong,

The line I toe zigzags, skips a page, wiggles the curb, scuttles like a night beetle, then, mid-fog, the center of a road appears . . .

I returned from the Berlin Literary Festival on the 15th and have been having a prolonged hissy because I was forced to check-in my carry-on bag, which then missed the connecting flight from Heathrow and was sent on to Phoenix the next day, then mistakenly rerouted. I have been singled out as a terrorist and searched since my first plane ride, a hop on PSA to San Francisco in 1967. I always pack tight to travel light, wherever I go, to avoid turning over my belongings to indifferent and sadistic airport officials.

My things arrived off schedule but intact, Truong.

I returned from the literary trenches, gift still functioning, as Black as ever, feeling deranged, with forty dictionaries in my metaphorical potato sack, lugging them across my back, seeking definition by exosmosis. This frustrating and ugly process has been complicated and exacerbated rather than helped by my best doings. Instead of being elevated into the heavenly echelons, I remain burning here in these mean margins, and subsequently writhing on the ever-shrinking edge, rerouted in a spiral that doubles back on itself, my destination no apparent destination, abandoned to squirm in excruciating isolation. The lines blur, wife vis-a-vis caregiver/taker. Sometimes I feel thoroughly dispatched. Ten years from now, will there be any world of books or lines left that matter?

*

Post Berlin Life: At the Western Literature Conference this week. Surprisingly, lots of fun. After the awards ceremonies, we went to the ballroom. Austin did his best to be a partner to me on the dance floor, but recurring ligament trouble forced him to sit it out. I boogalooed, ponied, shimmied, swam, and twisted up a reasonable sweat to terrifically imitated Beach Boy retreads, then we retired. On our way up in the elevator, a handsome, platinum-haired man shook his bespectacled head and said, "I'm too old for this." He appeared healthy, lucid, well-heeled and lucky to be so. "How old are you?" I asked. "Seventy-two!" I am thirteen years his junior and did not feel obligated to say amen. I pray I'm lucky enough to go out clawing, kicking and screaming. When I met Gwendolyn Brooks in spring 2000 at the awards ceremony for the Academy of American Poets, she was feisty and outspoken at eighty-three, hurt that she had been stereotyped for decades as a one-poem poet, her work after the Pulitzer Prize largely neglected by the literary mainstream.

Rilke argues: "We *are* solitary. We may delude ourselves . . . but how much better it is to realize that we are so, even to begin by assuming it."

What is it that one assumes in the arms of one's lover? How do lovers who share solitary natures become <u>realized</u> in one another? Should each return to that lonely state for the sake of creativity? Would that be the ultimate delusion?

The "aloneness" of the artist and writer is special. It is the inner topography of the seer as opposed to the (designated) social outcast, although they are often one and the same. And, too, there is a major difference between solitude and withdrawal, the former being within life, the latter against it. Like Ms. Brooks, I refuse to withdraw. I want to return to Berlin with Austin, perhaps spend a Christmas there, just being poets. But life as a contemporary Bohemian seems over now, the restless waitings and ludicrously awkward gropings toward what? That disgruntled shadow standing next to us? That enormous reflection that fills the mirror, cracks and all? That poltergeist who kicks up sand along the Russian River, now the Moldau? It was in Berlin that I saw that I was in danger of/becoming one of those tragic crones who stand useless at the periphery of events, begging the slightest attention. Ignored. Valueless. Ill-formed.

As to Berlin: I was the only writer to visit with inmates at Moabit Detention Center. The male prisoners are detainees awaiting trial and sentencing or release. It was significantly easier to make my reality clear to them, much more so than it was to impress a panel of literary peers, or a seminar audience. These prisoners could appreciate the fact that I might identify with them; how the American Black underclass is by nature imprisoned in the invisible walls of an artificial construct.

It was at Checkpoint Charlie that I met the ghost of my oldest son.

Will I arrive intact?

(The last time I saw you, she whispered, I thot you should be hospitalized.) I am in more trouble than can be contained in flesh. It leaked/leaks. That was the evening your friend ("baby sis" cute, dark, fuzz-ball ponytail, glints of amber and brown) came to see me read at Cal Arts, Truong—October 5th. I was so blind on psychic pain and over-the-counter anti-influenza drugs, all I could see was the abyss.

Oh, but Truong, we've only begun these shared perceptions, trashings over of pasts and presents, mothers and sonsofbitches, doubts that become certainties, only to be reestablished as doubts, (lust-loathing, denial-desire) the determinings of tongues and actions, the unsanctioned comminglings that fuel disjuncture and the poetry of disjuncture. Indeed, to become those exquisite masters of the art of reaching through one's skin to touch another's, one's being to enter another's.

We share a contradictory wish, Truong, to quote you: "if only it were as simple as that a line on the page in a book . . ." Studying the color photograph by Noah David Smith on the cover of within the margin, *it seems an emotional Rorschach test, "oriental" in intent, as if monumental obfuscated phalluses (cliffsides, clouds, rocks?) are marginally obscured by the branches in knotty red profusion, overcast or scrimmed at a bleak sunrise or sunset, the elegant scramble of possumhaw or winter-berry branches, the evidence of humankind, an intrusion of artifice in abstractly vertical luminous lemon lines announcing, defining and jetting along an invisible yet tangible barrier/demarcation . . .*

Let me say, finally, your power vaults the distance. Margin to margin. Your excellent last letter arrived today. Yesssss. Your missive has zinged me, my head opened and still ringing from the brick upside it, and with each rereading, that palpable heart thuds into my palms and bleeds all over my hands.

You are very welcome, Truong. It was my great pleasure to be of service. Until . . .

Your weary friend, and correspondent,
Wanda

Patrick Pritchett & Kathleen Fraser

Patrick Pritchett is the author of *Burn—Doxology for Joan of Arc* (Chax Press, 2005), *Reside* (Dead Metaphor, 1999), *Lives of the Poets* (Potato Clock, 2007), and *Antiphonal* (Pressed Wafer, 2008). His poems have appeared in *Colorado Review*, *New American Writing*, *Shiny*, *Bombay Gin*, *New Review of Literature*, *Hambone*, and *The Modern Review*, among others. Essays and reviews on modern and contemporary poetry have been featured in *American Book Review*, *Rain Taxi*, *English Language Notes*, and *Jacket*. Scholarly articles are forthcoming in the anthologies *Radical Vernacular: Lorine Niedecker and the Politics of Place* (University of Iowa, 2008) and *Ronald Johnson: Life and Works* (National Poetry Foundation Press, 2008). Pritchett has taught at the University of Colorado-Bolder and Naropa University. Currently he is a Lecturer in the History and Literature Program at Harvard University.

Kathleen Fraser has collaborated on artist books with Sam Francis, Mary Ann Hayden, Mel Bochner, David Marshall and Nancy Tokar Miller. Twenty wall pieces from **ii ss**—produced in tandem with NY painter Hermine Ford—were shown at Cambridge University and Pratt Institute of Architecture (Rome) in spring 2007. Fraser teaches in the graduate writing program at CCA/San Francisco in the fall and spends the spring in Rome, currently translating Andrea Raos. She has received a Guggenheim, an NEA in poetry and the Frank

O'Hara Prize. Fraser's recent poem collections include: *W I T N E S S* (Chax Press, 2007), *Discrete Categories Forced into Coupling* (Apogee Press, 2004), *hi dde violeth i dde violet* (Nomados, 2003), and *20th Century* (a+bend, 2001). Other collections include essays, *Translating the Unspeakable Poetry and the Innovative Necessity* (published in the Contemporary Poetics Series, University of Alabama Press, 1999), and *il cuore: the heart, Selected Poems, 1970-1995* (Wesleyan University Press, 1997).

Dear Kathleen,

So now we are writing letters. The question on my mind this morning has to do
with how we negotiate this task of lettering. Both the letters we pass back and forth
between us and the letters that deliver us to the poem. How do we keep finding
fresh ways inside of the same 26 letters? (God, according to the *Sefer Yetzirah*, the
Book of Formation, only needed 22 to create the entire world — how very thrifty
of him!) How, in other words, as we grow older in letters, and to some extent,
wearied by it, worried by it, do we re-invent the letter? How do we reinvent our
relationship to it? Is it like a marriage, which our reality-based, Protestant-flavored,
ideological script tells us can only be successful to the extent that we invest it
unremittingly with our dutiful labor? Wouldn't we much prefer instead a marriage
based on the pleasure principle? A relationship to the other, in this case, language
(the ultimate other?) that is founded on a principle of repletion and overflowing? It
would be something like Marcuse's utopian poetics, in which he envisions a re-affir-
mation of the early stages of the libido before it undergoes negation, suborned to
the harshness of the reality principle, and where eros serves as the foundation for
telos, pleasure underwrites existence. I think this attitude speaks for our desire for
the poem as well. The question and the anxiety every writer faces with respect to
her own work must be intimately tied up with the pleasure letters give. The ques-
tion on my mind this morning is simply this, then: how do we find new ways inside
the poem? How do we keep things from going stale?

Camus observes that to be classic is to repeat oneself. And he adds, it means
knowing *how* to repeat oneself. I think this is the real trick all right. Repetition is
the sign of obsession. To write is already to be obsessed. To obey and amplify one's
strangest impulses; the urgings of the word itself. The question of this "how"—this
however, this how-to!—has been weighing on my mind a lot lately. Not so much
from any grandiose anxiety coming from the chimerical appeal of what it means to
be "classic," as if anyone has any control over that, or that such a canonical designa-
tion could possibly mean anything. But from the deeper anxiety of how to keep
faith with my work (how's that for Rilkean resonance?), how to keep it fresh and
full of energy. I feel lately I've hit a barrier in my work, a place where I'm repeat-
ing myself all right, but in all the wrong ways. This is the place every writer

dreads: where yesterday's surprise and invention are today's cliché. The force of original thought that is a writer's style, as Synge calls it, can often decay into just a bag of tricks, a schtick of some kind. We all tend to repeat what proved successful once, but the risk we run by doing so is that the writing can just as often as not go flat. Even the most uncanny writing can erode into mannerism. I see it in older writers as well as those of my own generation, accomplished poets in their 30s and 40s who have hit on something forceful and new, but who then beat it into the ground. How do we escape this trap?

Your own work, it seems to me, offers a salutary model for reinvention. You continue to build on themes that have preoccupied you your whole life, but you do so in ways that infuse the language with vivid and demanding turns. *hi dde violeth i dde violet* is an extraordinary case in point. What incredible risks you take in this poem! It has the structure of a free-fall. But the thing is—as fractured as it is—it has a structure. It is very much a translation of the unspeakable, that is, it carries forward—and lavishes in a delirious spray all around it—the deep strangeness of English. Our own language comes back to us as though it were some other language. For my part, I feel lately as though I've become mired in everything I've done up to this point, marooned in stasis. Every time I start a poem I feel hampered by what I've already written, unable to see beyond the rhetorical strategies I've developed, or past rhetoric itself. (Gil Ott once told me I seemed overly fond of relying on rhetoric, a remark which stung at the time, but only because it was so on the mark. On the other hand, *pace* Gil, who doesn't rely on rhetoric?) Poets like Duncan, whom I've long held in the greatest esteem, have made an entire body of work out of an elevated, at times almost superannuated, rhetoric. (And now I wonder if my devotion to his poetry hasn't been somewhat misplaced.) The urge in my most recent poems has been to try to push things right up to the limit and then past it. To load up the language with as much tension as it can bear, straining it to some kind of infernal/internal breaking point. Then I find myself longing for some form of impossible and complete simplicity in the wake of such excessiveness.

The tension between excess on the one hand and austerity on the other seems central to poetry and deeply marks so much of the most invigorating work of the past century. To transit/translate back and forth between these poles is nothing but the longing to inhabit an idiom that obeys its own law. How to follow?

Perplexedly,
Patrick

Dear Patrick,

Does weather determine everything about human capacity? Is that why so many long-distance telephone conversations begin with: "So, how's the weather there?" It's morning in your letter and I'm guessing that the sun is fully blasting through the window, warming your back as you place your question with its elaborate sub-texts, on the table between us—a thesis already so eloquently developed that it might be launched as a dissertation topic. You despair of the dead-end position in which you find yourself at this moment while I, viewing you from the icy cold & drearily dark long European winter—"Rome's coldest in 200 years," warns *Il Messaggero*—admire your swift brain and your capacity to move flawlessly among the arguments and quotations you embrace as an important part of your poetic ground. I wish for that agility.

*

As soon as I arrived in Rome mid-February and unpacked my books, I pinned a photograph to the wall (just above the desk where I write) showing the figure of a woman running straight into a brick wall. On sudden instinct, I'd tucked the photo into my journal before leaving . . . knowing that the friend who sent it had intuited something of the life I was about to enter. The bricks are of uneven lengths, as if formed by a number of hands, and carry density unequally under the glare of a harsh light source projected from outside the top right corner of the photograph. [I think of a huge prison light, stopped in its certain surveillance . . . or a radiance outside my ability to name it.] The bricks—uneven in their sepia tones and pushed into beds of rough mud—fill the entire photographic plane, except for the woman's long white skirt of bunched tulle, her partially lit bodice wrapped hurriedly around her trunk, head erupting in a dark mass of feathers—or is it hair?—rushing away from her face as it collides with or turns slightly away from the wall, her outstretched hand braced for impact, her legs split apart, an isosceles measure in the air, feet still poised for flight.

Several other notable details: her black shoes, arching in opposite directions; a heavy geometric shadow pressing along the bottom of the photo, somber and irreducibly solid, rising abruptly to become the shape of a flat rectangular chimney—possibly, a doorway? And what is the dark stripe, three bricks deep, rushing along the back wall's lit momentum, marking an upper limit barely held in place?

*

In trying to describe this photo to you, my computer has jumped at least three times, erasing the shape or direction of my words, causing whole chunks of sentences to disappear from the screen. A groan of frustration can be heard by someone in the next room. My conclusion has been erased as abruptly as a theft on a bus. At first I thought it happened when I was tired and accidentally hit a wrong key. But I'm not tired today. There is no wrong key. I look again. Each time the erasure happens I'm required to start over and a slight divergence, a jog of invention occurs because of beginning at a different point in the established order. This is the only source I have at my disposal for answering your question because the brick wall is an image that chose me, one I didn't recognize or have a language for. It required my attention, brick by brick.

*

I wonder if the continuous surveillance of self, in the split context of one's private writing mind—re-phrased in the public glare of academic life—might not be a part of the problem for the poet who has grown up inside seductive, post-modern theory wherein subjectivity and self-referentiality, tricked out in their culprit costumes, persuasively lead one to the very self-tracking anguish that many writers of my generation were trying to distance themselves from in the Sixties?

I'm talking about the literal lexicon of narcissism that poets often seem to come up against, in this or that assigned guise—be it "confessional" or "objectivist" or "language" poetries—in the attempt to make something fresh and original from the tones and conclusions threaded inside an inherited language we admire and take for granted—the *drama* of self-consciousness, pitting the presumed "self" against history *and* in company with one's contemporaries. Seeking or doubting one's place in the reconfiguration of meaning as it is carried forward in alphabet and syntax, perhaps we allow too powerful a klieg light to be trained on our *most* private moments of privilege.

*

You feel certain that obsession—the heart of any vital writing—inevitably takes one back to a same starting point. I know well your feeling of frustration with a personal writing history that seems so often to have hit a wall after a certain number of years inside the same rewind of memory and cultural pressure. The problem appears to be not so much one's inadvertent return to the familiar but how to recover solitude and sufficient curiosity as to forego the personal drama and, instead, to untangle what has evaded your attention—to reconfigure the terms of investigation so that known grammatical paths are not so easily satisfied with their glamorous conclusions.

But you have addressed your own question, finally, by citing pleasure in language as the first working principle: Play as the highest form of work.

Kathleen

Boulder, Colorado
May 13, 2005

Dear Kathleen,

Well, my dear, if you can wish for my agility, then I can pine for your splendid, descriptive gifts and your singular ability to focus on and conjure up the elusive, moving target.

"Beginning again"—yes, that's it. The way the weather is always beginning again. But I prefer to skirt the fraught earnestness of this talismanic phrase, with its Rilkean echoes: the devout fetishizing of the poem as a mandarin passport for the soul on one of its haute bourgeois daytrips to Castle Weltschmerz. I want to try to unfold for myself what "beginning again" might mean.

Beginning again. What doesn't this phrase offer? Is it the promise of infinite renewal? A way to recharge the poem's energy field so that it becomes a negentropic device, something that impedes or arrests, for a little while, the inevitable slouch toward total decay? Or, more down to earth, is it simply the daily commitment to sit down in front of the poem and ask it what it wants of us? This is the stock writer's workshop response and it has all the resonating power of "use the force" and other empty clichés of self-empowerment. Perhaps the question of "beginning again" could be more fruitfully reposed as: what does form want of us? Beginning again, it seems to me, involves the question of form as such—of form's *desire*. Which may be nothing other than the desire *for* form.

So, how's the weather here? As ever, I'd say: a trope for reading all our shifts in mood, the exterior sign of our inner atmosphere. Poems are a bit like weather systems. Self-organizing systems of patterned energy. But they're also the instruments by which we try to read the flux of the world. Barometric devices for apprehending our subtle changes in pressure. Weather systems are said to be dependent on what chaos scientists call "sensitivity to initial conditions"—the so-called "butterfly effect" by which a hummingbird's flutter outside my window can set off a hailstorm in Prague. I think poems work this way too. The initial response to some change in the temperature kicks off the poem's epistemological engine. Because a poem, among other things, is what wants to know more, say more, see more, than we can already. And this can only be accomplished through the way we work through and respond to the longing for form. The longing *of* form. For what I want to call, in a hopelessly utopian locution, form's utopia. Why? Because form is what gives us the world at once more fully *and* more fractured.

I wonder if this extravagant thing I'm calling "the utopia of form" can successfully stave off "the glamour of conclusions," as you so aptly phrase one of the most looming and seductive of poetic pitfalls? I want to say that it can, so long as we learn to recognize that what drives form is not some slavish regulatory practice of *con*forming, but rather the urge of language to *trans*form: to continually morph into something else. Forget *make it new*, since the new is merely another brick in the wall of reification, but: *make it other*—*make it strange*. This is where the Objectivist mantra of learning to bring one's full attention to whatever one is looking at meets with Wallace Stevens' line, "And there I found myself more truly and more strange." And where is this *there* located, but in the strangeness of language itself?

Your description of the photo: a woman running full-tilt into a brick wall is a marvelous bit of ekphrasis. By the time we reach the end of this carefully nuanced narrative we know *more*—more about the photo than we would have had we been gazing on it ourselves—and more about ourselves and our habits of looking, our ways of seeing. But the other thing we know is how strange it is to focus with such singular resolution on *some one thing* and to allow ourselves to be saturated by that thing—and by the language we bring to that thing (and which it brings to us, in unexpected leaps of disjointed connection).

Benjamin, writing on Baudelaire, remarks that when we look at a thing we invest it with the uncanny power to look back at us, to return our gaze. This, he says, is the essence of the aura and its distanciating effect—*far away, so close*—the haunting intimacy conferred by a certain unbridgeable spiritual distance. Perhaps the aura begins at that point where form takes on substance, the point where the material weight of words, thick with saying, liquid and heavy, aspirate the body with a run of clustered syllables. So, the poem is what looks back at us and its gaze is a summoning to enter language. Language as a condition of longing that can only be assuaged by attending, with nuance and devotion, to language. The woman runs into the wall, yes. "A jog of invention" you say, and I say back, "yes," because now I am enclosed in what you see and know, too, and in what this photograph sees and knows. I am taken inside its ambit, to that point where seeing becomes a form of ethical engagement because it makes me implicit in your knowing—a bond has formed between us and that bond is form.

What you say about the poem foregoing personal drama in order to thrive really resonates. A poem can either be caught up in a host of little anxieties, in which case it will not amount to much, or it can summon us to a place of speaking, rich with its own force.

But summoning is not surveillance. "The continuous surveillance of self," as you put it, seems so much a part of this territory, but like you, I think it's a mode we've merely become habituated to. It has nothing to do with the poem *per se* and everything to do with the self-regulating dictates of ideology. The poem as therapeutic instrument or interface is a particularly pernicious instance of this ideology. As if what language in all its complexity required of us was simply that we take a spiritual inventory from time to time, checking off the appropriate boxes marked "trauma," or "mother," or whatever. What an impoverished, commodifying way to look at the poem!

This agonizing split in consciousness, though, surely didn't originate with the moment of theory (which, true enough, presents its own enticing bogs and hazards for writers). Theory only articulated it in a more legible way, tracing out its contradictions and allures, productively complicating much of what had become conventionalized in the script we employ to write about the self. Surely the split goes back at least as far as the Romantics. (Or does it begin when Adam first named the animals?) I think of Shelley's awful drama of bifurcation in *Alastor, or the Spirit of Solitude*, where the poet grapples with his daemonic other in a ghostly allegorical landscape as he threatens to dissolve under the very pressure of subjectivity into something utterly spectral. It is, admittedly, a precious drama, but it is, regrettably, much of what makes up our drama.

No, to be a self is always already to be haunted, I feel, since we come to find out who we are as much as by what we are not, as much by what has been negated, as by what we might become. This, too, partakes of the utopia of form—the spectral no-place that is also *someplace*—where to embody the self is to practice a kind of echolalia. How we listen to the echoes—and the utterance we shape in response to them—determines form's measure. The echo we hear pinging back off of our own words works to ensure that form's promise holds both continuity and rupture, identity and difference—that the utopia of form is founded on an order of repetition that is constantly repeating, yet always at variance with, itself.

Are we dancing yet? I think I need a drink—

Love,
Patrick

Berlin, Germany
June 25, 2005

Dear Patrick,

Again a wall—here, the grayish, hacked-out remains of it piled on little tables along the former Berlin Wall route where young men <u>still</u> sell fragments of "the

actual wall," together with other cheap trophies of the Russian/East German occu-
pation, lived through by their parents. During my walks here, I've found myself
startled by the visual push-pull of past and present, its effect something like a lung
breathing with effort, trying to expel its toxins. There are, as before, the extraor-
dinary classical museums unfolding one ancient treasure after another; they are
often located in bombed-out blocks of East Berlin neighborhoods now actively
restoring themselves with galleries, jazz clubs and bookstores . . . a little like the
Lower East Side in NYC in the Sixties, and a very lively and internationally hip
arts scene.

I'm very moved by—and take hope from—this urgency to go back to the drawing
board and rethink, remake habitable life. Seeing a freshly arrived generation in the
process of documenting its perceptions and critique connects significantly for me
with why poets need, on a regular basis, to re-form/re-articulate their own era.
Who can be adequately or entirely represented only by inherited arguments and
past ways of seeing? As practitioners, we itch to reconceive—to take apart and
reassemble the fundamental enactments of our language. Hasn't the great poetry
always been an invitation to turn the corner and catch a peripheral glimpse of
what's there, just beyond the comfy drone? Word architecture as antidote to
entropy's "ownership" effect? You know, the refusal of language as a set piece?

*

In Berlin, there is evidence of extremity. The once dominant and hypnotic presence
of Nazism is persistent, notably in the 80 lamppost signs posted in the Jewish
Bavarian quarter, each one enumerating a 1930s law that served to restrict Jewish
life in Germany. Even now, evidence of war and occupation persists in the formerly
occupied Eastern part of the city where bullet-marks and scars of WWII bombing
remain as lost graffiti on the facades of dreary apartment buildings, some fifteen
years after the once impenetrable WALL was dismantled, chunk by cement chunk.

Fortunately that's not the end of it. Suddenly turning the corner, you come upon
the radical geometric planes and vivid colors of recent buildings rising from the
bomb-leveled fields of Potsdammer Platz and feel grateful for the new century's
ability to create a different idea of human community without erasing the knowl-
edge of profound damage done. An extraordinary resurgence of architectural
innovation surrounds the walker with its vivid chromatic upswing of buildings by

Renzo Piano, Arata Isozaki, and Helmut Jahn. Nearby, a quieter kind of design takes an utterly different turn in the physically disturbing memory—conduits of Daniel Libeskind's Jewish Museum and the recently built Holocaust site, its city block starkly covered with black marble stelae of varying heights, leaning and subtly off-balance so as to physically overwhelm you as you walk the paths between stone rows and feel an overwhelming surge of sadness and dizziness along with the body's refusal to adjust.

Every day young artists and writers are migrating from all over Germany and other parts of Europe to absorb and respond to this history. For them, East Berlin also provides cheap housing and studio space where they can afford to live and pursue their art and craft. What has changed in this picture?

*

Thinking back to earlier conversations we've had about the weight of theory vs. poetry's need for fresh linguistic models, I recently returned to several books that had been important to me in the Seventies—Roland Barthes' *The Pleasure of the Text* and Ludwig Wittgenstein's *Philosophical Investigations*, both of which recharged my sense of the investigative potential of poetic language. Both texts also helped to suggest alternative vocabularies and to challenge the growing token use of abstract thought that had begun, at that point, to provide such heft and angst to the critical quest driving poetics studies since then.

This is the drama I was trying to address in my last letter to you. It is the drama carried around inside any potential poet when he or she contemplates—often through assigned critical readings—the heightened *theoretical* questions of subjectivity, gender, race, and class, quite before the physical materials or intellectual/ spiritual claims of a <u>particular</u> event have even landed and begun to register.

I would suggest that this potential rearranging of priorities should give pause to any poet already up to his/her ankles in the mud of words and inherited syntax.

*

My mind is tracking this **X** in our conversation because of shifting references to "form" that imprint your recent letter so that I can approximate your meanings by placing overlays of my own experience, like cut-out stencils, to bring me in some way closer to your use of this term. So here I am, at abstraction's impasse, feeling my way around a seemingly familiar *topos* of "form" but unable to seize upon a clear model of what you picture—what sorts of spatial movement or sonic notation you hold in your mind when you think *into* writing. I need to see your blueprint.

In your letter, these questions and statements regarding form particularly interest me:

"And this is the longing for *form*. For *form*'s utopia"; "What drives *form* is not some slavish regulatory practice of con*form*ing, but rather its ability to trans*form*. . . ."; and, finally, "to ensure that *form*'s promise holds both continuity and rupture. . . that the utopia of *form* is founded on an order of repetition that is constantly repeating, yet always at variance with, itself."

It is because of these—and other references—that my mind is hovering over this focus, but I remain uncertain as to what event you—the poet, PP—precisely refer to in your private set of equations. Your letter suggests a vividly embraced goal— perhaps a describable achievement, something agreed upon and already familiar to your academic and/or reading communities—but not yet connected-up for me, via particular instances or events of language that have illuminated your own writing practice. In fact, I'd love to hear more in this regard! It seems that for all of us the life behind form's somewhat illusive assumptions is worth a fuller investigation, so as to illuminate the presence of a term so continuously leaned upon as a cultural referent, yet largely under-described in poetics discourse.

*

Patrick, whatever happened to the ecstatic impulse we initially felt as young writers first encountering the unpredictable effects of poetic language, its delinquent Siren call? Barthes writes that: "pleasure wants . . . the seam, the cut, the deflation, the *dissolve* which seizes the subject in the midst of bliss." What I'm struck by is the precise, often filmic corporality of his critical vocabulary—seam, cut, deflation, dissolve—terms at once available to the body's understanding and the mind's ability to translate formally. These terms might suggest the *physicality* of *de*constructed rhythms and syntactical grammars that, employed with the intention and design of our individual brains and sensory skills, propel language's leaps forward, particularly in the realm of poetry.

Re-reading your recent letter to me, I note with delight the way you shift a reader's expectation via phrases embodying a certain physical liveliness—for example, "to live smack in the middle of turbulence," *or* "a kind of prosthetic advice"—phrases which bear the material evidence—the concrete image—of your mental processes, echoing your wit as it reorganizes familiar vocabulary frames. As you've written so brilliantly: "The sensitivity to initial conditions . . . works as the poem's tiny epistemological engine."

*

Am I wrong to observe that the language of critical discourse has *tended*—in the last three or so decades—to over-drench our thinking re the making of poems, by smuggling its own list of *au courant* abstract urgencies into poetry's more visceral territory? It would appear that many of the current choices *pre*/scribed from the sleeve of academic authority—patina'd with a certain allure—may have become, at the same time, too revered and yet too familiar, that is, once removed from the actual physical precipice that marks the uneasy edge of writing's activity. Is it possible that competing concerns (languages) of analysis/theory **vs**. the poet's invented syntactical/physical arrangements are capable of creating an *impasse*, even impairing one's working contract with the imagination?

Clearly, theorizing can be fun and necessary to illuminate the underpinnings of a new direction in writing or the arts. Am I then advocating a position of resistance to critical theory in one's own poetry practice? Not exactly, but I do wish to cause a flurry, to divert or subvert the poet's riveted attention *away* from the worship of any stylish cookie-cutter vocabulary or self-important drone that seems, too often of late, to precede or diminish a certain spirit of investigatory delight in doing what we do best. I can't help thinking of that old magic trick, performed with consummate timing and skill in which—with the proper flick of a wrist—two hands? two wrists?—the practitioner can part a tablecloth from the burden of its various place settings, leaving all solid objects perfectly intact while the tablecloth, meanwhile, is waved above the magician's head in a gesture of victory over entropy.

*

Wittgenstein's foregrounding of the term "investigation" in his *Philosophical Investigations* sets forth a *practice* of coming to the world without certainty, but rather with curiosity, *un*belonging to an established ordering, an openness to ambiguity and the unfinished—for a poet, the intentional pursuit of the untried, vs. the habituated default position of sound's organization.

I'll take mine neat with a soda chaser,
Kathleen

Boulder, Colorado
October 23, 2005

Dear Kathleen,

Your letter is so rich I hardly know where to begin! Your resonant and very affecting account of life and the renascence of art in a Berlin still recovering from decades of war and repression goes straight to the idea (the hope) that form will assert itself as the desire to shape a world even in, or most especially in, the most dire of circumstances. That it is, in fact, central to our way of living on earth.

Thinking about form is an invitation to enter a maze of the most intimate design. If it seems to me the central thing we must talk about when we talk about poetry it's only because I feel drawn to the questions it poses over and over. To wonder how form performs in a poem is to go back to the most basic concerns we have about art—to the primal regard with which we gaze on the world and the other. To the care we take for continuity, for going on. And to the places in that continuum where it is crucial that we break it, make a gap, a space for opening into and out of it, for letting in the strange, the discounted, and for leaping across, for striking a spark. For reforming our relationship to the world and each other by way of form.

About a month ago, I went to hear Jean Valentine and Julie Carr read at the University of Colorado. Afterwards they fielded questions from the audience and the thorny issue of "truth" in poetry was raised. There was a great deal of confusion about this notion, which I think speaks to some of my own concerns about how we should view poetic form. Someone in the audience felt that the "trueness" of a poem entailed some species of emotional honesty—the "write what you know" school of literary positivism. I much prefer to write what I don't know—that is, to be surprised by my own turns of language as I go, turns that lead me into wholly unexpected areas of the poem. (It's useful to bear in mind, all the same, Dante's enjoinder to poets in *De Vulgari Eloquentia* that they avoid tackling subjects that are too weighty for them to handle. Don't attempt a cosmological epic, he counsels, if all you're really capable of at the moment is a rather slight, if musical, love lyric. Right, then.)

So, what is *true* for a poem? And is this the same thing as expecting a poem to be true? Is it merely a case of producing something that seems emotionally verifiable, conforming to our available range of thought and experience? Does the poem have the moral authority to make certain claims it advances, or is it merely indulging in rhetorical posturing? That last seems important, but ultimately leads to an impoverished model of poetics, I feel, with everything weighed on a scale of nicety according to how closely it hews to the bourgeois reader's idea of a transparent, accessible self. It's a moralizing way to look at the poem, rather than an ethical one.

It seems to me more useful and more desirable to speak of the linguistic integrity of the poem, as a material object, rather than to assert any claims for it as a vehicle for truth-telling. What a poem *can* offer is precision of observation, or sincerity, as Zukofsky calls it: a formal category of perception and of knowing. In yoga, my teacher speaks of "the integrity of the pose." This is an appealing way to think of a poem. As a living structure in which opposing forces and tensions are brought into balance through breath and alignment.

When you and I were on the panel together at the Tucson Poetry Festival earlier this month, our discussion touched a lot on form's concerns. The painter Josh Goldberg referred to his own practice of generating a kind of "endless troping" in his work, a phrase I felt neatly summed up the process by which a poem generates and sustains its quest for energy. This "endless troping," Josh went on, moved in and around the desire to maintain a certain degree of doubt with respect to the work as it takes shape. What fed it was the "para-gestural"—the way the work moves both toward and away from something definitive on the canvas or the page, driving along opposing axes simultaneously, as it seeks to arrive at and reject closure all at once. This is a conception of form that keeps faith with its own process—that is *true*, if you will, to the process of its own composition and utterance, to its own internal procedures for mapping its space, for speaking otherwise. And though it often seems easily reduced to a mere slogan, it's important to keep reiterating that a poem is a form of language that speaks otherwise.

Poetry, and poetic form especially, entail learning how to see otherwise—that is, really see—how to recognize the other *as* other, whether the human figure of a person or some figure of the world, and not merely as something from which all traces of difference have been eradicated. The poem offers resistance to the hegemonizing and totalizing gaze of cultural systems deeply intent on reducing difference. Form itself must offer resistance to form—because even form—a stale, ideological version of form, one that fetishizes the history and reception of formal strategies—is prey to the same impulse toward totalization. Form is not something to be slavishly adhered to, but must be continually re-invented so that the human can always stand before the human, apprehended *as it is seen*. To acquire this kind of poetic or formal way of looking means, as Pound says, going in fear of abstractions, attending to what Blake called "minute Particulars." We need to unlearn how we see in order to be able to see freshly again.

At the Tucson panel, an audience member wanted to confuse a work's formal properties with its moral register by asking how poets and painters treat light and dark in their work. My reply was something like this: that the formal properties of a poem consist of its negative and positive space (type face, layout, the page considered as a unit of composition, with the white spaces "weighing" as much as the dark print). This suggests an arrangement or set of relations that seeks a proportion, a measure, a balance—the integrity of a pose—and this is the poem's ethical or moral center of gravity—this is how a poem stays true—to itself as an object. The urge to Sameness, rubbing at us from all sides, puts an enormous pressure on us to conform. Poetry offers a way to speak against that pressure—a heteroglossia—the possibility of a responding differently is an ethics of responding. The drive to the *otherwise*—doesn't this, more or less, represent "the victory over entropy" you speak of?

Denis Donoghue describes form as "the achieved, purposed deployment of energy, energy available on need and not there till looked for: it is never found before the need of it." I like this stab at a definition, yet it still feels far from adequate to me. Still there is the conundrum of form, the blank, white wall of it. The excess of saying, the need for it, and the need for containing that excess in a shape that will be useful, will carry over, from me to you, to my reader, to any proleptically imagined Whitmanian *someone*, whom, in this specific moment, I have such need for. You, my reader, saying "yes," as the form of a poem arrives. This is the utopian gesture the poem makes and lives in the hope of making—an apostrophe—a call to the other. Made to no one in particular, yet always with the implicit expectation of a response. The poem is an address to that other, a silent auditor whose very absence engenders the occasion of the poem's utterance. And this reciprocity strikes me as the very foundation of ethics. As my dear friend Ingrid Nelson puts it, the lyric "I" is almost an instance of pure tropism, the subject as an always-turning-toward the witness, the one who, even absent, is still present, and will hear my call.

*

Barthes, whom you invoke so aptly—he was that rare theorist whose great care for language made him not only, I feel, a master stylist, but a kind of lyric poet, at times (in this he is like Derrida—the Derrida of *The Post Card*)—Barthes speaks of the responsibility of forms, by which I take it he means that aesthetic form derives both its telos or purpose and its authority from the task of saying the world back to itself in a way that both recognizes and amplifies it. Beauty, then, can be viewed, as Elaine Scarry argues, as an instigation toward justice. And form becomes, to paraphrase Robert Duncan, the ability of the poem to respond to matter: the signature of the other, of the event of the other. In the place of whatever is felt to be missing the poem (or any work of art) tries to generate its own force field of singular presence, one that can assuage our ache for the absent other. I don't think this means that poems as such are somehow fetishes or mere substitutions for something more essential, elaborate mechanisms for staving off the void. Quite the opposite—in taking the place of what is absent a poem offers itself as the form of connection we can most rely on and draw consolation from. By speaking of what is lost, an achieved poem overcomes its exile and enters its own alterity. As such, it is ungainsayable.

Beckett urges us to seek new forms, since the old ones are insufficient. They can no longer admit the chaos of being. He spoke as someone deeply aware that form itself was in crisis and that for language to resist this crisis new ways of saying were required. They are required of us each day. Each encounter with the other makes a demand of us we can never fully hope to live up to and yet we must try, we must take up the poem as a way to say that encounter, as a way to make legible some signature of the event that is our daily meeting with the world.

✳

What if form is what actually *thinks* the poem's thought, not blindly, as in some mechanical motor function, but through a complex sensitivity to its own origin and evolution? A continual sense of itself as alive to an intricate network of possibilities which must always narrow to a single choice at a single juncture?

Form is the *body* of the poem, its kinesthetic mind. Form directing thought—the "content" of the poem—telling it how to take shape. This is more than the superficial notion of style as a wedding between sound and sense. It's more like what David Shapiro, in Tucson, referred to as "the wedding of loneliness and contingency." Form governs the morphology of a poem's intellection so that the turn of the line is also the substance of the thought.

I think finally what I mean by form is something like the continual response of the imagination to reality out of its deep dissatisfaction with each fresh attempt to articulate its desire to shape the real.

✳

The weather here is turning, green to gold to brown, and when shall we see each other again?

Expectantly,
Patrick

San Francisco, California
December 17, 2005

Dear Patrick,

As I drove home two nights ago through the early evening dark of San Francisco, my attention was abruptly pulled away from the familiar voice of NPR news by the sudden appearance of the moon—first, between two apartment houses, then rolling above or to the sides of high and low-rise buildings as I headed up Russian Hill.

It was so close. Almost "intimate" in its full presence yet entirely unknowable for the way it both retreated and advanced, a hovering and suspended white radiance emanating from the smoke-like fog surrounding it. Inside my car, the NPR interviewer was speaking to a shopkeeper in one of Iraq's northern cities where the election polls had just closed and last voters were still scurrying towards home, down the same dark alley where the two men stood talking, with only the full moon for light. The shopkeeper seemed happy; he explained to the interviewer that he'd been able to sell plenty of goods—even without electricity—because his neighbors still needed to buy rice and cooking oil. Election night was already in-progress, a rite of celebration . . . one could hear shouts of children and musical instruments in the background.

"That was the same moon *I'm* looking at, shining on *their* party," I thought, an obvious comprehension that never ceases to surprise me—that wherever one stands on the earth's surface, within any twenty-four hour period, the same moon displays, with equal power, its waxing & waning to every gaze trained on it.

*

I meant to note its strange beauty to Arthur when I got home but by the time I remembered, it had moved out of sight. The next night, an hour earlier and not yet dark, I looked from my kitchen window facing towards the east bay, where I expected the moon to appear. It would now be imperceptibly taking on more darkness, I thought. But it wasn't there.

I tried shifting position, moving a few feet to the left or right of the divided windowpane, checking closer to the horizon line. Then, quite suddenly, I saw it caught between the rungs of the over-built wooden stairs running up and down the backside of the building next to ours. There it was, framed and isolate—deep pumpkin-colored, definite in its contours. Formally re-contextualized.

∗

I much appreciate your willingness to go after a fuller exploration of the word "form"—your confessed obsession—as it pertains to the composing work of poems. You honor the continuum of one's writing while intentionally seeking a break from—a break into?—familiar territory to produce a stubborn record of, at the least, uneasiness.

Your yoga teacher's phrase "the integrity of the pose" eludes and seduces me at once, because its ethic seems to come from a still, self-contained point—a quality of attending within the body/mind that assumes a formal capacity in us to reach that final achieved place (pose) . . . something like the realized "form" of the well-made poem? You see where I'm going? I'm not sure I want my yoga mixed in with my poetics. Pilates invokes another body concept that may, for me, provide a better metaphor, i.e. "firing" muscles that have fallen into the inactive or default position while allowing other muscles to repeatedly take over, thus denying a given musculature its capability to help support the body's full expressiveness. Both these practices begin in deficit, and assume the formal capability for change, each keeping faith with its own process as a record of energetic embodiment.

∗

I'm intrigued by your quotes, in particular the Donoghue and Beckett statements. At the same time, I want to take my distance from any tone of absolute poetics issuing from both great and tiny minds, which appear to stabilize knowledge in a comforting way—self-assured edicts often circulated to correct others' waywardness—doubling as antidotes to a poetry that doesn't fit prescription, as if the poetic imagination were a disease to be finally cured.

I'm interested in why a concept such as "truth"—which pulls us into abstraction, a discernable "right" path—is a point of contention in the discussion following the public poetry reading you've described. What is the temptation here? And why are we writers so lured—we, whose passion for waking up the language has led us to seek a music and visual accuracy attendant upon our own peculiar, vagrant and unexplored claims on experience?

Take your Dante reference, for example—at least in the passage you quote, from *De Vulgari Eloquentia*—that poets should avoid tackling subjects that are too weighty for them to handle. "Don't," says Dante, "attempt a cosmological epic, if all you're really capable of at the moment is a rather slight, if musical love lyric."

"Ah," the impressionable writer might mutter, stung by the "truth" of Dante's wisdom. Will his/her mind then go into collapsed mode and agree to sign the contract: to keep modestly repeating his/her own "slight" versions of agreed upon "truth"? Possibly. What limits can hope to be exceeded if the poet recognizes this "slight, if musical" depiction as a possible characterization of certain of his own tentative poems written while "sick" with love? Perhaps our poet *enjoyed* discovering the anti-harmonics of a particular post-modern love entanglement, even as half-completed fragments struggled to find their intention on the page? Perhaps said poet had been contemplating—even drafting—a larger cacophony of voices, an incalculable jump from the high-wire?

I think Dante's got it all wrong here. How can one possibly know ahead of time what s/he is capable of? Why begin by courting someone else's fixed idea? Who decides what makes an epic work or how a love lyric should limit itself? Why measure one's own potential capacity only by what you've produced so far, or by what has preceded you? Why *not* take the plunge for love or planetary motion, even when you don't know if you can pull "it" off . . . or even quite how you'll begin? What is there to lose, should you decide to jump? Nothing other than someone else's historic surround and what that person has imagined as certainty ("truthfulness") of place.

Dante didn't understand, until too late, that he was like the Moon—porous to atmospheric change, refinement of lens, dependent on inter-connected phenomena—in his case, the capacity of the Church to empower his artistic vision <u>or</u> to reject it. He was on the run from their reigning power, on the wrong side of the argument between Church hierarchy and the secular leadership of the aristocracy who deviated from the Church's historic vise. The church fathers felt threatened by Dante's "truth" and wanted him in prison. In his visionary refusal of their bidding—his willingness to challenge the grasping and tattered dictation of church law—he found a way to produce the unavoidable pressure and demand that shaped his cadences and provoked the formal structure for his gathering outcry, an "otherness" that remains potent to this day.

✳

Perhaps one's "poetics"—or formal exploration—should be entirely tied to one's urgencies, wherein a writing practice may align its chanciness with the life being lived. You <u>are</u> "the other," Patrick . . . we are all "other," to varying degrees, given half a chance. What is this thing called "Truth" in poetry? Is it like "truth in lending," "the God's honest truth," "Truth or Consequences?" How are we to speak of the irreconcilable differences between two lives? Isn't "the truth" a concept dependent on movable parts, a point of decision measured and meted out by those before you who have controlled the perspective?

In a related email, Robert Gluck recently wrote me:

> To say one kind of poetry or thought purveys a truth and another does not, doesn't make sense to me. All form tells how the world is organized, it is an allegory of that, so that a linear poem, a sonnet, a poem by Mallarmé or a poem by you—each makes an assertion about how experience is organized, even if it only applies to one's own experience (though I don't believe it is ever so confined). The problem with an antique form is that it may distort the expression of my experience of the present. So, does my experience rhyme, does it have resounding closure?—sometimes, perhaps. Is it fragmented?—yes, more often.

✳

Our use of language propels and reveals us. It pieces "us" together when we are shattered. Such is the body of current re/formation, poetry's shifting formal ground.

Here's to you and the unexpected!

Kathleen

Hajera Ghori & Alfred Artega

Hajera Ghori graduated from the University of California, Berkeley in 2005 with a degree in English. She has decided to ignore the threat of future unemployment and is currently working on her master's degree in Creative Writing at Goldsmiths College in London. Her poetry has been published in the *Berkeley Poetry Review*.

Alfred Arteaga was born in East Los Angeles. He studied at Columbia University and the University of California, Santa Cruz. His writings range from poetry and personal essays to literary criticism and theory. His books of poetry include *Frozen Accident* (Tia Chucha, 2006), *Red* (Bilingual Review Press, 2000), *Love in the Time of Aftershocks* (Chusma House and Moving Parts Press, 1998) and *Cantos* (Chusma House Publications, 1991). Among his other works are the award-winning collection of essays, *House with the Blue Bed* (Mercury House, 1997), as well as *An Other Tongue: Nation and Ethnicity in the Linguistic Borderlands* (Duke University Press, 1994), a collection he edited on cultural studies, language and border politics, and *Chicano Poetics* (Cambridge University Press, 1997). He has received a National Endowment for the Arts Creative Writing Fellowship in Poetry and a PEN Oakland Josephine Miles Award for Literary Excellence. He was Professor of Ethnic Studies at the University of California, Berkeley.

Berkeley, California
April 26, 2005

Dear Alfred,

While wondering how to begin this project, and thinking of the issues that are most relevant to my writing, I was suddenly struck by how narcissistic being a poet can be. Do I write because I can or because I'm self-obsessed enough to think I can?

I imagine myself in a house full of mirrors, each one depicting the different ways I can be. It is sometimes tiring to feel stuck writing about what I know best — myself. However, my poetry can be a way to both keep myself from being trapped in this endless montage of self-reflection, as well as to project those images in a cohesive shape to others. In some ways, I admit, this is a form of self-validation. Don't misunderstand me; I write for myself, I have to in order to get words on the page. However, in the back of my mind, I also worry what other people will think.

I worry most over falling trap to clichés. For example, like many, I write best when I draw from some kind of pain or anger. I'm usually able to mold my pain into a form that pleases me and satisfies my need for verbal exorcism. However, lately I've been trying to escape that repetitious usage of pain as art. I feel that I perhaps shouldn't have to be depressed to write. What if I'm feeling content or dare I say, happy?

Recently, I've been trying to write romantic poetry, the ultimate forum for clichés. As a true product of my culture, when thinking of love I fall back on the mass-produced archetypes of love I was raised on through films and literature. The best of these attempts is, sadly enough, the following, where I express my fear and doubt towards this person.

At times
I see only
a structure of jaw
turned hungry. Tasting
my salted expectation

he plays me,
makes me believe
in the still moment
able to fall into itself.

I can see now
he hides
a hand behind his back,
holding the stone
I gave him
the color of sky.

I like this poem precisely because of the ominous possibilities behind the initial euphoria of falling in love. The rest of my earlier attempts consist of tired metaphors and adjectives I'm too embarrassed to quote. Herein lies my insecurity; should I be able to write happy poems or is poetry simply better or more interesting when there is an element of some more dangerous or subversive emotion? Perhaps when in that numbing haze of being in love or lust, I shut off some part of my intelligence. It could be the part that is a bit darker, more thoughtful and rebellious. Maybe what makes me happy is commonplace: kisses, sunny days, etc., but what makes me sad or angry is more unique and therefore more interesting a source to write from.

For example, if I look over recent scribbles in my notebook, I see a description of a small encounter I witnessed between two men the other night on the train. One was an older black man in a wheelchair and the other was a middle aged white businessman who had got on the train at the airport stop. The man in the wheelchair had a gaunt, prematurely aged face that slumped in a seemingly perpetual frown. He couldn't have been much older than the businessman. He asked the businessman for the time, who replied with a cheerful, somewhat patronizing tone. The man in the wheelchair then asked with a chuckle whether that was the right time for our time zone to which the businessman said nothing. The hopeful glint that sprang at his attempt at cheerful banter disappeared and he resumed his hunched frown.

I wonder why the elements of an incident such as this, with its representation of societal rifts and failed human interaction, is more of a source of inspiration in my writing than something such as my love life. It is odd to me that anger or sadness is so much easier to express than happiness. I feel that good poetry must be well-rounded and must speak to the reader through several senses, emotional, intellectual and to something a bit more, something that is just almost intangible. In doing so, the poet should be able to reach and tug in all different directions within their writing and scope of experience. Thus, my question to you is, what happens when a poet seems to write about the same subject? Is it simply the poet needing to expel whatever subject that insists on appearing repeatedly before moving on or does this imply a rut that needs to be overcome?

Sincerely,
Hajera Ghori

Palo Alto, California
July 20, 2005

Hajera,

Your letter so filled my thoughts that yesterday a walk in San Francisco could have occurred anywhere. For all that I missed around me, the Mission District might well have been Belleville, Cayo Hueso, or even, an anonymous desert dune beside an anonymous beach dune. If you had intended my *dislocasia*, then you were successful: the simple arrangement of graphemes and morphemes shook me loose from the world about me.

I had been heading toward Modern Times to meet Dana. Your letter came to mind as I passed Herbivore. It was close to sunset, the air, clear. The afternoon fog had already blown to Oakland. Light was rapidly leaving the Bay, the blue reddening as it reached across the Pacific. After that, I recall but your words. They performed the epistolary magic of writing, filling the present with meaning from afar.

Your letter interrogated what poetry did in words at once self-reflective and self-reflexive. And it posed the question why were pain and loss better expressed in your poetry than were romance and love. This mobius pursuit to interrogate the means making meaning is what so engaged me.

I am taken with how pervasive you were in the cafe, later when I was speaking with Dana Teen Lomax, how the epistle you launched at another time and place colored my perception and shaped my words. I kept steering the talk to matters poetic as if in effort to answer you. By means of the letter, you were there as a supplement, altering the course of the conversation. And though I draw attention to this here, this is merely what writing does. This bridging across time and space is a feature, an expression of its structure, and the magic of writing.

Which brings me to Narcissus. I agree with you, writing poetry often is an act of narcissism. In the myth, Narcissus sees his reflection, is swayed by its beauty, and falls in love. As it concerns poetry, I find it less significant that he falls in love with himself, or even that he falls in love with a beautiful image. It seems important that he exists apart from the object he comes to love. Narcissus is not his reflection; at the very least, he is spatially displaced from it. And it is that circumstance, the dislocation of self and perceived object, that provides Narcissus the opportunity to reach across and bridge the gap. In this case, the bridge is love.

In this way, poetry is narcissistic. For cannot it be said of poetry that like love, it too counteracts isolation? A poem is the meaningful quanta of connection. It reaches across the gulf separating self and other and conveys meaning, perhaps of love, perhaps empathy, perhaps loss. The other may be the known recipient of a letter, the unknown reader of a book, or even the self, as long as it exists at some remove, as it does for Narcissus.

By design, a poem connects. Love connects too. Because of this, a love poem is especially harmonious: the means and the meaning are the same. The love poem supplements the reality of dislove and disrupts the order of separation. It affects change. To some extent, it does what it says, it makes hearts, as well as minds, connect, harmonize.

But not all poems need harmonize this way. One that deals with the pain of loss, for example, can oppose the means to the meaning. While such a poem may connect poet and reader, its meaning, nevertheless, is one of failure to connect. The poem of loss is disharmonious: its means are a success, its meaning, failure. It is a structural irony and powerful demonstration of poetry's struggle against the entropy of isolation.

Your poem demonstrates that you value surprise, ambiguity, and the breaking of expected order. Yours is a poetics built on jumps where meaning is left unsettled and open. And you are particularly sensitive to disharmony. This is evident in the incident you chose to relate. You are profoundly moved by the failure of a man who struggles against isolation only to succumb to it.

So to answer your question, let me pose another. How could you not find poems of pain and loss more efficacious than those of romance and love? You prize the endeavor of poetry but lack faith in its efficacy. You write poems that reach out to the reader yet do extol the triumph of love. You are more interested and find more art in disharmony than in harmony. Love poems must strike you as naive and somewhat facile.

But because you espouse ambiguity, unfinished meaning, and the breaking of expected order, my answer cannot be that simple. Take the image of the stone at your poem's end. I cannot know without doubt whether it is of a ring or to be thrown.

Alfred

Berkeley, California
January 23, 2006

Dear Alfred,

It is very true what you wrote; I am naturally attracted to disharmony and ambiguity in literature and poetry. I feel a sense of morbid joy in seeing discord and confusion represented through a medium that is so painstakingly organized. I find it both discomforting and satisfying to distinguish between the pages of black and white something deliberately vague. My writing is not necessarily cathartic in the sense that, when writing a poem, I don't transmute through my pen, whatever pain or perplexity I feel at the time into clarity or resolve. I enjoy the process but I don't usually find an answer from the start of my poem to the end.

Instead, I embrace ambiguity and double meanings, especially in my endings, because I would feel dishonest to tack on some insipid resolution when I'm grappling with the issues at hand still. I don't want to provide easy answers in my poetry because I'm not provided any in my life, nor do I feel qualified for the position of creating answers. In the same realm of thought, I would feel insincere if I wrote a truly happy poem because I feel there might not be any such thing as a truly happy moment. Every happy memory I have contains a little bit of darkness to it. In fact, the faint reside of darkness accentuates the joy of that happy moment. For these reasons, I feel that a happy or romantic poem is beyond me because I can't seem to simplify my own emotions in my life to such definite categories of happy or sad, but rather, a wavering balance of the two.

I wish I could provide a recent excerpt of my work to exemplify my questions but over the last few months, I fell trap to a not altogether unfortunate bout of writer's block. I don't feel badly over it because it's not as if I was crouched over a piece of paper for hours in despair, pen in hand and waiting for words to appear. At the risk of sounding indifferent, I just didn't feel like writing poetry. This is not unrelated to a recent heartbreak, where despite the fact that this should have prompted me to write poems of epic proportions as many before me, I just couldn't bring myself to join the ranks of spurned and bitter poets inciting imagery of ragged hearts and floods of tears.

Instead, I have written a few random vignettes and children's stories based on some past memories. These vignettes differ from my poetry mostly because I wrote them when I was feeling the need to remember something calm. I felt that I needed these memories as an anchor to the kind of stillness I felt in these particular moments. These vignettes prompted me, in contrast to my more morose fascinations, to think of the reassuring value that lies in clichés. However, as I began to try to write poetry again, I realized the immobilizing power of this need for the familiar.

I'm reminded of being young and loving to have my palm read or my fortune told in some fashion. The story was always the same — I would grow up to have a big house, an exciting job, a husband and two children (one girl and one boy). However trite, I wanted to be reassured by these familiar images. There is merit to this kind of comfort but then there is also an inherent static quality in being comfortable. The flip side to all of my attention to disorder is, at times, a craving for something comforting and familiar. When caught in a period of transition, as I am now, this need grows tremendously. If my poetry is as you say, unpredictable, then my current state finds me at odds with my writing. I have preferred my journal writing and my little vignettes, just as in my reading I have preferred to re-read old books. I wonder if this will lead me to a new stage in my writing or if this will lead to a deeper rut. If my writing continues to dwell towards the familiar, could I lose my desire to write?

As is obvious, I have come to terms with my concerns with narcissism because I have decided it is unavoidable in writing. Whomever I portray, whatever topic I write of exists on the page only because it exists through me. If I am writing about a person, I am writing them how I see them. In effect, I am Narcissus and in my writing, I am chasing after something I visualize, that seems to be apart from me but isn't. Yet the lust and the fascination that Narcissus feels is there because he sees and desires a person he doesn't recognize. That space between self and projection, the mystery, is the ultimate inspiration.

Sincerely,
Hajera

Palo Alto, California
April 26, 2006

Hajera,

Don't confuse poetry with other sorts of writing. Poetry is not history or journalism and lacks their general impulse to represent facts in ordered sequence, to envision causality and to imply teleology. Narrative prosody suggests the revelation of reality, almost as does photography, so that such writing presents itself as a function of reality, structured by the real, by the order of fact.

History, journalism and scientific writing are good for some things, like logic, causality, like telling the story. Poetry is not so well suited for these endeavors. These narratives describe and recount and, perhaps most importantly for you now, they make sense because they establish order. For narrative imposes a structure that tells a story: beginning, middle and end. This caused that which led to this and so on. It gives clarity to a process and provides rationale for the outcome. The line of thought points to ultimate resolution. This can be very comforting, whether it is accurate or not. Hence, the efficacy of the fiction.

Poetry is art. It words a totally different kind of magic. It is powerful precisely because it is self-consciously a mimesis, because it is image, sentiment, trope. By avoiding the real it can speak the ineffable.

Because your heart is broken, you crave some stability, some clarification, understanding, and a sense of what it all means, where it is all going, how did things go the way they did. Writing in a journal, writing little narrative and descriptive vignettes, offers a means to engage the present. Poetry now would incite the fires of what might have been, of what could be, and at the present moment that might seem like nothing but raw chaos. In other words, poetry can speak the heart, but your heart is not in need of flames right now. The cool stability of a narrative can offer what you need: calm clarity. And in reality, it doesn't matter whether or not your words are perfectly accurate: you crave meaning and healing, and a strong story, which like your fortune telling, need only be well done. For in reality, who can gather all the truths in the correct quantity and order and envision the truth of the day and of the next?

If you don't feel like writing poetry now, don't. You are too talented and too young to worry about the end of your life as a poet. First, let your heart heal. If you can write, write whatever you can. Let your spirit dictate the form. Then worry about poetry later. If and when you need verse, you will find that it has been waiting for you all along. For now, focus on life on joy and on love.

Why the hell do you disbelieve in happiness? I understand you have been hurt and disappointed in life, but try to be objective a bit: you are beautiful, smart, healthy and talented. That some guy dumped you is fucked, but really, that is life. I do not believe in karma or in any balance of the good and the bad in life, it is all too chaotic for that. But I do think that you have to work at your misery, have to focus on the negative in order to deny the possibility of happiness. Both the good and the bad will come to pass in your life, you are, after all, human. But when joy comes, embrace it. And if you look hard enough, I am very sure that you could find much to be thrilled about. Forget trying to construct a narrative of gloom. Carpe diem.

Think of it this way. Your distance from poetry is your lack of desire to write poetry. Desire is very important, very important, but it is not everything. What I mean is, it is your desire that is lagging, not really anything to do with poetry at all. And while desire is good fire, it is essentially focused on the self. Desire is what I want. Love is even more important than desire and more important for a poet. And love need not focus on the self: you fall in love with another much more than merely realizing selfish desire. In other words, love is much more than what I want. Though desire is important, yes we can agree on that.

This is how people can stay in love forever, how they can sacrifice themselves for their lovers. As long as you focus on desire as the primary means of being, you fall trap to dangerous narratives of desire and its loss. In other words, yes you are miserable and are so for a reason, but to maintain your present state you have to construct a miserable narrative each day you live it. I say suffer while the wound is hot, that is the correct human response. Then bit by bit imagine something new. Then write poems again. Poems tragic or joyous.

I too am suffering broken hearts. Plural, because both my poetic romantic heart and my biological heart are broken. Alas. First, I managed to fall in love with a woman who is betrothed. And second, my physical heart is broken and my docs say I should get another. The problem is, as I see it, being a poet, I cannot risk a transplant and find myself in love with someone I've never met. That just wouldn't do.

So do I bemoan life in sad poems? I think not. Even if the gal in the first instance has the most poetic of names. Nor do I whine in sad prose. I'm not writing anything at all, except this letter to you, but what the fuck? I'll write poetry when I write poetry.

Alfred

Dear Alfred,

Unfortunately, yes, I have, for too long now, been wallowing in that addictively murky pool of self-pity, which I flattered myself to believe was profound self-reflection. What you wrote is true; it is absolutely ridiculous to create for myself a hefty burden of shit and then bemoan its existence. I want you to know that I started this correspondence believing in happiness and end it the same way.

Just sometimes I question the substance of that happiness. Remember that endless series of mirrors I see myself in? Well, when I recently started to lose what I depended on around me, I looked harder and harder at myself to gain some footing on the strength of some kind of absolute. I wanted to know what about me was true and what I only wished was true. In doing so for too long and incredulously, I started to see nothing. I felt that I was disappearing under my self-imposed scrutiny by losing my sense of fantasy or, in other words, creation. I think fantasy is what has always kept me afloat and this worried me. What I can depend on to be true is that we are all tiny, insignificant creatures simply part of a large mass of animals that have no fixed responsibility but to be born, live and die. However, my daily fantasy, my humming myself into a different place while riding the bus on the way to work, is what separates me, for my own purposes of survival, from droning into a sense of obscurity. I create my own significance as well as uncreate it at times.

In the last few months, when I tried to write, I feared that I had no right to put into physical form what I doubted existed in myself. Who was I to write of love, pain, the beautiful and the sordid? If poetry is indeed a mimesis, I felt that I had nothing worth replicating. I felt like I was an imitation of some false replica of a person and if I tried to mime that into poetry, it would be worthless, hence confirming my worst fears. In other words, I lost confidence. I never lost my desire but it was desire for the wrong thing. I wanted my words to give me definition, to give some shape to my being, instead of my life being the essence that defined my words into its own meaning.

Looking over this, I realize I sound unhappy, but I'm really not. I have always criticized apathy and flippancy in others and consequently never gave much thought to the vast expanse between being shallow and being ridiculously over-analytical. I got into the habit of embracing the bad and shying away from the good out of distrust. I have no wish to become one-dimensional, nor do I wish to whine away my life in moans and groans. I am looking, as most others, for a perfect balance, or at the very least, the ability to attempt it. I used to feel that I couldn't be passionate without being serious and unsurprisingly, I forgot to have a sense of humor.

I must admit, I'm sharing with you the experience of this letter being the only piece of writing I have attempted in recent months. I think these months of fear have benefited me by giving me this feeling of wanting to tell my imaginary scoffers to fuck off. It isn't worth losing sleep over wondering whether I have the right to be a writer. If I never write anything worth being shared to another person, what does it really matter? I read even my sappiest of works and though I cringe, I also enjoy a good deal of satisfaction. Even if that writing is self-important crap, it makes me happy that I have the audacity to believe in whatever I put into it. Perhaps it is self-deluding but maybe I need grand illusions to have the imagination to write.

Have I regained my desire to write poetry? Yes, but do I have the desire to show it to anyone? I'm not sure. Real confidence in my poems will take some time to come.

Alfred, I'm so sorry to hear about your heart problems, both physical and otherwise.

Hajera

Hajera,

It is my fault, this delay in responding. Things physical and metaphysical have conspired wildly, but as my muse, the minor Goddess Chaos, would say: this is not necessarily bad. A muse *sin control*, she abhors mirrors, those instruments of reflection, for their unyielding fixity and finality of sense.

The realm of Narcissus is that of reflection, and each manifestation of the mirror in your epistle is entwined with a narcissism, a concern for the self, perhaps with what is seen and not, but surely with poetry and truth. We've done Narcissus already, save for his ultimate drowning in self image, so instead, here, your words and mirrors make me recall the existential game: repeat a word enough times and it detaches from significance and devolves to mere utterance. The game really kicks in when one repeats one's own name. Damn if the self doesn't disappear.

It seems that it is very important for you to articulate the edge of poetry, of poetics, of language: that zone, that impossible breach, that always holds icon apart from divinity, a sonnet from the beloved, the simple breath of your voice from the about of your words. And why not? That is, after all, the whole of the trick, really. It is where poems be and where we begin. Always and always necessarily at a remove. It cannot work otherwise. Perhaps my muse can speak divinely without language, but I cannot, for language is the defining structure of being human. And since you is, you rhyme, as Descartes might have said.

To dwell in a series of mirrors is to get stuck in the wonder of it all, to attempt to see the workings of mirrors by looking in one before, seeing one behind, seeing one before, ad infinitum. A reductive task, actually. The kind of task that lends itself to aporia, to your focus on the disjunction of your self and yourself the poet. It is a funhouse game, nothing more. And I am grateful that its worst effect is that you might become disoriented, but that you won't drown.

A week ago I went to lunch at the Berkeley faculty club, that dark wood and beef den of truth-in-patriarchy. I go there about once a decade, and I hadn't been there since the big one, the Oakland Hills fires and way before 9/11. So I seemed due. I had the good fortune to meet Walter Alvarez and listen to him go on about how rare things are in the universe. He said that if you filled the Grand Canyon with grains of sand, the chances of picking a specific grain is the same as that of any of us having come into being. You, me, anyone. His point is: we exist, yes, but we do so at extremely unlikely odds. I like this. I find it comforting.

For example, there is the fact that I know you, but I am held in awe at the odds of my grain of sand actually coming to meet yours. In one sense, my Goddess Chaos might have it that we are as unlikely a couple of humans exchanging letters as there could be. We would not be worth betting on. And yet, existentially, we do exist, and we are writing, such as at this instant, this letter I will give you in four days when I see you at Strada, at 1:30. I think it amazing.

So while you might hum yourself to individuation on a bus of strangers, I, instead, consider the dark matter surrounding the both of us that is cancelled when we see each other, when we speak words, write letters, smile, touch. Yes, pretty amazing.

Write or don't write. But since your mirrors won't disappear you truly, won't submerge you in a wet image that is mere reflection, continue on with the stuff of being. In so doing, you cannot lose language. And when poetry does resurface, show the world. Send me some, publish books, give readings. Why? Because no matter whether you hum or not, you remain inexplicably unlikely and real.

Alfred

Jennifer Firestone & Eileen Myles

Jennifer Firestone is the author of *Holiday* (Shearsman Books, 2008), *Waves* (Portable Press at Yo-Yo Labs, 2007), *from Flashes* (Sona Books, 2006) and *snapshot* (Sona Books, 2004). Her work has appeared in *HOW2*, *Xcp: Streetnotes*, *LUNGFULL!*, *Can We Have Our Ball Back*, *Fourteen Hills*, *MIPOesias Magazine*, *Dusie*, *580 Split*, *Saint Elizabeth Street*, *moria*, *Feminist Studies*, *Sidereality*, *Poetry Salzburg Review*, *Phoebe*, *BlazeVOX*, *So to Speak: Feminist Journal of Language and Art*, and others. She is completing a book-length prose poem called *Flashes*, a collection of media sound bytes about war and community, *Gates & Fields*, meditations on death and death language, and a short work called *Who Is Mother Goose?* She is an Assistant Professor teaching poetry at Eugene Lang College at The New School for Liberal Arts. She lives in Brooklyn with her husband and their baby twins.

Eileen Myles was born in Cambridge, Mass. in 1949, graduated from U. Mass. (Boston) in 1971 and moved to New York City in 1974 to be a poet. She gave her first reading at CBGB's, and then gravitated to St. Mark's church where she studied with Bill Zavatsky, Alice Notley and Ted Berrigan. She was the Artistic Director of St. Mark's Poetry Project during the Reagan years. In 2007, she published *Sorry, Tree* (Wave Books), the most recent of more than a dozen volumes of poetry and fiction, including *Chelsea Girls* (Black Sparrow Press,

1994), *Not Me* (Semiotext(e), 1991), *Skies* (Black Sparrow Press, 2001), and *Cool for You* (Soft Skull Press, 2000). She wrote the libretti for *Hell*, an opera composed by Michael Webster, which was performed on both coasts in 2004 and 2006. Her novel, *The Inferno* will be out in Fall 2008. She ran the writing program at UCSD for five years and now she mostly lives in New York.

Young Male: I like the name Lindsay; it's pretty.

Mom: That's Lind-ZEE, with an 'e.'

Young Male: So tell me about your daughter.

Mom: Well, you could say she has a *chest*.

Young Male: Do you mean big boobs?

Mom: [Laughs]

Young Male: [Aside to camera] Uh oh, big breasts usually means big hips.

Young Male: So how much does she weigh? What's her body like?

Mom: I don't know . . . she's voluptuous.

Young Male: [Aside to camera] Voluptuous really means FAT!
I have a very specific body type that I go for in a girl. And the other girl is a runway model, which is more my type.

[Cut to commercial]

Selection Time: A limo door swings open, a skinny leg zoomed in on. Slit down dress barely swallows breasts. Young female embraces young male.

Young Male: [Aside to camera] This girl's hot as sin!

Dear Eileen,

I couldn't sleep last night so I turned on the TV and found myself watching, *Date My Mom*, where three moms go on dates with a dashing young male and try to convince him to ask out their daughters. I know I shouldn't be too surprised. After all, this is our "reality" right now. I think there's even a show about dwarves and dating, but I found *Date My Mom* particularly disturbing. Maybe because it seems to be yet another lesson on how to market sex and stereotypes, but this time the handiwork or the "sales pitch" is done via the lips of the very women who gave birth to their young, perfect, and marketable progeny. All in the name of money, fame . . . a date? I felt irritated by this freak show, imagining my students having a steady diet of it, hearing language carelessly thrown around, too many hair flips, lipglossed smiles, handshakes between mom and male; the deal is done. In a recent class I taught, my students were more critical of the female poets we were reading, saying things like, she seems "wacked," "angry," "a bit of a freak." I've been teaching the New York School, and everything's going well until we arrive at our first female poet, Barbara Guest. I explain how editors and critics excluded Guest from several books about the New York School, even though she was in the thick of it. I send out feelers to the students and nothing, not even a tiny shock comes back. Dismissal.

Once I had a famous male poet come to my classroom. This class had been relatively apathetic. The more I jumped, hopped, explained, expressed, the more their pupils crossed. Then the male artist entered. He scratched himself and looked down, he coughed, drank water, and asked what it was we wanted to know. He was unprepared. He referenced Shakespeare. He recited his favorite poems from memory. My class LOVED him. They thought his lack of preparation, his nonchalance took the cake. I called a good friend and she said, "<u>This</u> is how 'female hysteria' begins."

In *Cool for You*, you track the treatment of females within institutions. As a female artist working within the university, have you also been confronted with this kind of dismissal, and if so, how do you address it? I'm reminded of something you wrote in "The Lesbian Poet," from *School Of Fish*, "I want to say something else about my femaleness, which is what interests me, not feminism. Femaleness is owning my woman's insides." Can you tell me more about this ownership?

I first became interested in your writing back in grad school in 1995. You wrote about being a poet, a female poet. Each time I read the word "poet" I felt silly. Like being eight, wearing Wonder Woman underoos under school clothes. I had secret powers. You said you moved to New York to become a poet. This sounded self-permissive, powerful. It seemed also self-made. No royal carpet rolled out. You decided, you desired, you did. I'm interested in where are you now with this desire, gumption, how it shifts and gets played out in the poetry world, and how the more you become wedded to and webbed in this world, how easy is it to keep desire, female desire (?), afloat.

In *Maxfield Parrish*, there's a great passage from the prose poem, "The Poet," "It is not lost my century, thanks to us. We are the liars & thieves, we are the women we are the women I am full of holes because you are. I am the only saintly man in town. Don't be afraid to be feminine. A girl on a rowboat, full of holes. She saw words shooting through." Brighde Mullins (whose class I took at SFSU) writes: "This final, visionary image, of a girl in a sinking rowboat, is at once tragic and hopeful. The boat is going down, after all, but the girl in the boat is seeing and saying, not just sinking. This articulation is sustenance, is proof that 'poetry is strong enough to help.'" I agree and read this passage as an invitation to a world of imperfection, one where there is a connection with others about the imperfection and possibly even a transformation of this imperfection through imagination into art. I see the boat go down, and at the same time the holes are windows, openings to other arenas, particularly to the imagination. Though these holes don't necessarily offer escape, they are open and breathing. They also appear in another poem of yours, "Holes," "But I remember those / beautiful holes on / my back like a / beautiful cloak / of feeling." Even the repetition of the word "beautiful" acts more as a command than just an expression, where the speaker is able to understand and envision the holes as something that allows her to rise above, endure.

*

Thinking about femaleness (and *Date My Mom*), I picture our first lady. Would Laura Bush try to "win" the best date for her lovely twins? The answer is "probably." I can see her in a pink suit, with rosy cheeks, clenching a hanky as she awaits the male date's arrival, notwithstanding all her so-called "feminist beliefs" and marketing of her husband's war policies as a "fight for the rights and dignity of women" while ignoring its undermining of women's rights. Hypocrisy wins again. Eileen, what did you mean by the line, "Don't be afraid to be feminine"? How do you access this in your own life and work? You once said something along the lines of, the older you get, the more you are in touch with your mortality and fear of being obliterated because you are a female poet. How does this motivate you? How do you write/act against this obliteration?

This brings me to a recent conversation I had with Dana Teen Lomax. We were talking about the documentary *Rivers and Tides*. We appreciate Andy Goldsworthy's art and commitment to his vision, yet we were both struck by one scene where Goldsworthy's wife is cooking breakfast, the kids are running in and out of the kitchen, and Goldsworthy seems disengaged as he looks foggily into space, perhaps conjuring up his next environmental inspiration. Later, Goldsworthy leaves for the day to work on his art, leaving his wife standing at a long counter eating her breakfast while one kid sits at the kitchen table, which is cluttered with several dirty plates. This made me think, how selfish does a female artist have to be, how narcissistic? What sacrifices must she make?

You've talked about being inspired/mentored by a line of male mentors, Jimmy Schuyler in particular. How has the male mentorship affected your relationship to your art?

On a final note, it seems you're willing to put yourself (or a version of yourself) in your work if it allows you to get closer to the emotion and immediacy of an experience. That you communicate through a tangible "voice." In writing my manuscript, *Holiday*, I struggled with how to address the issues I had with *going on a holiday*. Although the writing takes a somewhat detached and journalistic tone, the self was also mixed in. I felt it would be disingenuous to write about issues of consumerism and travel without implicating myself in the process: after all, I did have the privilege to go to Europe, which *did* give me the ideas for these poems. Yet it's difficult to incorporate the self, knowing the criticisms that can trail behind. Though erasing oneself from one's work in order to comply with certain poetic trends doesn't seem the best approach either. What's your take?

Eileen, I've never met you. I'm writing to your persona, inundating it with questions, and projecting onto it who I think you might be. This seems false but it's what I have to work with. This falseness. And yet at the risk of asking too much, I'm thinking of something you once wrote: "There is a word in Italian, *affidamento*, which describes a relationship of trust between two women, in which the younger asks the elder to help her obtain something she desires. Women I know are turning around to see if that woman is here. The woman turning, that's the revolution. The room is gigantic, the woman is here."

Warmly,
Jennifer

Jennifer,

I hope you haven't felt like a jerk or anything since I've taken this long to
respond. It just was quiet tonight and finally I know exactly what I want to write
back so it feels like it's been worth the waiting. God you asked me many good
questions and it would probably be a bad idea to try to respond to them all. I
loathe the bit of dialogue you opened your letter with. What's horrible is that it's
not so new. I'm thinking of the young guy making asides to the camera — what he
really thinks. I'm thinking of George Burns on *The Burns and Allen Show* and
George turning to the camera, taking his cigar out of his mouth and saying some-
thing smart. George knew. That was the general bias of the show. George did the
knowing. And Gracie was. People will tell us that George and Gracie were one of
the great show bizness loves and I don't doubt that, but Gracie was a spectacle
and we never for a moment knew what was going on "inside" her. That's what
asides are all about. Divulging. Men are always divulging in a private powerful
way and women are divulging in a silly out of control way and we watch them.
They're like children, no? Unedited and delightful. Or "not my type." Right or
wrong, but not the guiding force. There to be judged. I also loved the dumpy guy
who came into your classroom, unprepared, quoting a bit and blowing them
away. It reminds me of a gay man I talked with at an artist colony who just hated
how straight men could be gross, out of shape, unshaven and treated like hot sex
objects. This gay man was infuriated by the entitled piggishness of straight men. If
you owned the world then of course you could sit there with your guy gaze
determining that some girl was fat or a slob because a straight guy sees himself as
the boss, and you know the procession of girls or opportunities or products are
there for his delectation. He doesn't have to see himself. I mean the guy's proba-
bly fucking old as well, and he wouldn't have any truck with an aging woman
either, never mind a fat one. So on top of it all you have that to look forward to,
too, Jennifer. If it's bad to be female now, just wait till you get old! Sorry I like to
throw my age around like a corpse or a skeleton. I've been sliding through yet
another breakup lately and I really wished I could not shave and have another
layer of disheveled protection to announce my sorrow and freedom through. I
mean I'd like to go through my breakup like an abject man, not an abject female.

Somewhere a divorced guy is being cooked for and I don't know what. Actually I don't want to be him, I want the beard, just the fucking beard, please because then I could have more hair on my head, less skin. I imagine my feelings would be less exposed. I mean a woman can grow the hair on her legs and I do. At school I was standing outside in the sun at the end of last spring's quarter and I was talking to a male academic, a kind of gnarly difficult guy but he was being generous and offering to hook me up with a curator in Mexico who would possibly show my work. Then he looked down and I had shorts on. And there were my legs covered with hair. It was like I had shit on them. He truly pulled away from me and in moments was looking back with scorn and I knew then that he wouldn't be sending me the email address he had been offering. Because I am such a fucking freak. How would he look good, then. You know how men like to help men. Helping a man is like helping yourself, but helping a woman is something else. Maybe my worldview is perverted. How bad can it be? Pretty bad. Really bad. Worse than you ever imagined. But somehow I also think it's pretty good and here's why. We are thrown radically upon ourselves. Do I have any interest in knowing who that shuffling poet who came to your class was? None whatsoever because I could put in a multitude of names that would utterly fill the bill. Do I need to know what his unprepared self had to say when he talked off the cuff about shit. No because I could write that dialogue easily enough too. We know what men have to say. Uncurated genius taking a little space and sharing the goods. Yawn. It's just another version of having a gut and not taking a bath and thinking you're hot. Your students sound pretty dumb. They don't deserve you. I think you have to care less about teaching and wowing them and spend more time going to the movies, and reading and writing and hanging out with your friends. Give less! It's hard for young teachers to do this, but especially for young female teachers. I really think students should be treated with more scorn and made to work more. You shouldn't read too much of their work because it's bad for you. They should be reading a lot and you should be writing a lot. I'd be curious to see your manuscript *Holiday*. I like the title. When I was in Europe a hundred million years ago I remember people asking if we (my friend I was traveling with, Anne, who I went to college with) were "on holiday." It sounded so much better than vacation. It reminds me of the far side of the sixties, the bossa nova side which was very la dolce vita, just stylish and Euro and hot in a light peachy kind of way, like really actually cool. Not hot but sexy. That's Holiday to me, the thick old school magazine – what was it about, fashion or travel? Whatever, it's gone. And Madonna's early great hit. I would love to read your book. We have no business writing letters without this basic exchange. Who's publishing it, how many pages, what's going on? I love Brighde Mullins. Did you stay in touch? When Bridghe taught your class I think she told me she was going to order my book for her class and that the class was huge, 100 or so – maybe you were not in that huge class, but a smaller one. I think at the time I was feeling bitter about always being fucking broke, or maybe just broke that day and I said oh great so I'll make like a nickel on each book i.e. $5. I don't know why I was such a grouch in response to her generous proposal. It was really sweet of her and I loved the picture of so many people reading my book but all I could think of was that like everything, it would bring me no money, nothing would.

I'm thinking about "a life of independence" – the difficult notion of being a free, unaffiliated poet in "a free market economy"– that nonetheless you pay a price as we do for everything – because so many times in my life in New York as a poet I wasn't able to see how wonderful things were because all I wanted was some help, I wanted to win, I wished someone would give me a big fucking grant or something. Being poor for a long time makes you feel small. I think my poems never got small. Oddly poetry seems to expand in relation to poverty – or at least it does for a very long time. That's probably why I'm urging you to be less nice to your students and try less hard. Because you need your time, they don't. But when you have it, it's like being young, know that you have it. Don't let fear get you down. Fear of the future, fear of poverty. Of your work not being important enough or read enough. It might be an injustice to present Barbara Guest as the New York school poet that got away. I think there isn't a woman I know who isn't familiar with how simply replaceable Barbara was in the eyes of whatever next young male editor was assembling some New York School book. Why not put in Bernadette or Anne, he thought. Should it be Alice, Bernadette or Eileen? This I've been told was actually said by one male editor when he was puzzling over which of us females should "represent" the east village. He chose Alice because of her relationship with Ted! What an insult to all of us. Female history is always destabilized by whatever guy is now watching the line of women parading by. It's maddening but those guys will never change. We have to think differently. We have to teach Barbara Guest differently. Don't teach her with them. Teach her with Amiri Baraka or Allen Ginsberg. Just don't even let the guys have her. I think females have to write new fictions to hold their truths. If someone introduced me as someone who didn't get her fair shake I'd feel terrible. And then some entitled guy stands up and he's gotten 97 awards and whom is the room going to listen to.

We have to set each other up better all the time and the terms of the world are always inadequate to women's true accomplishments. If she's received no awards then we have to give her one. An accurate and beautiful description would be enough if we weren't compelled to also say what's not there. Because your capacity to see value and state it in the present is adequate award for Barbara Guest and Eileen Myles. Your students are being set up too if they are told that a poet has been unfairly treated. They are like in debt before they've heard a word of her work. Then they have to save her. And they won't. Why do they have to fix it. It's like a threat. A guy stands up and he has nothing to give and of course they like him. He makes them feel comfortable and anything they can glean from him is a gift. He makes them feel good. He leaves them in the actual room. We just try too damn hard all the time and I think it's got to stop. I'm for female laziness and excess, female age and female hair and female fat. I actually like being kind of skinny because it feels good. Menopause threatens to put fat where it never was but if I didn't have to have a baby I don't have to get fat because I didn't have one. There are many wonderful ways to say no.

Thank you for reading my work. I really mean it. It's a wonderful feeling – that your work continues on when you leave it alone. It makes me feel very rich to hear that it's had its effect on you. I love holes. I've never been a continuous thinker – or I mean that I am very distracted and that's why I write poetry. Where am I when I'm not here. How do I track the move from thought to thought, vine to vine as I'm swinging through the trees. Holes seem generous. An empty way of saying there are other places to be, there have been other times and there will be still others to replace them. I like the anonymity of history. Your heart is broken today but later it will be filled with excitement or peace. There's something very romantic about loss. Hope's neighbor. I think the boat full of holes is as you say. The boat is not real, the lake is not real. So what if it fills up with water which is probably light. Shot through with innocence, a something else.

I think just when I'm a man, I'm a girl. The feminine line means that above all women mustn't be contemptuous of themselves. Just when the last thing that's going on is one's purported femininity, it erupts like a big bow. We're just so many things. I distrust my own jargon, my abandoning of the feminine for the female. I guess I was preferring sex over gender, but later thinking how arrogant to pretend not to be feminine. For anyone really. Why is the feminine the thing to hate. Something men, or mothers made to control girls. Surely it can free us too, then in some homeopathic way. I often forget words, that's why I like holes. All this quiet diving through the dictionary and a bird comes up tweeting.

I hated that Andy Goldsworthy movie with a passion. For among other reasons the treatment of his wife. The kids fared better, getting their heads rumpled etc. Being shot in a way that was proud whereas the wife was only a functionary of his and their needs. Ugh. But the movie was narcissistic in the worst way. The script was pretentious and foul. Making his every intervention on nature plodding and over-stated. The writer should have been shot. They undid Goldsworthy's work, but so does his beautiful life in his beautiful studio, that lonely and pathetic man. The beautiful furniture and desks in his studio and his contempt for his wife, a living person, everywhere. What a great man, an artist. Ugh. Enough of him.

Men have been entirely generous to me. Books and ideas and unending influences. Many of the men who had the most profound influence on me are already gone. We are supposed to learn from each other. That's what we're doing here. I have begun to learn from women more in recent years. I generally have younger girl-friends (and I learn from them) and also because I teach and spend a lot of time with people, mostly women younger than me, I've started consciously attempting to spend more time with women my age and older. Also I'm struggling to learn from the academy, a funny place to learn. The academy performed an economic rescue on me a couple of years ago and though I'm very grateful, I'm still trying to figure out if it's a good thing. I have three books almost done and I'll know more once that's happened. Soon I hope. A book is like a leash.

I hope I've helped you out tonight. You have really helped me. I had dinner with another poet tonight (Rae) and when she described her writing life I so distinctly saw the room she was writing in, the notebook she wrote in. I think talking among women about being poets and writing poetry is about as good as it gets. Writing about it tonight. Send me your book.

Truly,
Eileen

Eileen,

Since moving to NY I haven't stopped running. It feels countercultural to relax. The other day I was running to the subway and this guy yelled out offering to give me a spanking. I thought about whether my running seemed naughty, erroneous or just plain *bad*. I've lived in NY for three years. The first year I felt a strange sickness, the pressure of being in a place where ambition trumps exercise. Like it was a badge you had to wear proudly or it would be swiped off your chest. Yet suddenly I'm into being weathered. Of flying out crisp one-line emails. Of barking about no time. Feeling old and grouchy and busy, and jumping along with everyone. The fatty rats. I even smiled the other day on the subway when my friend yelled for everyone to move into the center of the train and this guy with a thick NY accent said, "I'll move your ass OFF the train."

What do you think about this city, and your switches between NY & CA? I'm in the middle of figuring out whether or not to move back to SF. When I lived there, I would get a rush from the openness of the space. I would drive south on 280 and love the wide highway.

If we move we'll probably head to the east bay, yet soon as I say this I can't visualize myself there. (Can I visualize myself here?) I wonder if I'd feel smaller there, swallowed. I've been thinking about your book *Skies*. In it, one of the ideas you seem to track is how varying allocations of sky, which fluctuate depending on geography, affect us physically, emotionally and intellectually. I think about locations, how my body feels in a certain space. I don't even know if I look up (into sky) that often in NYC. I'm constantly looking ahead, or looking to the right or left, avoiding traffic or some kind of harm that could be done to me. Plus there's so much to see at eye level. At first I felt claustrophobic by this, by all the commotion, and now I feel kind of comforted by the squished space.

I'm also considering connections, community. Maybe this is something I search for, particularly in NYC. It's strange how you can be on the subway, feel another body, smell another body, but have no contact. Of course this isn't always the case.

And there's the extreme other side of this. The personal made public. Tonight I asked the guy who was behind me in line at the corner store if he wanted to cut ahead. I had several items and he had a quart of milk. He kind of stepped into my space and blurted, "Oh no, thank you. I've eaten dinner. I've got nothing to do. I'm relaxed. If I go home now all I'm going to do is listen to music and watch the Yankee game." This isn't quite "community," but it's something. And during the Lunar Eclipse this winter I remember walking down my block and seeing small groups of people in their winter jackets, heads swung back as they all looked up at the sky.

Seeing your opera, *Hell*, was a community experience. Something about being packed into the Poetry Project, watching people sing, using language that was accessible and relevant. It was language that we felt okay to laugh with and respond to. The part that really stayed with me was when the character, "the poet," sings about the importance of "live" readings. "Well it's like/ the person stands in their body / breathing / their heart beating." And later when asked if people like these live readings the poet replies "They really do / They like to sit communally / And hear messages that / Aren't tinkered / With by the government / Or intended to sell a product."

Before I go further, I want to thank you for your last letter. I'm sorry about your break up, and hope you're alright. I think being in a break-up space as kind of murky—like you're not quite awake or asleep. I hope you are sleeping, eating, whatever it takes.

When you wrote in your letter you'd like to be able to grieve your breakup like the "abject male," adorning yourself with a protective and maybe schlumpy beard, I was reminded of an article quoting a physician's 1938 book, *Superfluous Hair and Its Removal*: "[facial hair] has induced in women mental states that bring on the direst of consequences. Such women may become morose and subject to fits of depression, develop a mania for seclusion, and it has even been known to lead to suicide." Imagine the reaction of the male academic if he saw hair sprouting from not only your legs but your face. I also loved your description of George and Gracie—George getting to be multi-dimensional, and Gracie a mere spectacle. I'm struggling with this. How to flip the gaze back onto the audience? When you feel you're there to be judged, forced to watch others sum you up. How to fight the force of the look and your own self-awareness? Sometimes I feel my body shoved into "the role." Oh boy, out comes a nervous laugh. Whoops, there goes intense and eager eye contact. Wham, the arms go out and I'm flapping my flippers together or bobbing balls on my nose.

About your suggestion of delivering scorn to my students: you kind of called it, my attention toward teaching (although you say for young females this is difficult and I'd be curious to hear more about why you think this is). I don't want to worry about being good or winning. To "earn" my way to the writing. But there's something else, is being scornful somehow being the "male"? Is that what I'm supposed to do? Step back? Not give? Be the asshole? I mean you are right, I've seen it over and over again. You give less and whoever/whatever comes crawling up sniffing with appetite. Yet I'm also feeling this itch to embody more of the "female," femininity. I know it's not an either/or, and I'm a bit concerned about throwing around labels. I can see my naiveté with how I introduced Barbara Guest to my class. I'm chafing against etiquette and standards. My friend Sarah Rosenthal talks about every time she eats with women who are taking quaint, delicate bites of food she gets overcome by this ravenous appetite and begins to gobble.

Thanks for asking about my work. You should throw *Holiday*, which I recently sent you, in the trash, as it is being reorganized. I'm getting rid of all the titles and sections and playing around more with space so a lot of the poems end up colliding. In writing the book one of the things I was thinking about was the "expectation" involved with going on a *holiday*. Not only is the tourist concerned she's getting her money's worth, but she's pressured to bring anecdotes and souvenirs for the people back home. Everyone vicariously wants to go to that "paradise" she's been to. It's unacceptable to talk about how the rooms she was staying at stunk or she had a sinus infection for most of the trip. People want the fantasy. I like how Susan Sontag's *On Photography* talks about our inability to relax. How the camera comforts us, distracts us, signals to us we are capturing, controlling, working. How people are into framing experience, thinking of memorializing their trip in a photo album.

Now I'm working on a new project, *Flashes*, (I sent you a few pages), which kind of took over in a sort of Jack Spicer-martian kind of way. I'm exploring what it means to live in NY during the here and now. The work switches between speaking as a "we" and a "you," a kind of collage of choirs, spitting out all the media speak and urban colloquialisms and corporate rants and stuff. I began working on this book last June at a residency. I was in upstate NY surrounded by lots of land, a wooded backyard, and a house enclosed by hills and trees. It was private and open, and there was a pond with frogs that alarmed me when I first heard them. I also heard screams of an animal getting killed outside my window late one night: I imagined a big animal being killed by a bigger one. One of those shred and tear scenes from the Discovery channel. I expected to look out in the morning and see lots of blood and body parts. I kept writing faster, not letting myself pause to sense the relationship between the pages, the lines. At dinnertime, artists talked about their projects and I kept quiet. Now and then I would wonder if my inability or lack of desire to talk about the work, to know what it was "about," revealed some deep flaw in me, the work, or both.

In a few days I'll be going to Deerfield Beach, Florida to visit my grandparents. They're in their late 80's and moving into assisted living. My grandma has a fantasy about bringing a brass headboard to her new home and so I'm going to help her hunt for one. We are also going to a flea market where she likes to look for knock-offs of very chichi perfumes. I'm excited for the ocean, for a different texture to the air and space. Last time I was there my husband was swimming in the deep end of the pool when a woman in a big hat yelled from her lounge chair for him to move away from that end of the pool. She told him that not too long ago someone drove his Cadillac right into the water.

Truly,
Jennifer

San Diego, California
July 14, 2005

Jennifer,

Okay I'm shocked at how long ago you last wrote and I haven't replied. And what a terrific letter you wrote. I have to bump up the font. This is tiny. I've been on a failing computer since March and finally it utterly died and I'm on a new one now. Generally, it's traumatic but this time I'm totally relieved. I'm not surprised that you liked *Skies* since though we're very different writers your *Holiday* book is a little similar. I mean you've picked a particular lens to write your poems through, kind of a literal concept and then you ran with it. Well I actually don't know what order it came in – idea or the procession of them started to fall in place? I read the book-length poem first and felt really pleased by the stab and the elegance of your lines and so I stepped into *Holiday* with a sense of what you do. I only felt you not doing it so much in the third section. Like somehow that frame took the wind out of your sails a bit. I think it spawned a slight dutifulness to the idea, which I think held you down a bit though there was much to like there too. The ones before were more surprising. I think you have a great economy going in your poems and I often think this thing about weights in poetry, how the poet is shifting her weight (of attention, I guess) as she moves through the landscape of whatever and again there was something always shifting in how you handled it, watching yourself too: "we are diligent about stars" was funny and yet not bursting you out of the flow. I'm glad I've gotten acquainted with your work. And I'm glad we're kind of a blind date here, not having known each other before the exchange so it can be truthfully abstract. We both get an opportunity to write this letter to *somebody*, it happens to be us. I suspect that was the quality of the original exchange (Rilke?) that made it work. *Skies* was entirely in response to New York and its space. Its lack of sky space. It just gets taken from you slowly, living in New York and then there's so much ecstasy in a tiny crack between buildings or what's out the window or the occasional walk to this river or that. The wash of color and light mostly doesn't happen because of us and our constructions and living in New York we become that. I was shocked living in Provincetown and I only experienced that shock because of New York so it was that urban thing again, just being vast making it so I could continually see the sky again and again it still being so completely new having been literally taken away for years. Now I'm living in this fucking suburban space which is pretty eerie. The first thing you think about here is the weather, on and on. It's always nice. They call it June Gloom because one month resembles New England. Otherwise it's nice. To live someplace where many of the people live here for the weather. Not the culture, not for a lover, or a job. The weather. Which makes people either old or from the Midwest, pretty much. Except of course for the military. And the many people crossing the border for work. But this general thing of coming for the sun makes the place just initially cultureless. I was getting a couple of tattoos last week (snowflakes – light blue) and the guy giving them to me told me he was from Milwaukee. He was young, in his twenties. It struck me that that's why he does snowflakes, though we didn't talk about it. But I did ask him why he moved here and he said the weather. I completely flipped. Why would somebody young care about the weather. Then I started to think about the notion of being comfortable. I had learned a bunch of years ago in the context of not drinking or doing drugs that one ought to aim to be comfortable. It was an impossible concept yet here it was afoot again, alive in the culture at large. Southern California is a comfortable place. New York is not. I have gotten incredibly defensive when anyone suggests I don't "live" in New York anymore. Dare they suggest New York is not my town anymore? It becomes a kind of badge, and it's threatening when people coyly try and slip it off your lapel. But part of being a New Yorker is you live with all that shit and mostly I don't. Another kind of shock. I love the voice of the New Yorker offering to move your friend's ass off the train or however. It's pretty Frank O'Hara to talk about how vulgar New York is, but that's a lot of it. The smell of the dirty stinking subways, the layered socializing, the endless opportunities to see and be seen. I find myself longing to get more "face" here. I walk among plants, I think about plants, I ride in my car. But you know stuff gets dropped in our laps. I moved here for a lot of reasons. I came here with a lover, for instance. The breakup's going well, thank you. Then I learn to live here by myself and it's a different place. It has a great prose rhythm. On and on. Nothing stops me. It's harder to write poems whereas in New York I simply get turned on. Put me on the subway, drop me in a cab and I'm filling a notebook. Did you like *Being John Malkovich*? I think there were these holes in that film. I can't remember how it worked. Were they falling through them into another identity? Poems seem like browsers to me in a way. I'm thinking of your work again, how the browser kept shrinking and expanding and that seems alive. I'm almost forced into a poem by being in New York (especially not having a job now or a schedule when I'm there so I'm just in its blind eye like I were young and poor) and here I have to get the shape of things again. One morning I wrote a poem on my cell phone. I was standing in the park with my dog early in the morning and I was stabbed by the impulse to write and no pen and notebook in my shorts but I had my phone. So I called myself and just talked it. Luckily I transcribed it before I erased it. I had to erase it. It was like a compulsion. I think I was getting on a plane that night so part of the poem was feeling that I was being here partially. The whole thing would be someplace else soon and that felt deep and a little beyond writing. I loved when you told me to throw your book in the trash. Immediately I had to read it. I did it with glee.

Truly,
Eileen

Brooklyn, New York
October 12, 2005

Dear Eileen,

It's been great writing to you. I loved your last letter. Weather, ugh. That is a strange subject to talk or think about. Although I like the word "weather." A student of mine wrote this nice poem that had the word "isobar" in it and the tone of the poem was flat and even-keeled. Once I assigned a class to keep a weather journal. (I got the idea after reading some of Jimmy Schuyler's diary entries). For a week they jotted down what was going on in the weather and what they were thinking or feeling at that precise moment. Their entries actually turned out better than what they were turning in as "poems." Nevertheless the idea of pure weather being a chief concern really depresses me.

Thanks for your generous and insightful read of my work. I really liked the movie *Being John Malkovich*. The characters had a portal they could chute into and land inside Malkovich's brain. It became a thrill ride, living through another, a famous person's, experience. And I think NY pushes you into these holes, portals everyday. You're sort of forced to look at how others see things. And yes poems are like browsers.

So here are some ideas and questions about writing. A recent trend in poetry seems to be to have a defined, well-articulated writing project at hand. This seems to run in line with publishers seeming less and less interested in publishing books as collections of poems versus poems working from a chiseled scope. I'm wondering what's going on, and I keep getting this feeling that the bridge between academia and poetry is shrinking.

I guess I'm letting onto my own anxiety around this issue. I like to do preliminary research for a writing project, but as I write this I'm wondering if there are deeper cultural shifts that are occurring that are making us turn to outside resources more and more: is there a feeling that we need to consciously KNOW what we're doing and how we do it? Is it fear? Distrust? I just don't know.

I also have trepidations around the word "project," about being too rigid about a work's trajectory. Sometimes I'll write process notes for future work, but then I'll feel like I just drew a container, looking at the work from the outside in. I loved your description of having poems just given to you when being in New York, the way you wrote a poem on your cell phone.

Recently I heard Leslie Thornton talk about her film *Peggy & Fred in Hell*. People were trying to get specific looks into her process. One guy in the audience said something about how she had these amazing compositions and that they seemed somewhat organic, like she just kind of fell into them. She responded, "I fell into them on purpose." And then, "I know when something is working when I'm falling backward and I'm just catching myself before I fall all the way. Just holding on enough to have it be meaningful and not arbitrary." When talking about audience she said that she wanted people to come into and out of the film, to like parts, to dislike parts, to be uncertain about it, just the way the film was uncertain about itself.

I've been questioning the value of things. Like I have a pair of new and suspicious eyes. The other day I was thinking I should spend more time publishing critical works. Yet this led me to consider where this questioning was coming from. Why am I finding new ways to make myself work so hard? Challenge is good, but if my writing or my teaching feels too comfortable or too pleasurable, I can't help but think that I need to do more. To pile on the duties. I struggle with the concept of utility, how I'm useful to and in this world.

I found an online interview with you that indirectly speaks to some of these concerns. You were talking about the whole enterprise of writing about writing, language poetry in particular and you said: "It was smart and it was what they wanted to make, but I'd rather make a novel or a performance rather than an essay about poetry. Or I like getting paid to do it, so I did journalism which surprisingly a lot of people in the poetry world think of as commercial. So then we're talking about class. I mean I do enough free things without writing about poetry for poetry magazines. But writing poems themselves feels like survival." I love this because you relate these choices and judgments to class, which doesn't seem to come up as much as it should. It seems that sometimes there can be these expectations as to whether one is thought of as serious-minded artist, but then there's not enough mentioning of how these expectations can conflict with time, money and yes, one's desire and/or ability to do just her own art.

I'm often ambivalent—maybe that's a good thing. I'm touchy when people are locked into their ideologies, where no exceptions are allowed. It makes me want to do the opposite of what they say. I sometimes struggle with the concept of being an "experimental" poet. I don't feel aligned with "mainstream" ideas, but I don't feel comfortable if the goal is to combat the mainstream, which seems like a convention in itself. I feel like you and your writing are able to navigate through several communities. I think that's refreshing. Is this a conscious effort on your part? (Like Harryette Mullen saying that her front cover and blurb choices for *Muse & Drudge* let her somewhat control how her book is received and, more importantly, who receives it.)

I'm drawn to writers who write from ambivalence or unknowingness. Cesar Vallejo's *Trilce*: "What is the name of all that wounds us? / The same as that which suffers / name name name name." I like how he repeats the word "name" over and over, as if maybe to exorcise or create meaning out of his questioning, his void. Or just to emphasize the lack of identity, possession, label. Or maybe this lack . . . is. Is "name." Or also, Carla Harryman's poem "Fish Speech": "In the beginning, there was nothing to hold and nothing to hold in mind, since there was no beginning, no nothing, and no mind. The end also did not exist. Nothing stopped. There was no gender, no extremes, no image or lack of image and no money. There were no pencils. In the beginning there were no names."

Even some of Rilke's comments to Franz Xaver Kappus: "Things are not all so comprehensible and expressible as one would mostly have us believe; most events are inexpressible, taking place in a realm which no word has ever entered, and more inexpressible than all else are works of art, mysterious existences, the life of which, while ours passes away, endures."

How to walk a tightrope, to have clear ideas, yet still be indefinite? This is how I sometimes experience your writing. There's a certain accessibility that I appreciate but also a slipperiness I find exhilarating. I'm right on track with the poem and then suddenly it's gone, though I can still feel the tracings in my hand. I love that surprise. That loss.

It's raining so much here in NY. The cuffs of my pants are wet. The trains have been delayed because there are "investigations" occurring since the latest bomb threat. I just came back from the Met. A photography and occult exhibit where there's ectoplasm hanging out of people's bodies, and mysterious words appearing on walls. It's a day.

Now I finish this letter to you.

Your letters have been important to me. I've told several poets the advice you gave me in your first letter about how I need my time more than my students do. I think of these letters as a kind of community. That our words can be bits of light traveling back and forth.

Thank you.

Truly,
Jennifer

San Diego, California
December 26, 2005

Dear Jennifer,

Am I getting the last word. It's right after Christmas, way late and I feel that I owe you a letter. I feel we've done pretty well despite the fact that these letters are a project. Right?

How did you do w/ the transit strike. Were you here? Are you going to the New Year's reading at the church. I think . . . people call it the Project now. I'm sort of extra aware of it since I just finished a relatively serious draft of my novel (showed to an agent) and in it I was a younger poet and she (the younger poet) was very excited about the moment when she began to call the Poetry Project "the church." And it also had a particularly excited creepy feeling since I'd come from a conservative catholic community growing up and look where I wound up. Back in a religious-sounding community. When I worked at St. Mark's I remember advocating the writing of religious poems. I guess religion has long been the last frontier it seems. If one is looking for space, religion could still be the place where no one wanted to go so you could have the field to yourself. I suppose self-help poems would have that kind of excess too. No one's knocking experimental poets over, trying to get there!

I'm thinking about your wonderings in the realm of ambivalence and unknowingness. And I'm replying that one strategy would be to be deliberately silly and then let seriousness rise up. If a poet were to do something as wrong-headed as to talk to god seriously you would be forced to find some new strategies for covering your ass which would yield a poem which was absurd, tangible, desperate, outré, embarrassing, self-possessed and many other things. I had an agent in the past (and not a successful past, so take this all as bad advice . . .) and I remember her telling me she was spending her vacation going to golf camp. Can you imagine anything any more wrong?

Yet wouldn't that be a fabulous venture for a poet to set out on. I'm thinking of the painter Malcom err what was his name. Malcolm Morley. British painter. Anyhow he was stuck (in his work) so he went on a "ladies painting trip." A group of women had a club or a class in which they met and piled into a rowboat on the Thames or someplace like that and it was so "artistic" that the class yielded wonderful stuff for him.

I hooted at my agent for going to golf camp and it was not the beginning of the end of our relationship but one of many. It was a lousy relationship but what a wonderful way for her to spend her time. I envied her. I think wrongness is always the right direction because it requires so much correction for anything to happen at all and that struggle makes a new texture. A friction would most likely exist for anything to happen at all. And of course it could utterly fail and yet there are so many other silly avenues to take. The possibilities are never exhausted. Just the fact that we know there are tendencies: to have projects, to be experimental, to write serious articles, to be more scholarly, any of the wonderful opportunities that exist for us should either be boldly ignored or else just pursued in such a wrong fashion that something quite nice could happen.

Hearing you I start thinking you shouldn't be teaching writing. Me neither! I really want to quit my job. I make all this money and my family – even my mother's neighbors in Arlington know I'm "a professor" and they are smiling at me in the street and I think it's absolutely gross. What would a professor know? Nothing.

I read in Philadelphia in December and I had a great encounter with Linda Hunt who was my professor at U. Mass (Boston) where I was an undergraduate. This Linda Hunt had unwittingly spurred (in one version of reality) my life as a poet. She had us write an inferno in response to Dante's and I wrote a poem and she read it to the class and the rest is the rest of my life. Well through the grapevine (a wedding I went to last winter) we got in touch and I sent her the chapter of the novel she's in and she invited me to contact her when I next came to Philly. There I was. It was amazing. To see someone after nearly 40 years certainly, but also to be the potential person in realization – I mean I couldn't talk to her then but she utterly moved me and spoke to me. But I couldn't speak. Now she was another adult, a smart one, from a class (w.c.) that explained why we had such a good connection and now we had a great amount in common including teaching in college.

I actually much prefer teaching literature is what I think about teaching. I had some great poetry teachers along the way but I've entirely worn out those thoughts I think and the ones that are new are about literature, or film, or art and how I as a writer see and implement those other media. I'm not sure what use my writing is but I'm very certain about how useful other people's work is to me. There's something undeniable about the excitement certain work produces in me and it seems the best thing I can do in teaching is try and explain to myself and the class I'm working with what that excitement is. What speck of the work, what turns, what possibilities make me feel gladder to be around.

The word utility really jumped out for me in your letter and I'm thinking as a writer we are simply translating what the human wants. I struggle with power, I absolutely want space. Whenever an idea or a body of work – a piece of weather, anything inadvertently opens up a new space for me, a sense of not being crowded and not being rushed, holding the moment for myself and reveling in it then I invariably have something to write about that needs no explanation. It's related to the production (and use) of energy.

And I still think femaleness is somehow at the bottom of what we are talking about. The search for rightness – which utility could certainly be a form of. Utility needs no explanation unlike female existence which is often merely appropriated or deemed empty if it is not. It's only useful in a way and one is always trying to be the better labeler of one's usefulness to sabotage some other narrative about yourself that may be getting written meanwhile without our knowing.

You girls alone? You know, like that. No, we're having a very important meeting. My building is full of wheezing spitting people. I love that your cuffs are wet. Which world isn't real? I think that when Leslie Thornton is falling it's very real and she lets it happen which gives her agency and she probably makes a mess. That's what she's claiming. A free wreck.

It's kind of a sport, which is what I'm urging on both of us this year, to take up some new kind of cudgel or club and swing it wildly and see what we get.

Love,
Eileen

Karen Weiser & Anne Waldman

Karen Weiser's chapbooks include *Pitching Woo* (Cy Press, 2006), *Placefullness* (Ugly Duckling Presse, 2004), and *Eight Positive Trees* (Pressed Wafer, 2002). Assorted poems have been published in *The Chicago Review*, *The Germ*, *The Hat* and *The Canary,* among others. She is a doctoral candidate at the CUNY Graduate Center and teaches at Barnard College in New York City when not caring for her daughter.

Anne Waldman is an internationally known poet, performer, professor, editor and cultural activist. She is the author of over 40 books and small press editions including, most recently, *Manatee/Humanity* (Penguin Poets, 2009), *Outrider* (La Alameda Press, 2006), *Structure of the World Compared to a Bubble* (Penguin Poets, 2004), *Vow to Poetry: Essays, Interviews & Manifestos* (Coffee House Press, 2001), *Marriage: A Sentence* (Penguin Poets, 2000) and the 20th anniversary edition of *Fast Speaking Woman* (City Lights Books, 1996). She

is also the editor of *The Beat Book* (Shambhala Publications, 1996) and co-editor of *Civil Disobediences: Poetics and Politics In Action* (Coffee House Press, 2004), and the forthcoming *Beats at Naropa* (Coffee House Press, 2009). She is a Distinguished Professor of Poetics at The Jack Kerouac School of Disembodied Poetics at the Naropa University in Boulder, Colorado, a program she co-founded with poet Allen Ginsberg in 1974. She was an Assistant Director (1966-1968) and the Director of the St. Mark's Poetry Project (1968-1978). She is the recipient of grants from the National Endowment for the Arts, The Poetry Foundation and is a winner of The Shelley Memorial Award for poetry. She lives in New York City and Boulder, Colorado.

Kyoto, Japan
December 30, 2004

Dear Karen,

Unresolved inter-connected-nesses, the need for the ancestor shrines, the way the imagination keeps playing back old (I am still stuck in romantic Heian period with Genji, Sei Shonagon, the sad diary entitled *Kagero Nikki*), yet newly activated images—holocaust/Hiroshima/Pachinko parlors. How does all this play here? And what to make of it? "Do" with it? "Do" anything? Is part of the poet's vow to perpetually catch, distill, refine, re-imagine where one walks, what one notices? Plus all the verbal wordplay and associations. The mysterious Noh plays' court backdrop reconfigures kingship/emperor/god/patriarchal power paradigm, and also—which is more important—engages "no action" which is what goes between the singing, music, stage movements, animal sounds. The big gap.

"Life and death, past and present—
Marionettes on a toy stage.
When the strings are broken,
Behold the broken pieces!"

CHORUS
(mimicking the sound of crickets)
kiri, hatori, cho, cho
kiri, hatori, cho, cho
The cricket sews on at his old rags,
With all the new grass in the field; sho,
Churr, isho, like the whirr of a loom: churr

—Zeami Motokiyo[1], *Nishikigi*
trans: Ezra Pound

Human life transmigrating between life and death, hell, ghost, animal, human, heaven realms . . .

But remember this is extremely evolved, refined art—on much older shamanic/Bardo death rites (which is where I am locating a lot of my writing and study) and confrontation involving encounters such as those with animal spirits and

---

[1]Zeami Motokiyo, born in 1363, was the author of many Noh plays.

"ghost" sound. And making/imitating those sounds of the animal. Modal structures. Though I have recently been impersonating robots. But is it all like *The Kingfishers/Wasteland*, etc. Are we just always writing in our Culture of Death? The old wounds/yearnings must be healed so the land will thrive? So everything can "go on"? My former Naropa student poet Kenji, here, as we were riding the Chuo train line, said emphatically "No more Kings!" which continues this line of theistic thinking re: death, its cycles. Those power mongers sleep with Death, using it all the time to keep us enthralled, in state of perpetual fear. Can we not do that? So I write to get out of my own Empire of Death and Fear, which is what I told students last summer at Naropa. Help!

Use of what we do? Relative to these cultural studies? I often wish I had been an archeologist. What is this self-appointed poet job? Is it always simple—on one level—re-act/response mode, which is why I have been so grateful to be out of USofA a spell and consequently not so primed to re-act, spout all the time what everyone in Our Camp knows, constantly replaying the delusion of the Masters Of War, their version of reality mimicking, commenting on their euphemistic vocabulary, etcetera, etcetera and recounting my own Nightmares vis-à-vis THEM. What a bore. Not to ever forget their horrific deeds, I will continue to record those in *IOVIS 3* under the title "Colors in The Mechanism of Concealment."

And what will the extraordinary richness of this "culture"—these cultures—which include praxis, religion, manners and mores bring? I am obviously excited.

Kyoto: Rampant with syncretic layers. Some fox shrine thoughts: had that red pelt in mind back in a time when animals roamed and we were one with them. A small clearing for fox assignation. What is it to love a fox? Brought to mind the rat shrine in Calcutta, the bat shrines in Bali . . . But saw similarities with stuff in Indonesia/Polynesia in the Shinto shrines—the animist/ancestor deal, now unfortunately associated with Japanese nationalism as the current prime minister keeps honoring the Shinto place (in Tokyo) where WWII war criminals are "enshrined." But most affected by the Hall of the 1001 Kannon bodhisattvas, "Sanjusangendo" founded originally in 1164 A.D., rebuilt after a fire in 1266—390 feet long, 54 feet wide. In the center is the chief image of Kannon (Quanyin, Avalokistesvara) with eleven faces and one thousand arms, 11.5 feet high. On both sides of him/her stand very close together, ready for "action"—like an army—1000 more images of Kannon with multiple arms and accoutrements. The idea is an army of compassion.

The rock gardens—meticulously raked white pebble carpets, with rocks that don't necessarily resemble anything, offer a nice conundrum. Like looking at Abstract Expressionism, someone said.

And on.

What are you studying? What does your world look like?

I wish I had a thousand arms.

LOVE

Later: Tokyo, Japan
                                                                                  January 2, 2005

Dear Karen,

One's mind is a place and a map indeed as per your chapbook *Placefullness*. My keyboard is Japanese hence lacking in easy access to quote marks, colon, semis. I miss parentheses and have written a piece entirely dependent on the parenthetical which is what you do when you can't understand most words and have an ongoing patter/mind-stream in native tongue but all the time thinking What is this I am hearing? Why is it alien. Or is it? Past lifetime in this language? How does it relate to animal sound. How does it relate to Korea, China, Siberia, Polynesia. What I know is some Japanese Buddhist chant. If only another lifetime to study Kana, understand Kanji. Both visual towers and topiaries. A kind of drama which includes the Theatre of Noh sounding, and at the same time: a temple, silent, with incense wafting. Many associations from movies, the shakuhachi flute. There's such grace in the calligraphic Kanji and the sense of the whole body making a stroke. Or the stroke being made with mind and heart as well. Stroke of the "warrior."

I also find the precision of the vast train system here in Tokyo daunting. There is a map here in my head of multiple cities—imagined, real, absent, pulsing, hardly any green. These mini-districts are post-war, constructs of wild dimension mounted on the fossil fuel of—hard to imagine. Complex history of Edo, the former capital, and the possibility of earthquake haunts the premises . . .

Population here is way over 12 million. Very few *gaijin*—literally "outside" people.

One has a mind of stone in the Zen gardens (Kyoto).

My mind is translating into yen from dollars. Dollars seem dirty, the Yankee crime. What does an American do here to counter all the negative karma accumulated by our bombing, nuking so many of their cities? You feel pain in the elderly, deep scars, many decades . . .

I have already begun a Buddhist poem triggered by a statue of a sow-headed *dakini*. What is Hebrew for "sow"?

My job here is a month's residency with the Tokyo Joshi Daigaku—Tokyo Woman's Christian University. Participate in a symposium, teach workshops, today a seminar on performance poetry. The campus bells are tolling "O Come O Come Emmanuel and Ransom Captured Israel"—apt words in current context, eh? So happy son Ambrose is with me, he's got his own investigations going—late nights in jazz clubs, has also made friends who play basketball. He's been invited to speak at a class on the novels of Haruki Murakami whom he admires.

I am seeing a Noh play tonight entitled *Kokaji* about a blacksmith and a fox. The Waki is the blacksmith, a witness figure. The spirit of Shite is a boy who is an incarnation of Inari Myohjin, the fox. My recent *Structure of the World Compared to a Bubble* seems to rest in some ideas from the animal realm—if we don't reclaim some of those origins, we're in trouble. You must know Pound's Noh, based on Fenollosa's notes. I almost got to Fenollosa's gravesite near Kyoto, not enough time. Think I passed Cid Corman's bakery though (and wrote a little poem). Thinking about the *gaijin* poets and Japan. Gary Snyder, Phil Whalen, Joanne Kyger, Clayton Eshleman, Corman. Huge source, here, for writing. And translation work.

Hmmmmmmmmmm

I need to get this preliminary bundle—an invitation—a summons—a bow toward our communication in missive realm off to you now.

What is the climate for your work life? History does indeed appear to flutter; the underground lost city. Your writing in *Placefullness*—ghost, view of time and the site itself very relevant here in my stint in Japan. And now we are even deeper inside this war and no matter what language we are innocent, people are suffering and dying without cause.

Love,
Anne
(the secular fox, the secular sow)

PS

I know poets have to keep traveling and placing themselves in other cultures, even as it gets more difficult for us norteamericanos. All the more reason. In fact, one experiences the heartbreak most profoundly from a distance. I want to dwell in "art time" the next years, but of course have always lived in "art time."

New York, New York
January 10-February 6, 2005

Dear Anne,

I have been thinking about Bardo death rites as a place for you to locate your work. Do you mean writing out of a state of in-between, or an emptying of consciousness? "The big gap" as you wrote? I want to hear more. Right now I am reading Andrei Codrescu's novel *Wakefield*, in which the main character gives a motivational talk about poetry and money while the devil looks on, and in the midst of the talk Wakefield says, "The difference between a modern artist and Buddhist monk is in the approach. The artist goes into the void empty and returns with a souvenir, if you will. The monk approaches the void with a traditional body of knowledge and arrives at emptiness." I really like this idea of the spatial movement of consciousness and having "encounters" within that journey, as you put it. Like Will Alexander's sense of astral projection, which I was just reading about in his interview with Marcella Durand in *The Poetry Project Newsletter*. Another useful way to think about writing.

There are so many: the image of the poet observing like a monk and recording, the poet who dictates—tuned into some other channel until the poem is revealed, the romantic poet active in exploring the movement of the imagination, the poet who plagiarizes or cuts-up language in order to reanimate or recontextualize it, the political poet who awakens, the poet who dredges up their inner emotional life, the language poet, the ecological poet; all of these ideas only begin to touch what it is that happens when a person sits down to write. It is a question asked every time someone writes a poem, and although the poet may think s/he is in control, it is still this inexplicable magic. Alice [Notley] once told me that she believes in doing elementary human things, like having children, and I think writing is one of these old human practices. It is an attempt to be active in the midst of existing—active in meaning-making anyway. And of course it is an activity that involves a certain amount of passivity, or not exerting oneself—the great paradox of creation. A way to build a nest within the always moving stream of consciousness, to capture and still the self, or not self?, at that moment, to see how the self is built by language, which is yet just another analog of the mysterious writing process. All the ways that poets conceive of their practices, and have throughout time, seem paltry and reductive metaphors for this basic human desire to shape reality through language.

And in this way maybe writing is a way out of—or through—the Culture of Death, as you termed it, because it is constructive and active work, like the bird who weaves a nest out of discarded, cast-off materials around herself, a work of living, a living work, even if the bird uses scraps of shroud. So for us poets, it is important. For the Culture of Death, however, I am not so sure. I have no idea if there is a real place for poetry within our culture anymore, since poetry will never really be able to fit into a corporate model (at least I hope it never will!). Is this because it costs nothing to write as long as you have paper and a pen, or a memory even? But the thing that is hard to swallow is that there is no bridge between our culture's need for poetry, (which became clear after 9/11's hundreds of poems tacked up all over NYC) and its actual living existence as an art form, as a practice that needs to be supported and paid attention to. Poetry is not a product for consumption but poets do need material support to keep creating their work. A dilemma.

A week or so ago Anselm [Berrigan] brought home a documentary about kestrels from the library—filmed in Sweden and without any dialogue. It follows a family of kestrels for a year and shows what they see; since their nest is in an architectural detail of a church and faces a well taken-care-of graveyard, they see people enter the frame to be buried, to parade, to marry, to shovel, to plant, to water, to walk the dog. The rock gardens around the tombstones are raked white pebble, like Abstract Expressionism, yes, but in the video you hear the repetitive and meditative sound of the rake across the stones. The birds watch and listen, on their own clock, in addition to hatching and then feeding their family of 6 young kestrels. What do they see when they see people? What is the use of human ritual? What kinds of rituals do birds have? Did you see that article in *The New York Times* about the scientific discovery that birds are way more intelligent and creative than previously thought? My parrot likes to ring his bell in the morning to wake us up—one of his many daily rituals. I don't know what it is to love a fox but I imagine it is no different from loving a person. I can't even picture a time when people roamed with the animals, but so many of the bedrock aspects of interpersonal relationships are the same for creatures everywhere—in herds, bevies, flocks, packs, families. Have the basic emotional realities of our lives evolved that much over time?

I am reading Edgar Allan Poe right now and thinking about imaginative decadence. Part of his excess is his insistence on a kind of absolute logic and reason, even in the no-man's-land of poetic composition. In his famous essay "The Philosophy of Composition" he lays out step-by-step the mental journey of connections in his writing of the poem "The Raven." I'm not sure I buy it. He details the same kind of mental stepping stone documentation process in his short story "The Murders in the Rue Morgue" where one character guesses another's train of thought and appears to read his mind through logical deduction. Poe makes reason and logic as magical and decadent as he makes madness. Or are they the same thing?

My world looks like this:

"clack" the summer parallel's
fine layer of shag

sticks,
breaks the eggshell
(speckled red containers,
head full of stars)
of merely
circulating
(citified yolk state)
schedule of buildings
sections condense, ease
dimension at that
dusk, immaculate opening of corners

You DO have a thousand arms!

Love,
Karen

Boulder, Colorado
April 25, 2005

Dear Karen,

"dusk, immaculate opening of corners" has a kind of Bardo feel. It's the in-between,
the *both both* quality of mind, that anything can arise and does and that there is also
there, experientially, a notion of purity. Bardo like the "charnel ground" is that
place of birth and death. And one can start from there and also end there. But in
the gap is—possibly—an emptying of consciousness, as you put it. Or that that's
some heightened sense of being less ordinary, or of ordinary magic and not so self-
conscious. I like to think that one can carry "knowledge," whether "traditional" or
classical or just street wisdom yet wear it lightly and it buoys you up, arises with
your thinking or has already become part of you if it is useful. "Useful knowledge,"
as G. Stein puts it. What is urgent to know about? I ask myself this every day and
get extremely dizzy. I made this poem construct below of "without" then what

"call" is heard? The idea was what can one do without and of course by saying those things you keep all those things. And it was triggered by the terrorists in DC pushing on the agenda that we are going once again to be attacked by the other terrorists—thus: "*coming? coming soon?*" I was thinking too the sense from Wakefield of the poem as souvenir. I couldn't locate my life without the poems over the years as signposts. Thus a diary of a particular kind of consciousness . . .

Agnès Varda's 3 films now showing (at the Film Forum) interesting as exercises in memory, emptying out, consciousness, politics.

Here I was thinking of Robert Duncan's poem of the mother being a falconress. I was thinking about being blind and being a seer. I was also thinking of Native American scholar and activist Ward Churchill's sense of the "little Eichmanns" in reference to Hannah Arendt's "banality of evil" and the whole predicament we find ourselves in being one of the "rivets," the "cogs and wheels" of the difficult exploitation/war machine. And this always brings up for me an issue of ethics, responsibility. Because everything is vastly inter-connected—more so than ever. Push a button, and a rain forest goes down in South America. Now Professor Ward Churchill finds himself in trouble over issues of the 9/11 karma, as does Amiri Baraka. So yes, encounters with the charnel ground which is like the World Trade Center site and like Rwanda and Cambodia not so long ago and like the gap where what we call our poems arises within.

Without Stitching Closed the Eye of the Falcon

without care without seed pearl without stitching closed the
eye of the falcon without seemly rectitude without the platitude
of o thou muddled media pundit without questionable
thermosphere without it working against you and when it does being
able to go on without it without gavottes without gazelles that you
study in neighboring Persian poetries without spallation and
without a diving bell how will you survive? without rapacious wildcats
without the sense of security you have always expected without your
familiar stage fright without the caves without the bombing of caves
without the mystery of caves without the caves in your memory of that
mystery that lives in caves without caves that long to exist in the
handprint in the cave of that memory without the rivets that hold

the wing together that hold the whole throbbing machine together that
assert the rivet dominion without which you do not have a plan of
fastening together of wings of arms for the automaton that holds
the capital together without its own mind of wheels and cogs
that run the show without all the pixels and efforts of more dominion
without borders to cross without needing to carry things over borders
the invasion of your homeland (*coming? coming soon?*) without it, what
call in the night what call is answered what nuance what tantrum in the night
or end of speculation what call what alarm is sounding deep in the home.

Yes, the elementary human (Alice's sense of being a real human being—humans
like to make things with their hands, they like to paint & sing & make babies)
which is why I wanted to bring this poem to home and hearth as it were. "Alarm?"
It is human to have children and be scared and want to survive? Ed [Bowes] speaks
proudly of us being "workers" being in the "cultural working class," being teachers,
citizens. Yet he makes movies that are a stretch, a struggle. A whole gamut of
imagination. He wants a sublime non-narrative-fiction, he wants to re-examine
story. He wants the democratic party to get its act together. So all the kinds of
poets you list and where they identify themselves are aspirational-ly summoned
above. I need to examine Persian poetries, I need to cross more borders and save
the Naropa tape archive, and so on. Exertion/passivity. I go blank and there's a
huge amount of energy expended that comes back later. Allen Ginsberg climbing a
hill to a campfire to give a reading on a chill night, exhausted, said that it would
give him energy to go there. The campfire as charnel ground, the cave as Bardo.

O yes that is the question about whether there is a place for poetry in our culture.
O dear, o dear. I will strive to continue to make a place for it yet with the revi-
sion-ing of history and the fact that someone dangerous like Bush & Co. could be
re-elected (or selected) after so much disclosure of the lies, pathology, the endless
examinations, books on the crimes, Enron, endless endless crimes exposed yet
what does all this get us? The fact that these revelations don't matter shows that
we are now OUTSIDE history, outside our culture, the story is coming to an end
(Baudrillard?). Or, rather, what do they mean? Are history and culture even rele-
vant at this point since they are a fiction! A version of the world that is markedly
UNREAL. Perhaps poetry is more relevant than any of this other stuff except that
there is very real suffering we need to constantly mitigate. Or maybe we should
start making more families with animals—as you have with your bird & all our

friends with cats, and canines, snakes, gerbils, turtles. Thalia Field is sure that dogs
have senses of humor and that they are making jokes when they sit on the sofa you
have forbidden them. One could go on & on thinking of utopian possibilities to
figure out how to live sanely in this post-capital avant derriére dark age. The
animals are certainly less dangerous.

So yes let's go to the bird realm. Their rituals seem more attractive, or stay with a
raking of pebbles. The repetition seems salutary. I keep flashing back on Japan. In
dreams Tokyo is still the Bardo between vast time periods and states of mind. And
how important the discipline of the "small" is and yet what is working on the disci-
pline of the "large" scale? Something awry. I find myself looking at symbols in the
dream (obviously the "kanji" letters) trying to unlock them. They look like bird
scratches, odd footprints. If I "get" them will I be able to get off the train—open
the sliding doors—and get back to the library in my study in Boulder? What the
devil do they say? I never seem to arrive.

And Poe maybe is methodical as an afterthought, you think? He seems to have a
dominating mind. Reason, logic, madness all magical and decadent—possibly. I am
not sure about decadence to wear as an artist, now that the body of our world
seems hopelessly sick with mental and ecological torment. The planet has AIDS,
perhaps.

> to the contrary
>   with-
> out
> authority the
>   dare, or
> pressure
>   point
>   a pebble,
> a true source
> Niedecker wrote
>   when casting
> a stone
>   was not a war crime
> should be
> a ground for

```
        truce & veracity
    o moral Annie
        sound
    the ground
        inside the head
    empty head
    between the word
        & the
    reach for it
```

Astral projection. Have you looked up at the moon?

Love,
Anne

Karen,

```
    Last year service in the eastern hills.
    Now the marches of the western seas
    How often in the span of an official's life
    Must he (she) weary him (her) self with these border wars?
```

        —Fujiwara no Umakai (694-737), from the *Kaifuso* (program notes)

Been thinking around the parameters of *Iovis III* (Colors in the Mechanism of Concealment) as I try to organize the rhizome it is. Borders and linguistic disputes seem so much at the root of what one is ready to die for. And because I am a poet so caught up with "polis" (the eyes, the public, those who will see for themselves unmediated by authority), I seem to constantly consider *both both* sides. And want to carry the epic sense of the total story as we are living it right now through the orality of our minds' ears & eyes. That's what I feel in this city, in this poem, noise and more noise. Trying to find the "C" train which doesn't run on weekends, although I can HEAR it, trying to find a language that isn't so common meaning prevalent (I love the common tongue). There seems to be so much more cruel racist graffiti around town as I make my rounds, have you noticed?

Seems like a bit of a dis-junct over the events of this week of Poetry Month April with PEN American Center/the rest of the community. The hierarchy of Salman Rushdie (who I see mostly getting in & out of limousines although I don't hold that against him as a formerly marked man). The New Yorker, which still doesn't consider poetry as a mind-changing & charging event, other arbiters of verse/prose culture and it's true the climate still feels somewhat "official" as in "official verse culture." We need to go to other kinds of neighborhoods or at the least widen the discussion. Include Etal Adnan. Maybe it's all hidden in books, between the lines. Maybe I just need to hide out in the noisy library. I want to study how things are said, so back into the streets again.

Chris Hedges talks about the Serbs, Muslims, and Croats distorting their own tongue as their "conflict" heated up, to accommodate the myth of their own sepa-rateness. How the Bosnian Muslims introduced Koranic expressions and Arabic words into the language, the Muslims adopted the word "shahid" or martyr from the Arabic and dropped the Serbian word "junak." The Croatians started "dusting off" words from the fifteenth century. In Zaghreb you couldn't use old Serbian phrases anymore.

Been counting more of the war dead the last century and where we sit now and wonder about the efficacy of counting in poetry. Piling up, naming. Name the poets, list their titles, count their lines? Counting coup. Hard to pay taxes this past week. Every cent a bullet, a bomb. Scent of death on the money. This epic has a somber "knell." I am thinking of more cheerful notes towards its completion any ideas? Young ideas! The Dark Arcana section ("Dark Arcana: Afterimage or Glow")—written out of the trip to Hanoi—maybe a bit more optimistic with a new generation some of whom I met all in their twenties, eager not to have to live out more endless revenge cycles. Ambrose who is heading that way soon, "How can they LIKE Americans in Vietnam?"

But there was a bit of a grumble during the Poetry Is News event this past Saturday (April 16) that so many SF Renaissance poets were being referenced over

NY School, or women even, although Bethany Spiers read a terrific Belladonna "mission statement" (for lack of a better term) with a host of our favorite women living breathing standing on the little performance zones of Zinc bar & CUNY. I mentioned the flowering fruit trees honoring O'Hara & Berrigan. But it's those texts of Olson, Duncan, Baraka, interesting to return to for the History. Only want my history now from the poets. Where do you go for history?

And so welcome in my own space and time an attempt to lighten up, but not the load which seems even greater with Creeley's death. What do I mean by that. Why do I still need poets to be heroes? What is this self-appointed poet warrior biz?

I wanted to send you the notes for the Intro for Poetry is News. And part 2 of this will be some of the epic.

Love,
Anne

P.S. Did I say I was inspired to write to you after your reading because I could hear youth music in your rhythm, in your tone? Was that it? Untamed a bit you think? Standing by her/your word. What is the shape of the new youth poems? They seem very propelled and full (rich) with stuff. Things & "memory." What does "political" mean to you?

New York, New York
June 22, 2005

Dear Anne,

Reading over the two letters you have written since my last one, I must tell you that I thought about you while swimming in the Colorado river—picture 103 degrees of Southwest heat, the freezing water contrasting with the hot, hot, dry and dusty air. Trying to push my body against the weight of the current, so strong it took a certain kind of determination to move against it, reminded me of you. You are filled with this kind of will and that it has given you the momentum to write what you write and push aside accepted narratives like an arm against onward water. Therefore I am not surprised that writing from out of the Bardo as you've been explaining to me is also a matter of will, of giving it up—harnessing the tension between exertion and passivity, telegraphing blankness as you put it. I'm reminded out in the desert that every inch of this country is charnel ground. And that is something to remember.

I finally successfully added John James Audubon into a poem I am working on—I have been trying to fit him into various works for months, and I find him fitting into this conversation quite nicely. Recently I read his *Mississippi River Journal* (1820-1) and discovered that all of the beautiful birds he drew and painted, all of those amazingly detailed portraits, were birds he and his company shot and killed. Here is this man, traversing the lush, "untamed" wilderness with thousands of birds flying overhead, birds never documented before, and he aims and shoots in order to create art. Was he thinking of arranging their corpses to paint them, of his hunger (he ate many), of the life ebbing from the birds themselves? He wanted to create life-sized portraits of the birds of the US (which he did in his famous *Birds of America*), and his journals document his respect for the birds while they simultaneously log his relentless murder of them. Talk about creating art out of the space of death! And the charnel ground of history.

To give you an example, here are two excerpts from Audubon's *Mississippi River Journal* published in *John James Audubon: Writings & Drawings* (The Library of America, 1999) from the log for October 14, 1820, the third day of his journey down the river towards New Orleans:

"We returnd to our Boat with a Wild Turkey 7 Partriges [northern bobwhite quail] a Tall Tale Godwit [greater yellowlegs] and a Hermit Thrush which was too much torn to make a drawing of it this Was the first time I had Met with the Bird and felt particularly Mortified at its Situation."

"We passd the Small Town of Laurenceburgh in Indiana, Petersburgh in K.y, We Walked in the afternoon to Bellevue. . . . We killed 4 Small Grebes [horned grebes] at one Shot from a Flock of about 30. We approached them with ease to within about 40 Yards, they were chassing each other and quite Mery."

Here is the poem I wrote in which he appears, entitled "Now Then":

It's an inconvenient kind of flatness accepting the offer of the road above.
You know alone flashes filmic in its own projection
curdling the light, moving forward into natural relief
with quick-handed horror-movie humor
the bodies pile up and disappear
clouds like magnets on the move:

O, to be a strippling world
with a certain thrown-her-glove-in sense of possibility
heralding forth the blanketing noise
underneath the familiar surface
like an animal stuffer shapes death into life
Oh right, but it's just noise
in a traditional hero rectangle of frame

On the Mississippi Audubon killed the birds then drew them
time held out in small delicate etchings
still warm though rapidly aging
in his hands, the paper's a trigger
big enough to walk inside
the chapel of a bird's body
is any body
breathing with ink

I think Audubon's love affair with vision involved seeing into something stilled—
an obsession with making alive that which he took the life from. Which brings me
to your poem "Without Stitching Closed the Eye of the Falcon" that you included a
couple of letters ago. The poem's questions about power, by asking us what we can
do without (can we give up the idea of invasion or dominion?) also expose the
connection between authority and seeing: how absence makes seeing possible, how
any representation is that kind of possibility. And your poem shows how words
allow us to conjure that which we can simultaneously evoke as absent, exposing
the nature of language in terms of power and possession. And although this make
me think of the beauty/horror of Audubon and his gorgeous representations with
their gruesome history, I think that your poem suggests how writing is maybe one
positive opportunity in a world in which one feels continually helpless—writing
allows you to address your own position in seeing, through seeing.

And so that might be what "political" means to me, which is a question you asked that I have been having trouble answering. The word itself gives me the heebeejee-bees, and at the moment I am loathe to enter into a "political" conversation, although I realize as I write this that I am happy to talk about political things (doesn't that include everything?) as long as the rhetoric of both the Administration and the left is set aside. When I encounter these bundles of rheto-ric (especially in poems!) I feel a vast empty field inside of myself shudder into existence. This might stem from the sense of alienation and disappointment I experienced (and continue to feel) after the election. So I only want to consider politics in utterly personal terms. What does the word mean to you?

Another thing I find helpful and hopeful to remember is that we are not outside of history or culture. For my studies I am reading very early American writing and writing on America like de Toqueville's *Democracy in America* (1835). All of these heady Enlightenment ideas and the power of their articulation in government— did you know that early Americans discussed the concept of doing away with inherited property to realize the promise of the Declaration? I love reading about the revolutionary potential in democracy.

On that note!

Love,
Karen

Boulder, Colorado
July 3, 2005

Approaching the 4th of July, 2005, not going to celebrate with fireworks this year.

Dear Karen,

"the paper's a trigger / big enough to walk inside / the chapel of a bird's body"

put me in mind of the plutonium triggers on warheads, and the sanctity of all our threatened reality with the talk of new nuclear power-plants and weapons. The power of "paper" with Audubon's "work," his scientific obsession, his power if you will. I think the human realm takes for granted its hegemony and in the course of this, destroys the things it loves . . . or could and might love. Some genetic propensity to conquer, to "know"—there's a deadly combination of curiosity with epistemology. I hope you push on further with your poem—how long is it?

I realized this taking a walk yesterday to a place called Button Rock Reservoir, a roundtrip 5 mile hike, but at one point the trail ends at a huge culvert and there's a rocky trail above leading to the actual reservoir and there is such a strong inclination to push on and see what's "just around the corner" no matter if it's high noon in blazing heat, and one is wearing the wrong shoes, etc. This is an area for water management. Scary to think of what harm could prevail (it is an unguarded pristine preserve, how easy to drop a few nasty pellets that could poison the whole Longmont populations (it serves that particular city)) (Ah paranoia!). Also forest management has a staging area with signs like "chop and scatter," "chip in." Magpies like to sit near the dam . . . quite charming. Also, there's the specter of water wars always in the back of the mind . . . How precious this substance, more necessary than oil . . . Harder to replace . . . And out west here, (as you know I'm right now in Colorado, our Naropa Summer Writing Program about to begin).

But there is certainly paranoia in the bird realm. Read recently that the black-capped chickadee singing its "chick-a-dee" brings its flock mates flying. The song is a warning that owl, hawk, or other predators are hovering nearby, thus forces are called in and arrive to harass these enemies. The warning call is a coded signal. Evidently by varying the call, the size of the predator is communicated, therefore the scope of the danger . . .

The chickadees were exposed to 15 different predators in a test situation. It also makes a high-pitched 'seet' call when they spot a predator flying in the air. But the most interesting thing is the variations of the "chick-a-dee-dee" call. The birds vary the numbers of "dees" depending on the threat. Sometimes as many as 21 "dees" can ensue—the Northern pygmy owl is deemed quite a threat! I remember once counting "dees" and wondering if the variations were random. Are our poems coded signals for help? The Greek meters certainly were meant to work the magic of love or conjure warrior behavior in battle. De DA DA DA! De DA DA DA! Back into *Iovis* mode—trying to pull together the strands for *Book III*. I think it's

the pedagogy of the Naropa summers that encourages and generates the "rhizomic"
nature of the epic and also the occasion to "perform" here—I pull together dis-
parate pieces for performance and my workshops this week. Here are some lines to
kick off my class something about being an occultist witness, and noticing details of
imagination and POLITICS. It's also supposed to be instructional:

Across from me is a crossing of leg, across from me, a gray striped sock,
long underwear, red which is a zipper which is an intruder writing
in a slant way, head turned right gazing on a slant curve, then it goes another
way, tumbled, as if to say Notice this, notice this detail before you
lose interest, before something interrupts the ordinary obscure moment,
and you stop adding on your long lines of narration, enter in your log
the premium story of distress, warning, desire or create
a cosmology, or origin myth on the relative differences between genders,
the way you receive the sun, the moon, the stars into your habitat, into –
dare think this oldfashionedly? – your occultist spirit, for that's what it seems to be,
a witness, seeing its way through a chaotic time, the face of these images,
turning blood to stone, stone to fire, make a limb dance toward
heaven, carried by a force you are capable of making this picture of:
the dream of a dust bowl, dream of a prophet, dream of a maimed soldier
(o please send me home now), labor of a blue collar mentor,
dream of a pre-Raphaelite, dream of a Machiavellian sports announcer,
the dream that leaves you cold, all the embers down, you have no refuge,
talking about Cambodian Paris now, vision when you stood in the doorway lintel,
 in uniform, informed and ready to march, and all did not seem strange –
 It was the day before the movie rehearsal everyone get lines down and
shoot, the day before the funeral, the day before the self-immolating attack,
when incendiary meant simply "hot," and you could say it about a lover
if you were so inclined, the day before the discotheque folded (it was bombed in Bali)
the day before so many suffered, and you could make something North American
about it, including all the continents that would keep a Polaris missile
out of their midst, and then it all came back to you, opposite me, you
leaning over your instrument of power – that new nuke –
that would record an inquisitive face, not Cleopatra's, not emperor Hirahito's,
not an Agrippa at the control, not a tyrant nor a super errant knight,
and you might ask about threads and stitches and you might inquire
about buttons and harnesses, about exigencies of destroying proof,

about all the colors matching, about a reversal of intention
before the Mayan long count, before the day we might go to practice our syllables,
and good intention needs to shine on those syllables, taking them out of the
bomb shelter, avaunt your paranoid behavior! out of the time warp and
onto the street where you stood waiting for the shutter to snap, shouting "Hold"
and then it was your face that was always needed, your face which was always with me
and it could hold anything it wanted to, an unforced perspective, a lunar calendar,
a kiss, a way of thinking, behaving, as spectator to the spectacle, a daily life . . .

messages from the atomic world

fly in the face of incredulity
it's a celebrity! it's a shoulder!
it's *auto-da-fe* for the mind
higher & higher the moon, plus all desire
an impatient one flexes her muscles

take here, dear one, your glass of sun

the planets have turned their backs on you

take, my love, your sullen people, your tribe –
angry and forsaken

take stock of the carnivore, of idle chatter, of the Kali Yuga
of a ideological cinema that shirks responsibility
cut-ups? move the mountain forward,
exhaust the petrol

your map is moving again,

you lost your way,

dispersal routes, elapsed time, biotic strains
have a hand on the throttle in this
terrestrial extension

get off the road, walk over, join the crowd . . .

and so on. All very much in progress towards the final chapters of Epic.

Politics is to me at this point trying to be awake, join the crowd, help the world ("everything else drunken dumbshow" as Allen Ginsberg writes), know the terms, terminology, the latitudes & longitudes, the names of things, and be an investigator of power structures here and everywhere. Poetry has to recover the word, the world. To look at the "empire building" in my own psyche, to let go, to give over to Other, sympathetically. But watch "idiot compassion" activate discriminating awareness wisdom at all times. This is a constant and often impossible job, but come back to the breath, remember, breathe out, towards Other. Keep the aspiration. We are connected through our breath. Stay connected to friends, family, neighbors, try to alleviate suffering (so much always moment to moment—dear brother poet, comrade Lorenzo Thomas dying of emphysema as I write this . . . say a chant to ease the passing as he "goes into spirit"). And it is incredibly moving as one grows older to acknowledge all those one has shared this work and life with—and follow what they are also going through, traversing "in sickness and in health." It's a vow, it's a marriage. What Alice [Notley] is writing, thinking, what Bernadette [Mayer]— the dear female comrades of my generation who moved experimental exciting writing along more than a few inches (W. C. Williams says our job as poets is to move the century forward a few inches—like some slow growing redwood tree!). What is the wisdom of these ones? Why does their writing excite me?

Study and respect other cultures, attitudes but examine how "harm" operates. Emphasize *doing no harm*. The environment/health of all the planet denizens issues the biggest I know and am reminded as I visit Japan, Canada, my own backyard out west, NYC and everywhere. Try to hold one's seat, be able to shift into modes and moods and multiple voices in the writing. In the Animal Realm section ("to hunt to skin alive to wear upon a body") in *Structure of the World Compared to a Bubble* I try to get inside that psychological space of the one being preyed upon. I really experience the "poetry is news" biz as a way to "become" other realities, both imaginatively, and then literally by doing the investigative work as witness and orator and *agit prop* perf poet! And just as the chickadees teach their offspring about "risks," that's part of our job as well.

Polis=city. Greek. Polis also carries a sense of "eyes." Maximus of Tyre, the image/voice for Charles Olson in *Maximus*, which focuses on the city of Gloucester (the way one might on Athens or Troy), wrote disquisitions called *dialethia* in Greek and he wanted in his teaching to help his students come to grips with a dissolving world. Olson attempts that in *Maximus* which is really the history of the rise and fall of an archetypal American city. "Istorin"—the discovery, the story, told out of one's own experience, with one's own eyes. I am a city person, a *polis* person. Civic-minded. How to get along in layered realities, melting pots of language, mores, imaginations, hopes & fears. I listened to a dear very political friend (we traveled to Nicaragua together in the 80s) go on at a party in my yard last night (probably 124 Naropa students present & it's not that big a yard) about Boulder being the New York City of the west. For its number of intellectuals, high Jewish population, he notices, makes Boulder unique in the state of Colorado, general diversity (not that obvious), its culture, its politics, mostly graduate students . . .We will see. I am going to work on that sense of communi-ty-civics even more this summer. It's not a suburbia, the Jack Kerouac school . . .

I had a question for you about the professionalism and careerism of the poetry and creative realm in general. I know you are a scholar too, but can you think of poets in your generation who do not hold academic degrees? Or have gone some other route entirely? Dropped out of the paradigm? I know it is an economic issue and also the academies are the zones and safe havens for the creative work. What the *polis* of New York City or San Francisco or Paris used to be—it just seems odd when I think back to my own generation (which started to go academic—Ron [Padgett], Ted [Berrigan]) the origins of the New American poetry and even further back, the ex-patriot urge, the drop-out urge. My own mother dwelling in Greece a decade, first heading there in 1929, dropping out of school age 19. Also poets seem to travel for holidays (& I can't blame them for that). But it was heart-ening to hear from Ambrose this a.m. about traveling to Angkor Wat investigating the killing fields of Cambodia. Not as a poet, more a Seeker. . . . He is definitely resisting graduate school at this point. He works a spell, then takes off . . .

Also I wanted to ask you about your sense of genre for your own work? I am in didactic mode right now, and oral mode. Ed Sanders has us writing new verses for *America the Beautiful*. I've begun: O beautiful for matriot's dream / sees beyond testosterone . . .

Well we will keep working on this *polis* definition. Maybe the city is a state of mind? Politics is a view, a state of mind, which engenders action. Projects action, projects voice.

Tomorrow in class back to the Noh which is still vivid in my mind, and did I mention previously that there have been red fox sightings on my block here? Also to Maria Sabina, a woman who never went to school, never wore shoes . . . and some of the Book of Events from *Technicians of the Sacred*. I am also invoking the term "orature" (oral literature—will be playing a lot of taped treasures from our own Jack Kerouac School archive). I have a woman who works for the CIA in my class and a war bride whose husband is in Iraq (she lives at the big base in Germany). The activity continues in 10 directions, as usual. The world is rich and strange . . . No more heebeejeebees. More birds!

Much love,
Anne

New York, New York
February 3, 2006

Dear Anne,

I am sitting in the main New York Public Library rereading our letters on an unusually warm winter day. This building, with its ornate, serious flourishes is perhaps my favorite institution in the city, though I feel sheepish in confessing it (with so many worthy choices!). Speaking of institutions, I have been somewhat troubled by your question to me about poets in the academy and careerism; I can only say that I am stumped—dropping out isn't a possibility for poets today, as far as I can tell, and definitely not in New York City. Every poet I know has a job, whether it is in academia or not, and struggles with how to balance making money and making art. Does having a graduate degree actually change this or make it easier? I am not sure but I suspect it doesn't (and yes, I know lots of poets without graduate degrees, and some without college degrees). Personally I feel very lucky to have a great poetry community here in New York, mostly centered around reading series such as the Poetry Project, Belladonna, Segue, the Zinc Bar, etc. Not one of the people I know is a "careerist" poet, though many of them slog it out on a daily basis in one kind of institution or another. I know there is a whole money-ed poetry world out there, but they don't deal with me, and I don't deal with them, and it suits us both just dandy. Don't get me wrong, I continually wonder about the Lily family donation of 100 million dollars to *Poetry Magazine* and wish some of it would funnel its way down to my friends and community, but on the whole I just write my poems and interact with people who are interested in the work and the work and the work and occasionally each other. Sometimes new anthologies come out that remind me of these odd fault lines between "scenes" but I don't feel too troubled in general. I think you might have a different kind of exposure to these other poetry worlds since you work in MFA programs and interact with lots of different communities all the time across the country and world. In terms of academia, I myself am very happy to be in the academy, with all that it implies, where people have jobs that require them to sit around and think about ideas and language and texts. And my degree is turning out to have little to do with poetry actually, as it focuses mostly on early American novels, a decision I made partially because I don't want to exclusively teach poetry workshops or direct my scholarly thought toward poetics. The experience of getting a PhD has been wonderful and exhilarating though stressful, and I have no idea how it fits into or affects my poetry. For now, though, I keep a porous barrier between these two creative, intellectual pursuits.

The question of what sense of genre I have for my own work is, as I am sure you can imagine, a matter deeply affected by the reading and writing I do for my degree and the class I teach on literature of the Americas. On some level, there is a kind of pleasure I find in writing poems now that I haven't had in a long time that arises from the motion of thought involved in it: giving my brain the kind of loping gallop it likes when I write as opposed to the more responsible laying out of connections that critical prose requires (feels like lumbering to me a lot of the time). When writing I try to let the poem happen without making it happen, to go in not knowing or directing the process. It happens quicker than I can write it down, quicker than thinking, and there is pleasure in seeing what the fuck will happen. With critical prose, I have to make it happen, and have a responsibility to my argument, to a critical history, and to the essay form. Most of the time I wish I could write a poem instead, but push through these barriers to be able to get to the creative connection, to the moment where something exciting happens, though it is a previously scripted idea. Since my critical prose is generally in long essay format, my poems have become rather short in reaction, short and using a quick turning line. Yes, my current genre would have to be the short poem in series. My influences have definitely changed; now in addition to Jack Spicer and Lyn Hejinian and the Howe sisters I am in conversation with Jonathan Edwards, Phyllis Wheatley and the James brothers. In college we always joked that if you stay in the academy your poetry becomes boring, but I think my experience in school as a graduate student and a teacher has made my work more interesting as a result, if only from reading texts from earlier centuries, in which the language and grammar are meatier. I'm interested in recouping the music from these earlier texts, in exploring the sounds of a lyricism, or maybe rethinking what it means in today's poetics. This might be the music you heard in my reading.

Since so much of this correspondence has centered on ideas of the political, I have to come clean: I really struggle with the place of politics in poetry and in my life. Reading your last letter made me realize that I am pretty uncomfortable, and have been for a long time, with claiming the political, although I try to do many of the things you discussed, such as staying awake and open, considering power structures, and avoiding idiot compassion (great term!). But these things don't seem to change the world around me, and I certainly don't see poetry having much room to do that kind of work, since so few people read and care about poetry. These things change me, and that is great (for me), maybe that is all one can do, but it seems like too little; and other forms of political activism seem to have completely failed in our culture the last 5 years. I love the idea that exploding the forms, jamming the machine, questioning what art can be creates greater change, but I am not convinced it does, or that it doesn't for that matter. And often when politics enters poetry it seems at the expense of the poem—not all the time, but often enough.

I really just want to sit down and read a poem and here is a poem to end this correspondence with, one I wrote today while working on this letter to you. Although now I am in another library in an ugly building on a rainy day, it is a poem that exists somewhere else, perhaps in some field of short and loving space between us, or between us and the person reading this:

The plant must grow tired, and I very sleepy

The potato says these things and admires them
for their quiet self languages:
"…a consideration of form and content,
glass and wine, breath and field,
gives me a grid to romance and order all eyes
here and a species there;
what is consciousness, a kind of rough platform?"

The potato says these things broad and comparatively:
"we are watching a potato grow
in the painting that is this poem
you and me, dear reader
insofar as genitals swing and remain in place
without notice or eviction
our magisterial gaze is this
quiet world of stanza, where
I be a lead male friend
you are a little earth anywhere
the female opposite of laughter
in how we react to one another
a sensitive regime change between
brooding stanzas of Earth."

"Your verbal tick is beautiful
a metaphysic wit of the longest blossom
illuminating your face as it drapes its own century.
Who knew the gaudiest peacock
would be the one without color
lying in an inquiry of our own gardens
sculpted to grow only biblical plants?"

Sending your thousand arms a thousand wishes.

Love,
Karen

New York, New York
February 7, 2006

Dear Karen,

One last response? Although you as younger hope-of-the-future should have the last
word. And you still should, but something felt incomplete without saying just a
little more. (Is there ever a last word as long as poets breathe?) I loved your honesty

in the letter, and bracing response to my old-hag-carping on poetry careerism and invoking politics all the time. It must get claustrophobic. I apologize.

I love the animist potato in your poem and the idea of consciousness being a "rough platform." And the image of the peacock/inquiry of our own gardens/growing only biblical plants. We obviously are on a spiritual path. Colorless=egoless? Paradise. And your poem itself existing "somewhere else,"—a "field of short and loving space" . . .

I read in the CUNY Grad Center's Rainbow Room last night—a kind of paradise—I mean that building, the old chic dept. store (Altman's)—is that what it's called: "rainbow room" where you can see the sky (the moon was out last night) and an angle of the Empire State Building? It was the opening of the Study-Abroad-on-the-Bowery semester and I also gave a talk on "hybrid writing" which referenced hybrid cars, genetic manipulation, "mirror neurons" and the biz of being a writer. I took the teaching stick a friend brought from Ethiopia, with Arab alphabet scripted on like an old-style hornbook and swung it about a bit. It's probably a hundred years old. I've carried it on the subway and it seems to make people happy, especially Arab-speakers. "Who are you? Where did you get this?" It is a cultural-appropriation-intervention, and inspires more interesting exchanges than reading anti-war poems outside the NY Public Library (e.g. "Go get it on with your Saddam, baby!").

In any case, I wanted to say because I am involved with making schools and communities I appreciate all those places that are havens and laboratories/scriptoriums for scholars and writers—such as CUNY (& we are discussing some kind of further partnership with Study Abroad, & Kerouac School at Naropa) but that yes, you're right, in my various rounds—primarily outside the NYC nexus, there's a perceived career path for poets that because of current economics needs the academy for the tenure jobs and it feels unhealthy and too competitive (& there's lots of gossip about who is in and who is out—who is getting the grants, the jobs, the interviews at the MLA). Where is the place for a Maria Sabina, the barefoot Mazatec seer with no education? Where is the place for the uncredentialed? It's my bohemian defensiveness. Maybe I have felt "left out" of the academy discourse?

But I so appreciate you and your intelligence and curiosity and poetry and your sense of the "porous barrier," the impact of your studies on the work. And so much of the community here in our world seems of your ilk, the real deal. I wept during Eddie's [Edmund Berrigan] presentation last week at The Poetry Project on the blues, his relationship to it, his making of it, where it comes from, the poetry he loves. And presented in that room in the Parish Hall which has seen so much love and grief and joy. Where else could you have that feeling, of community and generosity, modesty and respect? It seems so outside the world of capital and war.

Politikos (Gk) = citizen. You are a great citizen Karen. But I don't think we're in some kind of disempowered minority as poets. Many "rough platforms" of all kinds and capabilities and "magics" arise. I've been watching the NSA hearings, disturbed by the drift but also able to applaud some of our public servants across the divide. Get it on senators. An opportunity to just be informed, awake, stay connected, curious. Follow the language of master narrative and euphemism. Thinking and keep the practices of living and writing going.

Back into Japanese studies for this section of *Iovis* still in the making, I was looking at some photographs of a Noh performance where the "sea elf offers some wine of long life." That's the image for the day—for you.

      etiquette of all on stage

         wipe the sweat from your face my sweet

     exits of others need not hinder you

salute your formidable mask (3 bows)

     you are the "art of the flower of peerless charm"

          . places where you say "curtain" (maku! maku!)

        it rises

            and you miraculously appear

Dear Correspondent—I salute & bow to you,
Anne

Jill Magi & Cecilia Vicuña

Jill Magi is the author of *Threads*, a hybrid work of text and image (Futurepoem, 2007), the poetry collection *Torchwood* (Shearsman, 2008), and the chapbook *Cadastral Map* (Portable Press at Yo-Yo Labs, 2005). Her writing is anthologized in *The Brooklyn Rail Fiction Anthology* and is forthcoming in the *)((eco (lang)(uage(reader))*. Other writings and visual works have been published in *HOW2: Experimental Writing by Women*, *The Tiny*, *The Brooklyn Rail*, *Jacket*, *The New Review of Literature*, *Aufgabe*, *Chain*, *Pierogi Press*, and exhibited at the Brooklyn Arts Council Gallery, the International Meeting of Visual Poetry, and The Brooklyn Waterfront Artists Coalition. She runs Sona Books, a community-based chapbook press, and teaches at Eugene Lang College at the New School of Liberal Arts, Goddard College, and City College. From 2006-2007, Jill was a Workspace Program participant with the Lower Manhattan Cultural Council.

Poet, visual artist and filmmaker, **Cecilia Vicuña** was born in Chile and divides her time between Chile and New York. She performs and exhibits her work widely in Europe, Latin America and the US. Also an activist and founding member of Artists for Democracy, she creates workshops, seminars and collective instances of transformation with indigenous communities. She recently completed a performance tour of four Latin American countries along with Jerome Rothenberg. The author of 16 books, her work has been translated into several

languages. Recent titles include: *Sabor a Mi* (Ediciones Universidad Diego Portales, 2007), *Palabrarmas*, (RIL, 2005), *I Tu* (Tse-tse, 2004), *Instan* (Kelsey St. Press, 2003), *El Templo* (Situations, 2001) and *QUIPOem, The Precarious, The Art and Poetry of Cecilia Vicuña* (Wesleyan, 1997). *Spit Temple, Selected Oral Performances by Cecilia Vicuña*, edited by Rosa Alcalá is forthcoming from Factory School, Fall 2008. The *Oxford Book of Latin American Poetry*, which she co-edited is forthcoming 2009.

Brooklyn, New York
December 4-29, 2004

Dear Cecilia,

I write to you from Brooklyn on a sunny Saturday afternoon. It is almost winter and so the sun is low, its light angling right in the window and the warmth feels good.

To write with the light touch of gratitude—aware of you, reading this. So to begin, I want to thank you.

I am thinking of the round-shaped letters you sent to Chile. You wrote, "The letter is the poet's lifeline." This letter will be round in a different way—a meditation, coming around again and again to thoughts and questions I have about your work and mine.

∗

Dear Cecilia,

I remember that at the Dodge Festival of Poetry this year you said that the death or disappearance of a language occurs because of the shame of our own sounds. I am wondering—how was your Latin American tour? Were your performances well received? Could people hear the sounds of the languages in their histories, in their bodies and memories?

Now I am thinking of the sound of the Estonian language in my own family. How my father made extreme efforts to learn English well and to try and lose his accent. But I remember loving to hear the sounds of his first language.

This is the story I tell in my project called *Threads*. I gave the manuscript this name because I had an image that I was connected to the sound of my father's home language by just a thread. A delicate sense of the relationship, not forgetting, though I think he tried very hard to forget what he had seen as a child and the words that accompanied those experiences of war and separation.

Listening for lost sounds—that is where the writing and drawing comes in? I think so.

∗

Dear Cecilia,

Your sewn rooms and landscapes, threads connecting rocks and sticks, your pages in *Instan* where words flirt with the margins and gutters of the page/stage/frame. Pages where words are not separate from each other. A breath is drawn across the space between. It is about making silence visible.

Over and over, you lay threads down across emptiness and invite us to pluck at these strings. Instruments need empty spaces in order to sing—

How much of your writing comes from sitting still? How to find silences, how to write across empty space?

And another question: is your visual work a kind of poetics? Are your poems notes for your visual work? Or, there is no separation? Do words fail you? And then images fail as well? Both needing each other?

*

Dear Cecilia,

A memory: you performed in 2002 at the Poetry Project and I remember that you entered the space from the back of the room after you were introduced. You sang as you walked, unraveling a ball of red thread, draping it over the people sitting near the aisle. Some people held on to the thread and continued holding it like a kite string through the rest of your performance. Listening, I felt part of what was going to happen, that my physical presence depended on that thread, your movement, your voice.

And as you read, you wove languages together—English, Spanish, Quechua. There was no meaning problem. Because of your voice, I felt I understood everything and yet there was more I could learn.

I remember there were some chanting sounds coming from the dance performance next door. Instead of ignoring those sounds, you turned your head toward the wall and recognized these sounds, leading us all in a round of applause for the invisible (to us) dancers.

It was very human. None of us had to ignore anything anymore. There was no shame, no sense that you had been interrupted. There was a sense that it was impossible to interrupt a performance.

*

Dear Cecilia,

The idea that your work makes visible the unseen—this is what draws me to your work and this is what draws me to poetry. It is a spiritual concern, isn't it?

Do your spiritual practices inform your poetry and art? Did art lead you to these practices? Can that cause and effect be untangled? Is there a story there that you can tell?

I am thinking of something John Coltrane said. He said artists must work on themselves in order to make good art. Of course his quest for music was spiritual.

I probably use poetry and art to attend to my spiritual life. But I feel like something is missing.

*

Dear Cecilia,

I want to say that the sense of pause in your work is political. Your work seems to guide people to a place of compassion—first toward themselves and then others. It does so by inviting people to be in the moment. To not turn away. To stop a little. Your work lets us see ourselves as tricksters and scavengers, inheriting everything—problems and joys, justice and injustice. I am excited by this playfulness as revolutionary.

Later, I read these words in your book, *quipoem* "A work dedicated to delight wants to make the urgency/of the present, which is the urgency of the revolution, palpable."
I feel my most political act is still teaching. The classroom may be one of the few spaces left where the humanizing process, as Freire calls it, can take place. Teaching students to go ahead and take the adventure needed to make art and to

observe it—this leads to adventurous thinking in other realms? As citizens? I think so.

I am thinking now of Lorenzo Thomas' essays in *Extraordinary Measures*—about African American writers and modernism and then later, the Black Arts Movement. He articulates the inextricable link between politics and art in Black America. This is an important literary history to remember as a North American artist. To think there is a split between poetry and activism in this country is to disregard this vital legacy and ongoing tradition.

*

Dear Cecilia,

Sometimes I feel young and anxious about poetry. I'm anxious about "getting a book published" and yet that language about the publishing process feels passive and untrue.

I have been reading Agnes Martin's *Writings*. She says: "To feel confident and successful is not natural to the artist."

My struggle with recognition becomes less of a struggle when I am making work and distributing it through my own means. Right now I am making small books, decorated a bit with stitching. I make three or four of a kind and give them away. Little books, sized to fit the body.

Again, Agnes Martin: "I would rather think of humility than anything else."

The only rule for my small books is that I won't purchase paper to make them. That way they cost me nothing. That way they become good gifts.

*

Dear Cecilia,

What about your basuritas? Do you make new little monuments to garbage and from garbage now? And do you still decorate New York City streets? When I look at your work from the 80's all around Tribeca, I think of the fact that almost all of those empty spaces are now filled up with people, offices, restaurants, stores. Is there "a galaxy of litter" anywhere to be found downtown?

*

Dear Cecilia,

A dream: I was surprised to find out that my uncle had published a book of poems. He's not a poet. Nevertheless, it was a beautiful hardcover book and he presented it to me as a gift. I wanted to give him something in return and was frustrated that I didn't have anything so solid and seemingly permanent. I gave him a handful of my homemade broadsides, chapbooks, and pamphlets. Then I opened his book. I found two columns, almost a dual-language book, but when I read closer, I found that the column on the right was a commentary on each poem. Historical information was recorded there. One of the facts listed: "The bombing of Tartu." These events explained his poems. And so the book went on until I turned to a page where the language was unrecognizable. There, I read an italicized title: "Durne Durne." A gibberish I could not decode. Perhaps it meant "turn turn"—keep going, continue?

The next night I dreamt of a crane in flight, moving its neck wildly, so that it appeared to be writing something for me on the open blue sky.

*

Dear Cecilia,

The year is drawing to a close and I quit my job! I will still teach. It is a little risky financially but I believe that everything will be OK.

"I'm not afraid of love / or its consequences of light," writes Joy Harjo. This turning toward solitude, more light, days at home. Agnes Martin writes: "The silence on the floor of my house / Is all the questions and all the answers that have been known in the world . . . ."

So now, quietly and happily, I wait for your reply—

With love,
Jill

Denver, Colorado
March 5, 2005

Dear Jill,

Do you remember that day when we met? It was at Naropa, I was teaching a workshop called *Word Senses*. I wanted us to "feel" the way words "feel" us. Do you remember how hot it was? There was a drought, and the whole desert country felt ablaze. Water going away, water disappearing slowly from our lives, from the whole planet, as we pay no attention to her. Forgetful of our being water ourselves. We are in this workshop, and then there was an alarm, maybe a fire, or a bomb drill, and you were there, among all those girls. Only women, do you remember? It felt as a gathering of women from all over the world, of all colors, quietly sitting in a circle waiting for the class to begin. How can we begin? There is no other place but fire, and drought, this is our drill. Can we let it penetrate, take us somewhere? This is our place, our thirst, our only guide. And then I saw you, with your deer eyes wide open, a northern girl, Finnish, perhaps I thought, from the other side of the earth, a wild dancer perhaps, and then you spoke. It was Paulo Freire you spoke about, with such passion and knowing! I admired you right away, and felt so moved to see someone had taken his words, his practice, to heart! I said, I never encountered anyone in the U.S. who spoke of Freire like you did. As if this really mattered, as if this new kind of education were a matter of life and death.

Perhaps, you could write me about that experience in your next letter.

Then, I will try to answer some of your questions.

Yes, the day you wrote your first letter I was probably in Brazil, crossing the rain-forest (or the fragile remains of the mighty rainforest) by land on our way to Sao Paulo where the dead river Tiete receives the traveler with its stench. My performances around that city were about its death. I met a young poet there, Ademir Assunçao, who told me the only other people who noticed the dead river were the Tibetan monks visiting Sao Paulo. I am sure this is not true. Everybody notices, everybody has a nose, but we tell her don't smell, don't bother, we have to carry on.

He told me how magnificent the river Tiete was until not long ago, people bathing and swimming in the tropical gardens around it, until some companies created a very precise plan to pollute it. It was not an accident, or an unwanted result, it was a plan! He devoted a lot of time to research this, to mobilize public opinion, and nothing happened. There is no public opinion.

There is only public oblivion, he said.

So when you ask me how were my performances received, what can I say? I would hope that somewhere, deep down in their bodies, in a place their mind has not yet reached, or invaded with thoughts, someone may hear the cry that's coming from all that death.

It is beautiful the way you speak of your father and his sound, and you are right in your instinct to listen to that "thread of voice," the pain he was trying to forget. Maybe the listening, the connection between sound and ear *is* the thread of life. And to forget the pain, *is* to break the thread.

Have we "lost" a sound, or a way of listening, of attending to spacetime?

Maybe we are not losing our past, but a future possibility.

Love to you,
cec

Brooklyn, New York
April 12, 2005

Dear Cecilia,

Thank you for your letter—it was good to remember how we met—in your "word-sense" class at Naropa. I remember one student who came in to class late, complaining about the way her hair looked. Do you remember? You went over to look at her head and announced to the class that her hair made a perfect spiral and that the spiral is at the very center of life so she shouldn't be complaining! It was great! Speaking of teaching—you asked me to write to you about Paulo Freire. Where to begin? At the beginning—

I studied sociology as an undergraduate and began, in 1991, to study in a graduate program and found the seminars too abstract. I was interested in "social change." So I found my way to a community-based organization in Brooklyn that ran adult literacy classes. The teachers I worked with and learned from, first in Brooklyn and then in the South Bronx—Liz-Beth Levy, Fazeela Mohammed, Michael Willard, Paula Austin, Natalie Atherton, Maritza Arrastia, Stacie Evans, Sarah Wilkinson—introduced me to the ideas of Paulo Freire and I read and re-read his *Pedagogy of the Oppressed*. I was excited by what I read right away in Chapter 1, that "while both humanization and dehumanization are real alternatives, only the first is the people's vocation. This vocation is constantly negated, yet it is affirmed by that very negation." This made sense to me in a way I could not even explain— and I appreciated that I wasn't reading lesson plans or prescriptions for classroom management. Rather, Freire was saying that there was theory behind all teaching. I asked, "what will my theory of teaching and learning be?"

Of course Freire is writing about social change, not literary theory but I think he also loves language—that's something I think a lot of people miss in his writing, in his own story—he talks about being a boy and loving words, their beauty. I think his writings stem from that love, that desire to find the poetry in the language, liberating language from language itself! This kind of thinking—about how beauty and struggle can co-exist, is something that North Americans have a hard time embracing, I think. But maybe you can tell me more about the South American view—maybe the arts of language and other arts are not so sequestered there.

Again, another quote from Freire that set the stage for me: "Human beings are not built in silence, but in word, in work, in action-reflection."

So Freirian education, we thought, should begin with students' experiences and should include storytelling, reflection—toward what end? Making text. We taught that words are things that you can collect and use and even manipulate and make your own. Of course, this is something adult literacy students already know before they come in to the classroom. Words have power. And that power is in their sounds—not quietly sitting on the page. Perhaps this was my own first training in poetry.

I should interrupt here by saying that I was not "a writer" yet. Yet many of my fellow literary teachers were artists and writers and they had an immense capacity for listening, for creating. And that's the essence of Freire—that's the liberatory aspect—not necessarily action on a specific political agenda. Rather, liberation is education where learners and teachers are subjects and that's powerfully different from most educational systems that see all parties as passive—fulfilling traditional roles of powerful and powerless, knowledgeable and deficient. So Freire's theories are about transforming perceptions of ourselves into active agents in a world of dialogue.

I think an art practice also develops this sense of agency and dialogue, don't you, Cecilia?

Our adult literacy classrooms were literature-making laboratories. I have stacks and stacks of classroom anthologies that we put together. There were no textbooks and so it was a real gift—to have to invent everything. We would begin with storytelling on a theme, in response to a poem or newspaper article or even just one word—a word we'd call generative like "education" or "children." After, students would work in groups telling their stories, listening, and the groups would have to re-tell each other's story. Then came the writing. As the teacher I would sometimes transcribe a student's story if they were a very beginning writer or I would provide the occasional new word to a more advanced writer. We'd use what was called "invented spelling" to help students get their ideas down on paper without having to have assistance every two minutes. Then we'd have a "word session" where people would call out their inventions and together, as a group, we'd come to the correct spelling and so it was about the joy of the sounds and shapes of words. Then I'd type up the stories, make copies, bring them in the next day or the next week, and pass them out to the class. We'd read our work out loud, then students would talk to each other about the stories and sometimes write letters to each other about what they had read.

We sometimes improvised scenes from the neighborhood, our love lives, the welfare office, scenes from the park or the daycare center and then we'd write them down, revise, re-write, and put them on again as plays. And we taught poems. We taught Sonia Sanchez and Adrienne Rich. We read Kafka, Cisneros, Walker, Shakespeare, Baldwin. We asked our students what they wanted to study. They told us—they wanted to study child development, poetry, health, how to read menus, how to take the subway. We had monthly poetry readings and per-formances, chapbook-making lessons, and book signings.

Still, I wasn't "a writer" but we, as teachers, were all participating in the very lessons we were giving. We said, "to teach it you have to do it" and so we started a literacy practitioners writing group. We met for five years on and off, playing around with words and writing exercises that we'd ask our students to do.

I should talk more about playfulness. I think that adults love to play. Of course, making poems and stories can be about that. There was no single oppression nar-rative that had to be written—there was no polemic that we encouraged our stu-dents to write. Storytelling was now their tool and we, as teachers, didn't need them to explicate their hard lives. It's often the outsider's perspective that the poor and "oppressed" should write particular narratives—ones often devoid of joy and daily life. I think this is a common mistake of cultural imperialism which is always about objectifying, desiring a particular outcome for a pre-determined purpose. Freire warns against this.

And in terms of the forms their writings took, adult literacy students mixed genres freely. It was not uncommon for them to interrupt a short story with a chorus of poetry. It was not uncommon for them to start with a poem and finish with an essay. They embellished and changed identities when they needed to, turning autobiography into fiction without angst. They taught me that all stories are true.

This way of teaching came unhinged, for me and my colleagues, with the shifting political landscape of the mid and late 90's. There was a labor struggle, jobs were lost, good teachers were blacklisted and all over New York City, poor people on welfare were told they could no longer attend school. They were told to go to work for their welfare checks. I saw my students out on the streets picking up trash instead of going to school. I am not permitted by law to tell you details of the story—I had to sign a gag order and can only say that "we came to an amicable agreement." I was young and outspoken and I'm sure that I offended some co-workers—or, more importantly, I misunderstood them drastically—in my attempt to convince them "to do the right thing," to organize.

Those events were, for me, a quick lesson in power and activism. Because our students were so marginalized—blamed for their poverty and low literacy—so were we as teachers. We were told to be grateful we had any jobs at all. I began to get wise to the historical context—literacy in this country is still seen as an act of philanthropy. Literacy teachers—and many of them won't admit this—continue to be grossly underpaid, to go without health benefits, to piece together two and three part-time jobs. It's all just one of the signs that our country is and always has been exceedingly ambivalent about *all* people reading and writing critically.

I still reflect on why things happened as they did. Cecilia, I know you've experienced massive political upheaval in your life—and personal trauma as a result. What I experienced in my 20's was painful but nothing like what you went through. Do you ever reflect on what you learned? Do you experience a sense of gratefulness toward the experience—as a way to heal?

Adult literacy students taught me that we write for our lovers, our friends, ourselves, our colleagues, students, and teachers. As writers we don't have to think of our work finding that "big, anonymous . . . and weary audience" as the poet Jaan Kaplinski calls it.

I also learned that I share a rhetorical heritage with lots of different kinds of people. I read the Bible as a child. This language imprint was present in many of my students—it's present in me. So when I walk into the doors of the Poetry Project, for example, it might seem I have a lot in common with people there, but I may have just as much in common with the group I was just riding the subway with. Identity is complex. This, for poetry, is important to remember. Not to be so sure that we know everything about the writing community we come in contact with. But to be sure that poetry resides inside most people.

Finally, I learned not to be so sure of what people will do politically, even if I'm sure my argument is "right." The labor struggle showed me that I didn't know the depths of class and economic anxiety felt by some of my colleagues. I now feel wary of many political movements that espouse liberation and "rightness"—I feel cautious.

Teaching has changed for me though. I see many students in higher education as tired, interested in getting the degree as easily as possible and moving on because of the promise of a higher paying job. This is a tight-lipped, conservative environment we're in now. Working people are being asked to put in more time for less money. They're afraid of losing jobs, of speaking up. I don't want to generalize—I have some amazing students, just more students afraid or too tired to take risks, it seems, in their thinking.

Cecilia—how does teaching impact your writing and art? I'm also interested to hear about your work with Freire—did you know him when he was in exile in Chile?

Hoping that you are loving the springtime and the increase in light—

Love,
Jill

New York, New York
September 7, 2005

Dear Jill,

I have read your letter many times, it is so beautiful, so moving, for the pain you endured being denied the joy of continuing the Freire experience. I wish I could respond to your questions one by one, but it seems my attempts are struggling with not saying something. The pain and the horror of going there, the rage I feel is too deep. Maybe one day I'll be able to respond. It's been more than 30 years, but the pain is brutally alive. Especially now, having lived through a second Sept 11th. Most people do not remember the Chilean military coup of Sept 11th, 1973. It is just one more erased "fact." For us it was the end and the beginning of time. I just gave a long talk about it at Naropa, which will be transcribed, but feel that the many poems I've written about it don't even begin to touch the place I need to go to.

So, I'll stay on the frail surface of things, with your permission. But even that attempt is bound to fail. Freire is too dear, too important a subject for me. I never met him while he was in Chile (he belongs to my father's generation). He was involved in the great movement of the agrarian reform at the time (mid-sixties) and I was just a young poet. My vision of words was just beginning to unfold, and even though I came across his work much later (his *Pedagogy of the Oppressed* was published in 1970), I feel a profound kinship with him, as if we come from the same question.

If you click Freire on Wikipedia you will find a startling definition of his work as a radical vision of change based on one core practice: the reciprocal exchange between teacher and student, as a work of transformation. Where one becomes the other. Reading that, you can't help but think that, even though he is reputed to be such an influence on education worldwide, (this may be true, he was also appointed Secretary of Education for the City of Sao Paulo in Brazil at the end of his life), you wonder where, where, are people really putting it into practice.

Freire's story reminds me of another genius of South America. Simón Rodríguez, the master teacher of Simón Bolivar. Rodríguez evolved an extraordinary philosophy of language and education in the late 18th century, and who has heard of him? He is a national hero in Venezuela, but has his vision been embraced? Do you see his extraordinary visual texts in billboards, discussed or incorporated into people's lives?

And, this brings to mind my own struggle, the constant and long suppression of my work with words in Chile. Only now, there may be a change, it seems that my riddles and "palabrarmas" created in the sixties and early seventies, will be published in my own country for the first time! We shall see.

There's no need to fantasize about the South American difference. So many great thinkers and poets, so many visionaries remain forgotten over there, as they are here. Even more so, one would say. But then, you have the counter reality of the indigenous societies, still living, still fighting for their vision, and that, in itself, is a miracle. After more than 500 years of oppression! It is true that the struggle over there is alive with beauty, as you say. Beauty is the struggle, as far as I am concerned, and this is the ancient view of things, a deep, ingrained knowledge in all ancient peoples, in the Andes, the Amazon, Africa, Tibet, Australia, even here in the US. Wherever you go, you can see that wisdom displayed in life, and under attack. Imagine if we were to acknowledge that we all are "ancient peoples" and that we all have that ingrained knowledge, deeply suppressed in our souls, in our bodies!

From confluence and collaboration from all sides, a new tide of change may come.

I also wanted to thank you for telling your story. It confirms the power of the Freire practice, and I hope it doesn't put you in danger, being as you are bound by oath not to speak about it! (That's how "free" we are.) It makes all the sense in the world to know that you became a writer in the process of listening from that place of exchange.

Sept 8th

Our exchange took me inside the word "education," to the forgotten movement pushing its core. In Latin *educare* means "pulling out, leading out of." It opens with an *e,* for *ex*. Exit the usual definition and go back to its source in the body: the sense of direction is *duc*, the orientation we naturally follow into light, joy, and fulfillment, and there, in that *con duct*, the collective, mutual quest a possibility may arise. The original purpose was, and is, our desire to pull ourselves out of darkness, ignorance and fear as the ancients said. And the dream of poetries is that dwelling in feeling, in the memory of feeling, we may follow a deeper direction a shared energy that may lead us into a new understanding of life *and* "education." Not as a structure created to keep the system in place, but as a living force, a desire so powerful that it could "lead us out of" the present shape of things.

Education has been debased everywhere, because life has been debased, and all living organisms are now as threatened as we are.

And this debasement rests on definitions that separate, severe or cut the way we stand together. Pararse juntos.

Truth is we know, but don't want to know, that we are *teaching/learning* from each other continuously. Whether aware or unaware, we transmit our ways, our thoughts, to the children and the earth, and vice versa!

I think Freire is proposing to change our imagination first. To imagine change emerging from this basic acknowledgement: to see that exchange *is* the teacher.

Sept 9th

You ask me if I enjoy this teaching/learning thing. I do! I came naturally to it, as a child, I think.

My mother tells a story. When I was five or six years old I would disappear into the forest. She would find me in a clearing surrounded by other children, each with a little chair (that means we were organized in our playing!) as in a "workshop" where I'd be "teaching/learning" something with them. What, I wonder!

Sept 10th

I go back to the sixties, to the confluence of people in Chile at that time. Thinkers and artists from all over came down. Even Allen Ginsberg showed up. How we could re-create the feeling of potential of that moment?

At 20 years old, I was working on TV writing plays "to change the world" with "instructions" written by children. I invited them to contribute and they wrote from all over the country. Juanita Perez from Tierra del Fuego would see her name, her story on the screen transmitted nationally. And that is just one story, among many. And even though we had not been exposed to Freire yet, his ideas were somehow "in the air," infecting us with possibilities. His work was perhaps the most crucial in that great movement for change, which was taking place all over South America. Of course, that was the reason why brutal military coups were unleashed all over the region to stop the liberation movement. Thousands of intellectuals and so-called "educated" people had "joined the struggle," which meant working with people in all realms. And we started young, it was just a regular part of our lives, like breathing or partying. It seems everybody was bridging the gap between talking and doing, theory and practice. Politics for us did not mean manipulation and corruption as it does today. It was about change, and being part of it. For a short period, there were no limits, and no more separate little worlds. All spheres of life were mixing in and everything was possible. So, persecution began. Many people were killed. Many disappeared. What was killed was possibility itself. Freire went into exile in Europe, and soon enough I found myself in exile as well.

You ask what I learned from the coup.
I can say, the earth opens and swallows you.
I can say, you learn all of a sudden, and well before it happens, that the world as you know it can disappear in an instant.

I can say I learned that art anticipates life. I began doing my precarious, disappearing works in the streets and beaches of Chile in 1966.
Something in us, in our bones, knows before we do.
Something in us knows what we don't want to know.

Sept 11th

In other words, to undo the defenses we adopt in the wake of a tragedy takes a lifetime. Awareness of our deepest and most secret reactions, the ones that become invisible, inaudible to ourselves, is what matters. The way we take blame, and become small, feel guilty and ashamed, collaborating, without knowing it with the system that created the coup.

To undo that in ourselves is the work of peace.

After the coup most Chileans felt guilty (me included) like we had done something wrong, and the culture reversed itself. I called the new Chile *Elihc* spelling it backwards. No more idealistic, unselfish behaviour, no more self-sacrifice and communal values. It all disappeared *como por arte de encanto*, we say in Spanish. We felt it was wrong to be the way we were, an ontological change occurred. It was wrong of us to be poor, so now everyone wants to be rich. When a new mall opens, traffic stops, the whole of Santiago is jammed. It was wrong of us to be kind, so violence became ok, and now we have the highest rate of domestic violence in the world. I remember the first time I went back, after years of exile. I did not recognize the streets, or the people. Something so profound had changed that it will probably take generations to recover our humanity. Now Chile is fast becoming the capital of selfishness, the consumer's Latin heaven, the perfect colony where workers carry American flags in their buses, instead of Chilean flags. Very few authors have gone to that miserable place within us. I can think of Roberto Bolaño, of Elvira Hernández, to name two. I am not there yet.

To finish this now long letter, I have to mention Angie O'Gorman for the way she writes about this process of learning to allow our own humanity and that of the other, to unfold at the same time. To allow for the space, in ourselves, even when we are not ready for it. She says we cannot coerce people into freedom, that "the nature of insight and truth requires that they be freely accepted," that people have to be "allowed the freedom not to choose it."

This is true non-violence, and the core of Freire's education for democracy. As artists, or people, we can create, in her words "a context for con*Version*" (my alteration), a space for a new con*Duct*, in us and others: to follow together "the orientation of creation toward wholeness."

Cecilia Vicuña

Denver, Colorado
September 12, 2005

Jill,

Before I forget, there is something I still wanted to respond to from the first letter, the question of recognition. The "re" is very important here, it says "repeating," going there again and again. "Cog" in Latin is grasping, holding something until your body knows it. (In Argentina "Coger" is making love.)

If I think of your struggle with "recognition," I imagine a sweet shift to move you to the need behind it. I think what we really want is to see who we are. If we manage to look inside, and "recognize" it, maybe others will follow. And re, re, re as needed. That is the process of poetry anyway. If we do it, a response will happen of its own accord. Others may "recognize" you if you do. It may take time, or it may never happen. Who knows, but it is not for us to wonder.

"Healing" in the ancient traditions is "wholing," a completion, an acknowledgement of circulation and transformation, the two main qualities of the life force.

I can tell you how it happened for me, when I was still a teenager, and a first moment of "writing" from an inner "recognition" came, the instant when I think my poetry began. I woke up from a dream, and there it was, a force grabbing me by the neck. A "cognition" you could say, that came from a way of listening. All I could do was let it be. Write as fast as I could! *It* wanted "*recognition!*" *It* wanted for me to see its language, its form. It felt different from anything I had done until then. As if something had shifted in me. These words were not coming from a will to write or a desire to "be a poet," (I had done that for a few years). They had a "reality" of their own. It was like an animal encounter. A sensation so powerful it can not be mistaken with anything else. I suddenly saw that I was language, that something was being said in me, or through me.

Life created us, and yet we are participating in our own creation. Life speaks in us, the Upanishads say.

To "*recognize*" that language, the way it speaks in you, to discover where it is in you, is what matters, to find the source of delight that opens all doors: being in poetry.

The next step is extending that "*recognition*" to perceive being as a collective creation. To feel each one of our cells, each one of our neural connections as being part of that being. We are the work at work. It's poiesis. To "*recognize*" that is the real need.

Brooklyn, New York
October 12, 2005

Dear Cecilia,

Your last letter—it was overwhelming. I've read and re-read it, your words, your ideas unfolding more and more with each time I see those pages. Thanks for writing it, Cecilia. I will treasure the letter—recognizing what it took to write so many parts of your experience.

I have been thinking about reading lately. I mean "the reading" as a literary event. For some reason, I decided that I want to use my voice actually in just the same way I speak to a friend or to someone in my family. I heard myself as I read a couple years ago—actually, it was more like I "felt" my voice—it felt thin and high and maybe even strained. I've been working on this in my teaching, too. Working on speaking from a lower place, a place of comfort and a place that does not strain the throat. This seems very important to me lately and I don't know exactly why.

And in another way I've been working with my voice—a couple years ago Jonny bought me a guitar and I've been learning some chords and the songs that are the easiest to play and sing are old country songs. (Actually, they're not that easy—the further I go the more difficulty I am finding in the strumming patterns and voice inflections and so on!) So I've had this urge to sing which somehow feels related to the adjustment in my "reading" voice.

Tell me, if you can and want to, your thoughts on the voice. Your voice is very strong, and also very quiet in its strength. Do you practice this kind of speaking, singing, voicing? Where did you learn this?

How is it that you write? This might seem like an incredibly broad question—so here are more specific questions inside that question: Do you write often? Do you revise a lot? Or do many of your poems "come to the page" in the way they should be? Do you work in English? Spanish?

And meditation? Does this practice of yours play a role? Can you write about that?

Lastly, how does your visual work happen? Do you simply "sense" what needs to be done—the writing or the visual work—and then proceed?

I, too, work with images. Not sculpture or site-specific projects or installations, as you do, but small page-sized works. I've been printing words onto fabric, then ripping the fabric, sewing small pieces back together. The words are transcripts from congressional hearings or language from good legislation that can't get passed. Taking old paperback books about to fall apart, taking some pages and reprinting a revision on top. Fashioning the pages to make something else—a land-scape, some hills, for example.

I feel another part of my mind is working when I put words "on hold" and work with my hands, feeling the work as I'm making it. Unlike when I am writing, I feel the entire texture of time changes when I'm doing visual work. I begin to crave this texture change when I'm working with text for several days or weeks in a row.

*

Congratulations on the possibility of having some of your work being published in Chile! You must be happy about this. How did this come about? Is there a small and growing group of artists there who are interested?

This good news reminds me of your addendum to the first letter, your writing on "recognition." I keep repeating to myself: When we know ourselves, others will know us. Actually, there's evidence of this—it's not an esoteric concept—since I left my full-time job, something not too many people "in the poetry community" knew I was doing, I've been approached so many times to read and do things and to publish! How amazing—after I arranged that energy shift toward knowing myself as a writer. "A sweet shift" as you call it.

*

I want to share with you something that's occupied my thoughts for a while. And after such a great presentation by Juliana Spahr last night on Kamau Brathwaite's work and his influence on her work, I feel it's absolutely the right time to bring it up—

For a long time I have been thinking about how the avant-garde or experimental poetry scene appears to me to be racially segregated, and perhaps also segregated in terms of class. This kind of poetry is so very firmly rooted in the expansion of consciousness, the open reader, open listener. But why are so many participants and audience white? Not that there isn't diversity in whiteness—yet, with regard to class, I would say most are solidly middle class and "professionals," formally educated. Why is this so?

Should new literary ground be forged? If so, where would the space be? What borough? Who would come? For whom would the space be new? By forging this ground, what will our readers and audiences and performers look like? Will people be put together on a program because they are *different* in skin color, *different* in tradition or approach? Some self-taught, some with MFAs? From different backgrounds?

I remember going to the Nuyorican Poets Café in the early 90's. While the poets were truly diverse, the poetry seemed monolithic in terms of style. Are there scenes and venues, ones that are diverse and integrated, that I don't know about? This might be the case—I want to go out and find out what other communities are doing. It feels like border crossing—full of mystery and confusion, even.

To be self-conscious about diversity, is it problematic? Or does it problematize segregation? I think this, after all, is my point—to problematize the segregation is to see its effects and its intentions, even if they are unstated. And then go from there . . .

Because I teach in a racially and ethnically integrated college program, and all of my students are working people, I know that I am constantly being stretched beyond my own sense of "taste" in art. Yes, I ask them to stretch and read things they wouldn't ordinarily find on their own and they enter my classes expecting a challenge. And their readings and questions on the work challenge me. Like many other teachers elsewhere, I constantly have to open up canons and expose the gaps in "literary lineages." The students also expect that their racial and ethnic identities will not be reduced to a kind of fulfillment of a quota on the course reading list; they demand that multiple traditions and questions of representation be taught critically. Anyway, what I want to say is that in this context it isn't hard to see that measures of success, distinction, and publication-worthiness in the literary arts are socially and culturally constructed.

I'm also thinking "experimental" is a relative term. Experimental versus "tradition-al"? Whose tradition? As Juliana Spahr spoke about last night, the so-called "primi-tive" arts *are* experimental!

How did the cultural workers when you were young in Chile bridge class and racial divides? By what methods? What kind of organizing and decision-making process? Maybe in your next letter you could trace that process—what that kind of work looked like, how it challenged certain of society aesthetically—if it did.

*

Finally, I have no way to "wrap up" what this dialogue has meant, Cecilia—it has meant very much to me. I hope that we will continue—I feel we will!

Looking forward to your next letter—

With love,
Jill

New York, New York
February 12, 2006

Dear Jill,

It was hard to answer your letter about my going to Chile to have my book finally come out there, while witnessing the election of Michelle Bachelet as president. There was a resistance on my part to the questions you bring up.

Chile is one of the countries with the highest levels of domestic violence in the world, violence against women and children, of course. But women are not just the victims, they are holding up the **machismo** with their bodies and souls, they did not vote for Michelle *en masse*, as one would expect. No, women are still teaching their baby boys that they are "*el rey*," and ignoring their girls. I was one of those girls. I am still one, and the mystery, the horror is in knowing how we cooperate with our own disappearance, with the erasure of our thoughts and our works. This is what I am involved in, trying to see my own self, my own life with total clarity. It is much harder than one would think. The temptation is always there to fulfill a role, but I know that my voice will always be a threat to the dominant worldview and I have to accept the consequences.

You come up with this notion of "visibility," of trying to get it, and what is that? On the one hand we all need to be seen for what we really are, but on the other, do we really allow it? Do we see ourselves? This morning I was talking with James O'Hern and he said: "For a long time I was angry at my wife because she did not see me for what I was . . . until I realized I wasn't letting her."

The need for visibility per se, can also be a trick, a desire to conform, in one way or the other. A few years ago I created this poem:

IN side the VISIBLE

You wish to know how it happened that my Chilean book was published. Until now my books have been circulating in xeroxes. A couple of years ago, one of these copies hit a young student of design. He loved it and wrote to me. He said how can your work not be part of Chilean culture? and found a grant for it, and a publisher. All I had to do was come and sing those ancient poems as best I could. (The book was a reprint of *Palabrarmas*, published in Buenos Aires in 1984.)

You also ask about craft, but at this point I can only think of my favorite poem that says:

"Words go on failing and failing,
nothing like abiding in its midst."

—Tao Te Ching (translated by David Hinton)

I like what you say about the voice, about speaking from a lower place. Yes, you can also write from that inner low land. That place of moisture and change. To find the voice of that space you have to stalk it, until you don't know you are looking for it. As in the ancient myths, you have to forget about it to get there. People call it "surrender" and I wonder. Sound is the greatest mystery. It is there, and yet you have to learn to "drink" it, as the Chinese say.

You ask me where did I learn it, oh, nowhere. I don't know that I have learned it, all I know is that sometimes it happens of its own accord. It *is* its own reality and I try to live accordingly. Sometimes I tell stories about it, but that is just part of the stalking, of trying to keep *it* interested. To keep the relationship going, you might say.

And yes, about Chile in the 60's, and early 70's, to look at how that was done, you would require a whole book! For now the phrase by Che Guevara will do: "the method is improvisation."

And last, but not least, yes, I do remember Juliana's talk. There is a long line of poets who have seen the "primitive" as experimental. If you look back, this has been going on forever. Chuang Tzu, writing in the 4th century B.C.E. was already speaking of the power of the ancient poets, so did the ancient Aztecs, or the Arab poets of the 10th century. It seems each one of us has to come to that "discovery." For me, it happened in the 60's. Now, we have to acknowledge that it is a crime to call them "primitive," whether to elevate them or demean them. When you think of it, you see that naming in that way is really a weapon of mass destruction.

The attention to naming and its consequences is at the core of everything we are talking about.

I am sorry I don't feel like talking of New York now, except to tell you I arrived shortly after President Bush's discovered our addiction to oil, and the evangelists declared that Jesus Christ now compels them to solve the global warming crisis.

It is hard to keep still while writing these things. I feel like dancing them. My body re the *Taki Onkoy*, a "dancing disease" that took place in the Andes, where people danced themselves to death, believing their sacrifice would push the white conquerors away from the Andes forever.

Beware, beware, my heart says, as the ground slips away. And, I remember the old call "organize," "organize," but I have changed the meaning of that word in one of my poems! Changed it to remember the energy of the *org* inside the organ, the *orgon* in orgasm. Our life work is beauty itself.

I try to go back to your questions, but it is hard!

You say, the poems "as they should be." That is funny!!! Imagine a poem hearing you say that and laughing *its* heart out! Poems are wild creatures, they do as they please, as far as I am concerned. They are on the lookout, grabbing whoever is ready for them. And we never are, are we?

Do I write often? All the time! Do I revise? Forever! And to no avail! In English and Spanish? Hopefully! Other unknown languages intervene too. It is a complete mess. A maddening joy.

And meditation? Yes, regularly. What would I do without it? It is the mother of invention. A little taste of what *being* can be. Creating the void, to invite the wild ones in.

And yes, this exchange with you has been good and hard, to have to say things we usually avoid! So I thank you for that. And to say goodbye, a little pun.

Children pun before they speak. I remember Chløe, Barbara Einzig's daughter when she was only a year old. Standing by the fridge one day she said: "I-eye-ice" laughing out loud.

If we could only pun a little further, and remember that "I" and "self" both mean "same," we would know that language has been telling us all along that there is no separation. The pupil is us learning from ourselves as Elizabeth King suggests. We are reflected in each other's eyes as a tiny "self" standing at the opening of the iris. We float at the threshold of emptiness where light enters.

Cecilia Vicuña

Rosamond S. King & Jayne Cortez

Rosamond S. King is a poet, performer, and scholar. Her poetry can be found in *Xcp: Cross-Cultural Poetics*, *Beyond the Frontier: African-American Poetry for the 21st Century*, and *The Caribbean Writer*. She has performed her unique "Verse Cabaret" style around the world in Africa, the Caribbean, and throughout the USA at venues such as HERE Performance Space, the Bowery Poetry Club, and Dixon Place Theatre. King's scholarship on visual art, performance studies, literature, and sexuality from Africa and its diaspora has also been widely published. She recently held a Fulbright Fellowship in The Gambia, West Africa, and has work forthcoming in *Callaloo* and *Our Caribbean: Lesbian & Gay Writing from the Antilles*. Her manuscripts await publication.

Jayne Cortez is the author of ten books of poems and performs her poetry with music on nine recordings. Cortez has presented her work and ideas at universities, museums, and festivals in Africa, Asia, Europe, South America, the Caribbean and the United States. Her poems have been translated into many languages and widely published in anthologies, journals, and magazines. She is the recipient of several awards including: Arts International, the National Endowment for the Arts, and the International African Festival Award. Her most recent books are *The Beautiful Book* (Bola Press, 2007) and *Jazz Fan Looks Back* (Hanging Loose Press, 2002). Her latest CD recordings with the Firespitter Band are *Find Your Own Voice* (Bola Press, 2006) and *Borders of Disorderly Time* (Bola Press, 2003). Cortez is director of the film *Yari Yari: Black Women Writers and the Future*. She is president of the Organization of Women Writers of Africa, Inc. and is on screen in the films: *Women In Jazz* and *Poetry In Motion*. She currently lives in New York City.

Dear Jayne,

You have always encouraged me to do my work with the understanding that the work is both explicitly artistic and explicitly political.

I'd like to hear your thoughts on one of the other aspects of "the work" – specifically, seeing and being seen in the poetry "scene" in order to get your work out. I don't object to meeting new people or building community. But I am apprehensive about trying to be in the "right" place schmoozing with the "right" people more or less just for publication. Not only does it not seem right, it also doesn't seem to be the best way to spend time. What do you think? Perhaps this is just how everything in the world works, including poetry.

On a different topic, I was disappointed recently when I read somewhere that numerous nominees and winners of some national award stated that in the current times literature does not matter – either because it's not relevant to current events or because "no one" is reading it.

I suppose I bring this up less to ask you a question than as an example of how differently some folks think about and compartmentalize their work. I am (still!) so immersed in Yari Yari Pamberi and the idea that there is no separation between politics and art – and if you believe there is, you are doing someone else's work.

You've been doing this a long time—are these the same debates and questions rehashed, or is there some new spice in the stew?

Rosa

Dear Rosa,

Hello from Dakar. It is 12 p.m. and I am reading your letter. You might want to consider the following questions: ask yourself why you write poems and why you think yourself a poet? What is your purpose? What do you wish to achieve? Who is your audience? Why should anyone want to hear what you have to say? Is there such a thing as a poetry career? If you have career expectations, what does that have to do with poetry?

When I started sharing my poems with friends and audiences in California in the early 1960s, it was to exhibit and develop my poetic concept and communicate in a different way. At that point I was exploring life and death, life in death, and death in life, by fusing art ideas with political directions and using words and creating rhythmic patterns that could contain the content of struggle and aware-ness; constructing poems using the oral tradition and using words/phrases from African tonal languages like the Yoruba I picked up while visiting and later living in Nigeria.

When I first put words with music in performance in Los Angeles in 1964, there were no examples. For me it was a way of extending human rights and improving the condition of the community by giving examples of artistic performance possi-bilities. Except for the reading of poems in church or actors occasionally reading poems in recitals, there was no real poetry scene in the Black community until 1965 after the Watts rebellion. Then a cultural scene emerged with writing work-shops, alternative reading/performance spaces, art galleries, and Board of Education programs that included creative writing. Today in most cities there are many places to read poetry. There are a number of writing workshops and small press publishers. But it still comes down to you working on the work with pleasure and satisfaction, whether it matters to someone or not. I think being around people concerns information and maintaining relationships. If you are going to be seen you will be seen and what will happen because you are seen remains to be seen.

Rosa, being in the "right" place schmoozing with the "right" people in order to be published dulls the imagination. The so-called "right" person will have you jumping through hoops and still reject you and your work. So do not shake another limp hand or make yourself be somebody's mascot. Real poetry sits outside of that kind of activity.

Regarding literary relevance in the future, imaginative literature will always be relevant because it represents creativity and transformation which is a human need. As for me, I'm a poet in every situation and in all environments and it's my task to make poetry relevant.

Best wishes for happiness and peace in 2005.

Jayne

Brooklyn, New York
April 15, 2005

Dear Jayne,

Thanks for your letter! You mention that when you first put poetry and music together there were no examples. You have such a unique and exciting perform-ance style – and such great rapport with your band. I'd like to hear how you pre-pared that first performance and what spurred you to connect poetry and music in the first place. Is your rehearsal process now different? Do you think about per-forming the words as you are writing them? How much of the music and your performance are improvisation? I have been bringing song and movement into my own readings, in part because I am simply moved to bring these interests and skills together, and in part because I have been to so many boring poetry readings in which poets have put little or no effort into the presentation of their work. These are both fresh and "interdisciplinary" ways of presenting poetry, and harken back to how poetry used to be presented, don't you think?

Along these lines, I am also interested in your overall process of writing and revision — how much perspiration do you usually put in after the inspiration?! Are the pieces in your books mostly grouped chronologically or thematically or both? What do you think about when ordering the poems in a collection?

I'm also interested in how place has affected your writing. New York City is often a clear character or setting for your work. And I know you lived in Africa for some time — how did that experience contribute to your content or style? I'm finding travel to be incredibly enriching for my writing (and, of course, for my soul). I feel very fortunate to travel these days, to broaden my world and also to be a different representation of the USA than what many folks know from the media.

I just saw Mel Edwards' latest gallery show, filled with beauty and ugliness and emotion. While your deep connection with music is clear, I'm not as sure about any links to visual art — does your relationship to the visual directly inspire you, or is it more often part of all of the stimulation of life that affects your writing indirectly?

The rejections continue to come and I continue to write — what else is there to do?

I'll send this letter electronically, since we both are traveling, in the hopes that you will get it quickly wherever you are!

R

Dakar, Senegal
June 3, 2005

Dear Rosa:

We are having very good weather here in Dakar. Hope you are well and staying warm in Brooklyn. Thanks for your letter.

Most of my readings are without music. I never write poems with music in mind and I never write while listening to music. I select certain poems to read in a musical setting and prepare for every performance by not preparing to perform. For years I have been training my ears to hear everything that happens in my poetry music collaborations. The poetry comes first, the music comes out of it and after it. I work with professional musicians. They practice everyday and I usually write everyday. So we are skilled in what we do and have the ability to experiment and explore ways of entering, exiting and reaching the kind of aware- ness that will lead to spontaneity and allow for improvisation. Sometimes I rewrite and have several versions of the same poem. I'm always taking pieces apart, rear- ranging and intensifying. I count a lot on instinct. I believe you have to find the balance between your own voice and the content of your poetry. It's still about trying to do something unique and with depth. In rehearsals the poem is the focus and the root used to draw from. It's important to me that the players listen with fresh ears and not rely on clichés, unless the clichés are intentional. They have to find the poem and translate it into notes. It's a very special relationship that involves communion and transformation. If the poetry is happening it will work out. I'm interested in presenting our collaborations in a strong way. I want our presentation to be as significant and as powerful as the new technology used to document it.

When selecting work for a collection I do it as I feel it. I have studied the visual arts as long and as deeply as I have studied music, since high school. And I have been making monoprints for the past twenty-five years in New York, Asilah, Morocco and in Goree Island, Senegal. These works have been exhibited in gal- leries in New York and New Jersey and at the Haggerty Museum of Art in Milwaukee, Wisconsin. I also wrote poetry responding to the sculpture of Melvin Edwards, which was published 1994 in our book entitled *Fragments*. In 1971 I wrote a poem "Collage for Romare Bearden" in response to Romare Bearden's exhibition at the Museum of Modern Art. I published it in my collection *Festivals and Funerals* sent a copy to Romare and he sent me a notebook with my poem written in his handwriting and seventeen of his drawings responding to my poem. In the 1980s I wrote a poetic response to the paintings of the Cuban artist Wilfredo Lam. I also responded to a series of prints and lithographs produced by twenty-one artists at the Bob Blackburn Printmaking Workshop. To have a deeper understanding of visual art you have to pay closer attention to details and make the effort to understand what makes art, art.

I like to travel. I like writing in different environments and meeting people from different cultures. I like hearing other languages and checking out the various procedures for making art, music, and poetry. I have notebooks filled with words, images, observations and ideas collected while traveling. Traveling is very important. I have visited thirty-three countries in Europe, Asia, South America and the Caribbean and have been in and out of Africa at least thirty times since 1967, visiting many countries including Ghana, Nigeria, Egypt, Angola, South Africa, Morocco, Zimbabwe and Senegal. In 1967 I also left Los Angeles, California to live in New York City. Now I spend most of my time in New York and in Senegal, West Africa. Both places are a part of my identity. Both have been a resource for my poetry. I have family, extended family, friends and continuity in both places. This letter is traveling to you from Dakar, Senegal in the season of sweet mangoes.

Peace,
Jayne

Chicago, Illinois
September 23, 2005

Dear Jayne,

I am so glad you mentioned having different versions of the same poem and continuously revisiting pieces. The evolution of the poems is very important to me, but sometimes I wonder if people will feel "cheated" if the voice on paper and the voice in air do not match. Of course, that hasn't stopped me from changing and improvising yet!

I had no idea that you are such an accomplished visual artist – you're full of the unexpected, as usual. My travels and head trips have, in the past few years, been leading me back to movement (I've been dancing, as well as writing, since I was 3). I am now working on pieces that are movement only, text only, and on performances that involve text and movement. Still, everything tends to fall outside of the lines others have drawn: writing and movement which are too "weird" (read "experimental") to be "Black," work that is too "Black" to be included in "experimental" events or publications (as opposed to Special People of Color Editions), work that supposedly has too much music or movement to be poetry, or has too much text to be dance. Thankfully, as we discussed in the first letters, I am not dependent on others for defining or validating my work, even if they control some publication and performance opportunities.

It is, as always, a rich and exciting time to live purposefully, including the madness and devastation that surprise us and the madness and devastation that is familiar. Perspective is easily lost in these self-obsessed times; I thank you for being one of my reminders of this.

I thank you also for your suggestion and encouragement to go back to my Father's country and "see about my people" instead of traveling elsewhere in Africa – for now. The trip to Gambia was, of course, emotionally, creatively, and in every other way satisfying and challenging. I feel as you do, that travel is not just important to develop my art, but it is also a vital part of the life I want to live. I believe we've traveled to five countries, many US states and cities, and six seasons (fall, winter, spring, summer, dry, wet, and mango!) while writing these letters. So much more to do in our art, in the world, in ourselves. I hope our paths continue to intersect and sometimes join. Here's to art, friendship, and community; to creating, everywhere.

Peace,
Rosamond

Dear Rosamond:

I think you can have many versions of the same poem. You can do it any way you want. You can change it and change it back. Always feel free to change your work because it's your work.

I'm so glad that you made the trip to Gambia and found the encounter satisfying. I'm sure you will communicate the whole experience in one of your performances. You sound so fresh and enthusiastic about reconnecting the verbal text with body movement. Do you start with dance or with words? Are you matching the rhythm of words to the rhythm of body gestures or the body gestures to words? Don't worry about the lines drawn by others. Draw your own lines. Black can be color or action. Action and color can be involved: black revolution. Revolution is action and action and words together should function to raise the level and significance of the performance and to fill the space with all kinds of information and energy. In a region of Darfur, Sudan black people are targeted and are killed by bandits because of their color. Women are raped and humiliated because of their color. The people resist domination and are forced to seek refuge and take positive action to endure, survive, be secure and move beyond the impact of systematic destruction. There is a lot of movement and language in this story. No critic can control the events or control what is created in the process of understanding its meaning.

These are difficult times but as you said in your letter "it is a rich and exciting time to live purposefully." Indeed now is the moment to delete inflexibility and indifference. Without a doubt our paths will cross again because we will both be performing and both working on solving some of the same global problems and of course we will both be eating breakfast at *Junior's* in Brooklyn. Thanks so much for your letters and good luck with your projects.

Aluta Continua,
Jayne

Judith Goldman & Leslie Scalapino

Judith Goldman is the author of *Vocoder* (Roof, 2001), which won a Book of the Year Award from Small Press Traffic, and *DeathStar/rico-chet* (O Books, 2006). Her work has been anthologized in *Against Expression: An Anthology of Conceptual Writing* (Make Now Books [forthcoming]), *Bay Poetics* (Faux Press, 2005), and *An Anthology of New (American) Poets* (Talisman, 1996), among other collections. The *Wall on Terra: A Tragi-Comic Border Novel-Policy on BioPiracy*, a play on political, economic, and environmental issues surrounding the Mexico—U.S. border, was performed the New Langton Arts Gallery in San Francisco in 2005. Judith was a coeditor of Krupskaya in 2002 and 2003 and currently coedits the annual anthology *War and Peace* with Leslie Scalapino. Having earned a doctorate in English and Comparative Literature at Columbia University, she is now a professor and Harper Schmidt Fellow at the University of Chicago, where she teaches in the humanities core.

Leslie Scalapino is the author of thirty books of poetry, fiction, poem-plays, and criticism. *Day Ocean State of Stars' Night*, published by Green Integer in 2007, is six poetry sequences and an essay. *It's go in horizontal, Selected Poems, 1974-2006* is published by UC Press, Berkeley. Recent poetry includes *New Time* (Wesleyan, 1999), *The Tango* (Granary, 2001), and *It's go in/quiet illumined grass/land* (The Post-Apollo Press, 2002). Earlier books of poetry include *way* (North Point Press, 1988) and *Considering how exaggerated music is*

(North Point Press, 1982). Inter-genre fiction includes *R-hu* (Atelos, 2000), *Defoe* (Green Integer, 2002), and *Dahlia's Iris* (FC2, 2003). She grew up in Berkeley, California, and presently lives in Oakland. Her work has been published in many anthologies, and translated into Spanish, French, Korean, and Russian. Her awards include two NEA grants and a Poetry Center Award from SFSU. She has taught at Bard College in the summer MFA program and at Mills College in Oakland.

Dear Judith,

Sensing a difference or a shift (from a range of earlier contemporary and kindred work) occurring in your writing and that of other poets who are your friends and compatriots, I'm curious to ask you, and to consider myself, the subject which for simplicity I would describe as 'the relation of writing to events.'

As relation between political-social actions and writing: writing, since it is conceptual, is separate from action but may be a type of action by engaging that gap of separation.

A doctrinal writing (the impetus of which is to be non-narrative or anti-narrative) may become so stringent as to eliminate the individual's event and individual or single events (as say for the purpose of eliminating "expressivity"/ "self" leaving only the authority of its doctrine), may cross the line to forbid language as its gesture.

Doctrine may be anti-gestural if it is entirely authority-based without any means of or any intent to critique or examine that authority.

Or anti-gestural may be the conventional mode of representation (confessional writing is an example), the single event stripped of its actually infinite context isolated and thus without relation, which could only be revealed by event seen as in infinite context.

The way I would think to consider the contrasts is by giving different examples of choices.

My poem *way* (written between 1985 and 1988) is an example in my writing of the syntax (a sound-shape which is by line breaks, by words separated by dashes creating alternate interpretations across the dashes, alternatives even contradictory existing at once) being 'the same as' motions, yet these 'motions' not *representing* events (in the world), but being a language motion which is also an event at the same time.

I tried to express this in my *Autobiography*, published by Wesleyan University Press:

"'Life' / as occurrence as silent—or 'not itself' per se. The writing is doing the (exact) same motions 'conceptually'—so that one is not in one's life: So that one is not in one's life. So it has an impossible relation to it."

Referring to writing which is 'only' historical events, no commentary (commentary would be as: outside the motion of the events), the writing itself being event: "Later—writing *that they were at the beach* and *way* I was frantically trying to get the motions (as words separated by dashes and in line breaks) to be minutely the same—which is separate per se."

I struggled to do this and also to describe it, because it was being constantly taken for simply narrative of an event itself:

"Syntax is entirely different from physical motion. Thus (in early works, through the 1980s) I wanted the writing to be that gap: the writing being life, real-time minute motions (physical movements or events) but being or are these (minute motions) as syntax (not representation of the events).

Syntax is memory trace or conceptual shape. Yet it was to replace, or to be, the (its) present-time motion only. It can't be a memory, or a life then."

I always found it difficult to articulate this because although it was akin to the prevailing concerns of the poets near to me ("without content," "non-narrative," writing being "only its language" being key phrases), I was doing this somewhat differently to consider relation of 'being' to 'history.' On the one hand, events one does (and events in the world) are not the being (are not one). On the other hand, 'to fall out' of these events in the world and events one's in at their / one's instant, not 'to be exactly' 'as' (or in) the motions there (one is being whatever happens to occur in real-time outside?—no—and being is one's own mind movement as syntax?) is not to be at all, not to have ever been.

Descriptive language is an example of 'falling out of' (or never having been in, always separate from) one's own motions described there. Such as: to describe events or to reference ideas already in place or to discuss other people's ideas, rather than one's writing being the act of thinking, an action that would also be an invention occurring there. Sometimes poets (I noticed this in the 80s) would reject even writing a thought process (at all), taking this for descriptive rather than the act of thinking.

Different from narrative as such: In *way*, for example, I'd 'take' syntax motions that 'were' then physical motions in real-time and space (my seeing a mugger running, my being in the same time beside bums freezing)—later (as in *The Tango*) I'd 'take' a thought ("dawn" or "magnolia") placing it comparing itself in space, making the thought/the phenomena only words ("dawn" or "magnolia") to see mind-shape only: at the same time as real-time oppressive, or other, events are being registered in/as the same sound scheme. So, for one thing, the 'mind' is seen composing these events that are outside, which also exist (which also have occurred, are occurring).

Minute events are so in time (in memory), such as in *way* an event of an elderly man wearing a hat in a movie theater and a young woman shouting at him, him rising leaving, the audience chagrined wanting him to stay—many such 'random' occurrences (or randomly chosen while writing, registered as syntax as the equivalent of their movement). Time is eliminated (the past and present being even with each other and at once as the experience of reading) and an emotion is as much an event, is as effective or active in its being transient, in this infinity as any other event.

It means that anything occurring impinges on and alters everything else—equally effective in the sense of large and small are part of the context. There's no hierarchy (in existence, is my poetic hypothesis), though we see it socially created. The writing enables one to see hierarchy and removal of it, and to be 'without' it. A poem can be a terrain where hierarchy can be undone or not occur (in the writing), but obviously the writing does not make it not occur in the world. So, its subject is also the relation of conceptual to phenomena, conceptual being an action also. Yet even proposing conceptual non-hierarchy frequently meets with great resistance (usually).

One poem I wrote, a section of my book *that they were at the beach*, titled "A Sequence," was a series of segments with erotic encounters of a 'she' or 'her' (either in her thoughts or actions and these at once) with some men with leopard parts and with some men without leopard parts. Or she's watching groups of couples one or more of whom had leopard parts. The 'force'/erotic attraction is somehow based on the dissimilarity or on elements of similarity seeing them in their location, never on hierarchy or power between them. No one in this poem is perceived by virtue of dominance. Nor are the resulting erotic scenarios cathartic or even fully satisfying (in the sense of either reader's imagination or sexual response), the segments always a flat, one-dimensional space. Yet 'between' the spaces, alongside or concurrent with hearing the sound of them, at once or alongside the repetitive space and sound, is a (lower case) daily beauty not 'on' or 'from' any of the participants or called such. There is no exclusion of pleasure and no power structure or violence that creates the desire there. Although it uses negative space, the intention is not to exclude: So one would be free to have 'actual' pleasure and beauty somewhere outside a frame, the frame (as the writing, flat scenarios in which 'one' can't be) has to be proposed and maintained (in order to imply outside).

I reread, written some time ago, my essay that's in the anthology just published, *Biting the Error: Writers Explore Narrative*, and found that I'd described my sense of dismantling hierarchy and the relation to the illusion-as-writing one is making to events in the world:

"These are illusions in the practical sense of being 'only' writing (writing has no relation to present or historical reality—it has no reality, is it as well, being mind phenomena. So the 'ordinary' small action is [to be] as much 'reality' as events that are devastating). I am trying to divest hierarchy-of-actions. 'Hierarchy-of-actions' voids people's occurrences (that is, individuals' actions are relegated to inconsequential or invisible). Such hierarchy substitutes 'overview' of 'history'/interpretation/doctrine—therefore, to divest 'hierarchy-of-actions' is certainly a political act. (In one's/reader's/viewer's conceptualization then—[is the intention]). What I'm referring to as 'divesting hierarchy-of-actions' by definition has to be in oneself . . . Fundamentally anarchism (viewing that as being observation itself) is necessitated."

Part of the literary conversation, of my generation, and still a factor, is related to choices either of 'expression and expressivity' or 'formalism that changes the approach to and way of perceiving.'

What do you see as the issues or conversation now (in your milieu) and how do you conceive of your writing interacting with or being events? One characteristic I notice about your poetry is a type of direct borrowing from (use of) the exterior language of institutionalized violence, for example, in order to 'turn' this or perceive it, sometimes doing so by a direct borrowing of passionate language of soliloquy (such as from Shakespeare) so that the reader is not 'within' either language and is at once within both (only 'as' both) critically and not absorbed—or absorbed and aware at once? Is part of your subject one being 'borrowed language' negotiating being as such?

My Best,
Leslie

Berkeley, California
March 17-22, 2005

Dear Leslie,

The urgent attention you have always drawn to "'the relation of writing to events'" has meant a great deal to me for a long time now.

Your sense that the relation of writing to events is in flux in current writing by myself and others suggests (to me, at least) that the present extremity of representational infidelity and illocutionary manhandling and mangling by the powers-that-be (suspiciously vague term, I readily admit) has pushed us to react upon these breaches in ways that will meet, reveal, critique, and counteract them, through befitting strategies.

I suppose that any moment in history has been inhabited, en-dured by people feeling their time to be epochal, or even apocalyptic. I, too, cannot help but exceptionalize this era, my own and exceptional for me (trivially or naively) in that I live through it in the first phases of my intellectual adulthood.

Yet it may be, however compulsively I repeat the motion of clearing space for a state of exception, that this exceptionalizing action does, at this time, have some validity external to itself—that it is, as they say, a repetition-with-a-difference. In this, the first age of instantaneous global exchange, the quality of the authority exercised by the US as unique world superpower has profoundly changed, for all those subject, in various modes of subjection, to that authority, the parameters of possible political action, including and especially the political actions of speech and representation.

For me, right now, to work as a poet in this society is to function as a "participant informant," a role that must continually be re-thought as we witness and process and redirect—as vehicles of, as well as obstacles to—brutal, frightening, and new manifestations of bad faith, cancellation, deflection, inversion, manipulation, and open, yet still disavowed fictionalization.

Let me be clear: I don't mean to propose that I think of my work exclusively or primarily as a response (or an attempt to respond adequately or meaningfully) to an epochal change in the structure of political authority as manifest in representation and speech act. I mean, rather, to say that I intuitively agree with your initial observation and that I believe this shift, if we can pinpoint it, in "'the relation of writing to events'" is both materially and symbolically linked to current abuses of power and manifestations of violence in representation (in its dual sense) that seem not to have existed before. Or that seem to have been altered by the magnitude of their scope, the degree of their intensity, the new media through which they are enacted, the direness of the circumstances in which they both come to be and create.

This is just an initial affirmation. It is not a theory, or explanation, or description—yet.

*

One striking element of your work, Leslie, is its commitment to analyzing with great insight and care the very premises of the most basic relations involved in any interaction of a person in and with the world. "The writing enables one to see that and be 'without'" "hierarchy . . . socially created," as you say in your letter; one way your writing subtly erodes the deep hieratic frames orienting us within the world is through your continual return to the situational and relational grounds to which an event stands as figure. Your work also often takes notice of, places at center but then moves around, phenomena that would seem to be uneventful, or that our society would try to avert attention from, that we generally code as unseen and unseeable non-events.

To return to "'the relation of writing to events'":

I'm thinking at the moment of how, even before *way*, your work was representing the reciprocal pressures that writing, reading, thinking, consciousness, experience, action, appearance for and to others, and social demands exert on one another—in, for instance, the poem "hmmmm" in *Considering how exaggerated music is*:

> As Rimbaud said, I thought today sitting in the library
> absentmindedly leafing through a book on the habits of birds,
> isn't the way we find happiness precisely by losing our senses
> (oversimplified, of course. I was being facetious.) But still
> I can see imitating a bird's call such as that of the fledgling
> of a goose or a swan (here I referred to the book) by forcing
> myself into a swoon. And, by way of finishing the thought, I,
> for the sake of appearances, since there were people sitting
> in the chairs around me, merely sagged forward in my seat and
> whistled as if I were asleep. Ssss, it came out, sort of a hiss,
> like the noise of a goose. So, almost before I knew it,
> I followed this by a low and guttural cough
> and leaned forward simply to expel some phlegm. Then quickly
> I took a glance around before I wiped my mouth. Feeling weary.

The language here is perhaps more descriptive—less focused on itself as abstrac-tive, syntactical writing-event, performing itself less as such—than that of your later works. Yet it can be said, as you remark in your letter about your later writing, that "its subject is . . . the relation of the conceptual to phenomena, con-ceptual being an action also"—to which I would add, action's being in turn con-ceptual, harboring and informed by concept, though never exhaustively so.

This (to my mind, truly extraordinary) passage above discusses an experience of reading from outside the experience of reading. Mediated by external narration that is also temporally distanced from the action as past, this primary experience was *already* split: first, by reading's also being a physical act, involving "leafing through" pages in the physical space of a "library," and second, by your reading's absentmindedness. Your represented consciousness is not fully absorbed in the act of reading the "book on the habits of birds" because you are simultaneously thinking of, remembering Rimbaud's aphorism, reflecting critically both on its romanticism and on the problematic but still beckoning tradition (*e.g.*, Keats' "Ode to a Nightingale") of figuring Nature as holding the place of a version of the self we cannot know (as self) yet long to access.

You address this facile resolution of how to trace a (fictional) path to experience outside of consciousness by raising its paradoxes: not only do you receive an image of birdcalls, the medium or device through which you will merge with Nature, by means of a book, but you decide, with self-conscious intention, to "[force yourself] into a swoon," to exercise mind over matter such that matter or body is evacuated of mind or sense. At the same time, your consciousness of your social being in the library setting makes your volitional evocation in yourself of a nonvolitional act take on a theatrical quality: the swoon of bird-mimicry must be tempered so that it conforms to the physical and mental decorum a library demands, within which reading "should be" a quiescent, interiorized experience, not to be taken too literally, converted into action. However mitigated, your swoon nonetheless does effectively imitate "the noise of a goose"; this reading-induced action you then involuntarily react to with "a low guttural cough," a cough that you reflect upon in the action of coughing and that is not simply a physical spasm, but rather seems a profoundly social, though almost unconscious, gesture, an automatic covering over of acting out the bird pretense. The cover up needs to be covered up: you have "leaned forward simply to expel some phlegm." The poem further registers the banal oppressiveness of implicit surveillance to which you have responded semi-unconsciously: "Then quickly I took a glance around before I wiped my mouth. Feeling weary."

✳

To turn, for a moment, to what you write about the syntax and the importance of syntactical intervention in your work, which reminds me of the essays "The Radical Nature of Experience" and "The Recovery of the Public World" in your book *The Public World / Syntactically Impermanence*:

The purpose of that work (and others), as you describe, is not to present writing as standing in for consciousness or experience whether in the moment of writing or not, nor to give a "narrative of an event," but to produce a self-consciously non-literal, stylized syntax abstracted from and metaphorizing (and in this way commenting on, as well as equalizing) internal and external phenomena and their complex interchanges. (Your discussion calls to mind a few lines from Laynie Browne's recent poem "Anna Povlovna's Soiree" [in *War & Peace* 2]: "A simplicity not at all simple, a smallness not at all bare, though that is how I also wish to live, then must my words arrange themselves in a similar pattern?") This project has an added dimension of complexity or tension insofar as your writing is also aware of itself as action and as active, as well as distanced and imagistic; it points to how it itself rejoins the relations it frames, as part of "an infinite present" and process of discovery.

I have great regard and respect for your specificity in tracing the lineaments both of the agency of language, language as force or action, and of language (meaning writing here especially) as an essentially abstractive medium. Your depiction of language's proper efficacies is bracing: on one hand, as you note, "*anything* occurring impinges on and alters everything else—*equally effective* in the sense of large and small are part of the context"; on the other, you assert that, "A poem can be a terrain where hierarchy can be undone or *not occur* (in the writing), but obviously the writing does not make it not occur *in the world*." I need to read your essay in *Biting the Error: Writers Explore Narrative*; the idea you discuss there, as you mention in your letter, of "divesting hierarchy-of-actions" seems really important. (Perhaps we'll come back to this.)

*

I want to take up the question you pose about how my own work addresses "'the relation of writing to events.'" As you ask: "How do you conceive of your writing interacting with or being events?" I am wary of this question, not at all because I regard it as suspect but because I have a deep and fraught fascination with it. I guess there are various ways I will need to sidestep it as we write to each other before I face it head on, and this is because I take it quite seriously and have thought (probably too) much about it.

Much of my work involves theorizing and demonstrating—thinking through by acting out?—the linguistic event or speech act as the *primary* or *originary* model of action in the world and the modality of the force that language exerts. (I am thinking, of course, of J. L. Austin, who argues for this reversal of the priority of the paradigms of physical action and speech act.) When I draw on, as you write, "the exterior language of institutionalized violence" I am trying to foreground and to examine the violence of its authority and its authorization of violence.

This concern is linked for me to questions that came up in the "Is Poetry Enough? Poetry in a Time of Crisis" conference last spring at UC Santa Cruz, regarding (to put it in purposely overly capacious terms) the politics of poetry: What is political poetry? and more pressingly, Does or can poetry have any role in politics or political activism?, etc. (Juliana Spahr's paper, located at http://people.mills.edu/ jspahr/crisis2.htm, takes up these questions especially directly and clearly. As she notes, she draws on conversations with the Subpoetics-1 group.)

A few months ago, I came across the following quote by the (controversial) video and performance artist Andrea Fraser, which I found productive for my thinking about these questions. Asked by art critic Gregg Bordowitz over email, "What makes a work of art political?," Fraser responded:

> That's a difficult question. One answer is that all art is political, the problem is that most of it is reactionary, that is, passively affirmative of the relations of power in which it is produced. This includes most symbolically transgressive art, which is perfectly suited to express and legitimize the freedom afforded by social and economic power: freedom from need, constraint, inhibition, rule, even law. But if all art is political, how do we define political art? I would define political art as art that consciously sets out to intervene in (and not just reflect on) relations of power, and this necessarily means on relations of power in which it exists. And there's one more condition. This intervention must be the organizing principle of the work in all its aspects, not only its "form" and its "content" but also its mode of production and circulation. This kind of intervention can be attempted either self-reflectively, within the field of art, or through an effective insertion into another field. However, I'm rather pessimistic about the latter approach, except in cases of cultural activism based on collective movement. Most other artistic "excursions" into the so-called "real-world" end up reducing that world to signifiers to be appropriated as a form of capital within art discourse.

My poems and performance pieces do not usually take up the politics of the institutional domain of poetry, poetry's (and poets') material support, though they draw on and interpolate pieces of many different kinds of poems and comment on these works both directly and indirectly. My writing does, however, involve lots of "'excursions' into the so-called 'real-world'"—

[A short outtake here to give an example:

The title of my recent performance piece "FatBoy/Death/Star/Ricochet" is drawn from the names given to trading "games" played by Enron employees in their manipulations of the California energy market. My work (loosely) takes the form of apocryphal leaked internal memos and contains spliced, verbatim citations of transcripts of audio recordings of phone calls made by these traders, in the form of cell phone conversations that repeatedly interrupt the memos. The piece in part explores the conjunctions between the game theoretical aspects of war and of the market, focusing in particular on how torture short-circuits strategy, introducing an alternate logic of pure asymmetry and pained embodiedness. Other materials used in the composition of this work include the UN Convention against Torture and the US revisions of and exceptions to that convention, a dictionary of non-lethal weapons terms and references, the report reviewing Department of Defense detention operations, technical works on game theory and strategy, declassified White House memos, transcripts from animated video games, Emily Dickinson's poem "Split the lark," the song "The Big Rock Candy Mountain," and Louis Zukofsky's "A." The last memo in the piece is a reworking of "A"-7 (forthcoming in War & Peace 2). My rewriting relies strictly on Zukofsky's canzone structure, but inverts his promissory tone, as this darkened imitation takes up events at Abu Ghraib and intramilitary dynamics.]

I need to think more about why I believe my work nonetheless does not, as Fraser observes so often occurs, "[reduce] that world to signifiers to be appropriated as a form of capital within art [in this case, poetry] discourse." Obviously, I don't incorporate current political events and documents into my work to garner for it some symbolic caché. Yet regardless of wanting to accomplish other things with my writing, can I claim it is inoculated from enacting such problematic reduction and self-edification? Is asking this already to buy into a cynicism from which there is no exit? Or, if we do not presume the impossibility of "'excursions'" being pro-ductively evocative, revelatory, and analytical, how do we draw the line between work that is exploitative and parasitical, or at least insufficiently critical and self-critical, with regard to its forays into the political domain and work that is adequately responsible and responsive, interventionary?

*

I must draw this letter to a close, and thought I would do so by discussing the performance history of my piece "case senSitive":

"case senSitive" is another highly interpolative work that also tries to invent its own idiom in part through its self-conscious hyper-intertextuality. It presents the meeting of a war council that debates whether a case, in both a forensic and a casuistical sense, has been made to validate the initiation of hostilities with an unnamed enemy. This case contains inside it another case (or is it vice versa?), regarding whether war has *already* been declared. The two cases demonstrate the manifold interpenetrations of factitious reality and authority-effects. This work draws on, among other sources, the East Indian epic poem the *Mahabaratha* (which, incidentally, discusses at length mythical weapons of mass destruction), the Western epic *The Iliad*, and Gerard Manley Hopkins sonnets; it incorporates as well a redacted Google search on the word "combat."

As you know, since you were there!, I first read "case senSitive" the day the war on Iraq began—March 21, 2003—in Berkeley in the 21CP (21st Century Poetics) Series curated by Jen Scappettone and Julie Carr. I also read it in a compressed form at New College in San Francisco on the day of the "Shock and Awe" military missions (this was a reading I did with you, Leslie). At the latter reading, I first quoted from a *San Francisco Chronicle* article from that day: "In the case of Iraq, 'shock and awe' will reportedly involve launching as many as 800 cruise missiles in as little as two days and the rapid movement of ground troops—to 'make the situation look virtually hopeless for Saddam Hussein and his leadership . . . The pressure will continue until we run out of targets.'" (The speech in the article is from a high-up US military official.) Another time I read selections from this piece, I quoted from an article in the *Chronicle* on Arnold Schwarzenegger's victory in the California gubernatorial race:

> "Failure is not an option. It just doesn't exist," Schwarzenegger said in an interview with reporters in his conference room. "I didn't campaign this way, 'What if I lose this election?' I never went into a competition with

weightlifting or power lifting or bodybuilding, 'What if I cannot lift this weight? What if I can't make it? What if this movie tanks at the box office? What if I hurt myself if I do this stunt?' If you continue going through life like that, you just can't make it."

I want to think some more about why I chose to frame my work in this way, what purpose it served to introduce my work by means of these current speech and physical events, what kind of eventfulness it would produce in concert with my work . . .

My apologies for a somewhat un-wrapped up sign-off—

I look forward so much to your next letter, Leslie.

Yours,
Judith

Oakland, California
April 16, 2005

Dear Judith,

Touching on some thoughts in the first part of your letter, that this time seems epochal, though one cannot help but exceptionalize one's own era—I think many poets now are writing 'out of' that unimaginable actual. One way they're doing it is a language that is doing/imitating as at once dislocating rational construct and forms of such within rational discourse itself.

Recently I came to the idea of a poem as (it would be) vertical stacks, totem poles, with layers of 'exterior events' occurring also horizontally alongside and as 'interior individual's events'—not causing each other, not recurring as a cycle in it (though the events allowed to be recurred when they will), every single instance being *first*, at once with all. I began this in a writing I just gave to you, "The Forest is in the Euphrates River," but I want to continue outside that one and try to push it further (see later poem sequence "DeLay Rose"). Try to find a way, not to resolve, but as you say 'intervene' in the very occurrence that drives or is one. Regarding your mention of my early segment about Rimbaud and imitating bird language (from a poem titled, "hmmmm"), that was my first work, written in 1974. Its language is not to convey 'the irrational' or 'the non-rational.' The task of apprehending separation of one from one's language necessitated finding a way to jump outside of 'our' way of seeing, yet our 'seeing' is 'our' language. I began the poem during a period when dogs actually followed me, one all across Berkeley as I walked, various dogs doing bizarre motions on meeting me. At the same time I began to dream a recurring dog verging on attacking me. I had the sensation that what was needed was to jump out of one's skin, as well as to use language (as the poem) which is not discursive, not metaphorical, not conversational; rather the intention being the act of thinking is apprehended as same as object's motion rendered as the language's own sound-shape of its syntax. The language as motion isn't a *description* of an event or an imitation of the motion in event. The thing perceived (animation) is only that language, they're simultaneous; as such outside any defined or known state of 'being.'

I had a difficult plan in the poem (and was too inexperienced to bring it off, though it's also barely possible): it had to do with taking apart hierarchy rigid in ('our') thought as daily conceptions and actions that are at once social and (as such defining as seeing) one's physical 'being.' My intention was to see 'us' as strands of motions only (watching people walk, breaking 'us' down to the unit of lunging up the street, rather than translating that as emotion—which entailed 'seeing' guys making love visible as this by being barking seals mounted (on 'us'), because that sort of wigged out state, in which there's no difference between something being very funny and being painful as being access to beauty, made it possible to isolate 'emotion' also: as muscular motion only. Like laughter, any emotion a physical strand (languageless) is same as scenery or rocks, thus removed from doctrine of psychological (the effect of doctrine being merely to translate, any description being ideology). The segment you mentioned, citing Rimbaud as a source, was a commentary on my failure to do *being* as language: in that, there couldn't be any commentary, either, because that reinstates hierarchy of thought. Intervention of any thought is doctrine (obviously), there is no extrication of the human from the human. I 'am led to' 'to have to' pretend and to perform what is then silly (as slight, minute) 'rebellion' (young women do not cough up phlegm in the library, nor is imitating a bird enough since I cannot change my basic structure as human—just as language is only itself, can only imitate by disjunction of itself an emotion or motion). The Rimbaud segment was to directly perform thought: pretending to be a 'girl' (which I was, but aware of not defined by this in my own view)—this pretending girl as if pretending to be an old geezer is 'thinking about' coughing phlegm, these in a 'minor' frame of sound scheme in order to note being trapped in language, in performing states of rebellion as being oneself, etc. Performing states of disengagement is different from dramatizing states (the former being the act, the latter is representing them).

Sources of that early work ("hmmmm") were romantics: Emily Brontë (*Wuthering Heights*, for its extremity in seeing people as savagery in the way that the moors are savagery) and Rimbaud (though not Keats) because Rimbaud's poetry makes a very specific, detailed, odd place where one is as reading (just as Brontë said, words to the effect, 'I want to be there, really with it and in it, not merely outside looking in at it,' something like that). I was, as I say, just beginning to write then—but the thing about "hmmmm," for the purposes of our exchange, is that although this isn't evident in the poem, it arose from the sense of changing of reality perceived through the US war in Vietnam.

I think there's some resemblance in this to your discussion of performance as language, and to, say, the video performance of Andrea Fraser.

I wrote "hmmmm" just emerging from being a graduate student in the UCB English Department where a large room filled equally with men and women (women who nonetheless were mostly, maybe all, failed later, coming before orals boards composed exclusively of men, right before the instituting of written exams on which names were withheld resulting in an almost equal number of men and women passing) submitted in one class to the weekly baiting of the women: we were screamed at as the professor paced in front of the class railing that women cannot be scholars, are not creative, do not have ideas (which is the creativity of men's minds)—we were challenged to prove the contrary and were mocked in any reply. An exam (testing only memorization) in which all the women did better than all the men demonstrated for the professor that we were not creative. In one seminar in which I was the only woman, another professor, chairman of the department, firing questions at each man in the circle always pointedly skipped over me as if I were not present, also skipping me at the end of the course when he asked the men what they wanted to do in their careers. We were not ready and organized. Further, these professors were middle-aged men in the midst of the violence of the exterior war literally savaging women, mostly like myself twenty-two years old. I realized I was already outside, certainly in regard to their gender customs, and hopefully to everything. Many of the men in this circumstance were against the war, for example. Yet their way of conceiving of the nature of thinking in how and what we were being taught was intrinsically conservative social hierarchy, as such also implicitly imperialistic. It was unseen by them, an invisible whole that was the language itself—I thought at the time, not having written a word yet, 'we have to take this apart (our) entire social/as thought fabric, that fabric as separation (itself an ideology) of thinking and being.' And we have to take apart the separation (such as mind-body separation), that as an action.

For me in beginning, writing was a language experiment (similar to Artaud's description that his deranged state of mind was meant exactly as writing to see mind (his)—though he was sometimes insane and I was not that). What was happening in the world then (as always) was simultaneously seen in individuals. In order to take apart social as thought fabric, it has to happen in writing being a present act.

This leads me to the part of your letter I find very crucial, the performance aspect of your writing, which I see to be not only occurring in your delivery or presentation of it, as you point out, but in its performance as its written occurrence in 'silent' reading, its intrinsic characteristic as writing. You question your writing in one passage:

"[C]an I claim it is inoculated from enacting such problematic reduction and self-edification? Is asking this already to buy into a cynicism from which there is no exit? . . . [is it] adequately responsible and responsive, interventionary?"

You describe your interventionary tactic as demonstration of "manifold interpenetrations of factitious reality and authority-effect." I first misread your word "factitious" as "facetious," conceiving of performance as taking on all the faces of the authority-effects including your own. The distancing of yourself (oneself) from "Shock and Awe" becomes at once the experiencing of (every)one in shock and awe, by the apparent exclusion of oneself in the imbalance (in reference to the world) but inclusion of one as discursive jeering as imitating being the imbalance at once. That is, self is in relation to massive, continual invasion and transformation. The very smallness of the individual, as you place them/her in your works, becomes an interventionary tactic. I don't mean to compare what I just said about my writing (early or later) to yours because the feel of your language and its mode of inquisition is different. You're making it tougher (in a different way than up to now) for the self to manifest its particularity by it being the social references, by your apparently subsuming it (as if one is entirely social) in a stream of subvertings, even making the font hard to read (as font language, social in the sense of mechanized)—yet font which can be easily 'heard' in listening in the presence of the individual speaking (thus subverting the process even of reading, since it has already been subverted in the outside). A salmon fighting its way up stream, this tough dialogue of yours between the 'outside' and one in it (in which characteristics of the individual mind are not allowed in the dialogue except as her ventriloquism in her speaking?), seems necessary to the tough time, otherwise the dialogue wouldn't broach the reality. I find no exploitative or parasitical aspect of your writing.

Further, the performance of it (both as written, the exchange within it as the multitude of sources in which no one source prevails—and as demonstration/presentation of this to an audience) is interestingly the lively manifestation of 'one,' Judith 'before us.'

My Best,
Leslie

Berkeley, California
August 1-4, 2005

Dear Leslie,

It's taken me so long to return [to] your letter!—there were several readings to prepare for, as well as dissertation chapter deadlines.

[Writing academic prose makes me long so for poetic argument: in the former, you are expected to avoid exemplifying the tendencies of the object of criticism/analysis, whether you debase or heroize it; in the latter, the point (or at least my point) very often is to enact what I want to point to in as many variations as possible, to get at its limits, contradictions, potentialities. Apparently, I am having a hard time making my project into a proper dissertation commodity; have been characterized as creating insufficiently polemical "shadow texts" that lack critical distance. Such ungenerous engagements with my academic work seem particularly farcical considering that 1) I have taught expository composition/argument for five years and have focused on working with students to develop intellectually demanding theses and rigorously tried/tested/analyzed support for their ideas; 2) I'm writing in part about eighteenth-century theories of rhetoric, focusing on the affective relationship of author to audience and on the expressivity of language. Interesting that the close reading I'm doing translates into an entrapped, epistemological closeness/parasitism; wish it could be just "interesting," and not also painful, frustrating, catalyzing of self-doubt/self-punishment. I bring "all this" up apropos your graduate school reminiscences, which are, of course, really poignant for me, caught in the midst of this credentialing process to which I have such an ambivalent relationship.]

So much has happened, to be proverbial, since last you wrote that is relevant to our conversation—a few things that spring to mind: Cheney describing the Iraqi insurgency as in its "last throes" and the subsequent administration recuperation of this remark (in a CNN interview he later said, "If you look at what the dictionary says about throes, it can still be a violent period, the throes of a revolution"); the fight over filibustering and the Republican "nuclear option" (this would replace the 60% vote needed in the Senate to kill a filibuster with a simple majority vote, in effect eroding to the point of disappearance any pretense of oppositional politics); the election of Cardinal Ratzinger, ex-Hitler Youth and longtime head of the congregation of the Doctrine of the Faith (the Church's committee preserving ideological orthodoxy) as the new pope; the about-to-be implosion of the Supreme Court with resignation of Justice O'Connor (no leftist but not as rabidly conservative and dogmatic as other members); the London bombings.

Even in the last two days, Bush has appointed Bolton to the UN (this "back-door" assignment made with Congress in recess), signed the Central America Free Trade Agreement (a set of highly disciplinary parameters for trade favoring US corporate/hegemonic interests), and evinced that he supports teaching the "intelligent design" theory in public schools.

I know you share in a daily outrage/grief/disappointment/frustration/disbelief with regard to these actions. You especially have done so much to show that we are not simply implicated in being (mediated) witnesses (as well as deprived of responsible witnessing/forcibly ill-informed) of these events and in being members of the political entity however convolutedly represented by this government, but that we are also, as subjects of empire, scrambled, twisted, manipulated by our culture in incredibly violent ways. Living on the obverse, triumphalist side of the post-late capitalist nightmare, we sustain or are at least continually exposed to modes of exploitation, cognitive, affective, and otherwise, proper to our privileged positions in the head of the beast.

To return to my attempts to "intervene in," *i.e.*, reveal/do local harm to/redirect the nexus/logic of informative currents operating in imperium central through making performance poems:

To get at what exactly these poems are doing/how they do it, I need to think through a description of the "epochal change in the structure of political authority as manifest in representation and speech act" (as I stated earlier) that's occurring.

[Let me note that I am a little disturbed at the self-importance implicated in such a purpose. Yet these concerns really do intrude, as they do for many, every time I use my web-browser, with all the (narrative) threads of social agency brought together to enact themselves on that flat, little stage as it opens, for instance, onto Yahoo or Google or other meta-site. I regard theorizing our current "condition," the internet experience (and also the issue of computer access/literacy and the new articulations of class through the digital divide) an important part of our predicament, as something that can only be a collective project, that my thoughts about it are in flux daily, can't hardly hold 'em still.]

I've broached this topic or task—that of specifying the ideological/imagined/discursive lineaments of our society that support the direct and indirectly, transitive and intransitive, prosecution of empire—with a number of friends.

All agree (as is popularly intoned) that the dialectic of mystification/demystification, secrecy, misrepresentation/truth has been thrown into a tailspin with the Bush administration's novel policy of openly lying and its *1984*-esque (or not even —esque) euphemistic/scientistic/and otherwise intensely oxymoronic nomenclature for its stances and actions/violations. But what to call, how to get a handle on what they are doing exactly, as well as our epistemological/psychological/practical position in relation to it, the "our" here referring to the public at large, but also more specifically to those holding more critical, dissenting views? Also, I don't quite buy that veiling is not in play—after all, Cheney is having closed-door meetings with Enron—but then again, that secrecy, as well as the absurd conflict of interest it covers up, is a public fact?

Konrad Steiner (experimental film/videomaker making a vision-track to your book *way*) noted the other day that the internet has made the government more, rather than less, transparent than it used to be. What I immediately thought of, however, was the warning I saw a couple years ago on the American Library Association's website to the effect that librarians should print out government documents the moment they appear because the Bush administration alters the official online record of its statements in order to make them consistent with its current position. (A good antidote to this: http://www.archive.org/.)

Drolly observing recently that it seems like Bush will have a third term (meaning, I guess, that this self-perpetuating nightmare feels like it had no beginning and has no end and will keep us trapped), Geoffrey G. O'Brien also remarked that people go along with the top-down/overdetermined version of reality because they believe in "the truth of the lie," this paradox, as he clarified, a version of a "willing suspension of disbelief." Again, part of me agreed but part also was struck with contrary thoughts: isn't the willing suspension of disbelief a mode of regard to be applied to known *fictions*? What happens when this willingness to entertain true (realistic, probable, as pertaining to a preferable world, where we're not the world-monsters we are) lies is directed to propositions describing reality?

This reminds of Bush's characteristic assertions of a circumventing-of-all-responsi-bility-between-me-and-my-conscience belief in a certain picture of things, rather than directly of facts, as well as of the administration's debasement of the "reality-based community."

[This phrase was reported by Ron Suskind in the fall of last year in "Without a Doubt," an article on the (psychotic) state of self-grounding, unpuncturable, unrevisable self-confidence in Bush's cohort:

211

In the summer of 2002, after I had written an article in Esquire that the White House didn't like about Bush's former communications director, Karen Hughes, I had a meeting with a senior adviser to Bush. He expressed the White House's displeasure, and then he told me something that at the time I didn't fully comprehend—but which I now believe gets to the very heart of the Bush presidency.

The aide said that guys like me were "in what we call the reality-based community," which he defined as people who "believe that solutions emerge from your judicious study of discernible reality." I nodded and murmured something about enlightenment principles and empiricism. He cut me off. "That's not the way the world really works anymore," he continued. "We're an empire now, and when we act, we create our own reality. And while you're studying that reality—judiciously, as you will—we'll act again, creating other new realities, which you can study too, and that's how things will sort out. We're history's actors . . . and you, all of you, will be left to just study what we do."
(The rest of this article is worth reading.)]

About two years or so ago, I was in an extended email conversation with Taylor Brady about how to locate/map the reality of performative and authorizing utterances and in turn the reality that they bring about. I was interested in the statements Bush kept making at the time about how any "collateral damage" in the war on/occupation of Iraq would be "worth it" in order to liberate the Iraqi people. He was, in other words, again and again scripting the (putatively) accidental civilian death/civil destruction that would be a (putative) by-product of the war, somehow trying to own and preemptively(!) exonerate the (putatively) unintended consequences of very questionable uses of force he was to authorize.

[To give a formulation of this by literary critic Angela Esterhammer: *Even if language seems to be an inevitable component in shaping the experience of reality . . . its power is limited by other formative components of experience. Coincidences, contingencies, and temporality . . . constantly interfere with the proper operation of performatives according to linguistic rules and sociopolitical conventions.*]

(Surely Bush2 had in mind the massive amount of civilian casualties the Iraqis sustained in the first Gulf War prosecuted by his father?) When the war actually started, however, the administration decided to use quite a different self-indemnifying logic: they refused to recognize the existence of any collateral damage at all; civilian body counts were declared illegal, all dead were declared insurgents, etc. (I wrote about this in my paper at the UCSC conference, as you know.) During what the military itself called "all-out assault on Fallujah" last fall, the US army threw piles of Iraqi cadavers into the Euphrates; they also refused to admit ambulances and the Red Cross into the city, determined to hide the traces of reality not authorized by their representation of the war and the "enemy."

I think, Leslie, that our discussion about this when it was happening led you to compose "The Forest is in the Euphrates River" (the "totem" poem stacking, both horizontally and vertically, recursive but also simultaneous interior and exterior events) you mention in your letter. One way I interpret this description is that this piece shows how the dynamic organizing fields of representation riven by antagonism/asymmetrical power relations operates homologously in a personal and a larger "virtual" or political framework. You are touching on a difficult family situation in these passages and also a fantasy sequence involving the character Circe, yet they also reflect the current impossible political climate/machinations:

> There's no way to directly articulate. [. . .] A bully or fascist 'is' as if they were interchangeable because there aren't words here. They sneered as a pack as if they were expressing feeling and as if the other, in favoring treatment, were criminal in which the bully sustained, speaking so that the blank couldn't speak, speaking when one spoke.
> [. . .]
> Circe seduces others, charms without her sensation or touch there, other than her words, which flatter men in their hierarchies only. So she creates these in people who would ordinarily not do it. As if other women did not exist, the forest is in the Euphrates river. [. . .] C asks to hire one to find someone, and asks her to do secretarial work. But one isn't a detective or secretary. C is imitating one [the speaker of the poem]. At a present moment she changes one's thoughts in what blank says to be something else—C imitating blank but altering it in front of others. Thus, for C, history is passive, without actions even. Always already altered. Yet C cannot change blank's body to be something else (such as a deer) in that one isn't a man. For C, men are separate, superior, though blank can't comprehend this as it makes no sense, isn't there.

To get back to Taylor's point: Taylor argues that ideology does not amount to providing a mystifying picture of reality, but is rather a dynamic interpersonal, transactional web, organized by pragmatic protocols we might call belief practices, *i.e.*, rather than belief in truths independent (of belief). According to Taylor's reading of, among other texts, the West Indian, postcolonial theorist C. L. R. James' reading of *Moby Dick*: *The very understanding of ideology as a falsehood masking a truth is itself ideological and works in the service of the cap'n . . . Ideology is more accurately characterized as a set of institutions, protocols and methods of working than as a set of false precepts . . . Ideology is the fundamental belief in the givenness of reality that founds practice, and not a distorted lens of beliefs through which actual practice is viewed ex post facto.* (I hope he won't kill me for quoting from his email!)

*

Your framing of current politically engaged/redirective projects in conversation with a potential apocalyptic future in which US imperialism is halted by world depression:

> I think many poets now are writing 'out of' that unimaginable actual. One way they're doing it is a language that is doing/imitating as at once dislocating rational construct and forms of such in discourse.

reminds me of Blanchot's concept of "writing the disaster." As Blanchot's *The Writing of the Disaster* begins:

> *The disaster ruins everything, all the while leaving everything intact. It does not touch anyone in particular; "I" am not threatened by it, but spared, left aside. It is in this way that I am threatened; it is in this way that the disaster threatens in me that which is exterior to me—an other than I who passively become other. There is no reaching the disaster. Out of reach is he whom it threatens, whether from afar or close up, it is impossible to say: the infiniteness of the threat has in some way broken every limit. We are on the edge of disaster without being able to situate it in the future: it is rather always already past, and yet we are on the edge or under the threat, all formulation which would imply the future—that which is yet to come—if the disaster were not that which does not come, that which has put a stop to every arrival. To think the disaster (if this is possible, and it is not possible inasmuch as we suspect that the disaster is thought) is to have no longer any future in which to think it.*

The disaster is separate; that which is most separate.

When disaster comes upon us, it does not come.

To relate my work to these ideas: to begin to "think the disaster" requires that any representation of it not issue directly from me. To (only perhaps) do so entails staging a collision of discourses, forcing an implosion of various authoritarian stances, in part through inhabiting them. This indirection/not-quite-parodic ventriloquism rhymes with the mediatedness of my own experience of the current disaster the US is forcing upon various elsewheres. Speaking *immediately* of and from the locus of disaster would demand that one destroyed by it speak from beyond the grave, living in, and through the aftermath of, one's own death. There is yet another mode of mediatedness in the protected (but also compromised) position I inhabit vis-à-vis the divide between occupied/seized territory and imperial state.

I would agree with you that the collage techniques I'm using right now involve a crowding out of any voice that could be apprehended as an authentic, subjective voice, or even an abstract representation of a place of unsubsumed subjectivity (the residue we all are in that our interiorities are never wholly colonized/dictated). Hmm, I guess it's the total squashing of subjectivity/personhood that I'm after, by the human, yet other-than-human personae that end up crowding the poem, whose usual job is to solicit us in order to engage and dominate us. I'm trying to replicate but also derange how we are hailed in the virtual age.

The distinction you point to in the performative registers of my work read aloud (by me) and read on the page (by others) is interesting . . . For instance, in a work I composed this past May, "Prince Harry Considers Visiting Auschwitz," the graphical/diacritical presentation in the second section, "Vesting Order 259: HOLLAND AMERICA TRADING CORPORATION (Oct. 1942)/GeorgexW.xBushxpaidxtribute /quotetoxrecallxthexevilxquote" is like so:

GeorgexW.xBushxpaid*pays*xtributexonxSunday/~~by which investigations into the financial laundering of the Third Reich~~/toxthexsoldiersxwhoxdied-*die/dying*xtoxfreexEuropexfromxNazixGermany/~~a de facto Nazi front organization in the US~~/60xyearsxagox

Thexquotebank,quotexfounded*found / made / founded* / xinx1924 / wasx
UnionxBankingxCorporationxinxNewxYorkxCity / axdexfacto / cemet
eryxinxthexNetherlands / PrescottxBushxaxmanagingxdirector / ~~for the~~
~~financial architect of the Nazi war machine~~

This work plays on the strange recent troping of Nazis and Nazi-signifiers—the
new pope's *Hitler Jugend* past; what was popularly referred to as Prince Harry's
"fashion gaffe" in February 2005, when he wore an Afrika Korps uniform to a
"colonial / native" theme party at the home of the British Olympic champion
equestrian Richard Meade; the ravings of extremist pro-life websites insisting that
Nazi Jews are behind abortion murders and the supposed "culture of death" in
America; revelations about the Bush family connection as American money laun-
derers to the German industrialist who bankrolled Hitler's rise to power and
bought him the Brown House (Nazi headquarters), as well as the Bush family own-
ership of Polish steel companies using concentration camp slave labor; and then
W's audacious presiding over the 60th anniversary of VE Day. I use mostly news
sources and websites on these phenomena, but also incorporated into the work
citations from translations of laws instituted in the Third Reich and a play by
Hanns Johst (a Nazi apologist), an art history article on the self-referentiality of
images in illuminated psalters illustrating God's speech, a few news articles on
Laura Bush's fashion sense, the gate crasher to a royal birthday party who dressed
as Osama bin Laden, and Prince Harry doing very poorly on his Army aptitude
entrance exams, an Umberto Eco essay on "Ur-fascism," a book of Ratzinger's
memoirs called *Milestones*, Holocaust denial literature, the Tennyson poem I*dylls
of the King*, and a contemporary ethical treatise in which WWII resistance fighters
tell their stories. The poem is organized into 4 sections, each titled with a Vesting
Order that records the seizure of a Bush family property made by the US Office of
the Alien Property Custodian during WWII, under the authority of the Trading
with the Enemy Act. The section above juxtaposes and is meant to render the
absurdity of the current president speaking at a cemetery in the Netherlands about
the human cost of the second world war and the business practices and political
machinations of his grandfather, who kept the German side supplied with steel and
who lobbied to delay the bombing of Auschwitz so as to have continued its access
to free labor. The text dealing directly with the Bush family-Nazi relations is
crossed out; the rest of the text has no blank spaces, but rather fills in an "x"
between words. These graphical marks are meant to make the text difficult to read
(when I read it aloud, I forced myself to use the same version of the text as it will

have in print), but this in turn is meant to force on the reader a sense of deeper cognitive dissonance involved with the Bush dynasty rewriting history. Their past is covered up; the present filled with empty homilitic rhetoric (the crosses also fetishistic reminders of a forgetting, like grave-markers). I used super- and sub-scripts to play with verbs in W's VE day speech to foreground the stiltedness of his words, to create the illusion of alternate, subjunctive histories nesting in his ver-biage, and to demonstrate the history-stripping, stalled temporality of everything he says: the triumphal yet pietistic, nursery school moralism he spews about the past war he also spews about the present one, the enemies of the past he points to were bankrolled by his own family, as the bin Laden family is now, etc. The section thus demonstrates/enacts the reality-cleansing of the Bush administration and turns it inside out.

Ok, there has still been no big push here to theorize my poetics—I am still just describing what I am doing—but look forward to hearing back from you about these meanderings.

Ever yours,
Judith

Oakland, California
August 12-15, 24, 2005

Dear Judith,

You are raising in your letter what is now the issue of writing: utter transforma-tion of reality. Iraqi casualties, their torture, legal rights, etc. are apparently not conceivable. The occupation may be predicated on humiliation and subjugation of the Iraqi people as war strategy. As for US casualties, Bush has stated it's worth it. In regard to language, perhaps it's a difference between discursive language, which will always be behind following after the events, judiciously studying or marking but in your case one's emotional comprehension as well—and your poetic lan-guage which can alter a reader's recognition or hearing of the events.

For example, your long poem, "case senSitive," in its use of, is it Elizabethan? phrases, as one of its language elements is a simulation (or imitation or perform-ance) of emotion bespeaking tragedy, the 'speaking' rendering a range of emotions such as grief, horror, outrage, sarcasm, as if in spoken exchanges (about US in Iraq) in relations between people in the poem (or signifying The People), perhaps (there's the sense of) one person who is at once also a chorus in the poem. This speaking in the poem is the creation of a subjectivity, which is marked as bor-rowed, therefore recognized as manufactured or fake, while at the same time this 'outside,' or foreign as from a different century, thus not-US, speaking voice (or voices) is the poem's 'authority' (that of compounding, enhancing, even mocking, response, not embodiment of US power) in whose 'subjectivity' the events of the war are cycled.

> wrong alas but necessary, but
> wrong alas
> aggress alas
> wrong alas but un/necessary alas
> Combat Shock will fuck you up
> burning chunks of/why it happens/you are
> anonymous user, you/can register
> beat him under with hands/out of the strong encounter
> fitty cents/cold sweat/vouchsafe the distance/from earth
> > to heaven
> the case was not-made/the case is made
> Such is the privilege/Absolute of force
> reckless disregard/to anyone in the/actual world
> Love wing'd my hopes
> and/or taught me how to
> fly/as dim lights vanish in the rays of
> > the sun

It seems that now 'the difficulty' (the necessity) of writing is both to be and to apprehend utter transformation of reality, by everyone at once, at every instant of the writing. If this can't be done the writing becomes a saying about something particular (some episode in history) that has already happened, has gone, and reality has altered in relation to it as well as in relation to all perspectives 'at once.' Thus I'd slightly question Taylor's comment, in that it seems that ideology is both "the fundamental belief in the givenness of reality that founds practice" (the givenness of reality for the Bush adviser is that being "empire" is acting which forms and creates reality?) and ideology is also at once (simultaneous in time) "a distorted lens of beliefs through which actual practice is viewed ex post facto" in the sense that all events are 'over' and there is no 'outside.' 'world,' or 'reality,' in the Bush adviser's view no reality that is outside of their own actions—no 'one.' Falsity is practiced openly for this purpose.

For myself, another way of stating the problem of 'apprehension at all' as the central issue for writing (given that you've cited my piece "The Forest is in the Euphrates River") might be phrased as 'the problem of Circe.' Comparable, I think, to your description of sources for your piece, "Prince Harry Considers Visiting Auschwitz," I do not plan a work of writing, I put in as I go along what comes to hand, what's occurring side-by-side in the world. I happened to see a beautiful painting in Washington DC of Circe (can't remember the painter), white, snubbed nude lying on an emerald green knoll with the creatures she'd transformed around her, all, including herself, with muted naïve expressions of body as well as face. What was fascinating to me was that the creatures were not simply swine (the Odyssey's portrait of Circe as woman sorcerer who turns men into swine, not from their desiring her: they eat her food—can be flattery?): the creatures were a deer, an owl, and other individualized strange little creatures. The nature of Circe is that the men are accepting a conventional 'relation' of themselves in actions at all. Yet in the painting transformed they are individualized and as such beautiful, their naiveté. Robert Grenier read "The Forest is in the Euphrates River" and asked me What's Circe doing there? He's a good reader, so I had to consider what is the fantasy sequence 'itself' doing (later, when I read it), placed there acting subconsciously as a side-line?

I'll consider "its laws of movement" (my poem's). I find in reading that the realms that are in "The Forest is in the Euphrates River" are separate, do not mirror each other, yet 'act the same' at once: the 'outside' world, the 'not inner and inner' world of the family, the no-existence of 'one' therefore "blank" (as in 'fill in the blank'), a place however ("one" which as you say can be "the speaker of the poem", if that's also any reader, but it's also 'single, solitary, individual' rather than many) creating separate realities in which no one would accept or even understand the accusation of their lying because their own reality can't include any other person's (except to deny, alter, or obfuscate what negates their own). Circe's charm is to continually praise people, giving them what they want, but in relation to this phenomena an accusation of lying or delusion wouldn't make sense because 'there' there is only the state or the pursuit of 'being praised' (being accepted, acting within, being reality, successful, etc.). There's no moral standard outside this desired state, none in which that as delusion could even be mirrored. Thereby only 'all' of these realms of the text exist (though the speaker in the midst of there being no "one" is placed under such stress to the point of blanked out, similar to being alive past one's own death). Though the 'speaker' (apparently the writer) takes a moral viewpoint (as do you in your writing) this only occurs by repeating (citing) what the actions already are (history). It's a question (must be) of going past that to be *with* the actions. Can this be done in any art? Which action, if it did occur, would alter other relations? Change 'only' alters 'how everything is seen later.' An aspect of the totem pole 'figuring' (in spatial relation), as a conceptual model of the writing, is one not being 'within' any single level or place, not inside or out, making there all 'come up' and be first at once. This 'coming up and as being first continually yet already there' can be heard when read (heard also, especially, in silent reading) and as such is an action outside oneself but apparently 'from' oneself. So there's a shadow of one. The so-called 'political' reality-that-is-the-turmoil-of-world-at-this-instant is in a sense the only 'inner' of the poem "The Forest is in the Euphrates River."

I did have a sense, before writing, of the written 'sound' 'structure wave' of the totem pole being 'all coming up *first* at once.' But first I had a sense of a sound shape in the air (not the totem-pole-vertical-stacking-at-once, that came later as a way of translating) that occurred when I listened to you speaking. You walked into my kitchen, having just entered the house—in speaking you were passionate with a pure, utter despair (no description of emotion or of yourself) and said the phrase "They are throwing the bodies into the Euphrates River . . ." The event was a shadow and you were a shadow in the speaking. The sound shape you 'caused' (in the air) was separate from the occurrence (Fallujah) but inseparable from apprehension of it as the distance between 'what is occurrence as being one's apprehending' and 'the languageless action.' It's past and present at once. I could not directly render or describe the shadow that was sound-shape.

The American cultural mindset of dividing into categories such as 'political' versus 'personal' is itself an ideology that prevents alteration of the conception of the phenomena undertaken. There are no actions that only exist in separate realms (one's life versus 'there, world'), the actions are everywhere, thus if the writing can be being contrary-simultaneous-transformation (that is, the writing mimicking other actions rather than being 'about' the events themselves as description, rather than commenting on them—in fact possibly even negating actions which are simultaneous there) the process of the writing may allow or provoke an action (of the poem) which (action itself) becomes a change of reality (by being an apprehension, or making a thought—a thought such as a new placement together, for example). Causing a transformation of one, however painful. Which is to say, people's subjectivities (distinguishable or not from their intellects) make actions that are reality (side-by-side with the actions being created by Bush and his senior adviser as they alter our future). Simply, we're as much reality-machines as are events.

The race to be ahead of the event (one of Creeley's modes, for example) is in your "Prince Harry Considers Visiting Auschwitz", language racing to render "x" the event fleeting as now past (and being already in place in its effect), to "x" it out on the part of the poet, and to alter the "x" event's effect—these at once, an action which can't occur except as language of contraries visible together.

Definition of personhood is itself an ideology of US puritan dualism: (the split) mind is not matter/is separate from matter; physical body is separate from its superior that is soul (or intellect, in the terms reflecting views of elites). 'Our' culture as 'only' that ideology of division and conquering is implied in Susan Stewart's description of 'our' language being for or having the purpose of to reverse night (as night being only terror in that it is not controlled) and 'our' language imposing 'day' as a language of rational construct, which as conception is imperialism of/on 'reality' itself (there'd only be ours) from the inside-out as being the language of western or anyway American individuals, who would then be *everyone*. It's so embedded it can't be undone? I wanted to 'get at' and undo 'our' sense of subjectivity by placing it alongside my language (individual mind shapes, such as a thought or experience in its process) at once as beside language of US soldiers (speaking in the newspaper) in Afghanistan—and beside night as phenomena, the word—in order to find the edges of (any) mind's instant being outside that construct (division as 'rational as being conquering,' and that division supposedly being mind per se). This was in my poem 'Can't' is 'Night.'

Similarly, it's probable you intended to "squash" your actual subjectivity, whatever it is unknown, because you 'feel' it indistinguishable from socially-proscribed "personhood." We're Frankenstein. In Iraq, the term "The Freedom" means (without irony, as possibly the ultimate irony) *US censorship rules*, imposed on the citizens, violation of which results in imprisonment. And, in "case senSitive," you imitate (there being) a subjectivity (someone else) by imitating it simultaneously with its authority and also with undermining its existence. Nor is the emotion of the poem "expression" only (though that's not excluded as its inseparable). The rigorous syntax of juxtapositions makes 'thought' the same as 'emotion' be 'as if' this subjectivity that is itself a way of seeing itself and (and as) context differently from the warp that is it.

My best,
Leslie

Berkeley, California
March 25 – April 1, 2006

Dear Leslie,

Your letter returns several times to the question of an "outside"—a potentiality/ negativity inhabiting our social (non)totality—and joins it to the idea of writing as performance, in both senses of that term: a theatrical "mimicking" or shadowing of the speech acts executed by political officials/authorities, and, at the same time, a deforming performative in its own right.

As you say: "It's a difference between discursive language, which will always be behind following after events, judiciously studying or marking—and poetic language which can alter a reader's recognition or hearing of the events." I would add: not by explaining or refuting and offering another information set, but by repeating and altering the earlier performance, thereby challenging its self-referential, self-authorizing and thus seemingly sealed off and protected (in other words, disturbingly ontologically tenacious and consequential) act of social/ political making.

In "case senSitive," this deformance (I refer to Jerome McGann and Lisa Samuels' discussion of "deformatives" in "Deformance and Interpretation") involved a few poetic texts, but mostly focused on the poiesis of "official" reality-making, repeating and deranging it. I really liked your reading of the poem as creating "a subjectivity . . . marked as borrowed . . . recognized as manufactured or fake" to be its poetic "authority," its being a "response to" and not an "embodiment" of totalitarian power, its "outside." It is precisely through the use of so many citational structures against themselves and each other that the poem refuses to "sanction the primacy of reality," as Adorno puts it, carving out a viable "outside" position from which to speak that cannot be a whole-cloth naïve exteriority, but rather tries to draw out the exterior within, working (to use a metaphor you brought up) virally—or to invert this (as you also suggest)—as chemotherapy, if we imagine the social whole (or its self-representation in media and official discourse) as itself a cancerous waste of facsimile personhood. I find Adorno's formulation/injunction that "art must turn against itself . . . and become uncertain of itself to its innermost fiber," to become thereby "qualitatively other" richly suggestive: poetry does not make itself "other" through "abstract negation"; rather, by destabilizing the distinction between art and reality on which it seems to be predicated, it can simultaneously work to corrode reality and de-totalize it, as it also undoes itself, pointing to the "uncertainty" of its citational redirections and detournement of citability.

"We're as much reality-machines as are events": your work engages radically with representing thought's texture, its uncontainable, riven, processual nature, towards changing frameworks of apprehension, perception, affect. This is another way the outside is inside—over against the strategy of challenging, by repeating from a self-reflexive, constructed exteriority, (speech) actions/events, you point to and perform a tactic of demonstrating thought as interference pattern, rather than a stable impressibility or context enabling the remaking of the real.

You're reading of the temporality of the x's in the "Prince Harry Considers Visiting Auschwitz" piece is right on. Adding superscripts or exponents to the verbs in the section using Bush's speech on the 60th anniversary of VE day at the Dutch cemetery was, too, meant to create a layering of time; in addition to heading the event off at the pass as you interpret, I wanted to reveal its ghastliness, the pressure of the alternate, subjunctive histories with which it is swollen and opposed to. I was also working with a synchronic structure in that poem, trying to render the fetishism (state of "divided belief" [Freud])/amnesia conditioning that language-event and making it possible. Using x's, I was inserting history back into the speech in the mode of its being subjugated or x'ed out, doing so such that the interpolation would literally make the present (both inside and outside the poem) unreadable and signal its radical, violent incoherence.

*

I'm currently teaching an MFA creative seminar at SFSU called "Violence and Representation." Amanda Davidson, a fiction writer and poet in the class, recently posted an interesting 1998 interview called "Infowar," sponsored by the organization powerfoundation, that took place between Ian Douglas, director of the organization, and James Der Derian, author of *Antidiplomacy: Spies, Speed, Terror, and War*. Two statements from it seem especially to relate to what we're discussing:

Regarding war in the age of new media, even before the Iraq war started, Der Derian presciently commented: "This is a war of maneuver unlike what Gramsci meant. It's a war where you have to be willing to concede that you're not going to have time to develop a story about the truth of the matter, à la Noam Chomsky. Instead, you're going to have to develop a counter-simulation to the simulations that are surfeit, that are in super-abundance at time's crisis." This is one way of putting how "case senSitive" is meant to work, as "counter-simulation" to the "surfeit" of "simulations" . . .

Der Derian also prefigures the domestic spying crisis happening now, stating: "Increasingly the military is seeking out a policing role. Technology allows them to intervene in civil society. What we traditionally conceive of as war—being organized violence between nation states—is clearly devolving into new forms, often invested within civil society; what [Paul] Virilio calls 'endocolonization.' It's a fusing of peace and security, and this is what Virilio is trying to resist. All too often in the discourse of security peace is simply the absence of war." Der Derian seems slightly to miss the point, the real contradiction in calling the security state "peace": the problem is not that such a peace has no positive content, but that totalitarian "endocolonization" is really a form of warfare.

I'm worried about the reality of totalitarianism all of the domestic spying disclosures are resolving into. This coming Friday there will be a Senate hearing on a formal censure of Bush for secretly authorizing (30 times!!, and that's by his own count) illegal wire-tapping of US citizens' international calls after 9/11 (the warrantless tapping has been going on for over four years). Cheney calls the NSA activities a "terrorist surveillance program," although about 5,000 Americans have had their calls tapped, with fewer than 10 people per year (as per *Washington Post*) who could be described as evidencing "probable cause." In December, Condoleezza Rice stated that whoever had disclosed the existence of the program should be prosecuted for spoiling its efficacy.

The Pentagon also recently entered UC Berkeley and UC Santa Cruz student war protestors into their Threat and Local Observation Notice (TALON) database. According to the ACLU, "The TALON program was initiated by former Deputy Secretary Paul Wolfowitz in 2003 to track groups and individuals with possible links to terrorism, but the Pentagon has been collecting information on peaceful activists and monitoring anti-war and anti-military recruiting protests throughout the United States."

I recently found out that in 2004, CA state funds earmarked for "anti-drug programs" were secretly appropriated (i.e., without the legislature's knowledge) for the CA National Guard "to create domestic surveillance units to spy on antiwar protestors." The units, which have since been disbanded (?), were called "Information Synchronization, Knowledge Management, and Intelligence Fusion," and Schwarzenegger apparently authorized at least some of their activities. Supposedly, the spying exploits a hole in the law: "Using the California National Guard to conduct spying is an attempt to make use of a loophole in the Posse Comitatus Act of 1878, which prohibits the military from conducting domestic spying. However, the act does not apply to state National Guard units." But the National Guard, the Army, and the governor's office deleted much evidence (for instance, wiping a subpoenaed computer clean) and refused to hand over some correspondence based on "executive privilege." The Schwarzenegger administration finally turned over some documents, on condition that they would be shown only to the budget committee; the Army took over the investigation of the National Guard, waylaying anyone else's access to evidence, and immediately ruled—also in a report not shown to anyone on evidence also not shown to anyone besides the general who wrote the report—that they didn't do what they did. A National Guard memo from last year acknowledged the presence of intelligence "Fusion centers" in Arizona, California, Colorado, Georgia, Minnesota, Missouri, New York, Pennsylvania, Washington and West Virginia.

And yet another very recent incident involved agents from the FBI's Joint Terrorism Task Force questioning Miguel Tinker-Salas, a Latin American and Chicano history professor at Pomona College who is an outspoken critic of US policy in Venezuela, during his office hours. Tinker-Salas, a Venezuelan, said the agents told him they were seeking information about the Venezeulan community in the area and were concerned that it may be involved in terrorism. And, of course, a number of professors from the Middle East and from Latin America have been prevented from teaching (by being denied visas) or have been harassed by the government.

All of the putatively "anti-terrorist" gaugeure mostly secretly put in place by the federal and also a number of state governments seems chiefly to be being used against critics of the war and of the Administration.

*

Border issues are also really heating up, with undocumented immigrants and allies demonstrating everywhere against the anti-migrant policy being proposed in the House and Senate. I am currently working on a new book entitled *Civilian Border Patrol, a border novel-policy on bio-Piracy* (commissioned by Atelos). It focuses on a formative chiasmus in our current political imagination and in US policy: Americans are phobic about a perceived Mexican scourge; a potent rhetoric of contagion is used to represent a Mexican invasion of our culture and society, licit and illegal immigration figured as enacting damaging incursions into the English language, the Anglo race, and the US labor and welfare structures. Aside from the public's refusal to acknowledge the indispensable contribution of this immigration population to, among other sectors, the economy, both in terms of its exploited labor and its tax contributions, key to this ideological formation is our failure to connect migrant labor to US economic and agricultural policy, set up through, among other policy measures, the post-WWII GATT treaty (General Agreement on Tariffs and Trade; signed in 1947), now supplemented by NAFTA (North American Free Trade Agreement; 1994) and CAFTA (Central American Free Trade Agreement; 2005); the sale of heavily subsidized US agricultural products in Mexico at a cost lower than that of production has destroyed the livelihood of small farmers in Mexico and forced them to seek work opportunities north.

Here is where the double-cross comes in: the material and phantasmatic "invasion" of America by Mexicans is countered by a movement from north to south of genetically modified organisms that are radically threatening Mexican consumers and also the biosphere of southern Mexico, a precious natural resource in which many of the species the world uses as food first developed. In addition, multinational corporations are poaching on Mexican cultures and ecological domains through what has been dubbed "biopiracy," the practice of patenting the genomes of species cultivated over centuries by indigenous peoples, who must then pay corporations for the right to use seeds once "owned" collectively.

Civilian Border Patrol exposes this chiasmus of cross-contamination and attempts to revision it through the juxtaposition/deformation several hundred documents and artifacts, including news stories and blogs documenting the vigilante border patrols in Arizona, Texas, and California, GATT and NAFTA, speeches by key political figures, food patents and patent law, science articles on biopiracy, the script of the *Terminator*, websites advertising maid services and labor studies books on domestic labor, Hannah Arendt's *The Human Condition*, Walt Whitman's *Leaves of Grass*, and other works.

I will be performing part of this work in the performance writing series at New Langton Arts in SF in June. I am currently working on a section about walls (*i.e.*, about the proposal that we build 700-plus miles of "fence" between US and Mexico but also about cultural, economic, and political work of walls/borders more generally). This section will be a discrete play within the larger piece in the form of a puppet show (perhaps with humans playing puppets), that will cite and borrow from the "Pyramus and Thisbe" play-within-a-play in *Midsummer Night's Dream*, in which one of the players takes the role of the (speaking) wall that parts the lovers. In my version, Thisbe and Pyramus are on either side of the Mexican border, the puppet-player playing the wall being Bush (since he really was AWOL for so long). The wall will be "eavesdropping"/wiretapping the lovers' discourse—there will also be an execution scene, in which someone is shot against the wall, with references to Sartre's "The Wall," a story about the Spanish Civil War—a scene of a midnight meeting of senators discussing Wal-Mart's (fictive) role in building the wall—a scene of lovers' talk containing references to legal briefs on the Israel-Palestine wall as violating international law—and a musical finale with a Spanish translation of Pink Floyd's "Just another brick in the wall" warring the hymn "Joshua fit the battle of Jericho (and the walls came tumbling down)." As you can see, it's not all worked out yet . . . .

In a press conference last week, Bush stated, in answer to a question about Iraq exit strategies, that the issue " . . . will be decided by future presidents and future governments in Iraq." Can it be that we are doomed to remain in Iraq until 2009? How could a devastating and extreme decision on our most important foreign policy issue have been casually made public this way? I know you (helpfully) keep reframing my questions in terms of "consider the source," but still . . .

I have so much enjoyed this exchange, Leslie. Thank you for the enrichment you have brought, in so many ways—through your work, your friendship, your press, your editorship, your example—to my life. I value it more than words can say.

It is April Fools Day.

With love,
Judith

Traci Gourdine & Quincy Troupe

Traci Gourdine's poetry and stories have been published in numerous literary magazines, and she has been anthologized within Shepard and Thomas' *Sudden Fiction: Continued* (Norton, 1996). She is co-editor of *Night is Gone, Day is Still Coming* (Candlewick, 2003), an anthology of writing by young Native writers, as well as *We Beg to Differ* (Sacramento, 2003), poems by Sacramento poets against the war. She also co-edited the *Tule Review* with poet Luke Breit for the Sacramento Poetry Center. Traci Gourdine is a professor of English at American River College and chairs the Creative Writing department for the California State Summer School for the Arts as well as the Sacramento Poet Laureate Committee. For ten years she facilitated writing workshops within several California state prisons. Originally from New York, she lives in Davis, California where she has raised two daughters.

Quincy Troupe has authored 17 books, including eight volumes of poetry, two children's books, and six non-fiction works. T*he Pursuit of Happyness* (Amistad, 2006), an autobiography, was a *New York Times* best-seller; *The Architecture of Language* (Coffee House Press, 2006), a book of poems, won the 2007 Paterson Award for Sustained Literary Achievement. T*ranscircularities: New and Selected Poems* (Coffee House Press, 2002) won the 2003 Milt Kessler Poetry Award and was selected by *Publishers Weekly* as one of the ten best books of poetry published in 2002. Troupe has written two books on jazz great, Miles Davis: *Miles: The Autobiography* (Simon & Schuster, 1989), by Miles Davis with Quincy Troupe, and *Miles and Me* (University of California Press, 2002), a memoir, by Quincy Troupe, soon to be a movie in 2009. His books for children include *Little Stevie Wonder* (Houghton Mifflin, 2005), and *Hallelujah: The Ray Charles Story* (forthcoming in 2009). He is editor of *Black Renaissance Noire*, a literary journal of the Institute of African American Affairs at New York University.

Hey Quincy,

I hope this letter finds you well during the opening weeks of this new year. I'm
just gonna riff with you awhile and not try to show up "proper" and "refined."
Here's my starting point: two quotes from two fine men.

"I don't sing a song unless I feel it. The song don't tug at my heart, I pass on it. I
have to believe in what I'm doing."
    —Ray Charles

"Jazz music has always been for me, as well as most black writers, an inspiration . . .
The ideas that emerge magically from this music often provide clarity in the work
I am doing."
    —Paul Carter Harrison

I can't tell you how many times I have reached for jazz in order to get to the soul of
a poem I am writing. In silence I may hear whispers or pick up a hazy shadowy
someone moving along a street, but as soon as I put some jazz on, suddenly there's a
woman in a red dress measuring herself in a mirror while her small sister looks on.
The whispers become a crisp and clear narrative of a piano player limping home
after an all night gig, wishing he had made it to Paris in his youth. I can see the rain-
slicked streets, the floor in a tenement, and even hear a baby crying down the hall.

For some reason, jazz takes me back to all that is familiar to me. Somehow I find
my way "home" again. And when I say "home," I mean back to my origins, the
women in my family who sang a few lines of a song when all other words wouldn't
do, my father crooning "Moody's Mood for Love" whenever my mother sucked her
teeth and turned her back on him, and the crystal clear memories that never fail
to come at the first few notes of Bird, Monk, Miles, Brubeck, or Coltrane. My
father had a huge reel-to-reel that ran most evenings while he was in his den,
smoking a cigar. The music seemed endless, but of course I took it for granted.
Jazz was as solid and as constant as the family around me, but when it became
time to define my own generation, I turned towards the popular music and left the
old folks to their own.

It's funny how we come back to the things that shaped our early memories. Jazz pleased me when I happened across it, but I didn't truly embrace it until I realized how essential it is to my creative spirit. I always worked off of pure imagination when I began writing my first hesitant stories. I'd stare at people on the bus, on the street and "suppose" about them. However, once I moved away from the East Coast and into the heat and weeds of Northern California, I didn't have the vibrant cityscape to inspire me. I found myself without the music of family, the cadence of speech and laughter, how shoulders move when dipping and dodging through the crowded avenues, the rhythms of the subways rollicking on the tracks, and what sad notes can be heard on rainy Mondays. Popular music wasn't taking me anywhere near home because it was too new, so with some form of instinct, I found myself listening to a local jazz station to ease the blank of my imaginings.

I found I had to compose with only instrumentals. Lyrics had me shaken from my chair and singing along. With just a sax, I had the tempo or mood I needed to complete a poem, and a piano helped me add texture to a setting that would otherwise appear flat.

I believe jazz helped me through the toughest class in graduate school. I took a class that concerned itself with poetics. We read theory, critical analysis, and learned the terminology of poetics. It was deadly dull and I could barely find anything very palpable that I could grasp or identify as my process. As the semester went on, I still felt as if I could not articulate my own poetics, how I come to image, how I frame my poems in line and rhythm.

One day while commuting to the Bay Area, I played and replayed Miles's "Sketches of Spain." Amazingly I found myself drawing imaginary line breaks in the air as he played his horn. I understood the connection and the reasoning behind the manipulation and timing of the poetic line. It was a major breakthrough for me because I found an explanation for my process. People stalled in that traffic must have thought I was insane, watching me draw a flurry of long and short lines in the air.

I immediately experimented not only with lines, but I also fooled around with mimicking actual tunes by Bird and Davis. My work moved into new ground. I had more control of my process than ever before.

Once the piece is written, I "play" it with my voice, listening to the notes I've laid down. I then tune not only for meaning but for the musicality of the thing. As with music, I feel that a poem also has emotional value by its sound and timing. I can hear when a word may stumble the piece by breaking the mood, or a line break is ruining the tempo. Once I have that down, I feel that the piece is complete and I can play it back with its original intent no matter what mood I'm in. I hope that makes sense; it sounds so obscure when writing it here.

I know that jazz has played a major part in your work as well. Who or what influenced or changed your work the most? Have you other outside influences as well?

What do you reach for when a piece stalls out or you need a boost of inspiration? I'd also love to hear how you fine-tune a piece to your satisfaction.

Again, hope this new year is going well for you and that your travels were safe and serene. I look forward to hearing from you.

Traci

Montebello, Guadeloupe
February 23, 2005

Traci,

When I got your letter I was in Guadeloupe where I have a little house and where I go these days to write and clear out my head, so that I can live clear-minded here in New York City, which has a lot of noise and sounds—as you know—that interrupt the peace I'm trying to plug into my brain.

But I love New York City, especially Harlem where I live, because there's so much music and language in the air everywhere and I can just go out and be submerged and surrounded by it all. The food smells, the car horns, the subway, the myriad languages and voices and yes, even the stupid arguments!

But, like I said earlier in this letter, sometimes I have to get out of all the music and language I hear and feel here, and try to get through to my own rhythms, the music and language I hear inside my own head. And that core linguistic sound and rhythm comes from where I was born—St. Louis, Missouri, and that mid-western thing that Miles Davis and Chuck Berry come from too—and from all the other places I've been that have added their beauty and rhythm to the language I write: that means everywhere I have ever visited with my ears and tongue wide open.

I'm going to get to your specific poetic concerns and questions a little deeper in this note, but first I would like too say that when I'm finishing a book, as I'm doing at the moment, I like to go to someplace where the air is clear and fresh and silent like Guadeloupe is in the countryside where I stay, because I really want to hear myself think out loud.

I'm finishing a book, an autobiography—with a man who also like Miles Davis was from the mid-west, Chicago to be specific, and I'm just about through with it. When I go to Guadeloupe I can really hear his voice clearly in my head: his name is Chris Gardner, so look out for the book because he's lived an extraordinary life, one which Will Smith will portray and bring to the big screen soon—it's Will's next film—so look for it. The book is titled, *The Pursuit of Happyness*, which is also the title of the film.

Yes, I too was influenced greatly by the music of Miles Davis, John Coltrane, Charlie Parker, Billie Holiday, Sarah Vaughan, Dinah Washington and other so-called "jazz" musicians and singers of that genre. But I also felt the pulse of Chuck Berry—whom I grew up down the street from—Little Richard, Fats Domino, The Platters, Frankie Lymon, Sam Cooke, Marvin Gaye, Jimi Hendrix, Sly and The Family Stone, James Brown, The Beatles, Mozart, Beethoven and the music of so many others that threaded their way through my early and later poems.

Then I got into African music through hearing Hugh Masekela and Miriam Makeba, and they led me first to visit Africa and hear Fela and Sunny Ade and then to the music of Franco, Rochereau, Salif Keita, Sam Mangwana, Youssou N' Dour and so many others. But during my formative years I grew up in households where all kinds of music was played.

My father was a great baseball player and traveled to Cuba, Puerto Rico, Mexico and Venezuela, and sometimes he took the family with him, so I heard music from these countries at a very early age as well. After my mother and he divorced, she married a blues bass player and then I had the pleasure of meeting and hearing great blues musicians like Howlin' Wolf, John Lee Hooker, Bo Didley, B. B. and Albert King and so many others in my home.

So all of what I have said above influenced the language, sound and rhythm in the way I spoke, not to mention the friends I was hanging with and the voices I just heard up in the air, even before I started writing poetry. After I seriously began to write poetry, it was first the work of Pablo Neruda, T.S. Eliot—also from St. Louis, even if later in his life he didn't want to be from there—Langston Hughes and Gwendolyn Brooks who influenced my poetry.

Then I discovered the poetry of Cesar Vallejo, Aime Cesaire, Garcia Lorca, Jean Joseph-Rabearivello, Allen Ginsberg, Amiri Baraka when he was LeRoi Jones and after he became Amiri Baraka too, Melvin Tolson, W.S. Merwin, Sylvia Plath, Leon Damas, Nicolas Guillen, W. B. Yeats, Jean Toomer, Robert Hayden, Derek Walcott, Sterling Brown and others that also impacted my work in profound ways.

But music continued to impact my poetic language in significant ways.

Later I saw Pablo Picasso's great painting, *Guernica*, and that just blew me away and I began to look at painters and sculptors, and there are so many that I will only mention a few here, like Matisse, Romare Bearden, Jacob Lawrence, Wilfredo Lam, Salvador Dali, and later Al Loving, Melvin Edwards, Ed Clark, Jose Bedia, many Haitian painters, Jean Michel Basquiat and so many others.

All of these things began to fuse inside my head and help me to fashion whatever language I began to write in my poems from the beginning of the 1980s until today, even though my work in my opinion continues to evolve and change.

As you have mentioned, I too agree that poems have "emotional value like music," and like music poetry is important for the "sound and timing" it can bring into our lives and the way we hear the flow of language. That's why improvisation and surprise are very important ingredients for me in poetry, the way both these things can enhance the joy and pleasure of reading a poem.

In that regard, and because of my appreciation of music, I am always aware of what might "break the mood and flow of a poem when a word stumbles," or that a badly made phrase or rhythm might fracture the synthesis of a heretofore beautifully made, blooming poetic line.

I'm writing a long poem now titled "The Architecture of Language," which is the title of my next book of poems. In this poem I'm very cognizant of the mood and flow of language and not breaking the "magic" that hopefully is evolving inside the voice. This poem is also trying to comment on how poems and a poetics are put together, and my idea is that they are put together like a great architect might construct fabulously beautiful great structures and environments/places that we live and work in. I try to employ the devices of surprise and improvisation in the way an architect or a musician or a painter or dancer might use these things to enhance what they are trying to create: I hope it works for me.

I reach for great music and writers and poets I love when my work stalls, which hasn't happened that often—knock on wood, Traci!—but when it does, I think of what Toni Morrison once told me when I asked what she did when her writing was blocked. She replied: "I'm supposed to be blocked and no matter how much I might try to write through it, I've never been able to do it because I'm supposed to be blocked. So I just do something else like listen to music or read a good book."

That's what I do too, and I might even take a trip to a place I've wanted to go to if I can afford it.

I'm always fine-tuning my poetry and sometimes I rewrite too much as I did with "The Architecture of Language," which was called "The Architecture of Speech" when I first started writing it back in 1988. I rewrote it so much I lost the magic and feel of the poem, and so I put it aside until August, 2005, when I rediscovered it when I was writing down in Guadeloupe and thought I would take another fresh crack at finishing it, which I did on May 19, 2006.

So far it's worked out and I'm just trying to let it flow this time: wish me luck.

There you have it.

Let me know how the visual arts and nature's boundless beauty affect the way you write, how California has impacted the way you hear and shape language, you know, whether the hissing waves of the Pacific, and how all that snarling traffic out in that otherwise wondrously beautiful place you live in has been a positive, soothing or negative influence on your truly fine poetry. Let me know.

All the best to you, Traci and I hope this letter provides a frame for our continuing poetic dialogue.

Take care and until we speak again continue to let the poetic spirit wash over you and provide inspiration for your work, but don't forget to always keep having a wonderful time.

Quincy

Davis, California
May 18, 2005

Quincy,

I'm truly inspired by all that you said. Your letter made me want to rush out to find Berry, Little Richard, (oh yes!) the Platters, and I remember the sounds of Masekela and Makeba too. You provided quite the shopping list with Rochereau, Mangwana, N'Dour. I've laughed, nodded and cheered right along with Etta James, and find myself wanting more.

So many of my fellow poets hold poetry in one hand while embracing another discipline in the other. Some even amaze me with their incredible abilities with poetry and music, poetry and painting, poetry and photography, bonsai, dance. Oh yes, poetry and baseball! When you wrote that Toni Morrison doesn't fight "the block" but instead finds her study and outlet elsewhere, I recognized the sentiment. Aren't we as poets and writers working whether or not we are seated and spilling ink? Photographers are seeing and composing whether they have the lens in front of their eye, the same way a sculptor sees possibility in a snow drift, the dancer in the steps of a harried waitress, the musician within the tease of hesitant rain in wind on leaves. I believe all artists are present and living within an inch of their lives in order to create. And I'm not referring to great risks of limb in adventure or booking tours through the seven circles of hell (be it lifestyle or couplings) to get one's work done. I'm referring to being present in the world and seeing the grand to the miniscule; star shine to pin prick, old oak to raw bud.

Sometimes in this racket and routine, I must remind myself that I am suppose to be listening, not speaking, receiving and not responding, feeling, and not grasping.

That brings me to how I've come to understand the natural world and how it's found a place in my work. I was insolent and bored when faced with earth. Having been raised on concrete half my life with hardly a slit of sky visible above my head, I swore only pigeons and ragged blue jays claimed the sky. I was under the belief that life happened only if people and buildings were present. When I moved from the East Coast to Northern California, I had to be taught to see all over again as well as learn the language: swollen river, ribbons of tule fog, white caps in April sea, muddied old horse patient in rain. The change of landscape required that I had to learn a new way of seeing.

Here I've come to know how to find the dark seams on an orchard's horizon and watch the serrated black wings of crow start their eastern commute. Did you know night will fall within 20 minutes after the crows' flight? Out here the crows fly in from their daily work somewhere west of me. They take their happy hour in the fields where I walk my dog. They light, stand tall, yellow/black eyes set in the direction they will fly, and they mingle like blue-collar steel workers, socializing before heading home. Then as if on cue, they all rush up, climbing the air above us. I love to shut my eyes and listen to the sound of feather and wing ascending. Such a magical sound, silence and wing. Walking my dog out there in those fields has taught me how to love the earth. I can't name a plant or tree beyond the obvious, but I know the call of Canadian geese, and the mating calls of California ground squirrels. I also know that my dog prefers it if I let her act big and beastly out there with her brethren. I have learned how to come down off my bi-pedal platform, crouch low and watch how ants create civilizations, how they haul their infants from the dark and into the light, war, and reconstruct, only to start it all over again. I even carried home a snakeskin shed as neatly and as whole as a woman's peeled nylon. Amazed me for days.

I am currently working on a series of poems based on family stories, primarily from my mother's point of view. Since my father's passing, she finds herself in need of having her side of things told. My father had an enormous presence, greatly respected by so many in life, and even in spirit he stands strong. My mother, however, is determined to reveal how she sustained herself, her sanity, her dignity in the midst of his fame and persona. Her phone calls are not fireside chats of warm reminiscence; far from it. They are harrowing scenes, softly told without rage or venom about being eclipsed and stunted by his blaring influence. The pre-scribed role she had to play as obedient West Indian wife and mother left little room for her to speak up for herself or carve her own path in life. She is a clear depiction of the 1950's woman married too young, loving too hard, and tied to a kitchen sink with a faint smile twitching in rage. Now clear of all those narrow boundaries of virgin bride, dutiful wife, and unrealized dreams, she feels this need to reveal what went on in the periphery of my father's fame and public personae.

These tales are haunting yet universal in their way. I found myself reluctantly writing them down, but I was compelled to because I needed them out of my ears and onto the page. I felt she was deconstructing the father I have loved and held in such high regard. I came to avoid our phone calls for fear of what new revelations I would hear about their relationship. Somehow she understood my discomfort and said that these were the stories about a man and a woman in love, during a time when men had full reign and women had only a handful of options. "These are not father stories, child," she said. "These are stories about the man I loved. Know the difference." She does not know that I am carving these bits into poems, juxtaposing her truth beside the public charismatic hero that I knew. I would rather write about other matters, but I find my parents appearing on the page time and time again. It is unusual for me to write about personal truths; it's not my style, but somehow the work comes uncalled and demands to be addressed. I obey. Have you had the experience of feeling pushed in a particular direction you were reluctant to follow? I'm trying to be careful with this work and respect the two of them here. Who knows what will come of it, but isn't that part of the journey after all?

I hope this letter finds you and your family well. I apologize for my delay. Mom was recently diagnosed with breast cancer and has had surgery and two rounds of chemo since you and I last spoke. The siblings are gathered near, bringing comfort, hilarity and exasperation with them. They have no idea how they make my mom feel stronger as they tease and banter, sing and pamper her at bedside.

She is well and healing quickly. The semester is ending and the students are trailing off towards long summer months without essays and exams. I look forward to the lull when I can choose how I will fill my days.

Take care Quincy!
Traci

New York, New York
August 24, 2005

Traci,

I've been so busy in this over-the-top hectic place called New York City. Sometimes it seems as though some of us who live here are moving so fast we pass ourselves on the treadmill without even knowing it. Then finally when I decided I had to stop making excuses for not writing and just sit down and do it, New York City was hit with the most insufferable heat wave, coupled with the highest humidity that I have ever lived through: it just seemed like we were all living in a very hot and wet steam bath, and those kind of conditions completely shut my writing down. Today is better, so I'm penning this long overdue letter to you.

I'm sorry to hear about your mother's breast cancer, and her surgery. Parents are very important to our lives, especially mothers, so I know what you must be going through. Like you, I lost my father also, just about 12 years ago, in 1993, and hardly a day goes by that I don't think of him and of all the good times we had together. I also think of all the things we failed to do together, those missed opportunities that turned into deep and nagging regrets after my father died, and so it makes me happy to hear of you and your siblings gathered around your mother "bringing comfort, hilarity and exasperation" into her life during this trying time. And you are right, all of the "banter," singing and teasing makes her "feel stronger" while she's going through chemotherapy, because all of you are there with her, and I know this is very comforting for her spirit and well-being.

I just threw my mother a surprise party in St. Louis to help celebrate her 88th birthday. All of my life she has always told me how much she hated surprises, but I thought I would incur her wrath this one time and see if she was telling the truth. She wasn't, and as it turned out she was absolutely delighted, and completely surprised, so much so she jumped up and down like a happy little kid. I was thrilled that she was so happy. We filmed it, and it was memorable for her, and for all of the 50 people gathered there to help wish her a happy birthday with great food, cake and endless champagne! Eugene Redmond was there also and took a lot of pictures.

I'm trying very hard not to have the same kind of regrets with my mother that live on inside me when I think about my father. So I'm spending more and more time with her, inviting her to New York to spend time with my wife and me, talking to her over the telephone, trying to see her every chance I get in my hometown. I'm about to go to St. Louis again in August for my family reunion—whew, talking about hot and sticky? St. Louis in August is almost unbearable, but I'm going anyway, just to be with my mother again and experience the rest of my beautiful but crazy relatives. I too have been thinking about how I can turn some of these memories of my mother and relatives and some of my old St. Louis friends into a series of poems.

My mother was the very first feminist I knew, because she always stood up for her rights—with her three husbands, her jobs, with everything and everybody. She was always political, said what she felt about the local and national government, and if you wanted honesty she would give it to you, whether you could handle it or not. Most people couldn't, so they thought she was arrogant. But she didn't care what most people thought and so she never had a large circle of friends, which seemed just fine with her, because the friends she did have loved her and her them.

One of my latest poems is titled "Diva," and it is about my mother, because that's what she is—a "Diva." In the poem I'm attempting to really describe this fierce little woman who is my mother, who has such "certainty" in the way she views things. Yet, she is "delicate," almost "bird-like" in that she reminds me of "a ballerina" when she walks by. She is also charming, highly intelligent and beautiful, with such a "sunny" disposition when she is happy. But don't push her the wrong way because the mood instantly changes, "like a sunny day suddenly goes dark, and a tornado drops down from black clouds." This is the way my mother is, has always been, and I and everyone else who knows her walks tippy-toe around her mercurial disposition and personality. One moment she's all smiles and the next, well, you get the point.

Anyway, I'm trying to get some impressions of my mother, my father, my grand-mothers, uncles and cousins, along with a few old friends, into a series of poems. Some of these moments will turn up in my auto-memoir *The Accordian Years*, but I still would like a poetic record of our journey together.

The difference I see in your approach and mine is that you're writing your series of poems through the voice and eyes of your mother—am I wrong?—and I'm writing mine exclusively through my own experience and eyes. But I am interest-ed in what you will come up with, in hearing your mother's voice on paper, however "haunting" and "deconstructing" of your father it might be, because that makes for a certain tension in a poem that I find myself drawn to. By the way, what did your father do? He sounds very interesting, as does your mother.

These narrative poems about my family will be a shift for me in tone and approach because my poems lately have been going more in the direction of attempting to create a voice that is less narrative, one that is more fragmented if you will. I am a little reluctant to change direction at this time but feel that I have to get down on paper the experience of my family, because I don't see anyone around in my family yet who will do it.

In the past I was a little reluctant about writing about "personal truths," but I think I have gotten over that feeling because it is essential for me to be as honest now as I can when I write about my own life and others, including my mother, father and the rest of my family. I have even gone as far as to tell them to expect some harsh truths in my auto-memoir, the novel I've been writing forever, and in some of these planned new poems. I'll just have to wait and see how they take it, because I'm definitely going to write about them, and truthfully. But I will be careful and respect all concerned. Sharon Olds writes really honestly and well about her family. Have you read her poems?

On the other hand, I have been trying to accommodate more natural elements like the sea, wind sounds, mountains and birds and flowers into my poems. That's why I love going to Guadeloupe so much, where I'm able to watch birds, especially hummingbirds, egrets and pigeons, and not all these concrete buildings that surround me here in the "big apple"; buildings also have their own kind of power, majesty, and beauty. There are so many different beautiful birds in Guadeloupe but I just don't see enough of them, or recognize which ones they are yet.

I have, however, been enthralled lately with a family of chickens, who have somehow found the big yard around our little house accommodating. There's a confident king rooster, who runs everything, his son, prince rooster, who gets chased by his larger father, who is actually a magnificent creature, with a crowing voice deep as Paul Robeson singing "Old Man River!" I mean his voice when he cacadoodledo's is the envy of all of the other crowing roosters in the entire area! He struts around giving everyone orders, running after them, giving them sharp pecks in their behinds whenever any of them do anything that displeases him. . There is also the queen mother hen, who rules with an iron fist over the other four hens, chasing them around like king rooster does whenever they piss her off, and finally there are five or six little chicks, who undoubtedly will be larger when we see them again in the middle of August.

I love going to the mountains and forests in Guadeloupe, because they are so beautiful and bountiful. There are mango, banana, cherry, lemon and lime, and papaya trees everywhere you look! There are stunningly beautiful scarlet and pink, orange and purple, yellow and lavender flowers that jump up and arrest your eyeballs. Everywhere you look there is lush green foliage surrounding your senses because of all the rainfall. And when "rainstorms come swooping in wearing veils of dancing mist," they remind me of the "switching, swishing motion of women's skirts when they swing wondrous hips." These storms seem to wash and sing through the leaves and branches of trees. It is a hypnotic experience for me, mesmerizing, totally enthralling in its sensuous beauty and rapture. And it cools down the hot day!

But this kind of natural phenomena requires another kind of poetic voice for me than the one that might capture the experience of my family or New York City. Derek Walcott can capture this Caribbean experience effortlessly because it's what he grew up with, experienced everyday. But I have to work at it, feel it, let it all course through my body with its many, many voices and rhythms, so I can capture it also, make it a part of my on-going poetic muse. I tell you it is a challenge for an urban spirit like me, but it is a challenge that I will not shy away from, and one of these days I hope to get it right.

Actually, this need to embrace nature in my poetic voice started when I was living in La Jolla, when I was teaching at the University of California, San Diego, which is also a very beautiful area of California.

Well, I think I've said enough, although I will say that I agree with you that we "poets and writers [are] working whether or not we are seated and spilling ink." I know I work inside my head everyday, all the time, even if I don't write it down; I still think about stuff.

That's what creating is all about. And yes, it is about "great risks," "living within an inch" of our "lives in order to create." But that's what we sign on for when we decide to become artists, isn't it. Those of us who survive this tortuous path and keep creating realize there are pitfalls — huge ones — and accept this as part of the journey. Others, like Kurt Cobain, or John Berryman, I don't think ever fully embrace the concept of "great risks" as part of their journey, and when they encounter a failure, or a pitfall then sometimes they commit suicide. That card is not in my deck of cards. I fully realize the "risks," and have prepared myself to deal with them, however dispiriting they might be, as I believe you have too.

All the best to you, Traci. Writing to you has been an unexpected joy.

I look forward to your next letter.

Quincy

P.S. Part of busyness in New York was reading the blue pages for *Black Renaissance Noire*, which contains your fine poems and which should have been published in March of this year. The MS was finished and ready and was sent off to the printer in December of 2004. But when the bill came, the university thought it was too high, even though they had first signed off on it, and refused to pay the bill. So we had to switch printers and get the price down and so now we expect the finished product in about three weeks. It's a beautiful issue, full of a lot of great writers, poets and artists. I think you will love it when you receive copies.

Dear Quincy,

So much has gone on since we last talked. I enjoyed your last letter; it took me
around the world. Today I watched the memorial for Coretta Scott King. It made
me well up several times. It wasn't just the speeches or the soul stirring choir that
moved me; it wasn't the comforting tones from Maya Angelou or the rhythmic
timbre of the preachers who praised her work that made me want to weep; it was
the very atmosphere and the people in the pews who moved me most of all. I
became homesick, terribly homesick for the ladies in the big hats with slow
nodding heads and knowing smiles. I listened for the calls and responses that
rippled in the air whenever someone spoke some truth and how folks laughed and
amen'd just like any other good Sunday service. There was so much history in that
church today! It took me back to when my dad wore shiny pants and a cocky hat
with a tiny feather in its band. I can hear the music playing and smell hot combs
warming on the stove for the weekly torture of little girl's hair. Who's on the radio?
Ray Charles. He's singing, and so are we. I remembered line dances. I saw Saturday
night card tables littered with cards and beer bottles, bowls of potato chips and
peanuts. I heard my mother's young laughter and the political talk about marches,
church bombings, boycotts and integration. I was very young at the time, but those
days resonate in me tonight. It's amazing how the small moments and everyday
people in my life worked themselves into important landmarks of history.

When I was a child, we lived in New Jersey, and my father would sometimes
entertain himself with a bit of shit-disturbing. He was a physicist with his own
company called Gourdine Systems, later known as Energy Innovations Inc. In his
free time, he loved to start debates with the most disparate characters he could
scare up. He'd match folks up and step back to watch them go at it. Thinking back
on it, it was his form of cock fighting. One of his favorite rivalries to watch existed
between two men: my Uncle Skeets and Amiri Baraka (then known as LeRoi
Jones). My father would drive deep into Newark and bring Skeets up to the house
where LeRoi would be visiting and enjoying his peace. But once Skeets arrived,
my father would introduce a hot topic and then step back to watch. Skeets was a
loud, rambunctious and extremely opinionated man. He prided himself on being a

Negro, and had little patience with this new turn of phrase "Black." He was a card carrying Republican, while Amiri was ready for a new consciousness. Oh how they fought! My father would tip back his chair and laugh at their arguments. He'd laugh until tears came; then he'd drive a sputtering enraged Skeets home.

One day, he and Skeets were driving through the streets of Newark when all of a sudden Skeets demanded that my father stop the car. He sprang out of the car and ran up the street towards a line of rag tag men and young boys lined up military style at attention. Pacing back and forth in front of them was Amiri being a drill sergeant, preparing the ranks for the Revolution! As my father tells it, "They looked like F-Troop but with squirrel rifles!" Old men, the corner drunk, some restless teens and a handful of true militants practiced their turns and presentation of arms. Skeets tried his hardest to disband them, yelling and cussing that their rusty old squirrel guns would only blow up in their faces. I can still hear my father's laughter as he told that story. Those were the early days of the Panthers, when they were just coming to be, and Amiri was introducing the party to the folks in Newark.

I also recall when the cities burned and the police came to our house and surrounded it believing that a bunch of radical Negroes had taken a house hostage. We lived in the suburbs then, in West Orange, New Jersey, when the Newark riots broke out. My father had business associates over to the house for an afternoon party, but when the cab driver dropped off two white people and noticed the house was teeming with Black folks, he called the police, stating that the Newark riots had spread. My father was trying to close a big business deal one moment, and the next a SWAT team swarmed the outside of the house aiming their guns at the heads of the Black men. It was a terrifying and true sign of the times.

My brother, sisters and I became so used to our cartoons being interrupted for days because of assassinations and funerals. Looking back on it now, the TV was constantly beaming turmoil. If a program was interrupted, it surely meant a good man had died: Kennedy, King, Malcolm, Medgar Evers. We saw dogs on short leashes backing young black women against walls, felt the force of fire hoses knocking people to the ground; all of it became common but truly frightening to us. One night my parents went out, leaving us behind with the sitter. Halfway through the night the TV was interrupted by a newscast stating that James Meredith had been shot. My father's name is Meredith, and we being children took everything as literal. Oh the howling that went on in that house! We swore every black father would be killed, and now ours had fallen too. Ironically James Meredith's wife's name was June, same as my mother's. We thought for sure our world had been torn! It was a terrifying and yet historical time when everyday people were standing up for themselves and for each other at the risk of death.

My parents and grandparents straddled a society steeped in blatant racism and oppression while at the same time they experienced the breaking dawn of possibility. They could actually see the fist that beat down so many lives begin to unfurl and relent. They could see great opportunities for their own kids. How invigorating that view must have been! What is most interesting about that time is that no one thought they had to wait for a vote or an elected leader to make a noise that something wasn't fair or equal. People simply stood up and said, "Enough!"

I'm telling you these stories because of how the Iraq war, Katrina, and Coretta's passing have made me look over my shoulder to see where we've all been and how much has been forgotten. I've started writing poems centered around those times when people realized passivity could mean their death. Unfortunately, I don't sense the end of the passivity I feel around me. I try to rally my students, urging them to please pay attention to the irreparable changes taking place in our country. I tell them to get mad and claim their direction. Too many of them seem so numb to me, and there is no collective memory that allows them to see. Some barely recall Desert Storm, and only a smattering were breathing air when Vietnam ended. I feel as if I'm watching a terrible replay, but for many of my students, Iraq, the Supreme Court, and the destruction of the Gulf Coast's culture is just an incident that has no connection to them.

Coretta's memorial on February 6, occurred on the same day that FEMA shut off the money to pay the hotels housing the scattered Gulf Coast victims. On that very day thousands were evicted and officially without an address; therefore, they can no longer be counted. Something's wrong here, and I hope the young LeRoi Jones' are ready for a new consciousness.

So what role do we as poets play in all this? Emerson wrote, "Doubt not, O poet, but persist. Say 'It is in me, and shall out.' Stand there, balked and dumb, stuttering and stammering, hissed and hooted, stand and strive, until at last rage draw out of thee that dream-power which every night shows thee is thine own; a power transcending all limit and privacy, and by virtue of which a man is the conductor of the whole river of electricity." Wish I said that. But it is better that I recognize the truth in it.

When the world seems to tantrum like a baby neglected or creates tyrants and disease out of simpletons, isn't it true that the artists set to their most heaviest work? Like little machines we get to churning creating and saying everything the news refuses to bear or what politicians divert our attentions from. While markets shove nonsense down our throats, in our ears and on our backs, the artists and writers keep recording and warning, hoping the ship might turn. From what I know of history and times, the most unlikely of men and women have caught the reins to stop all sorts of wars, oppressions and evils. Some were kings and rulers but most were everyday civilians tired of sitting still. Some were poets, some were painters and sculptors and some were small town preachers. But in all of them there was a need to act, and they did.

I'm just proud to be in the company of so many poets and artists who aren't afraid to write it down, speak out loud and not care if their lights go out. It gives me hope.

That's where my rant is these days. I've been drawn away from my personal challenges to look up and see how troubled this country is. Now I've got my ear to the ground and I listen for the sounds of rising voices and determined footfalls moving towards yet another stand.

In closing I want to tell you how beautiful the edition of *Black Renaissance/Black Noire* is. I quickly shipped a copy to my mother in Baltimore. It made her very glad and gave her long hours of good reading. The edition was worth its long labor. I look forward to purchasing more editions. I hope your travels are always good ones. You are blessed to have both city and country, cement and neon, and flower and meadow to wander. A change of view feels so good and definitely allows for great writing. I can't wait to read your new experimentations with your work! Enjoy your approaching spring, and I'll talk with you soon.

Blessings,
Traci

Dear Traci,

At the moment I'm in your adopted state, California, down in Los Angeles, doing—you guessed it—readings, workshops and lectures. I'm also dealing with "Hollyweird"[1] people about the screenplay I sold based on my *Miles and Me* memoir. Everything seems to be going well, especially with the poetry end of things. As for the discussions about the Miles movie they too seem to be going well, but with "Hollyweird" one has to just wait and see.

I too watched the funeral of Coretta Scott King and found it very, very moving at times, as well as very political, as it should have been. I found myself trying to get inside President Bush's head as I was watching the proceedings, wondering what he might possibly be thinking as all those deserved political attacks came his way as he sat there for three hours. I know he had to be furious, because he couldn't just get up and leave with much of the nation watching. It was surreal, bizarre, and I thought I might write a poem about it. But in the end, I didn't think whatever I might write could come close to topping what the TV cameras and microphones caught during that event, so I just left it alone.

These are very troubling times we live in, and I think things are going to get far worse before they get better. It hurts me to say this but I feel in my heart that it's true. So with that in mind, I feel that poets and artists must speak the truth from their hearts as they see and know the world they're living in. This has always been the role of committed, serious artists, wherever they have lived in the world. Great art has always been made and written by those poets, musicians and visual artists who live and create in the moment. I know that's what I try to do each and every day I wake up and attempt to write.

It's depressing for me to listen to and watch how many young people adopt a head-in-the-sand attitude about the contemporary political environment they find themselves living in. Perhaps that will change, I certainly hope so, but I'm not

---

[1] "Hollyweird" is an expression some people use to characterize many Hollywood film people.

holding my breath in anticipation that a progressive shift in their political attitudes will take place. I know my own children are too self-centered in pursuit of achieving their own goals to risk saying, or doing anything political—in public, that is, because they say a whole lot in private—that might rub up wrong against the right-wing American status quo. They don't like what's going on but think—and I might add correctly—to say something that might be considered subversive will mitigate against their future goals. It's a quandary we find ourselves in as a nation, but that's the dilemma we're in: between a rock and a hard place.

But we poets—those of us who have the courage to speak out, and I place myself in that group—can speak for the many who are too fearful to do so. Of course we might pay a heavy penalty for doing it but that comes with the territory of being a committed artist, or human being, doesn't it?

I too remember stories from my past that involve both my mother and father, though I didn't witness anything like the episodes/scenes you saw with your father, Uncle Skeets and the young Amiri-Baraka-in-the-making, LeRoi Jones. What great stories! And colorful, and instructive, politically, that is.

My own stories involved baseball players, numbers bankers, other assorted gangsters, weirdos and musicians. My father was a great baseball player, and after my mother divorced him she married a blues bass player, so that's who was hanging around my house: the gangsters, numbers bankers and weirdos just happen to live in our neighborhood.

I remember Sachel Paige, the great black pitcher coming to my house: he came often to see my dad and mother and he was always dressed to the nines. One time he came by dressed again like he had just stepped out of *GQ magazine*, and I ran up to him calling out his name. He picked me up with a wide smile on his face—just as he always did when he saw me—just as I spit out whatever stuff I had been eating, that had turned to goo, and it spilled all over his fabulous shirt and razor-sharp suit. Well, he couldn't believe it, and with a shocked look on his face put me back down on the floor, stepping away from me to survey the damage. My mother who was standing close by picked me up and took me quickly from the scene and scolded me.

I know Satch and my father spoke about it because my dad told me not to ever spit up on Satch again. I must have been about 4. Well, the next time the great man came by I ran up to him again as if nothing had happened, but Satch stopped me this time and held me away from him at arm's length, and with a stern look on his face told me: "Naw, little Troupe, you just stay down there on the floor, because my clothes cost too much for you to be spitting all over them. So you just stay down there on the floor."

And I did. I was hurt to the bone, but Old Satch never let me jump up into his arms ever again. I've been thinking lately that this story would make a pretty good poem if only I could find my way into it without being too mushy. I know it's going to be in my auto-memoir, but I can see it as a poem, too.

Unlike many American cities during the 20th century, St. Louis never burned because Black people never publicly revolted there against the rule of White people: we took our anger out on each other maiming and killing whoever looked like us with alarming regularity and brutality. St. Louis was and still is a gigantic plantation and there's a bunch of ass-kissing Black folks living there, who hate themselves with such a vengeance it's really scary. And it doesn't matter if they are poor or make gazillions of dollars: most keep their mouths shut when it comes to dealing with White folks. It's a sad state of affairs, but it's something I try to deal with in my novel, *The Legacy of Charlie Footman*. It's grist for my fictional mill, something I try to look at on a deep, deep level. But White folks too are in a sorry mental state in St. Louis, as they are all over the country: they just have power, and many have a whole lot of money, though that doesn't mean many of them aren't crippled, or terrible excuses as human beings, just as are many Black people.

I think extreme false religious beliefs have damaged and corrupted the fabric of this country. It's terrible to hear and watch people tearing at each other's throats because of religious difference. It's like we didn't learn anything from the Crusades. The same thing with racism. Sexism. All of this bullshit that we humans continue to dump all over each other. It's a sad, very scary state of affairs.

But for those of us who love it, there still is art and poetry, the beauty of finding a deep way of expressing ourselves through the act of creation. I feel I am blessed to have poetry in my life, and for me to be able to express myself through this magical, ancient art is an act of faith, and is close to a religious epiphany every time I am able to successfully create a poem. I hope you feel the same way, Traci, though deep down I know this is true about you.

It has been a great thing for me to have been involved in this communication with you over the past year. I have learned a lot about myself and I have learned much about you. It has been a blessing for me to have been involved in this creative act with you, and I hope you have enjoyed it as much as I have. I also think we will come out of this exchange being friends for life, carrying a deep respect for one another. In the meantime thank you for helping to bring to the surface things in me I didn't know were there.

I'm on my way back to Guadeloupe three days from now to get a little respite from this pressure cooker that is New York City. Take care of yourself, and all the best.

Quincy

Brenda Iijima & Joan Retallack

Brenda Iijima is the author of *Animate, Inanimate Aims* (Litmus Press, 2007) and *Around Sea* (O Books, 2004). *If Not Metamorphic* was runner up for the Sawtooth Prize and is forthcoming from Ahsahta Press. She is the editor of Portable Press at Yo-Yo Labs (http://yoyolabs.com/). Together with Evelyn Reilly she is editing a collection of essays by poets concerning poetry and ecological ethics titled, *)((eco (lang)(uage (reader))*. She is the art editor for *Boog City,* as well as a visual artist. She lives in Brooklyn, NY where she designs and constructs homeopathic gardens.

Joan Retallack is John D. and Catherine T. MacArthur Professor of Humanities at Bard College. Her books of poetry include *Steinzas en mediation* (Format Américain, 2002), *Memnoir* (The Post-Apollo Press, 2004), *Mongrelisme: A Difficult Manual for Desperate Times* (Paradigm Press, 1999), *How To Do Things With Words* (Sun & Moon Classics, 1998), *Afterrimages* (Wesleyan, 1995), *Errata 5uite* (Edge Books, 1993), *Circumstantial Evidence* (S.O.S. Books, 1985), and *WESTERN CIV CONT'D: AN OPEN BOOK*, an ongoing serial poem

in various formats, including installations and an artist's book (Pyramid Atlantic, 1995). She is one of the foremost interpreters of the work of John Cage and has published numerous essays about his work and a book with him, *Musicage: John Cage in Conversation with Joan Retallack* (Wesleyan, 1996), for which she won the 1996 America Award in Belles-Lettres. The University of California Press brought out her theoretical text, *The Poethical Wager* in 2004 and her *Gertrude Stein: Selections in 2008*.

Brooklyn, New York
September 20, 2005

Dear Joan,

It is so exciting to suddenly have this forum in which we will communicate, con-
spire: I have wanted to approach you about various issues, ideas and thoughts
about modalities of writing but so far the frenzy of daily life added lag.

THE POETHICAL WAGER is plentitudinous! Your work addresses explicitly how
writing manages participatory actions that shake it loose from abject paradigms.
You strike upon a holistic functionality for the diachronic and synchronic—that
they might work in conjunction—fused up and phased. Time and its implications
are not so straightforward and linear as supposed, where Destiny waits at the
(pre)prescribed (ad)vantage point compartmentalized as a microscopic, unap-
proachable bit chained to the horizon. It seems like what you are espousing is a
glittering state (of being, writing) where the charge of varied, swirling particulates
make time as they absorb and release energy (utterance). The powerful project is
the invention of the polymorphous future in an atmosphere distrustful of openness
to multiple—sensual as well as rational—logics, as you state in :RE:THINKING:
LITERARY:FEMINISM: I find myself focusing on formation in your work, instead
of fixating on forms themselves (static, inert) (emphasis on the making, not the
reenacting). The pulse is where situations for language arise (and dissipate, as is
the case with *AFTERRIMAGES*). Or along the craggy edge of meaning as it melts
into each fractal crevice. It seems repressive to maintain that language participates
in language systems only, that language is somehow segregated out of life. For me
this discussion signals a return to an anarchistic/autonomous mode (in the sense
that each body matters)—all-inclusive: waiting not for the behemoth superstruc-
ture to cooperate, but endeavoring to create pathways for our autonomous selves
to link up with the social-ecological fabric.

The designation of thingness seems a culprit, as resisting expanding perceptions—
forcing and determining separations and encapsulations. The liminal is granted
little space. States are favored over transitions. A prejudice against undisclosed,
unrefined matter—but herein lays potentiality! Heidegger acknowledges the
murky position of a thing is in its pre-ontological existence. I notice how your

256

work peruses vectors instead—you make registers within permutation. Elsewhere in your work it is the use of macaronics.

I am reading from *MONGRELISME* now:

> A SENSATION OF FLOATING AT THE MOMENT THE ROAR
> of the roar of the blast ends the silence lifts everything into the air &
> then the whimpering & sobbing & screaming begin Carnation Lily Lily
> Rose four little girls in a garden with luminous paper lanterns in the
> museum & world might intersect in such a way that the the twin pho-
> tons parting to carry their little electro-magnetic packs to different ends
> of the mathematical spectrum of the unexpected in which hue one finds
> impossible calculations the deterministic random the stable unstable
> dissipative and turbulent systems catastrophic theories teeming unknown
> variables this is the start of a sentence and seems to be the end too

If a human were to be inserted into a metal cube that had a breathing and speaking vent the thingness of the cube would tell very little. Thingness can't realize absurd-ity. It seems that our present system of ----------, (this phenomenon of intangible global exchange) relies on properties of apparentness to prop up its power.

Anyway, conscious energy abounds and is not limited to humans. Non-human energy is not as easily aggregated, so is useless in a capitalist system, therefore escaped excessive scrutiny though the symptoms of ecological destruction are felt. I guess this is what is referred to as primitivism. The way *way* back exists in the present—in fact, there is a way in which everything is the same (comprised of) time, the same age. A rock sits there nonchalantly telling a trajectory from beginning(s). I am engrossed in making deeper animate connections. Rapport: ferment: details.

My concern of late has been to study the ways in which Western culture in partic-ular compartmentalizes humans from animals—there is this astounding polemic that exists to disrupt our interaction with animals as *animals*. What got me inter-ested in this again, most recently, was the viewing of *Winter Soldier*, a documen-tary of the testimonials of returning Vietnam veterans. The description of the film from the Walter Reade Theater flyer reads as follows:

On the first two days of February, 1971, one month after the revelations of the Mai Lai massacre, a public inquiry into war crimes committed by American forces in Vietnam was held in the second floor ballroom of a Howard Johnson Motel in Detroit. The event was organized by *Vietnam Veterans Against the War.* . . . Over 125 veterans spoke of atrocities they had witnessed and, in some cases, committed. 'The major that I worked for had a fantastic capability of staking prisoners,' continues one piece of testimony, 'utilizing a knife that was extremely sharp, and sort of filleting them like fish.'

Several of the soldiers spoke of their 'having to become animals' to commit these torturous acts—that they were told to think of the Vietnamese (civilian as well as military) as sub-human, animals, that they had to be eradicated because they were animals. Much of the justification went as follows—ascribing animal(istic) qualities as transformative events that made these killings conceivable. After hurricane Katrina struck, animals were, for the most part abandoned, their lives deemed less significant than humans. And based on class and race, humans are being treated with varying degrees of dignity and concern. The mutual aid that Kropotkin talked about is all but missing from these scenarios. I am interested in this veiled history of the United States as it continually makes solidified attempts to neutralize, control (stolen land from indigenous peoples) and by extension, decimate nature (while existing in and *as* nature simultaneously)—at best natural expanses are understood as ornamentation, at worst, used for their cash value alone without other considerations coming into play. When I think of the war on Iraq, my mind wraps around the impact on the environment—the ecology of the living and how the body count doesn't include this incontrovertible damage. Dropping thousands of tons of depleted uranium on civilian and military populations effects universally the ecosystem—porosity is the word I continually utter in alarm. I try not to pour my experiences through the lenses of eschatology.

I paid particular attention to your statement:

I sometimes wonder whether the attitudes that propel my aesthetic come down to instinctive hope, strategic optimism, or an unaccountably cheer-ful—always precarious—retrofit of despair. Perhaps it's more truthful to say I'm in search of a poesis that wagers on all three in unsettling but syn-ergistic conversation.

It seems you aren't hybridizing so much as interrelating, which seems to me to have social dimensions that interconnect outwardly. Hybridizing would more so bring forward an individualized new One, a more internalized new thing. Later on in the interview with Quinta Slef you say it is the inventors who interest you most . . . not only in the arts but in every discipline. What about cultures that focus the least on invention, whose main emphasis is a flexible, adaptive maneuverability that sustains and is in kinship with an environment? Sometimes I think the impact of Western culture and its built-in burden—big tools, expensive paints, glossy books, the de rigeur plastic plug in computer and the necessary attachments, and all under the heading "property" etc., etc.—a clogging by stuff where could be experience—should be less acquisition-driven. Of course, inventions don't have to involve bulky materiality. John Cage seemed not so much to have invented a way to do without these excesses as remembered and encouraged a way to do so. Every so often I find I am romanticizing Hunter-Gatherer societies—one of the lasting effects of having been raised in a zone of unrestrained nature.

What was your childhood like and do you find the residual of this in your work?

How have your notions of your work changed?

What projects have you taken up of late?

With happy anticipation of your reply!

Yours,
Brenda

Annandale-on-Hudson, New York
October 17, 2005

Dear Brenda,

Your letter is so generous and full, I've wondered how I can adequately respond. It's been an interesting text for me to read several times over. And, first, I want to thank you for it—for your engagement in it with some of my projects. Your own poetic texts have this richness as well, and more! Much to puzzle about amidst arresting darts (Zeno's arrows again?) of what I take to be intensely purposeful clarity. I've loved their presence in the minimalist format of the October *Primary Writing*. The selection there begins almost immediately with a wonderful statement of the nature-culture agon we don't necessarily always recognize as such (agonistic): "You see a beautiful sight / Caused by erosion." I wonder if you're assuming something of the ancient prophetic role of the poet in this work—*Eco Quarry Bellwether*—since the role of bellwether is to both lead the flock and augur the future. Is your use of capital letters to begin every line a statement of wanting to reinscribe or acknowledge certain kinds of poetic traditions as well?

You ended with a series of questions and, as you can see, I'd like to really begin with some of my own about you, but I'll try also to comply with some answers: You asked about my childhood. It was urban and chaotic with eccentric parents in NYC—Chelsea in Manhattan and then an immigrant, working class neighborhood in the Bronx with continued ties to Manhattan since my father lived in The Cornish Arms, a residential hotel on west 23rd St. But it wasn't all city. There were summer vacations in a (then) sparsely populated part of the Maine Coast and my teen years were in the semi-tropical beauty of the Carolina low country surrounding the pre-civil rights meanness of "the south's most civilized city," Charleston S.C.—a beautiful place built by slave labor. My academic training and subsequent interests have been in poetics and philosophy (of language, ethics, science). I'd say that every bit of this experience has affected everything I've done. (It's been conducive to a certain kind of practice-based research and thought experiment and an interest in qualities of attention). A not very interesting truism, I'm afraid. What about your growing up? Where, when, how? Actually, I'd rather that the other things you asked come up in our epistolary conversation as it proceeds.

I like your idea/project of making "animate connections." It does happen in your poetry! This may or may not relate to my interest in invention, but "animate connections" are at the heart of what I take to be poesis—a continual revitalization of language/attention through forms of composing, forms of reading that bring together the sensual and the rational.

So, in reply to your question, I value invention because it must start with noticing a need (probably more so than a desire) and is inextricably linked to a questioning, experimental attitude. I see no part of our world that we are not affecting. A noticing, questioning, inventing of constructive ways of being a non-destructive part of our world is essential—to my mind—to combat conservative smugness and the destructiveness that comes out of a greed for "MY security, MY nostalgia, MY preferred stability." Living in mutual acknowledgment and respect for others is not a simple I-Thou Ah Ha!—as one can see all too well in the Middle East. It requires the invention of new ways of being together, new forms of life, as Wittgenstein puts it, new language games.

I suppose I'm saying that it takes inventiveness to maintain what you so nicely call "a flexible, adaptive maneuverability that sustains and is in kinship with an ['our'?] environment."

In fact, we *are* animals, aren't we?, and like all other species we seem only to rise to the ethical when we contravene those parts of our own nature that are impulsive, on the brink of fear and anger, and drive us toward self-defense and self-interest alone. It is in our nature to be cruel and to kill. A civil society is an amazing, fragile construction built with the help of those other parts of our nature—the capacity to bond with others, to empathize and to love. All these varying capacities make it tough to get along. I have a new puppy right now so I'm experiencing this everyday—in her; in me.

Yours in continuing conversation,
Joan

Brooklyn, New York
January 4, 2006
Alice Coltrane playing in the background

Dear Joan,

Happy New Year!!

I relished your intense, variegated letter. Your positions are energetic and create a positively charged space that opens up for dogma-free conviction. After the onslaught of consumerism (in the face of war, poverty—so ugly and brutal the contrast) accelerated by the holidays, I feel recalibrated when noting the sensitivity of ethical purpose proposed throughout your letter. Thanks for this fortification!

It was lovely to witness your performance of Jackson's piece: *Nuclei for Simone Forti* at the Granary Press book party for the release of Jackson's *Doings: Assorted Performance Pieces 1955-2002*. For me personally, it was such an honor and a thrill to perform pieces that night as Jackson's work has been ever so important to me. Where was my generation (in the audience, as performers), I wondered!

Here's the gist of my background (it feels like fantasy to embark on an account having lived in Brooklyn now for 10 dynamic years). I grew up in North Adams, Massachusetts. My parents' house is situated on the foot of Mount Greylock, so surrounding the house is what seemed like endless forest (you can only hike so far until you hit a road) as a child. The town was and is in the throngs of a severe economic depression (not to mention environmental devastation by the likes of Sprague Electric, a tannery, hat factory, and shoe factories that massively polluted the land and rivers). The population was and is mostly working class of French and Italian descent. I grew up within a conservative set of motifs (which I tried to disband). Although my parents insisted on a stark and stringent protocol religiously, Massachusetts thankfully is a liberal bastion and North Adams specifically has an offbeat, anything goes undertone of wildness (and untampered wilderness) that buoyed my own sense of possibility—Yankee fatalism and somberness notwithstanding. My mother immigrated to the United States from post-war Germany and my father is 1st generation Polish. Though my parents are consumed by a religious fervor their lifestyle is exceedingly quirky and thankfully doesn't echo the fear-based politic of what seems to be a fundamentalist rhetoric prevalent in America presently—the church they attend advocates for gay, lesbian and transgendered ministers and is quite liberal as far as Protestant, First Congregationalism (of the United Church of Christ) goes. Throughout my childhood, my parents opened our house up as a kind of safe haven and open shelter for people from the community to come by and recover (from nervous breakdowns, alcoholism, etc.). My parents were always on call for anyone in any crisis. So the household was teeming with nervous, provocative energy, the aim always therapeutic: advocacy (chaotic for a child!). In the background the timbre, resonance and harmonics caused by my parents' comprehensive classical music collection. We never really embarked on pop culture, my sister and I were dissuaded, notably we didn't have a TV for years. Also, my mother took it upon herself personally to beautify the town—North Adams in the 1970's was a wasted post-Industrial Revolutionary "backwater town" in shambles (it had a very defeatist self-image when contrasting itself to neighboring communities like wealthy Williamstown). This meant that I, as her assistant, would have to (for years) sweep city streets, pick epic amounts of trash out of hurricane fences, chisel weeds out of sidewalk cracks, etc. We were an odd band of helpers because often the people my parents helped would inevitably help along. Was this the Protestant work ethic taken to new civic heights or my mother's own energetic eccentricity, I can't say. These projects were grueling, interesting too—I learned so much about materials! A subproject involved the recycling of all the Urban Renewal refuse that was being wasted. We stacked tons of marble, slate, lumber, cobblestones, etc., in our yard and with this material my mother created gardens throughout the city, within our backyard (a truly grand botanical garden) and finally anyone who commissioned her to landscape architect. Some of these projects spiraled—particularly her commitment to shut-in people. As a child I felt somewhat overwhelmed by her exuberant giving and the time and energy it took to sustain so many people in tentative conditions. (I was liberated when I left for Indonesia as an exchange student my senior year of high school.) This is already leaving out so much, like how my mother also recycled as much as she could from the town landfills, from government welfare rations that went into the trash—it goes on . . . or her predilection for flat stones . . . My father likes to build totemic figures out of found materials and my mother paints on found materials. Joan, I wanted to summarize this background information, but it is impossible!

I am anticipating the ecopanel that Evelyn Reilly and I are hosting at the Bowery Poetry Club in a few weeks. I want to examine how considerations of language are affected by considerations of the environment and vice versa. I am still hung up on *thingness*, it seems drastically clear that the notions like "no ideas but things" need to be abandoned ASAP. I don't mean to single WCW out, but this utterance is emblematic of a crisis at large. Since WWII, at least two hundred new chemical (synthetic) compounds have been entered into the environment, into the language. The ramifications of this epic dumping are almost totally unknown but signs of stress stemming from the careless use and waste of these new substances are manifesting. Classically, what gets affected first biologically is *wildlife* and so is easily ignored by all but a distinct community of scientists, ecologists and civilians. That frogs are commonly growing two heads or two penises that don't function may or may not disturb civilization—or the news is watered down so that the severity of the crisis is not matched by clear description. Clarity about interrelationships comes across via description—a mode that is disparaged. An adjective or adverb is *in connection* with something—it transmits. A noun can be as falsely separate (an object) as intended. By thinking of two bodily analogies: prosthetics and phantom limbs (and resultant pain: causalgia, phantom limb pain and the neuralgias), I am trying to understand how technology and a philosophy of distance (racial, environmental) create paradigms for the varying degrees of health (functionality), or distress (disfunctionality). Language can be a conducive intermediary between time and space, body and mind, and all other dichotomies that disrupt a flow of interconnection amongst the labyrinth organism that is life. Do you have any thoughts on this matter, any suggestions? I am definitely thinking along the lines of your:

> & the world might intersect in such a way that the the twin photons parting to carry their little electro-magnetic packs to different ends of the mathematical spectrum of the unexpected in which hue one finds impossible calculations the deterministic random the stable unstable dissipative and turbulent systems catastrophic theories teeming unknown variables this is the start of a sentence and seems to be the end too

Remembering Animals (the project I'm now working on) has elements of lyricism and sensuality but I must tell you, it is brutal and the words have been blasted into smithereens. Empathizing with what the language is capable of in extreme conditions has led to a scattershot modality as each utterance gets sort of cellular. I'm actively reading Kamau Brathwaite's recent book, *Born to Slow Horses* as well as his older work, for example, *Middle Passages*. Going through Diane Ward's work gives me psychic guidance. What are you working on these days?

A friend sent me the following quotation and it resonates with what you said in your last letter about invention: "If this is not the garden, / allow me to go back, / into the silence where things are invented." Olga Sedakova wrote this. Evidently she is an obscure Russian poet, how obscure I cannot tell . . . . And yes! The egotism, ethnocentrism of "MY" that you point out . . . so much danger in it for its destructive consequences, the MY that wants to urge on Armageddon or some such symbolic mega fiasco as if a sixth extinction will be a sanctified, *holy* occurrence. On a local note, I relish the way Susan Howe recuperates or establishes Emily Dickinson (and to some degree, Gertrude Stein) in her book *My Emily*

Dickinson (how did Emily Dickinson feel in the newly minted town of Amherst, placed neatly on a killing field, her family's heritage (cultural heritage) of replacing forests, indigenous Indian populations for centers of white intellectual institutions (government, law, the studies of these at Amherst College) all accomplished with perseverance, moral certitude—a continuum that has only accelerated, verbing its way through). There is a way in which every person's civic and moral fiber needs to be operative in maintaining a mutually sustaining, healthy world, but what does that moral fiber advocate is always the concern. The Ford Motor Company is soon to release the biggest SUV yet, no!! Land mines dot landscapes ubiquitously. How habitable will life lived in a McMansion be, say in ten years . . .

With kinship and collaborative spirit,
Brenda

Annandale-on-Hudson, New York
April 23, 2006

Dear Brenda,

As I've dated this letter, I realize our correspondence has spanned almost a year. The epistolary impulse clearly doesn't fare very well with the rest of life barging ahead. So I'm glad that this staged correspondence makes it a necessary pleasure. The question you raise about your generation in relation (or absence of relation) to Jackson Mac Low's work interests me, i.e., I wonder what *you* think about it. Sometimes the innovations of a pioneering figure lose their urgency because the new contemporary moment is presenting different kinds of problems and/or because they've been incorporated into the battery of poetic strategies succeeding generations take for granted and/or because they've been met with a critical (negative) response, as have many of the principles of Language poetry. All of that seems healthy and understandable and, yet, in this case premature—because there hasn't yet been widespread use of Mac Low's performance pieces and there's so much to enjoy and learn from them.

My performance from Doings used several of the instruction "cards" called *Nuclei for Simone Forti*, 1961. I was happy about how fresh it felt, how nice the balance between directives and improvisational liberty. It was a vitalizing experience for me to figure out how to realize a performance of these spare texts. I think Jackson's pieces require thoughtful purpose and discipline, as well as humor, otherwise the performers can become "anything goes" silly. I'm planning to use the *Doings* book with students at Bard for one of our performance events next year. JoAnne Akalaitis and I have started a series called *Black Swan Nights* at a local tavern of that name with programs that are put on half by the theater department, half by the poetry program. It's all performance of course, but particularly interesting to notice differences in the poetics of performativity as presented by poets and theater people.

Though I've never heard you read your own work, I imagine—because it's so active on the page, at times so transgenred—that you're after a language that makes things happen, more than, e.g., a meditative approach. I enjoy the sense of your exploratory projects and their surprising vocabularies, and the periodic humor of it: "accounting systems / Where precisely there is a notion like incompletion." You have the ability to make the reader wake up and think. You also make the reader want to trust that you really know what you're talking about—so one can feel one is learning from a poetry that is happily not taking on trivial matters. I tend to think there's no greater responsibility than to be a poet while not by any means claiming it's the greatest responsibility. If only there were an equivalent of the Hippocratic Oath for poets that added to the enjoinder to do no harm a pledge to avoid phantom eloquence.

What you write about your parents enacting their values in the community where you grew up seems pertinent to what you're taking on as poet. You don't say what their professions are, but they sound like people I've known who were committed to lay ministries. Poets can be like that too, active citizens of the polis, lately the globe. It's part of what makes poetry credible (maybe the only thing!)—that it's a vocation, not a profession.

"This is already leaving out so much." I read that and smiled. But I also smile at Beckett's and Cage's sense of giving the unsaid or silence (not the same thing), the most secure place in the work. It's the attempt to tell a straightforward story that brings on the anxiety of incompleteness, isn't it? I feel a kind of vertigo when I try to talk about (explain) any part of my past.

You mention the ecopanel at the Bowery Poetry Club and I'm curious about how your thinking has been developing since then. I agree with your rejection of Williams' injunction. At the same time I wonder, would you change your mind if you thought of words as things? The materiality of language has been an important postmodern construal of modernist objectifications. It does depend on how one defines "thing." And yet, even as words litter our environment, language *is* an environment—is one of many environments we live and breathe in—part of the global chaotic environment of Nature/Culture enjambed, as our species experiences it.

Your interest in reclaiming description to clarify relationships between human action and natural disasters invokes in my mind a sense of the need for widespread scientific literacy, so that the way a cellular structure is changed by chemicals comes to be understood. This is about the actual intimacy of what can seem to be widely removed events—uses of certain chemicals, cells growing in mutant forms. Description here would have to be knowledgeable and methodical and might employ adjectives only sparely. My language paradigm is frankly Wittgensteinian. There are many adjectival language games. The language game of scientifically accurate naturalist description seems to me to fit with a poetics that refuses to accept uncritically the metaphorical baggage of conventional descriptive strategies.

I'm teaching a seminar at Bard this semester called *Poetics of the Experimental Attitude*. We're just now reading Niels Bohr's 1931 essay "Atomic Theory and the Description of Nature." His argument is that, given our (then) new understanding of the quantum of action, we must change the principles of scientific description. We can't, for instance, assume continuity and non-contradiction in our accounts of how photons behave. I think the anathema toward description as a core principle in literature has had in part to do with a somewhat similar realization—as we've noticed greater complexities (including discontinuities and chance elements) in our experiences of the world, the descriptive artifices of "naturalism" (which tend toward illusions of logical completeness and continuity, and "capturing" reality in isolated events) have seemed inadequate, if not misleading. Whether or not that's something about the nature of adjectives, as Stein thought, it is, I think, a legitimate problem. On some other hand, what adjectives bring into the picture is individual impression, subjectivity. The question of how to compose linguistic forms of life that enact responsible subjectivities and concerns about the world, beyond individualistic ego-impulses, may be in part about how to inform one's desires with a heightened knowledge and caring about consequences.

What this has to do with adjectives is not obvious—an interesting puzzle. I've tried to do some work on these kinds of questions in *Memnoir* and in my current project "The Reinvention of Truth," but don't claim to have gotten anywhere with the urgent implications you suggest in your letter. I imagine you'll be investigating such things, among others, in future work.

As you can probably tell from the interrogative cast of much of this letter, you've set me to wondering about a lot of things. I'm glad you're so worried about the mess we (our species) has been making, the skewed values our government sends young men to die for . . . and that you're thinking about how to respond as a poet. I look forward to your future work!

Yours with warm best wishes,
Joan

Brooklyn, New York
June 20, 2006

Dear Joan:

I am slow to reply because of the extenuating circumstances: my 70 year-old mother, the stalwart gardener that she is, chose to prune the crown of a 50 foot white pine tree at sundown. This was common practice for her. This particular tree had been damaged in an electrical storm months earlier and evidently its root system was weakened—the tree fell with my mother in it. I had headed to North Adams for my father's 83rd birthday—inexplicably I changed my plans and left a day earlier than I planned—I found my mom unconscious by the fallen tree with all of its dagger-like sawed off limbs. At first I thought she was hiding on me—that's her kind of humor. She was severely injured: two broken hips and a broken arm. I've been in Massachusetts for the greater part of the last two months, making sure she gets the best medical care, helping my father (he was hit by a truck 3 years ago and is semi-handicapped) and tending to their garden. . . . Needless to say, it is a life-changing happening. She's relearning to walk and is finally able to exert some pressure on her arm. It happens that the life expectancy of the white pine is similar to humans living in the same geological location.

Before drafting this letter to you I was reading Slavoj Žižek's *Organs Without Bodies* and had arrived at the passage where Žižek introduces Spinoza's thoughts concerning power and right. I feel compelled to share it with you. Žižek tells the reader that, "A right is, for Spinoza, always a right to 'do,' to act upon things according to one's nature, not the (judicial) right to 'have,' to posses things. It is precisely this equation of power and right that, in the very last page of his *Tractatus Politicus*, Spinoza evokes as the key argument for the 'natural' inferiority of women":

> But, perhaps, someone will ask, whether women are under men's author-
> ity by nature or institution? For if it has been by mere institution, then we
> had no reason compelling us to exclude women from government. But if
> we consult experience itself, we shall find that the origin of it is in their
> weakness. For there has never been a case of men and women reigning
> together, but wherever on the earth men are found, there we see that men
> rule, and women are ruled, and that on this plan, both sexes live in
> harmony. But on the other hand, the Amazons, who are reported to have
> held rule of old, did not suffer men to stop in their country, but reared
> only their female children, killing the males to whom they gave birth.1 But
> **if by nature women were equal to men, and were equally distin-
> guished by force of character and ability, in which human
> power and therefore human right chiefly consist; surely among
> nations so many and different some would be found, where
> both sexes rule alike, and others, where men are ruled by
> women, and so brought up, that they can make less use of their
> abilities. And since this is nowhere the case, one may assert with
> perfect propriety, that women have not by nature equal right
> with men**: but that they necessarily give way to men, and that thus it
> cannot happen, that both sexes should rule alike, much less that men
> should be ruled by women. But if we further reflect upon human passions,
> how men, in fact, generally love women merely from the passion of lust,
> and esteem their cleverness and wisdom in proportion to the excellence of
> their beauty, and also how very ill-disposed men are to suffer the women
> they love to show any sort of favour to others, and other facts of this kind,
> we shall easily see that men and women cannot rule alike without great
> hurt to peace. But of this enough.

(The bolded part of the paragraph is the section Žižek quotes, I went back to the chapter of the book in its entirety to see what I'd find. . . .)

One of the most baffling and infuriating aspects of this is that his statement is BLA-TANTLY UNTRUE. Spinoza's statement flashes across our eyes as if it were contemporary—constantly revived by male philosophers like Deleuze and now Žižek—does no one bother to fill in these egregious blanks of awareness! Ignoring the historical-social truths allows fantastical speculative philosophical analysis to continue. . .

I've compiled a quick list (it most certainly is incomplete because I spent less than an hour on the internet) of women who ruled prominently between the years 1640-1670, 1670 being the year in which *Tractatus Politicus* was published! Perhaps Spinoza tried to repress from himself the fact that numerous women in Africa had ruled. His book was written during the (Enlightenment) period when Europe was actively involved in the trade of slaves. In fact Queen of Matamba, West Africa, (Nzingha) lived from 1582-1663. As I researched her accomplishments I came across this depiction:

> She was a brilliant military leader who fought for thirty years in struggles against slave-hunting Europeans. The Jagas, (which she was a member of), were a militant group that acted as a human shield against the Portuguese slave traders. Her struggles compelled others to take a strong stand against imperialist, slaving interests.

His only mention is of the Amazons who "are reported to have held rule of old." And what about *all of the other* female rulers, for example: Amina, Queen of Zaria, a province of Nigeria, Candace, Empress of Ethopia, Cleopatra VII, Queen of Kemat, Dahia-Al Kahina, Queen Kahina, Hapshepsut, Queen of Kemet, Makeda, Queen of Sheba, Nefertari, Queen of Kemet, Nefertiti, Queen of Kemet, Tiye, Nubian Queen of Kemet or Yan Asantewa of the Ashanti Empire? Here is a partial list of the women who held power from 1640-1670 in Europe, Asia and The Americas:

Around 1640: Queen Regnant Pea of Morning (Myanmar-Burma)
C. 1640-ca. 60: Moäng Ratu Dona Maria Ximenes da Silva of Sikka (Indonesia)
1640-49: Princess-Abbess Sedonia von Oldenburg-Delmenhorst of

Herford (Germany)

1640-53: Guardian Dowager Countess Juliana Elisabeth zu Salm-Newville of Reuss zu Schleiz (Germany)

Until 1641: Princess-Abbess Agnes Elisabeth von Limburg und Bronckhorst of Elten (Germany)

1641-75: H.H. Paduka Sri Sultana Ratu Safiat ud-din Taj ul-'Alam Shah Johan Berdaulat Zillu'llahi fi'l-"alam binti al-Marhum Sri Sultan Iskandar Muda Mahkota Alam Shah of Aceh (Indonesia)

1641-94: Sovereign Duchess Claire-Clémence de Maillé-Brézé of Fronsac (France)

1641-92: Sovereign Princess Marie de Bourbon of Condé-en-Brie (France)

1641-ca. 50: Princess-Abbess Isabelle van Kerckem of Munsterbilzen, Dame of Wellen, Haccourt, Hallembaye and Kleine-Spouwen (Belgium)

1641-44: Reigning Abbess—General Francisca de Beaumont y Navarra (Spain)

1641-42: Dowager County Sheriff Maren Skram of Mariae Kirkes Domprovsti (Norway)

C. 1642: Ruler Karenga I Pucu of Sanrabone (Indonesia)

1642-4: Lieutenant-Governor Madame Colles of Alderney (England)

1643-51: Regent Dowager Queen Anne d'Austrice of France

1643-5: Regent Dowager Duchess Anna Eleonora von Hessen-Darmstadt (Germany)

1643-64: Countess Leonora Christine (Denmark)

1643-76: High Sheriff Lady Anne Clifford of Westmoreland (United Kingdom)

C. 1643-46: Sovereign Countess Elizabeth zur Lippe-Alverdissen of Schaumburg (Germany)

C. 1643: Princess-Abbess Henrica Raitz von Frentz of Brutscheid (Germany)

1644-ca. 57: Queen Regnant Cockacoeske of the Pamunkey in Virginia (USA)

1644-53: Princess-Abbess Barbara I Weglin of Baindt (Germany)

1644-45: Reigning Abbess-General Ana María de Salinas (Spain)

1644-46: Dowager Sheriff Anne Bek, Laholm Len in Halland, Denmark (Now Sweden)

1645: Regent Dowager Empres Yudokia Lukyamanova Stresneva of Russia

1645-54: Dowager

His statements are concurrent with the European witch hunts and those taking place in New England. I've been reading Christa Wolf's impressive collection of essays (*The Author's Dimension*) and I found this passage:

> We all know that at the beginning of the modern era women were burned at the stake in such numbers that many authors have been moved to compare the witch burnings to the Jewish Holocaust of our own century. But how much do we know about the reasons the inquisitors gave for these executions? Two noted authorities recorded their opinions in the notorious *Hammer of Witches* (the *Malleus Maleficarum*): women in reality are "imperfect animals"—the book says—and are completely delivered to "fleshly desire . . . which is insatiable in them . . . . This is why they consort with demons, to satisfy their desire . . . . No wonder if more women than men have been found to be polluted with the heresy of witchcraft." And the men must have experienced the threat emanating from these women as aimed directly against their potency: for the book says that women could also afflict men with "sexual" disorders through witchcraft.

This excerpt is taken from a lecture she delivered at a conference of the *Work Group on Psychosomatic Gynecology* held in Magdeburg in 1984.

Coinciding with these witch hunts Europe experienced repeated epidemics. Mary Kilbourne Matossian's book *Poisons of the Past* highlights the fact that the incidence of witchcraft persecution is distributed in proportion to ergot poisoning. Cold rainy winters cause rye (the staple of European diets) to form into an alkaloid poison that, when ingested, causes bizarre erratic behavior. She states:

> Prior to 1650 it was commonly believed that a supernatural being, benign or malign, was the cause of ergotism. In the century that witnessed the beginning of the scientific revolution, however, many educated people began to seek natural causes for the symptoms. New labels were given to the disease—"hysteria," "vapours," "hypochondria," "nervous fever," "fits," and "frenzy." But the search for natural causes did not succeed for over a hundred years.

I wonder the extent of this era's cognitive/emotional duress due to poisoning caused by synthetic chemicals being dumped without scrutiny into the ecosystem.

How does the social and intellectual space become defined by this—and how are these considerations gendered? The binary of nature/culture breaks down in the face of nature's equally active involvement with culture, at least in my observation. I find it difficult to see nature as inert or passive. Elizabeth Grosz evokes this clearly:

> If we understand the relations between nature and culture as a relation of ramification and elaboration, or in the language of science, as a form of emergence or complexity, rather than one of opposition, the one, nature, providing both the means and the material for the other's elaboration, and the other, culture, providing the latest torsions, vectors, and forces in the operations of an ever-changing, temporally sensitive nature, cultural studies can no longer afford to ignore the inputs of the natural sciences if they are to become self-aware.

Nature has been gendered feminine and this association has been used as a justification by "those with various paternalistic, patriarchal, racist, and class commitments to rationalize their various positions" (Grosz). How do you parse this Joan? How can feminism link up with issues concerning the environment? Grosz makes this vivid declaration:

> With the exception of the ecology movement, with its eco-feminist and eco-philosophy off-shoots, with which I am loath to be identified, virtually all forms of contemporary political and social analysis continue this tradition of ignorance of, indeed contempt for, the natural, which today remains identified with either passivity or inertia.

Nature, seen in the light of Spinoza's utterances is indeed spurious, explosive ground. Hurricane Katrina was hardly a passive happening. Global warming and species extinction are certainly not inertness. I don't think these events can easily be depicted in romantic terms. Romantic distancing is certainly moot. As Tim Flannery, a mammalogist and paleontologist argues in his new treatise, *The Weather Makers*, the Darfur genocide is essentially a function of climate change, as the desiccating desert land in western Sudan drives nomadic herders into areas of sedentary agriculture and into conflict with farmers for scarce resources. In your last letter you said that there is a need for widespread scientific literacy—I hope you'll take this up in more detail. Please tell me more about your project, "The Reinvention of Truth"!

I can't wrap up this letter—the provocative sparks keep me humming—thinking about how you might respond, how these thoughts might be converted into direct action/activism.

Cheers!
Brenda

Annandale-on-Hudson, New York

December 10, 2006

Dear Brenda,

First of all, I'm very glad to know, from our interim emails, that your obviously remarkable mother has recovered from her injuries.

Her accident would be quite spectacular for anyone, but for a 70 year old woman—now that it's turned out alright—I 'd like to say it's quite impressive.

I feel certain that at any given moment in the US and EU there are more men up in trees than women. (I restrict the territory because I'm prepared to learn, albeit with surprise, that in other regions on our planet it's the other way around.)

In Ovid, quite a few women are turned into trees because of lusts and desires gone astray, but that's a different (quite fascinating) matter. From the point of view of Western rationalism, it is clearly more powerful to climb a tree or to prune a tree, than to be a tree—A tree whose every limb is bent / To unfold Nature's argument.

The non-ascension (except for the Virgin Mary) and/or fall of woman in the eyes of men is a staple of Western history and all the East Asian history I know. It's hard for me to believe that it's been significantly different in a good deal of Africa, given traditions of female genital mutilation and other conventions that leave the majority of women powerless over their own bodies and in servitude to men. Of course, one would have to look at this by surveying one tribal culture at a time.

That there have been particular contexts where particular women had power over men (Elizabeth I of England is a clear case in point) is undeniable; but I think it's also undeniable that there has been a chronic historic imbalance of political power favoring men for all of written history. This seems obviously to be linked to cultural and historical positions of women in relation to family planning and birth control. (Elizabeth I was the Virgin queen!) Before the late 1800's married women of all classes routinely underwent as many as twenty pregnancies during their lifetimes. The stories of Mary Wollstonecraft and Mary Shelley are remarkable wakeup calls. Childbirth (early and fatal) accounted for a large part of who they were. (Wollstonecraft died two weeks after giving birth to Mary; Mary began *Frankenstein* at the age of nineteen nursing a second infant who would die less than a year later.) It's shocking that it wasn't until the late 1960's, early 70's (in the industrialized West) that women gained the possibility for complete control over their (our) reproductive functions.

History provides such a deeply inscribed template of male domination, the fact that the dominant authority of men went, until recently, largely unchallenged is not very puzzling. The cultural vectors were all aimed at keeping women aware that their first duty was to bear and nurture their children and (another sense of "bear") their men.

What's more puzzling to me is why the post-pill and post Roe v. Wade (1973) period hasn't been more revolutionary in terms of women assuming/creating powerful gender identities and roles. A long-range view of the puzzle is very forcefully articulated in the well-known essay by the anthropologist Sherry Ortner, "Is Female to Male as Nature is to Culture." Ortner points out something depressingly similar to what Spinoza was saying in the quote you found in ZŽ's book (one I haven't read), though without the implicit moral judgement and with a good deal of anthropological evidence that has been attacked by some critics since, but not by any means discounted.

Questions that come to mind: Is Žižek agreeing with Spinoza's attribution of natural weakness to women? This is hard to believe. Or, another way of putting this, to what use is he putting the passage from Spinoza? I'm also puzzled about your assumption that Spinoza would/could know what was going on in African tribal politics in his time? What website does the list you quote come from? I wonder why it was assembled and I wonder, quite frankly, about its reliability if its designed to prove that women had substantial power over men as well as women. Abbesses, for instance, had power only over other women as far as I know.

Ortner points out that in every known culture to-date (the article was originally published in 1972 but she continues to stand by her findings) women are identified with nature, men with culture and the cultural identification is, by definition, more highly valued. You rightly question this binary. There is a healthy tradition of questioning it in the making. But it nonetheless has been pervasive. (Binaries seem to be the intellectual agonism of our species.) The accoutrements of being "closer to nature" are of course cooking, child rearing, emotional (or, as the ancient Greeks thought of it, animal) intelligence, and even some of the characteristically "feminine" diminutive (childlike and/or submissive) traits so often trained into women—high-pitched, childish voice (undescended voices analogous to unde-scended testicles in men?); dressing in ways that impede vigorous full movement of the body, and/or that reveal enough flesh to reassure spectators there's been no hostile takeover by "disembodied" mind.

There was an interesting article on shoe styles in the *National Geographic* recent-ly. The writer pointed out that women's shoe styles throughout history and across cultures have been a kind of index to what women have not been allowed to do (e.g., in certain Chinese aristocratic cultures, to walk comfortably or even without assistance). Stiletto heels, recently back in style, are dangerous and inhibiting. They literally weaken the stride of the woman who wears them. Interesting, no?

Imagine a man delivering a lecture teetering on high heels with a little skirt that requires clamping the legs together and taking very small steps to and from the lectern. You'd be imagining a man in drag. The trouble with gender binaries is that they are the extreme cases at either end of a biological continuum of sexual char-acteristics and those extreme cases are caricatures. The hyper-feminine woman is as much a drag-queen as the man who takes on that role.

Luckily, we have awareness of many more than two gender possibilities now; unluckily, the preceding "we" doesn't include the major part of our society.

So, to my mind, not enough has changed over time with our tight little cluster of dangerous isms—sexism, racism, ageism (particularly with respect to women). What can we do about this? I think poets should be offering intelligent (if not always intelligible) and inventive alternative visions for human society. Linguistically enacted thought experiments of various kinds. Alternatives to entrenched language usage that perpetuates current power asymmetries and unwarranted assumptions are always a good start. Language is a powerful directive in our forms of life.

But to be useful to even the small audiences poets court, we should be among the smartest, best informed, most consistently thoughtful, intellectually responsible of the culture—i.e., do our utmost to know as much as we can about what it is we're exploring as poets. With all that, we need to develop powerfully informed intuitions about language that come partly from courageous purposeful play (apart from official logics). All in the service of lucid and startling poetics that are more than impulsive self-expressions.

The planet is being killed by self-absorbed competitive capitalists supporting (mainly Euro-American) lifestyles that depend on the oppression of women (still) and dark-skinned peoples (still) and the death of many forms of hope. When John Cage wrote in his manifesto, "The History of Experimental Music in the United States," (published in *Silence*) that in his view we must not seek success, fame, money, but must do what needs to be done at our moment in history, he was and continued to be an artist whose energies were so entirely devoted to understanding what he was doing and why—to extensive study—that he had little time for developing career strategies.

Because we live, generation by generation, in somewhat different "contemporary moments," members of each generation have to figure out what they feel needs most to be done. Something one can only discover in the development of one's own (and communal) poetics.

I wonder what you would like to be contributing as a poet. The perils—wars, global warming, racist perpetuation of exploited underclasses, gender struggles— are all obvious. What isn't obvious is the genre struggles that need to be a vital part of all this turmoil—struggles that can through their poethical force give cause for improbable optimism.

With curiosity and all good will,
Joan

Dana Teen Lomax & Claire Braz-Valentine

Dana Teen Lomax is the author of *Currençy* (Palm Press, 2006) and *Room* (a+bend, 1998), a chapbook which was awarded the San Francisco Foundation's Joseph Henry Jackson Award. She is a fourth generation Californian who teaches poetry and writing in a number of institutions and serves as the Interim Director of Small Press Traffic Literary Arts Center in San Francisco. Her writing has been supported by the California Arts Council, the Marin Arts Council, the Peninsula Community Foundation, the Academy of American Poets, and others. Recent work appears in *War & Peace 3* (O Books, 2007), *Bay Poetics* (Faux Press, 2006), *sonaweb*, *Dusie*, *580 Split*, *mem*, *Shampoo*, *Moria*, and elsewhere. Currently she is making *Q* and *Disclosure*, two book-length experimental documentary pieces, and writing a series of poems called *Shhh! Lullabies for a Tired Nation*. She lives in San Quentin, California with her daughter and husband.

Claire Braz-Valentine lives in Paradise, California. She conducts writing workshops with incarcerated writers through the California Department of Corrections' Arts-in-Corrections Program. She is a widely anthologized poet. Her plays have been produced in New York, Los Angeles, across the United States, in Finland, Greece, Italy, and Canada, and published by Samuel French and Smith & Kraus. She has been a freelance writer for both children's and adult fiction and non-fiction, and a newspaper columnist. She has worked as a playwright in residence through the California Spectra Program in middle schools, taught through the Poets in The Schools Program and also through the University of California, Santa Cruz Extension, and Butte College.

Dear Claire,

I'm really glad to be in touch with you again. It feels like so long ago when I was living in that little room in the back of your Santa Cruz house, when we were swapping cigarettes (we've both quit, yes?!) and watching late night TV. I remember one station ran a political biography on Bob Dole and you were all pissed off. You said something like, "Damn it! They're actually trying to make me like the guy." It's been about 10 years since then, and I'm happy to be rereading your plays, poems, and essays. I wonder if I would have pursued poetry if we hadn't met. I love my work and the people I know because of writing; I owe a great deal of this to you.

And I'm a mom now. Una's always in the backdrop wanting me to read *Fantasy Beasts* again, "inside out" her dress, or just hold her. I know you raised three boys pretty much on your own and kept writing. Is that part of the reason your work has often been overtly political—your boys? (I'm thinking particularly about the Susan B. Anthony and Amelia plays, the more recent "Open Letter to John Ashcroft," and your poem "To Laura Bush.") I've noticed a different level of urgency in my concern for social justice since having Una; I can't tell whether it's because things have gotten so fucked up and far to the right or whether having a child has been the key factor in my shift in perception. Probably both.

In the midst of the "war on terror," I've been questioning again the efficacy of poetry in the social sphere, at least in this country. Here we are with a second term of George Bush, wars raging, the death penalty firmly in place in California, creationism on the rise; the planet's dying. In a recent note you wrote, "it is our mandate as poets to record it all. We must go out into the world and feel the pain and then write about it." I agree, but to what end? I've been thinking about the many poetry anthologies: Joris & Rothenberg's *Poems for the Millennium*, Hamill's *Poets Against the War*, Forche's *Against Forgetting*, Hoover's *Norton Anthology of Postmodern American Poetry*, Waldman's *Civil Disobediences*, Sloan's *Moving Borders*, this one. When all's said and done, do these books serve the same social function? It's unclear to me. Is protest in poetry record-keeping? I'm haunted by the recent events in Ukraine. Incredible. Where are our masses? I know change is incremental, but I'm losing faith.

A good friend, Richard, is certain that the arts are inadequate tools for any real social change. When talking about artists, he likes to say, "Resist bourgeois scum in their ruthless search for authenticity," and "Your consciousness is formed by withholding food for money." Part of me thinks he's right.

These questions remind me of when I first started teaching in the prison system. You'd given me some great lesson plans and a lot of reassurance. You showed me the Godzilla poem you wrote for the guys getting out. I had unreal expectations. I believed (and to some extent still believe) that the arts could change the inmates' lives and that it would help keep them out of prison. I thought that the William James Association's Prison Arts Project mission statement was above reproach: that creative risk-taking and high quality arts instruction would offer incarcerated men and women the tools to stay out of prison and use their creative energies in socially constructive ways. I had an outstanding group of poets at DVI (Deuel Vocational Institution); they'd been together for years, were excellent writers, and many of them had release dates. When I was teaching there, I was in the second trimester of my pregnancy and hopeful as hell.

Now it is clear to me just how naive I was. Although I still absolutely believe in the restorative abilities of the arts, I'm just more realistic about the social and economic realities that the incarcerated face. Just a few months after their release, all but one of the five inmates from that DVI class that had been on the streets were all back inside. Soon after finding this out, I read Angela Davis's "Masked Racism: Reflections on the Prison Industrial Complex": "Imprisonment has become the response of first resort to far too many of the social problems that burden people who are ensconced in poverty . . . Homelessness, unemployment, drug addiction, mental illness, and illiteracy are only a few of the problems that disappear from public view when the human beings contending with them are relegated to cages."

One of the best writers in our group struggled with reading. Another wasn't receiving treatment for mental illness, because he was (rightfully?) suspect of the system. One of the guys told me that he hadn't had a visitor for five years; he said, "mama doesn't like to drive in fog." Several of the inmates were admittedly "self-medicating." These men are up against far more than my poetry class might remedy. Yet I'm sure art does change the quality of a life. I wouldn't be able to live here at San Quentin (benefiting from an institution that kills people), if I didn't know it to be true. I still teach in prisons. But is there something more useful I could be giving the guys? Did you have these feelings in Soledad? Because I understand that poetry can be limited in its ability to alleviate suffering, I am committed to other forms of community involvement. And I realize it's not an either/or proposition, but the questions remain.

Related to these questions of poetry's influence are questions of language. Several mentors at SFSU insisted that poetry must not be decorum on culture. They discussed the tyranny inherent in structures of language and syntax; they showed how words, their histories and common use, serve to perpetuate oppressive understandings of experience and the world. We read Celan. We read Oppen and Stein. We read Brathwaite, Olsen, and Cha, writers all trying to reorder language, break it, expose its agendas and misgivings. Then there are my first loves: Adrienne Rich, Anne Sexton, June Jordan, T.S. Eliot, Frank O'Hara, and Walt Whitman. Informed by these projects, the manuscript I've been working on for a while now, *Currenȼy*, struggles to be a book that my brother can read and grok while also taking on the project of challenging common diction and the development of meaning. That's the poetics I've been working under.

On the page and in practice, I read in your work a conscious decision to use everyday language as a pragmatic tool. It is as if you are working within the system to change it. You read in community centers, in art studios, in libraries, in national readings, in pubs. In your workshops, you deconstruct a wide range of literary experiments in all genres, but continually you come back to questions of "access." As in your poem to Laura Bush:

> Who wants to hear about the Mother of All Bombs
> which we will drop on the mothers of Bagdad?
> There are better things to write about.
> Laura Bush tells us to go away,
> If we can't say anything nice, don't say anything at all.
> Laura Bush, first lady librarian, knows about these things
> knows that poets have always been the canaries in the coal mine
> And she knows the poets are lining up now singing their heads off
> because they know
> what's coming down the shaft just a few feet away . . .

I read this poem with the clients in Napa and you were their hero! One of the therapists said, "This is how I feel, but I didn't know how to say it." Your writing reaches people. Remember the scene in *Harold and Maude* when Harold says something like, "You really love people, don't you?" And Maude says, "They're my species." There's this tone in your writing. Like Whitman, like Oppen, you are talking to your kind. And the work is brave. Recently a great poet in San Francisco read and when I asked her how it went afterwards she said she could tell that her peers were a little uncomfortable with her references to motherhood, as if it isn't hip enough, isn't "in." She felt that talking about raising children makes the work "lite" somehow in their minds. In your work, you champion these issues.

I feel a bit anxious about this discussion because it flirts with a "schools of poetry" rehash. I saw a lot of "I'm an experimentalist—have a cigar" attitude in graduate school. And an equal amount of disdain from writers who thought some innovative poets "needed composition classes." In the years since college, it has been odd and disappointing to realize that there are nationally recognized poets whose ideologies supercede their abilities to communicate with writers not of their ilk. Weird. Ultimately, I've learned that the categories aren't so useful and that Harryette Mullen is right when she talks about "shared aspirations of social and aesthetic movements that envision a better world." She writes, "While I celebrate the differences that create distinct aesthetic preferences, I seek to overcome the social segregation that enforces aesthetic apartheid." This makes a lot of sense to me.

Since my work has changed radically since we worked together and because I never explicitly asked, I'm wondering: what is your philosophy of language? How much do you consider audience/access in the making of your poems?

Well, it's late. Una's sleeping, but is an early bird. It kicks my butt when she gets up before 7:00 a.m., and I'm fully expecting this tomorrow. Just a last thought. Steve and I have a bookmaking friend named Beth Thielen (do you know her from The William James Association?) who's a visual artist and has worked on edible art projects. One of the things she has done is to letterpress words into organic produce while the plants are still young and watch them distort and expand as the vegetables grow. A while back she stamped a Chris Desser quote, "larger than our commerce, larger than ourselves" into lettuce leaves which she later ate and served to friends. Maybe on a much grander scale this is utopic. To feed ourselves completely. Any suggestions on how to get there?

I love you Claire. Hope these holidays are the best yet.

Yours,
Dana

Paradise, California
February 14, 2005

Dearest Dana,

What a blessing to be part of your wonderful project and how proud I am to work with you individually. Oh yes, I do well remember when, for a short time, you lived in the little room in my garden, six blocks from the beach in Santa Cruz. What a joy it was for me, the mother of three grown sons who never had a daughter. How I loved seeing you come up the deck stairs in the morning to the main but tiny house, saying to me, "I slept so hard last night." Even then before you had allowed yourself the title of "poet," you were speaking in poetry. Even now, when I sleep well, I think of you, and I say also to myself, "I slept hard." And yes, it's been many years since I gave up smoking, although when I quit I thought I might never write again.

There is so much I could tell you about poetry and what it has meant to me in my life. I think though, I want to start by saying every poet has his or her view of what it means to be a poet. Each of us differs from the other, just as each painter, or photographer, or sculptor differs. I do not think there is one right way to look upon the reasons people write poetry or the way poets use language.

For me, my poetry is and has always been the lens through which I view and interpret the world. But I find this time now extremely difficult. We live in an age where the horror of the tsunami is broadcast into our homes with visions of Asian children drowning, and we live with the daily count of death in the war. Somehow, being an American poet during this time becomes the heaviest of burdens. I see my mandate as a poet to record. It is what I must do. Without words or comments on the pulse of the world as I see it, I feel like a camera, unused, gone dead in a drawer.

I am so very troubled by your friend Richard's comments about art and how it cannot affect social change. Perhaps he himself is not an artist to make the accusations that "consciousness is formed by withholding food for money." I find that such a curious statement, perhaps because I was a child of the poor. I wonder if this comment by your friend comes from his experience, either by practicing art or by living poor. I am a poet and I have gone without much money much of my life. There are many things in life I can live without, but I cannot live in this world without poetry.

Poetry has always been a powerful tool for social change. Why is it so many countries under oppression imprison their poets? In 1988, a year before the Tiananmen Square Massacre, I had the pleasure of meeting two young poets from China. As they shared their poems with me they told me that probably by the end of the coming year they would be imprisoned. Perhaps the Chinese government saw it differently than your friend Richard. Perhaps social change can result from a poet's words.

I remember reading my anti-war poetry on the steps of the quad at San Francisco City College during the Vietnam War. A well-dressed, clean-shaven young man held a "cigarette pack" up to his eyes and took my photo with a hidden camera. Perhaps also our own government thinks poetry might cause social change. Maybe the reason Laura Bush turned away the *Poets for Peace* from the White House was because she feared the power of the poet.

This of course brings up your questions about the work you and I do in the prisons. I felt so sad when I read your words about how "naive" you think you are when you grapple with the hope art will change inmates' lives. Of course it changes their lives Dana. I have sat in hundreds and hundreds of poetry workshops with inmates in almost every maximum-security prison in the state of California. I have worked with the most hardened of criminals, with murderers and rapists, with drug dealers and smugglers. I have written poetry with the women of Chowchilla prison, with women who killed their abusive husbands, and the young mother who accidentally killed her own baby. I have sat behind the razor wire in Juvenile Hall and written poetry with kids as young as nine years old who have done horrible things in their short lives. I have given out probably a thousand pencils and a tower of blank paper to the trembling hand of the offender who is drying out from drug overdose, alcohol abuse, or trying to settle into his or her state-issued psychotropic drug prescription.

From what little I know about the parole system and the difficulty parolees have finding employment and housing, when the only employment they ever knew was pimping, prostitution, or drug sales, I can't even imagine how poetry could affect the recidivism rate. What poetry can give them, however, is a way for once in their lives, to write about their fears, to finally put down on paper those terrible feelings of loss and waste and despair.

So many times over the years I have had new inmates walk into my workshop and say, "Well I'm not a poet, but I'd like to sit in and maybe learn how to write." I always tell them. "By the power vested in me, I now pronounce you a poet." In my deepest core of beliefs I know I am right. Everyone who wants to write poetry is a poet. The call comes to them like music running through their minds. The words haunt them. They just haven't had the chance or the permission to spend time on it. I feel very strongly about this. Some poets are blessed with more talent than others, but if someone feels the desire to sing, they should not be silenced simply because their voice is not as perfected as another's. When we are writing poetry, we are singing the songs of our hearts.

I think the greatest gift we as poets can give to those behind bars is their dignity and the opportunity for them to use words as a path to their deepest feelings. I remember one specific day in Soledad Prison. An inmate I will call Dave, about forty years old, exceptionally handsome and muscular, attended the workshop for months and just listened. He was convicted on a drug charge and close to parole. Then he began to write love poems to his wife. Week after week, the poems got more and more amorous, how he would take her in his arms finally, after five years. He showed us pictures of her, a pretty little woman smiling at the camera. Then about a month before he was released Dave came to class and his face was all swollen. It was obvious he had been crying. He sat silently and no one asked him what was wrong. That wasn't our role there. After about an hour Dave said he had to read something. He got up in front of that class of the men in blue, his peers, those hardened convicts, and read a poem about how he had lied to all of us about his wife, about how she had divorced him a year ago and then married another man. As he read, his hands began to shake and the tears flowed down his beautiful face. And he kept reading. He read about how his mother had left him when he was a child and how his father beat him and told him he was stupid and ugly. As he read, he cried and cried and the tears just rolled down his face onto his poem, and the men in that class sat as still as stone. Dave struggled with his words and his pain. Then he finished. He put his paper down and looked out over the silent class. I took a moment and then said, "What you just read to us took more courage than anything you will ever have to do in your life. I commend you for your strength."

Then something beautiful happened, a very old convict who was incarcerated for several murders walked up to Dave and put his arms around him and held him, and said, "It's okay to cry man. We're all crying in here." Then one by one each of the students stood and applauded him. Some went up to him, slapped him on his back or gave him a hug. When he finally went to take his seat my own face was covered in tears. He stopped by me and said these beautiful words, "Why weren't YOU my mother?" In a strange way, at that time I felt like his mother. Before he met me he had never written a poem in his life.

This thing I know. When those inmates are with us in our workshops, we open up the doors of their minds. When they return to their cells they walk with dignity. They carry their notebooks and their pencils like medals. In the dark of night they write, in the middle of the day they write, when they cry they write, when they are afraid they write, and when they are angry they write. Writing gives them the tools to cope with their lonely and terrifying lives. We cannot take the burden of guilt and pain away, but we can help them lay the burden down for just a little while.

While we are there with them, working on their words, giving them the freedom of their minds, welcoming their thoughts, building the bridge that only poetry can build, they are model inmates. They are not interested in running with the bad guys in prison. One inmate told me that groups of inmates in prison are called "cars." He said there's the druggy car, the weight lifter car, the card-playing car, the gangbanger car, and then there's the poetry car. He said all the inmates in the poetry car stood together in the yard and read poems to each other. He said no one ever challenged them or threatened them. He said the poets were the scribes of the prison, that for a pack of cigarettes or a couple of candy bars or some Top Ramen, they would write a personalized mother's day card for an inmate to send home or a birthday card or love poems. The poets are treated with respect and they act with respect.

I know I have not answered your questions about my philosophy of language. I do not know if I have one. I am the daughter of a Portuguese longshoreman and an Irish housewife. I am a second generation American. I have never been to college, although by now I have guest lectured in many and taught for UC Extension. I got married when I was eighteen and divorced when I was 37 and have never been married since. Poetry has been my crutch, my spirituality, my savior, my in-road and my exit. I cannot imagine a day in my life without reading a poem, anyone's poem. My house is filled with poetry. I write the way I speak and I speak the way I did when I was raised on Potrero Hill in San Francisco. Poetry has played the most important role for me in plays. The highest compliment a theater critic can give me in a review is that my plays are poetic. And yes, I do think of the audience when I write. I think of them standing on the docks of the city. I think of the winos I knew as a child who leaned against the buildings on my way to school. I think of the inmates who will never see a night sky except through bars. I think of my children, my grandchildren, and the grandchildren they will have eventually. I think of the day they will go through my papers and read my work. I want them to understand what I say, and I want to make them proud. I want them to write poetry also. This is the gift I want passed down through my ancestors.

I am honored that I had a role in helping you toward your path as a poet. Many blessings to you and your beautiful little Una. What a lucky little girl she is to have such talented and loving parents.

With loving thoughts,
Claire

San Quentin, California
May 1, 2005

Dear Claire,

I've been mentally writing to you a little everyday since you left and been delaying sitting down in front of the computer. Right now Una is in the front room busy acting out all the kids' parts to the *Annie* Soundtrack. Her "Hard Knock Life" number rocks! She spreads out baby blankets for rags and frantically scrubs the wood floors, getting a forward roll in whenever she can. Steve is cleaning the kitchen. I'm glad he's domestic, and work really hard not to take all he does for granted. By the way, he found the missing corkscrew in our teenage roommate's room—we're all rookies not to have thought of looking there! So I'm sequestered in the office to get down some ideas. I have so many questions and these topics feel bigger than I am.

I've been thinking about how prison gets sensationalized in lots of insidious ways. It's like the night you came here. You and Scott Peterson arrived at San Quentin within hours of each other. All the lights and TV crews and satellite dishes. Because we live on grounds many people were saying things like, "Soooo, you guys are getting a new neighbor . . ." As you saw, the hype and attention for the story was incredible. I'm curious about people's curiosity, their lust for retaliation. It goes without saying that murder is a tragedy. But the vengeance our society craves remains illogical to me: kill because killing is wrong. Loads of people think this way, including my best friend since childhood. She's glad he's sentenced to death. She swears she wouldn't feel differently if she had "to push the button." My friend actually said, "No, really. I'll be glad he's gone. There's enough freaks in this world already." Or like the lawyer I sat across from on a flight last year put it, "I'm for isolating all the death row inmates on an island together and letting them hash it out themselves. It would be a lot cheaper and more reasonable. They deserve each other's company. Now *that* would be good reality TV."[1]

I have this theory that our culture loves prison stories to the same degree that we despise prisoners. We consume the morbid details of the murders, whether out of fear or fascination. We internalize the injustice done and act out our own rage at whatever wrongdoing we've encountered in our lives. We compare our personal levels of insanity or anger and come out ahead. Current legislation in California certainly bears this out. And, of course, the media's hand is also in this. I realize there is a broad spectrum of people's concerns that ranges from mere intrigue to civil rights activism, yet there's an overarching demand for revenge that gets called

---

[1] I've been checking in with friends (Rose Najia and Jon Morrill) and together we've discussed the very real difference between the act of killing on one hand and the practice of killing someone who has killed someone on the other. For some, this difference justifies the death penalty. But since DNA testing has shown that several people who were sentenced to death were wrongly accused, it seems that the death penalty is at least short-sighted and problematic (read moratorium in Illinois). Even if we could 100% guarantee that a person was responsible for a given crime, capital punish-

retribution. And that is front page news.

So here we are writing letters that we know will be published that explicitly address our prison work. On one level, I'm fine with it; if we can't talk about poetry in prisons, who can? But, in part, our dialog reminds me of something I once heard about critiquing advertising. If you hold a Starbuck's cup in a performance that takes on commodification, you defeat your objective by providing free advertising for the company. Also in talking about my experiences inside, I want to be very careful not to mis/represent what goes on in there for the men and women and don't want our work to be merely part of the prison exposé.

If anything, I'd hope to complicate/humanize the issue. In *The Wedding Dress*, Fanny Howe writes:

> A prisoner or a patient becomes a double monster—despised and then despising of self and others, unless she can redraw the content of experience, and give it a new name. . . .

> The prisoner, when deformed [by the prison system], is required to endure the gift of self-loathing. When a prisoner, contrarily, finds something recognizable in herself, then she can be at least mentally liberated. Remembrance is one approach to self–recognition and reorganizing the facts through writing them down as transformed moments is another.

And this echoes what you said in your last letter: that the work of teaching art in prisons matters. Since we as a society know for sure that the vast majority of those serving time today will be back on the streets in relatively short order, we/society have to address this "double monster." Arts in Corrections is one way to do this.

---

ment is highly questionable. There is something not ours in the taking of another life.

This discussion often leads to the question, what if someone hurt or killed one of your family members. How would you feel then? People in my family have been seriously hurt, but not killed, by others. It's hard to guess, but I would like to think my view wouldn't change. I've read stories of families who lost members in the Twin Towers. Many of them did not support the war in Afghanistan, did not want more killing. I'd like to say I'd be like them. I can see detesting the act, even detesting the criminal, but for me this leads to wanting to make sure that the crime couldn't be repeated, not to wanting to end a life.

The state does have some responsibility for the circumstances and conditions of *all* of its citizens, so doesn't it just make sense for us to supplant our punitive desires for inmates with restorative ones?

Since I have worked inside for over ten years and live now at San Quentin, people ask me about the prison system a lot. Even my best responses seem inadequate—my experience and privilege so far removed from those serving time. This said, we both know how much play "I teach creative writing in prisons" gets at cocktail and dinner parties. So while I rail against the association, I know its appeal for others, notice both its limitations and allure.

I was really taken back by what you said regarding your philosophy of language. That you write for your grandchildren and want to be understood by them and make them proud. I have to confess that all my graduate academic training has made me skeptical. What, no poetics other than this? No "language around" your language use? I really had to check myself. You wrote, "This is the gift I want passed down through my ancestors." This stance challenges my priorities in very real ways, ways that I'm continuing to consider. I appreciate still learning from you.

Claire, so long ago you gave me direct advice which I followed almost to the letter. You told me to get myself into graduate school, to apply for all the grants I could, and to dream big in terms of my writing. So I did. (You also told me to get a PhD—I got pregnant instead and these days school seems refreshingly far away.) But I've been wondering why you were adamant about the academic route. At some point most poets rely on universities in one way or another, but you haven't and are going strong. How do you think operating outside of the academy has benefited/hindered your career? I was surprised, curious, (unbelieving?) when you said you "don't care" about ambition these days. Is that really so? How have you dealt with the push to be seen, to be recognized, to further your career? What are your big dreams right now? I'd love to hear more about your writing projects and who you're reading, what you're up to . . .

In my own poetry, I'm fighting with being clever. I think I have several good ideas in this new manuscript, but some of them feel flat because they resonate at the idea/conceptual level instead of sinking down into lived life more. I'm struggling with my own fears of "sounding smart." (Busy as I am recently with books on health and raising children instead of the latest experimental or philosophical works . . .) Last year I sent *Currency* to a press in Brooklyn, and they were great. They didn't take the book, but they read it well and wrote a reassuring rejection letter, if there is such a thing. One of the editors appreciated the work, but said that ultimately parts of manuscript were as frustrating as they were interesting. I agree. I've been working on this for a long time. Maybe too long. Sometimes I wonder if I shouldn't start another project just to shake things up a bit, but with Una and work, I'm fighting for time as it is. I'm acquainting myself with the tougher aspects of writing; at other times it's been much easier for some reason. I try to keep in mind that some of my favorite poets weren't so prolific, but some of my other favorites were long dead by my age . . . Anyway, I'm sending you a poem or two from the manuscript that shows what I'm up to; "One" is the first poem of the book and looks at value and community vs. value and the individual. It's a mini poetics for the manuscript.

I haven't felt singular in a long time—Una goes where I do for the most part. This past Friday we had an incredible day. Two months shy of four is an awesome age, my favorite so far. We went to Muir Beach and set off exploring for a sea anemone. Barefoot, we climbed tall rocks covered with mussels and judged the currents so we didn't get soaked. We could not have traveled this same terrain even 6 months ago. Una was singing *Pippi Longstocking* and after some maneuvering was just about to put her fingers into the spongy center of a brilliant green anemone. A brown crab creeped along and freaked her out so badly that there was no continuing. Before I knew it, she was way off down the beach muttering to herself in some strange accent, "I'm not goin' back there to mess with a mean nasty crab . . ." It was a great time. Parenting is much more fun now; those first years were kind of rough—poetry and mothering haven't always complimented each other well for me. It's not been an easy balance. Sometimes I'm convinced illness has had a hand in this, but I'll save that for another time. . . How did you manage to keep writing as a single mom with three boys? Please advise.

There are a lot of loose threads here Claire—I realize. I'm glad we'll be in touch. And thank you so much for your last letter, what a kick-ass Valentine. I'm looking forward to seeing you again in a few weeks! Please write with all the news.

Love,
Dana

Dearest Dana,

Oh how I love your letters. You are in that wonderful stage where one gets married, has children, chooses a career. These are the years that lay down the paths for the map of your life. So now you have the beautiful little girl Una and your loving and supportive husband, and your MFA and you teach at a University! Bravo!

You deal with health issues now also. I supposed I bring this up to ask you to think about what role health plays in a poet's life, in an artist's life. When I researched the artist Frida Kahlo, for my play, *When Will I Dance*, I was recovering from my third spinal surgery. I found her work to be particularly compelling because she had twenty-seven spinal surgeries. I discovered I could write about her pain most realistically while I was suffering pain myself. I learned from her that we must use what we are given and put it all into our art. What are your feelings about this?

Yes, I agree with everything in your last letter regarding the work in the prisons and society's obsession with crime and violence. The work in the prisons has been a gift for me, a gift I give and I receive. Since I had no higher education, I had to learn where I could, study on my own, and find my own individual voice without guidance, without support. When I meet inmates in a new class, I often begin by telling them some of my accomplishments and then tell them that I began my writing life without opportunity. I do this to assure them that if I could do it, they could do it, that what it takes is a fully open mind, the ability to focus, to dream, and the willingness to work, and work hard.

I try hard not to get involved with what society thinks of our work behind the walls. Sometimes I write about it, as in the play I wrote with the women at Chowchilla prison. But I think I am completely confused as to what society thinks in the first place. I am stunned when I read the TV program lineup. How many fictional killings are there on television each week? There are so many TV programs that have been smash hits for years that I have never seen, nor will I ever see. I also refuse to watch movies that have violence. I simply do not find violence entertaining. That isn't to say I don't enjoy a good mystery novel. But if the novel focuses on the gore or violence, then I just can't read it. When the inmates in my poetry class at Soledad Prison discovered this about me, they were stymied. One of them said to me, "Claire, look around you. He opened his arms to take in all of his classmates around the table. "We're murderers, batterers, thieves, burglars, rapists, perpetrators of violent crimes. What do you see here?" Of course my answer was simply, "When I look around this table, what I see are poets."

You wrote that we both know teaching Creative Writing in prison makes for good conversation fodder at cocktail and dinner parties. Frankly Dana, I try to stay away from parties. I've never been very good at them and I find that being in a room with many strangers sort of makes me nervous. Once I mention that I teach in a prison, it makes me the center of attention, which is not where I wish to be. I would rather listen to people tell about their lives than sit and talk about mine. I already know my life. Occasionally in a gathering of friends, I will perhaps tell a story about something that happened in the prison that I found particularly moving, or read a poem written by an inmate that I found to be exceptional. But I do this with friends only. There is no need with them for me to explain or justify what I am doing in the prisons. They understand I may never be able to truly describe my desire to reach out to those inside, behind the walls. I have often thought of how moved I was as a child in Catholic School when I first heard the quote in the bible from Matthew, "I was sick and imprisoned and you did not look after me."

But I want to try to answer some of your questions in your last letter. You asked me what are my thoughts on poetics, what do I want to do with my career and what difference it has made to my career because I never attended college.

First of all, I want to emphasize that I have never thought of being a poet as a career. We actually began discussion of this issue in my little house in Santa Cruz many years ago. You decided that you wanted to have a career as a poet and you asked me how one could do that. Since I was at that time working to support my three sons in an administrative position in the Literature Department of the University of California, Santa Cruz, I knew exactly how you could do that and I told you then. If you want to focus on poetry as a career, you need to get an advanced degree and teach it. If not, then you will probably do as I did, work at something else to support yourself. Yes, I did work around faculty/poets. In fact, there is one day impressed on my memory when a poet with whom I had given a

294

poetry reading, walked into my office to apply for a teaching position. When she saw me at the desk she expressed surprise. I told her that I was on the clerical/administrative staff. She blushed and apologized to me over and over, and insisted to me that she didn't know, as if I had told her I was a member of an untouchable caste. But this was a rare instance and not from the regular faculty at the University who were always supportive of my work. There were many times when I was invited to a poetry class or playwriting class and asked to read, to give input about my work.

It always gave me particular joy that I was the administrator in charge of getting Lucille Clifton to take a position there. I in fact set out by myself to secure a home for Lucille and her children. I remember the first day she arrived on campus and how I told her that her poem, "Miss Rosie," was one of my favorite poems ever written by a woman about a woman. In her first poetry reading in Santa Cruz, she read it for me. What a gift!

I think rather than poetry being my career, that in my core, the center of my being, I am a poet. I have always been a poet first, before I was anything else. That is absolute truth. I am a poet who gave birth, a poet who loves her children, her sisters and her brother, grandchildren, a poet who loves animals, a poet who loves to cook and a poet who requires friends as much as she needs air, a poet who loves the man in her life when there is a special man in her life. When I buy my clothes, I buy clothes the poet loves, when I play music I play music for the poet. When I write anything else at all, I am the poet writing something else.

I have never been, nor will I ever be, very interested in marketing my work. The exception to this was the few years I worked as a free-lancer for magazine stories when almost every story I wrote got published. I soon found no joy in that endeavor. Since then, with a few exceptions, almost every publication I have had was requested from a publisher. I rarely scout around looking for places to publish my poems. Even my little book of poems was solicited from a publisher. I have never written poetry to be published. I have written poetry because I cannot stop. I have always found great solace in Rilke's words, "poems come, then you will not think of asking anyone whether they are good or not. Nor will you try to interest magazines in these works for you will see them as your dear natural possession, a piece of your life, a voice from it." Of course he meant that for the younger poet, when he first started writing poetry, but nonetheless, it is what takes the anxiety away for me and settles my mind, allows me to focus.

Then again, I have written many poems for the ongoing *Celebration of The Muse* poetry festival given annually in Santa Cruz. It is an honor to be invited to return there to read every year. I find that knowing I will be reading a poem to hundreds in the audience puts such colossal pressure on me that sleep is hard to come by while I am writing those poems. It took me three months to write my poem, "An Open Letter To John Ashcroft." That poem got posted on the Internet and was finally published in over fifty different publications, and I received over 350 emails in response to it. Some of those responses were terrifying, threatening, and condemning me to hell and some of them were so supportive and loving.

As far as what my writing projects are right now, I have just written the final sentence of my memoir, *Potrero Hill*. It chronicles a few years of my childhood and the extraordinary life of my family. When I was in the fourth grade in Catholic School, I was fencing stolen goods my father stole from the waterfront where he was a longshoreman. I wore my Catholic school uniform and went into fancy San Francisco stores on upper Market Street and traded the goods for money and saw no problem whatsoever with it. The book is funny and gut-wrenching. In writing it I had to eliminate any thought about anyone who might possibly read it, but most of all my family. I simply sat day after day, week after week, and year after year and wrote it. I was compelled to write. Then I rewrote it. Then I rewrote it again. Then last week, I wrote the final sentence. I am still writing the final sentence. I am suffering over that sentence.

Now I would love to see the memoir published. So there you are! I don't think of poetry as a career, although now that I have "retired" from the University, I teach poetry. I don't want to write to be published, but then again some things I do want published. I am contradicting myself all over the place aren't I? How frustrating! Please forgive me.

Also I wanted to address your statement about poetry and motherhood not complimenting each other. Oh Dana, poetry doesn't compliment anything in our lives really, other than solitude. I am sure there are others that will not agree with that, but I have found poetry to be a needy lover. The more you give to her, the more she wants. But just read aloud these exquisite lines you wrote in your last letter, about your visit with Una to the beach. There is a poem right there in the rough.

Look at it again. You will see the poem, already written, waiting for you to recognize it the way you recognized the beauty of that day.

You ask me how I could find the time to write with my boys in my life. My God, how could we as poets, survive motherhood without writing about it? And of course you are writing about it! In both of your letters so far there are beautiful words about that delightful little girl of yours, and she is a poem unto herself anyway. And many more poems will come for her and from her. Just get out of the way and let them come.

As to your questions about the death penalty and trying to find reasons others use to justify it, I simple refuse to think about that anymore. My mind is made up. I am against killing. I am truly without apology, a pacifist. I do not believe in capital punishment and I do not believe in war. I hate that our country is in a war right now. I hate that our sons and daughters are dying along Iraqi roadsides. I hate that I have not met one American who has any idea how many children and innocents we have killed in our bombing campaign of "Shock and Awe," and since then. If we care so much about saving lives, then why don't we know those numbers? This is the blood on our hands as I see it. Others shut their eyes to it. This is what it means to be a poet. Our eyes don't shut.

All through the Vietnam War I marched against it, and I marched against the Iraqi war and the war in Afghanistan also. I went to San Francisco on a two-hour bus ride with people I did not know to march all day and make my voice heard. Where I live in far Northern California, this is not a popular stance.

The only killing I could justify would be to do so in self-defense and I am so grateful that I have come this far in my life without having to put that belief to the test. Then again, if there is a spider in my house, I smash it so hard I almost put my shoe through the wall. So I guess I will now get off my soapbox.

I think your poem, "One" is perfect. Is there a "Two"?

And congratulations to Steve on the excellent article in the *San Francisco Chronicle* about his art programs at San Quentin. You married well my dearest Dana.

With Much Love,
Claire

San Quentin, California
October 16, 2005

Dear Claire,

Thanks for all your notes and letters over the summer. In short, the past 4 months have been the most difficult in my family's life. As you know, Steve's younger brother died in an accident in June. Allan was one of the best people I ever knew— and I'm not just saying that in some kind of JFK, now he's gone, remember the best, bullshit kind of way. He was one of the few that made the world and the people in it "better." There were over 1,000 at his funeral. The poem I wrote in your 1st Napa class, the Uncle poem, was all about Allan and how I was so happy that in Northern Washington, Uncle Allan was waiting for Una to come up and visit. I felt lucky just knowing that. He died a week or so later. Then in July, another of my favorite people died, my paternal grandmother, someone who along with my mother's mom was really formidable in shaping who I am. She was funny, self-taught, incredibly strong, and she loved language. Due to a brain meningioma, she spent the last 3 years of her life a quadriplegic and never complained once. She loved having her family around her and felt fortunate to live the end of her life at home. At 92, she was twice as old as Allan when he died. Most of our family was with her when she passed away. In fact, we were all laughing; she would have loved that. (It's a long story...) Then, toward the end of summer, my mom had a series of stents put in her heart and right carotid artery. This past season was emotionally exhausting. I'm glad my mom's OK. We still need her around! Ack. What a summer.

The whole turn of events has made me think about the value of a life. Maybe value isn't the right word—worth/meaning/understanding/use/hope/? Language isn't holding up. Just before my mom's procedures, she and I talked. She's not a real process-oriented person. She hasn't been to therapy for any length of time. There we were, driving to her heart procedure, listening to the news and she was busy scratching off BINGO Lottery tickets, about 5 of them. I kept thinking if this is our last day together, is this the way to spend it? We ate out at a brew pub. We drove by the ocean. Finally I asked her straight up, "So mom, if this is IT, if you might die, tell me what's your life come to? What matters? Teach me this." She said, "Life's about what you accomplish, for me it was raising you kids, and helping people out along the way." That was it. There was nothing undone between us. We said we loved each other and she kept scratching her Lotto cards. Punto. Finis.

Then, at the end of the stent placements, when my mother was in ICU, I got a phone call that Palm Press took my manuscript *Currency* for publication. I've been working on that manuscript longer than I like to admit—years—and the timing was really odd and complicated by the fear of my mom not doing well or having a stroke or taking a bad turn. Any other time, I would have been thrilled by the news, and I was happy, but in the context of everything else, the "book," "getting the book," was far from first on the list.

In your last letter you asked about health and its role in a poet's/writer's life. I've been thinking about this a lot. It's weird; all this recent illness and death has taught me something about my poetics. Illness has made me much more empathetic to all kinds of writers and projects. When your world gets blown open by losing two of your favorite people, by living in that grace-ridden and scary place of complete surrender and grief, more ideas seem possible, if more fragile. And you see every-one around you in this same mortality boat trying to fulfill some need or other, and you soften to them, love them even. I'm reading differently and in some ways less critically. But in other ways, paradoxically, I have stiffer, more rigorous, over-arching questions of the work. "So if this is IT, if THIS is what a poem comes to, what matters?" I want the poem to do something, say something. Fucking change something. This is what I want my poems to do anyway. Our time here feels more crucial than before.

Having dealt with an illness for years now, I've known these distinct ways of listen-ing. But with all the day to day things to do, I lose the weight of how prized time and experience are all over again. It's like the end of that Flannery O'Connor story, "A Good Man Is Hard To Find." Sometimes I think, *she'd have been a good poet if she'd just had someone to hold a gun to her head every second of her life.* Time would be cut down to the essentials. No crap in the way. I'd be awake and see—I'm not even sure what.

And yes. I think you and Frida are right. We take it all, the health issues, the loss, and pull it into our art. Shortly after Steve's brother died, he started writing a short story called "The Ride." It's an intense piece about going out and riding the horse that his brother was killed on. He was trying to find any answer any way he could. The story talks about his father who caught and broke wild Appaloosas, about the breed itself and how it was raised by the Nez Perce who through selective breeding created a horse that was a combination warhorse, racehorse, hunting horse and a long distance mount, and about dealing with death. I was surprised by how quickly Steve, who is a woodworker, not a writer, turned to writing to help him deal with the loss—he was surprised too. Death has a helplessness about it; our inability to do anything is built in. We grieve and keep living and make art out of the pieces. Steve's short story is incredible. When he'll let me, I'd like to send you a copy.

Most of my questions now are about how to reach loved ones in their deepest pain. Steve and I are very close, and yet I know I'm nowhere near to fully understanding his grief. I realize you've gone through this recently as well. If you have any ideas beyond grief counseling and the Hospice resources, please pass them on.

In our everyday lives, Una keeps going to the Co-op, we keep working, planning things for the weekends, and eating out too frequently. I want to cook better and more often, do the laundry on schedule, love dogs more than I do. On Tuesday, we're getting a Catahoula Leopard dog/Spaniel mix named Windy, a three-year-old Stinson Beach stray. I'm wary (read: dog shit and hair). Steve and Una's enthusiasm is winning out and I hope it's contagious. I'm writing when I can.

And when I am writing, I'm thinking about institutions, not just governments and prisons, but schools (I'm on a Kindergarten hunt for next year: Sudbury? Waldorf? Charter? Public?), universities, and homes—the elitism and hierarchy, the built-in racism, the economic discrimination, the caste systems you mentioned in your last letter. If I want Una's education to emphasize "reverence for and stewardship of the earth," it will cost me $12,000 a year. But with that money, she'll become "aware of the interconnectedness and diversity of all life forms on it." Yet, I wonder how diverse this school really is. And truth be told, this is one of the schools at the top of my list, even though we could never afford to pay the full tuition.

So I'm reading more now, spinning in my own ignorance and how much there is to know. I've been thinking over your idea of what it means to be a poet. "Our eyes don't shut." I wish that rang truer to my experience. It seems that Americans in this country are so comfortable, poets included, that hypocrisy and certain drowsiness afflict the best of us. Even the poet who taught me the most in graduate school vacations in Las Vegas.

As I've been writing this correspondence, I've been well aware that this is the "last letter" of the formal exchange between us for this project. Everything feels so urgent with this one, so pressed. In its final stages, I've been reconsidering the project, the *Letters to Poets* anthology, and been driven to question the format we've chosen, and more acutely aware of the challenges endemic to the "mentoring" process. Even in letters, which are more intimate and "honest" than email, there are gaps—threads that get lost, veneers of discussion, misinterpretations. We're lucky that ours is an on-going conversation: 10 years now, is it? And I've no fear that this is indeed the "last letter," but these scrapes do call into question the endeavor. The constraints of productivity in action. And mentorship is a tricky business. It has all the pitfalls and hazards of any hierarchical discourse, but these can be interrogated, at least, and perhaps dismantled, overturned. I've been wondering who your mentors are. I've heard you speak about a group of readers you have. To whom are you apprentice, and how has this relationship evolved?

I'm looking forward to your next letter and I can't wait to read *Potrero Hill*. That last line will be a dusie.

All this said, I have been honored to be in dialogue with you again. I have taken the apprenticeship you offered me so long ago in Santa Cruz seriously and still hold it dear. It has helped to shape my life in ways that I will always be thankful for.

With my love and respect,
Dana

Paradise, California
December 15, 2005

Dearest Dana,

It is difficult to believe this letter exchange is almost over and this is the last letter I will send to you for the project. It has been an enjoyable process, one that I haven't taken lightly.

First of all I want to say that I think about you so much and the overwhelming anguish you have endured these past few months, with the loss of two beloved relatives, and the dire sickness of your mother. This burden is too much to endure all at once, but then here it is, and you must carry on, and you do carry on, being the mother, the wife, the teacher, the twin sister, the daughter, the poet.

You wrote in your last letter that most of your questions now are about how to reach loved ones in their deepest pain. I do not think there is a path here Dana, that anyone can place you on. My own brother who is very close to me lost his high school sweetheart after 46 years of marriage last Christmas Day. I spend time with him but I cannot even see how deep his pain is and all I can hope for when I am with him is to allow him a safe place to cry. In my private writing workshop that I conduct in my home, I have a woman who lost her husband to a drunk driver. She now writes the newsletter for the local Hospice Society. She has given me support over this past year on how to help my brother. One of the things I know he appreciates is that I keep his wife's name in our conversation. Last week at lunch he cried while telling me that his grandchildren have stopped staying the word, "Grandma." The sounds of a name can comfort, keep memories close and alive. I suggested to him an exercise that my friend had suggested, that is to spend time with family, each giving a wonderful memory of the person who is no longer with us. My brother has decided to do this at a Christmas lunch with his grandchildren. His wife died around noon Christmas day last year. I hope it will comfort him a little and also keep her memory alive for the youngest children.

I think possibly the worst thing anyone can do is to expect that there is a pattern or a timetable or any special way to grieve and comfort. There are of course so many wonderful books written on this subject, but I have found with time, grief comes and goes. It renews itself suddenly, maybe while walking down the aisle of a market, at the sound of the phone ringing, and then after a while the periods of sudden wracking pain get farther and farther apart. Then we go into a place where we remember our loved one with joy and appreciation for our time spent with them.

I tried when my own mother died, to write about her as much as possible. I knew that eventually I would forget some of the little things she would say or she would do. I smiled when I read your lines about your own mother scratching off her lotto tickets, while giving you her answer about the meaning of her life. The last thing my mother and I did together was work a crossword puzzle. I was holding the book and she was flat on her back in a hospital bed, giving me answers, remembering exactly where each word was placed. Her sharp mind was alive and well as they wheeled her into surgery for an operation that she would never recover from. I held on to that crossword puzzle for a long time. Then after several years, I simply threw it away. It brought me too much pain to think of it. I try now to keep mostly the good memories. I have her photo hanging above my writing area. I look at her often. She is smiling in the picture. Some days when I'm really messing up, getting too frantic, overloaded, overwhelmed, it seems to me I see a frown on her forehead.

I remember when my book of poetry was published. There was a big party in a friend's garden. My mother was there. I remember her saying, "She's my daughter. I'm the poet's mother."

It is important to me that I keep that identity. Yes, I am a playwright, and I have written fiction and newspaper columns, and my memoir, but at my deepest core I am a poet. And this statement brings me to your observation that the poet who taught you, vacations in Las Vegas. Yes, we are everywhere. Perhaps the bright lights, the fast pace, the constant stimulation takes that particular poet into a merry-go-round of stimulation where the words can stop for a moment. Perhaps that's what it takes to rest her mind. If she chooses Vegas, rather than alcohol or drugs or self-destruction, then good for her.

I am so wonderfully proud of you Dana and the fact that your first book is to be published. What an amazing accomplishment. I know that the timing seemed so strange, with your mother in Intensive Care. But then what else in the world could have eased that worry, even for a few seconds? That's wonderful news, the culmination of years of work will bring you joy for the rest of your life, and now the world can see into that brilliant and zany mind of yours and grow to love you the way I have.

You ask who my mentors are. This is difficult because my mentors are not someone I can telephone, send an email to, or even a letter. I suppose my real mentor is the woman whose photograph hangs in my living room. Her name is Katherine Hallahan. She came from Cork, Ireland in the bowels of a ship when she was a young woman. She fled famine and poverty and said goodbye to her mother and father forever and set off for the new world. She was held at Ellis Island with her two sisters and then went to San Francisco where she became a servant. She married a teamster who had a wagon with six horses and she had three daughters. The teamster left her and her three little ones and they went hungry most days. People would leave baskets of food on their doorstep on good days. Eventually all of her daughters were taken from her and placed in foster care. She died very young in San Francisco General Hospital in the TB ward. She gave her life for those descendants who would come after her. I never met her. She died 7 years before I was born. She was my grandmother, my mother's mother. When I need strength I look at her photo. When I want to try a new path, have courage, keep going, forge ahead, I think of her. When I feel that I have no right, no credentials, no education, no training, no path laid in front of me, I simply remember her deep in the dark of that ship, pointed towards America.

I vowed to her memory that I would never go to New York until one of my plays opened there. Then I would go as a tribute to her. My first trip to New York was for the opening of *This One Thing I Do*, my play on women's suffrage. My sister went with me. On our first day there we visited Ellis Island. It meant more to me than opening night at the theater. It was my way of saying thank you to Katherine Hallahan and letting her know she didn't die in vain.

When I finish a big manuscript I will always have my friend Philip Slater read it. I respect him enormously and he has the courage to tell me when something is not working. He also knows just the right words to say to keep me working on something. I tend to dismiss myself. My theater mentor is Michael Griggs, the most talented director and actor I have ever known. It is so interesting to me that the two people this feminist writer turns to are men. But then again, they have made their mark in the world and they have in kindness and brotherhood turned to many women and held the door open. Any woman who thinks we are artistically liberated should try playwriting. It is a humbling experience to find that most theaters go year after year without ever producing a work written by a woman.

I am now at that place in my life where I don't know what to write next. I have a longing for more poetry and that's probably what I will concentrate on now. Winter is right around the corner and it is very cold here in Paradise. I live in the pine forest. Living alone can be difficult. I bring in wood for the fire, rake up pine needles by the ton, and constantly seem to be cleaning my house. I irritate myself because I cannot live in clutter and chaos. My house is so tiny that anything out of place is obvious. Then there are my two adored dogs. They are like my children with their toys and the floor is covered with things that squeak.

I suppose where I am going with these random thoughts is that this process of discussing what poetry means to me, what advice I can give to you as a young poet, has caused me to do something I don't do regularly, if at all.

That is, think of myself and what it is I want and who I am. I have spent so much of my life running to keep up, being the main financial support for my sons because their father never forgave me for leaving him and the only way he could pay me back was not to pay me. Yes, I did receive a pittance for child support, but it was pittance nonetheless. I retired from my administrative position at UC early because I was so exhausted and I wanted more than anything to live my life as writer. And that is what I have done these past 13 years and it has been good. I now teach two days a week, one day in my home and one day at Napa State Hospital for the incarcerated, as you know, since you had this position yourself up until this year. But still I must reign in my fierce wild mind every morning and stop staring in the mirror and thinking, my god you look like hell, and simply say good morning poet. I can obsess about a wet dog nose smear on the window and the fact that papers are stacked all over my desk and the damned toilet has a ring in it. I swear the water in Paradise must have gold in it because the cursed toilets always have gold rings in them.

I worry about EVERYTHING! I am the oldest sister in my family with two younger sisters. My youngest sister lives across the street. She is a retired Engineer from Hewlett Packard. My other sister lives in Arkansas and my brother lives in Chico just about 30 minutes away. One of my sons lives close and the two others are a day's drive, which as far as I'm concerned is too far. I am the glue of the family. I am the one who calls all of them. I am the one who plans holidays and passes on news. I am not complaining at all! This is the way I want it. If I lose touch with them I am nervous, grumpy, out of sorts. It is a rare week that I don't have a family member or two at my table. I obviously NEED this. I used to long for life in a commune where everyone I love could live together. When my sons moved out for college I simply wept and wept. I still miss them and the youngest is 40. At night alone in my house in the woods with my two little dogs I wish I had a son sleeping somewhere in the house. There is such a wonderful comfort in that. I had a foster son for a year and our house also turned out to be the house where all the runaway boys came. I have to fight myself often not to adopt another boy. I know that wouldn't be fair to him and also not to myself, because I am past that time in my life.

I often think of myself as a woman who writes when the fancy hits her. From my first memory of poetry when that nun in the fourth grade read "Sea Fever" by John Masefield and I got hooked, I have been hooked. I cannot see something clearly unless I write it down in words on a piece of paper. Even now after so many years working on the computer, a blank book, a piece of paper, a pencil, is often the key that opens my thoughts.

The truth is that we all are uncomfortable in our own body, our own life. We want so terribly to get it right. We look to others and think, if only I could have done it that way, looked that way, written that way. We are a constant whip on our own back. We never let go. We need to breathe, relax into that person we were born into, be her. Let her think, create, love, and rest. Let her laugh, even at the wrong moments, and let her weep uncontrollably when she needs to. When all is accounted for I want to have evolved into that woman I have always wanted to be. And I am working on her. Every day of my life I am working on her. And as time passes I am getting closer and closer to her.

You have been one of the jewels of my life Dana. I have always been fascinated by you, and your facile mind. It seems trite to say that if I had a daughter I would want her to be like you. It is more than that. If I had to come again in this life and I could choose one more sister, I would choose you.

You are a blessing to all you encounter. You are never predictable and I for one am so grateful to be counted as your friend and honored to be called your mentor.

So many blessings little sister of my heart,
Claire

Albert Flynn DeSilver & Paul Hoover

Albert Flynn DeSilver is the author, most recently of *Letters To Early Street* (La Alameda/University of New Mexico Press, 2007) and *Walking Tooth & Cloud* (French Connection Press, Paris, 2007). He has published more than one hundred poems in literary journals worldwide including *Zyzzyva, Jubilat, Chain, New American Writing, Hanging Loose, Exquisite Corpse, Jacket* (Australia), *Poetry Kanto* (Japan), *Van Gogh's Ear* (France) and many others. His visual work has appeared at The Armand Hammer Museum, and a recent visual poem will be included as part of a large public sculpture—designed by the artist Paul Kos—to be built on the banks of the Sacramento River in 2009. He is also the editor and publisher of The Owl Press, publishing innovative poetry and poetic collaboration. He is the 2008-2010 Poet Laureate of Marin County in Northern California.

Paul Hoover is the author of eleven books of poetry including *Edge and Fold* (Apogee Press, 2006) and *Poems in Spanish* (Omnidawn, 2005), which was nominated for the Bay Area Book Award. He is editor of the anthology *Postmodern American Poetry* (W. W. Norton, 1994) and, with Maxine Chernoff, the annual literary magazine *New American Writing*. His collection of literary essays, *Fables of Representation*, was published by University of Michigan Press in 2004. He has also published a novel, *Saigon, Illinois* (Vintage

Contemporaries, 1988). With Maxine Chernoff, he has translated *Selected Poems of Friedrich Hölderlin* (Omnidawn, Fall 2008). With Nguyen Do, he has edited and translated the anthology, *Black Dog, Black Night: Contemporary Vietnamese Poetry* (Milkweed Editions, 2008) and the poetry collection *12 +3* by Thanh Thao, one of Vietnam's leading contemporary poets (Vietnamese Writers Association, 2008). Born in Harrisonburg, Virginia in 1946, he is Professor of Creative Writing at San Francisco State University.

Dear Paul,

I write to you thinking of thinking, thinking of letters. I've been revisiting my manuscript of letter poems, *Letters to Early Street*, written from 1998-2001 and since continually tinkered with. Many of the individual poems have been published and the manuscript as a whole has been finalist for numerous book awards (I think five to date) and yet it remains unpublished. And so now I question the desire to publish, the want to want to want. What are my motives? Ahhh, the perpetual pines! In the Literary World you don't exist without a book and even less so with a book that's largely ignored which seems to be most poetry books. And so perhaps not existing isn't so bad, especially in the narrow eyes of a so-called "Literary World," whatever that is. I mean the literary world is largely an idea, a projection I have of a bunch of people who read and study and write books, who judge the worth or interest of others based on what they think is "good writing," or "good thought." And these things change constantly—modes of writing, hip ideas, accepted philosophies of the decade. They fade, and what about all that is inevitably excluded? And this judgment of "good thought"—the mystics from any spiritual tradition might say the best thought is no thought or "now" thought— which is ultimately where I aspire to reside. Yet how much of mind gets consumed with thoughts of acceptance by this largely amorphous, imagined literary world? It's difficult to operate (write) in a vacuum or a void, and yet I once read this interview with my friend, the poet Anselm Berrigan, who said, "voids are hard to colonize" which I've always loved, and is profoundly true. I know each person has this void, emptiness within them which is untouchable pure potential where all thought, ideas, poems come from, but we mistake that place for the mind when really it's what makes the mind tick. (Don't mistake "yourself" for this mind or this body, says the great Indian visionary Nisargadatta (amen brother!). Jealousy is a gnarly colonizer, so is envy, so is hate, so is lust, so is infatuation, so too desire, etc. . . There doesn't seem to be much of a place for these emotions to cling to for those who dwell in voids.

I guess I'm wanting to speak to a sense of timelessness or emptiness in poetry, a poetry that evokes an experience of self and the world that is profoundly *inc*lusive.

I think of Whitman. I think of Dickinson. I think even more so of Hart Crane with his exquisite verbal acrobatics. I'm not sure where I'm going with this other than to say my own commitment to poetry is to reflect this sense of timelessness via a contemporary use of language—one that may quicken the senses, open the heart, inspire a mind to be cracked open a little wider to let more of the mystery of life in. The wild diversity, the wild magic, the gross absurdities, the blind violence, the immediate and boundless <u>Love</u>, what we all need now more than ever!

And yet I still would love for *Letters to Early Street* to make it to print, because I believe it's a "good," dynamic read. And so cultivating the art of patience is what these same visionaries might recommend . . .

Lagunitas, California
December 2, 2004

Dear Paul,

I am currently drinking Twinings "Lady Grey" tea on a Thursday morning, feeling like an elderly English woman out on the heaths as if in a Brontë novel and yet have just written "Says Phoebe" in my notebook. Actually it was the other day— "the English other day" as my mother would say, which really means several months ago, when I saw or rather "spotted" a Says Phoebe near Wilbur Springs and all its sayings were mapped in its movements, its wings, saying "fence post" "dart out over meadow" "hover with invisible cloud of insects" "ingest" "return to fence perch for another round of the invisibles" "fly off into small distant bush." It was this curious erratic hovering behavior that caught my poet-eye.

And then, more recently, I wrote down "noetic fences" while reading Diane Ackerman's new book, *An Alchemy of Mind*, which is a semi-poetic/scientific riff on the brain and mind (a bit mainstreamy—Discover-magaziney, but catchy). I love "noetic fences"–seems a bit of an oxymoron, but I love the word noetic and its ethereal nature being reined in by the hardness of fences. And what of fences and being and poems and saying phoebes? Saying untamable things with body and wing.

So begins "The Letters"—a correspondence hoping to say something profound and revealing, elegant and inspired, about process perhaps, thought—questions of longing, literary desire, or some such other humanness to speak to the younger poet—the elder poet—the spaces between and what can be gleaned, ignited, immortalized, historicized by the exchange—a sense of judgements, peculiarities, personalities, unkempt truths, lies, fears—generalities aching for particulars . . .

Back to beginnings. I write to you from The School Bus, a 1971 Gillig—refinished with bed platform, composting toilet, heaters, mini bathtub, tile counters, etc. Marian and I and Garp the dog have been living in it for a year and a half, halfway up the flanks of Mt. Barnabe in West Marin—surrounded by a mixed forest of Fir, Bay, Oak, Buckeye, and the occasional Madrone. Today the sky has filled in with a rush of warm air and thickening clouds stretched low across the meadowed hill-tops—I guess rain by nightfall.

We have been working on building a house in Woodacre for the past year which has consumed much attention—and so poetry to some extent has been existing on the periphery while always brewing internally in the center—no matter how dormant for a time. Recently I have been over re-editing *Letters To Early Street* which I thought was finished 3 years ago and since has been finalist for four book prizes and had almost 40 of the individual poems appear in magazines. Blah, Blah, Blah—I'm ready for it to be a book and I think so is the world, but there seems to be little fussy incongruities that need tweaking—so tweak I do. In the meantime, I've three other full-length manuscripts, and a new collection of concrete poems based on Serra's *Torqued Ellipses*. Plus, I'm working on a collaborative project with Edwin Torres about 'place'—our respective places—of mind—of land/people-scape—of culture—of language, etc. So far it's very amorphous, incoherent, and place-less which is exciting—(it's in its infancy).

Oh yeah and last April I started sketching out a "Novel"—in a month-long flurry of inspiration—I got a shell of a story—some characters, and a few good scenes, a bit of dialogue—can't imagine when I'll revisit that. I need a house first, a focused place to compose—and some time would help—the bus is challenging, cramped and now very cold, and my computer is over the hill in San Anselmo and so I have to drive to type a poem which is exhausting—coupled with the guilt of burning ever more fossil fuels, and there are infinite decisions to make in the last four months of house building—aesthetic decisions no-less—vying for poetic mind.

And so, am I supposed to ask a question of the wise elder? Pine for acceptance, praise your genius, or just be with the words and write a letter as it comes in direct correspondence from the void, in the moment? I suppose there's no "supposed to" in art and poetry. No "shoulds." No "musts." Just immediate creation via heart and mind! I'm looking forward to this exchange. It's a great honor and delight!!

Sincerely,
Albert

Mill Valley, California

December 18, 2004

Dear Albert:

I received your letters of 11/28/04 and 12/2/04 in the same envelope two days ago. I love that they are hand-written on graph paper, with all the cross-outs and errors intact as well as the weavings and intersections of after-thoughts, better thoughts, the whole flesh of thought apparent at first glance. Marjorie Welish published a book called *Handwritten*, though her own procedure or shall I say tone as a poet is hardly dashed off; it is, rather, assiduously thought through & precise, as philosophical texts must be. I usually hand-write my poems first on the same kind of lined school paper I'm using here. Then I move the text to the computer, where it undergoes (or suffers) its revisions. But it must be completed first in the hand, by hand, not as visual artisanry but because it's the most casual and private way of proceeding—no clacking of keys that can be heard in the other room. Poetry is a secret, for the private mind, a private trial perhaps, that strives to be made public.

Which brings me to your dilemma with *Letters To Early Street*, the unpublished manuscript, and the near hysteria that results from repeated rejection. It's terrifying to think that one's voice will not be heard among all the falling objects at the dump site, the seagulls calling and insanely ranting, the odor of refuse and failure. It's useless to try to calm you with a rosy wisdom or two gained with age. If anything, such fears become sharper with age, since the whole career seems in jeopardy. Young poets fear death at birth; older poets may fear that history itself will fail them, fear extinction. But in truth, good work always finds a way, and your work is good. I knew it for sure when I read your miniature volume *A Pond* published by your own Owl Press and which you presented to me:

> look at the light
>   in the pond life—
> an orange moth landing on the
>   surface is
>   exceedingly quiet with
>   out even
> wetting its wings
>   and shiny

I keep the book standing upright, open like a door, on my windowsill, where it suffers the elements such as window condensation and cobwebs, some of which I have just now removed in finding a quote. But this is sounding too poetic. The book fits the sill; I like the book.

Thought and non-thought are forms of expression. There's no escape from the grind of time and desire. I enjoy the human and natural facts of your poems, their ease, and I know you are also ambitious. One has to be insistent, but this poetic ambition works best when it pushes toward silence, the unspoken & unspeakable. Both the measured noise and disorderly silence find equilibrium in art, in being crafty.

As for the "Hip," it's probably a liability in the long run. Nothing dates quicker than service only to the moment. The Beat poets and New Critical poets bear witness to that. It's not the social moment that counts but the jostling drive toward eternity like Dickinson's horses. In other words, in Ginsberg's lovely and durable poem "To Aunt Rose," what matters isn't the 1950s reflecting back to the Communist 1930s (Abraham Lincoln Brigade), or even Ginsberg's vulnerable confessionalism, a period style; it's his fierce and generous recognition of the passing of time for one lonely woman. I write this knowing that we are both more or less identified with the Hip. Finally it's a matter of writing through one's limits and desires to the object beyond, which is the poem (I almost wrote "ramshackle poem"). You call it, via A. Berrigan, "Colonizing the void," which is fair enough. Crane's "verbal acrobatics" (lovely noise) against the background of a great silence (grandmother's love letters "And liable to melt as snow"). You write passionately of "immediate and boundless love," which in poetry is felt in the tension of syntax and a generosity toward the world at large including, especially, its words.

Yours,
Paul

Mill Valley, California
December 20, 2004

Dear Albert:

My eyes are fiery from cooking onions for my renewable Cajun chili recipe. Everyone ate all the meat and beans in the first course, leaving lots of saturated and delicious broth. So ours is a recipe (or kitchen) "pruned to a perfect economy," at least in this case. I'll resist the temptation to comment on the economies of poetry—the fully spent wealth of Whitman's expansiveness and the knots and conundrums of Dickinson, both poets finding power in wisdom, both poets *observational*, taking points of view on the things they devour, and what's wrong with that? Your phoebe at Wilbur Springs (a good title) is observed in the relaxed admiration of an event as it develops, the bird in mid-field, mid-air, seeing all that's available in its range of movement, which takes skill. The seemingly erratic movement of swallows over a field when something has caused the insects to rise is one mode for the mind in writing. It knows what it wants (it is hungry) and in general the place to find its semblance (it has craft).

Inevitably such modeling brings us to "language" writing; that is, the limits of "scatter" suggested by erratic movement, which leads also to thematic limits, ranges of resource. Is it wrong to observe, to take a point of view, especially lyrical? Irony and distance are required of that approach; is that limit also the border of "hipness"? Does a cultural positioning like hipness—see also identity politics—push the "poetic fences" too close to home and thus into a safe period style, the postmodern fragment and so on? Well, the phoebe has its natural range. Polar bears swim for hundreds of miles from the arctic to Canada and back, sometimes coming up through the home ice at exactly the same place as last year. Some poets are at home in highly dispersed conditions of language that seem barren wastes to others, and their point of view is also multiple like Hobbes' Panopticon: "The night has a thousand eyes." My neighbor Jane Hirshfield comments: "You know how to read such writing." It is not a matter of advantaged mind but rather of preference. Home is where cognition allows a person to dwell.

I too feel uneasy with the elder/younger frame of this project. The young poet asks Horace a question and Horace goes on for hours.

You know the names around you: Mt. Barnabe, fir, oak, buckeye (I thought that was Midwestern—how strange). Now I realize that the polished, beautifully brown "nut" I picked up in Mill Valley was a western buckeye, fatter and less elliptical than the ones I saw in Ohio. Madrone—I wouldn't know it from a California Oak. My naming (therefore gaming) options are limited.

About projects: since being virtually cast from Planet Chicago in Spring 2003, I've completed 3 poetry manuscripts: *Edge and Fold* (the 49-section serial title poem, my first such endeavor, and another long poem called "The Reading"); *At the Sound* (4 long poems in short sections, each written in first draft in a single day, that being the planned compositional constraint); and *Poems in Spanish*, which consists of 25 poems written "as if in Spanish," that is, fully under Ibero-Hispanic influences such as Vallejo, Pessoa, and Lorca. These poems are lyrical, ironic, and *voiced*. Writing as if in Spanish allowed me a mood and point-of-view otherwise inaccessible because so unashamedly ripe in expression. Ripeness has been a frequent trope in my recent work, the going into fullness that promises soon to turn; that is, go over into liquor, vinegar, and perhaps even bitters. It's the most conventional of my recent projects, which also means potentially the most daring.

A fourth book is near completion. Based on the books of the Old Testament, it's called *Testament*. But I'm not actively working on it because of the hundred pages of contemporary Vietnamese poetry I've translated with Nguyen Do and another hundred pages of Hölderlin I've translated with Maxine Chernoff—this second project instigated by your invitation of last year for a collaborative volume. Both translation projects have a way to go, esp. the Hölderlin. We've done most of the hymns and fragments—of Richard Sieburth—but unlike Sieburth we translated all of the *Nachtgesänge* (Night Songs) and also several of the odes, early and late.

Sadly, the Hölderlin collected is massive. We must decide on a limit or frame. I've been reading lots of secondary materials such as Susette Gontard's love letters to the poet. A married woman, her husband a wealthy banker, she dropped the notes down to him from the high window of her small reading room. She often describes him as "pale." He would soon be mad for the last 35 years of his life, and she would soon die of measles.

Your Edwin Torres project sounds exciting and your other activities too. We published some of the Serra-influenced work in *New American Writing*. Torres will propel you in yet another direction. The novel is an intensive mode. I gave up 5 months to write one in 1986, and it was published in the Vintage Contemporaries paperback series and in *The New Yorker*. It's all, good, as they say, but I know that novels were never mine to do. A second novel, a half-hearted academic farce, lies in a file cabinet and may receive no further attention. Novels steal attention from poetry, long prose also. This happened two years ago in putting together my book of essays (*Fables of Representation*). The theft is of time and labor, not of inspiration.   .

Best,
Paul

Lagunitas, California
December 22, 2004-February 8, 2005

Dear Paul,

I started this reply on the back of your envelope because it all just felt so urgent. Thanks for your terrific letter—what a great read—and the simple joys of getting a handwritten letter in the mail! The last time I received one of those was from a friend who I hadn't seen in a long time who was just diagnosed with lymphoma (what a word). Fortunately it was not a farewell letter. I just got a holiday card—she's in remission. Anyway, it says on the back of your envelope to me that writing letters somehow feels easier than writing poems, lately. And... And... I feel like telling you about the copper pipe I "laid" today.

First I spent a couple of hours with Mike and Marian digging this heinous trench from the water meter at the road to our house. Copper pipe is gorgeous stuff, but then again I've never been to the mine or the smelter. In South Central Utah there's the largest copper pit/mine in the world. I'll have to visit it next time I'm in the neighborhood. I was sad to see the pipe buried and trench backfilled, but I will think of it glowingly every time I turn on the water. And perhaps I'll think too about the copper mine/pit in remotest Utah. And what about the miners? Do they have a health plan? Union representation? Oh don't get me started! This copper pipe also reminds me of my most immediate neighbor--Tam, a gruff, dour-looking guy—lives in this ancient redwood cabin with a perfect view of the whole valley. He's been skeptical or suspicious or something, of us, and our house project since the beginning. (He's a contractor.) He came by the other day with some copper shingle samples recommending them for durability and "curb appeal" (great title). They're notoriously through-the-roof pricey. Ha ha—I said, "you buying?" That was the end of *that* conversation. I think he's a bit disturbed by our choice of "Galvalume" which most people use for sheds and outbuildings, but which Marian and I find rather "Industrial Chic"—and cheap—it's all about cheap. Do people really want to read about this? Wait, isn't this "Letters to an Elder Carpenter"? I'm confused, you were a carpenter before poetry, right? Do I have the right Paul Hoover? Will the right Paul Hoover please explain to me what a "Trembling Auger-Nut" is!?

The boss said we could write about anything we wanted to, right? Trembling Auger Nuts it is! There is a connection (I think?)—I was just thinking about a next poetry-writing project when I came across this fabulous list of occupation titles from the U.S. Dept. of Labor's *Dictionary of Occupation Titles*. I'm using some of them as titles for prose poems. Did I already mention this? I can't remember what I ate yesterday for lunch—let alone what I wrote in a letter three weeks ago—so anyway, my favorites are "Doper," "Jollier," "Head Chiseler," and "Lingo Cleaner." I've written sketches for three so far. I envision a spin off of Studs Terkel's *Working*, which I first read in high school and completely loved. My take is to tweak the narrative a bit, pump up the music, funk out the syntax, etc. Perhaps I will send you a draft of "Lingo Cleaner" next round. It begins "My name is Brawny like the paper towel." Which is what I heard the other day when I called Home Depot. This guy answers in the paint department and tells me his name is Brawny, "like the paper towel." I love Home Depot for this only—otherwise I find it to be an apocalyptic capitalist/consumerist nightmare. But hey, this is America, the price is right and I'm soon to be a homeowner. There must be a divine plan with Home Depot and Costco as key components, because here they are to stay for a while anyway, and then like all monuments of empire, they will dissolve and fall to ruin. Oh the tangents--I feel like one big blazing tangent lately barely able to spell let alone focus on one idea for any significant amount of time. Just now I'm overhearing this bearded Fairfax fellow talking about "Awareness" and "Lucid dreaming," "Your thoughts create everything around you," "Your mind can shape your reality, dude, peace out!"

True tho, ain't it? I've been reading this physicist named Goswami, a book called *The Self Aware Universe* about how consciousness creates physical reality—it's quite mind-bending. There's this very interesting film that just came out a couple months ago called *What the Bleep* about physics and "Spirituality" (Whatever that is . . .). But it's a film worth seeing, and I went to their website to find their "reading list" which I've been slowly devouring—*The Self Aware Universe* (was at the top) has some complexities in it that are beyond me, but other lucid parts about mystical traditions around the world and how physics is ultimately a similar search for "the truth" about existence, physical reality, the nature of consciousness, etc. The only difference between the physicist and the mystic is the physicist keeps searching outward in external physical realms--while the mystic looks inward into the depths of his own mind, heart, and soul. The physicist discovers many interesting and brilliant things, but along the way many horrific and dangerous things— but ultimately I think they're searching for the same thing! Love—connection— understanding. And so too with any self-respecting poet. Making connections, exploring consciousness—Who am I?—I mean REALLY—Who am I?" Not this body—Not this mind.

I forgot to mention last time that on February 6 (Sunday) at 3:00 pm I'm reading with Mary Jo Bang who will be out here for a reading at Berkeley on the 7th. I find *Louise in Love* to be an exquisite book. And she has a new one just out. I met her last summer at the Napa Valley Writers Conference. She's a terrific teacher as well. She gave this fabulous talk on Whitman, or rather a talk on I can't remember what, in which she read sections from *Song of Myself* that I'd never heard read aloud with such attention and sweetness. It was completely beautiful! And so I hope you and Maxine can make a day of it out in Pt. Reyes—did I mention it's at Pt. Reyes Books? And by all means, spread the word.

This isn't in much response to your letter but here we are, after a nice tall Chai Latte and a cramp in the wrist.

Sincerely ours,
Albert

Happy New Year!

Mill Valley, California
February 26, 2005

Dear Albert:

You asked if I was a carpenter before poetry and in a way I was. I spent the summers in high school working for a small, two-truck construction company in North Hampton, Ohio, mainly grunt work like lifting plywood up to the roof and my favorite, "framing in" the walls of the house while they're still lying flat on the deck unassembled. I became pretty skillful with the hammer and could "lick in" a 12-penny spike in two strokes. I also enjoyed nailing the plywood to the joists of the roof and floor, using the smaller 8-penny nails. This was before nail guns—all manual, back-breaking labor. But power and exactitude are required, as well as concentration, and as we know these are also features of poetry. I can do basic electrical work and don't fear jobs like replacing ceiling fixtures and fans. I can also weld and use an acetylene torch to cut metal. Both welding and cutting metal are very poetic because of the metal's transformation to liquid, which the welder "runs" or "puddles" just right to get a join: not too hot, not too cold, not too fast and not too slow, as the metal literally crumbles under the welder's touch. And all this is done behind a smoked glass mask in close proximately rather like reading. I love welding and cutting. Once while working in a U.S. Gypsum plant in Wabash, Indiana, I successfully built a metal box out of slabs of 1/4" steel, first the 5 sides to fit and then joined them together so they wouldn't leak the heated glue that was to be contained in the box. You have to prove yourself to the boss and fellow workers, especially as a "college boy" summer worker, and there was some hazing about that. They made me do the nastiest jobs you could imagine, like scraping clean the walls of a cooled-down furnace used for producing "batts" of "rock wool" insulation for the walls of houses. Rock wool is made of spun rock (another furnace produces fiberglass, which was always floating in the air, and covered our skin by the end of the shift). At the end of the shift, I'd go home and pour a very hot bath and sit in it until the sweat raised the rock wool silicates out of my pores. Only then was it safe to rub yourself with soap.

Which is another model for poetry as receptiveness, like Robert Duncan's emblem of the shaggy-antlered moose (as opposed to struggling salmon), receptiveness and patience—don't push it when it's not ready; wait for the cure of attention.

I don't know what a "trembling augur-nut" is, but I'm tempted to run to the OED to check the connection of "carving out" to "prophecy." Scratch and you will uncover; truth waits for your investigation; and so on. I know what wing nuts are. Ron Padgett called them "metal angels." I said to someone last night, "If poetry were as good as sex, poetry would be hugely popular," a dumb remark, and someone said, "To be good, sex has to be like poetry." I've been thinking lately what recent poetry lacks is intimate contact. It is at risk of losing all semblance of "funk"—dirt, grind, and get-down. I see lots of perfectly well-tempered, active poems, sophisticated in their obliqueness, fledged and syntactically suspended like the good late symbolist works they are, but there's no earth tone, and that's the base note/bass note that brings forth the real. Even Mallarmé cited earth as the first and final appeal of poetry in his essay "Crisis in Poetry." Just as an aside, it wasn't Rimbaud who sent indeterminacy spinning into the discourse (as Marjorie Perloff wrote in *The Poetics of Indeterminacy*); it was Romanticism—the thrust toward negative capability, spontaneity, and evocation which Mallarmé made the turning point toward Stein's "continuous present," the material signifiers and the recent hymns to indirection we've been calling "recent innovative practice." But Rimbaud makes a more interesting progenitor as a public figure, leaning as he does toward the physical and psychological urgency. At any rate, you used the words "funk" and "tangents" in your recent letter and I've been teaching "The Poetics of Indeterminacy" as a course at State.

I think awareness in poetry is double. You watch, and in writing you watch yourself watching. Lyric poetry seems pretty confident lately that no one is looking but us. There's beauty in such a cold assessment: Stevens' "The Snow Man": "Nothing that is not there and the nothing that is."

I'm sorry to have missed your reading with Mary Jo Bang. It was a nice pairing and in a beautiful setting in West Marin. Thanks for your descriptions of her teaching, a beautiful moment because it's exactly for such realizations (emotional awakenings) that we come to poetry. But the door is only briefly open, and we have to be grateful for whatever we find there. Mary Jo was my student for a year or so in the early 90s. I've also been in a kind of hermitage lately due to the recent loss of my teaching position in Chicago. The parting was inevitable, but knowing it makes the finality no easier, and the loss of friendships in Chicago wipes out an entire world. "Snap out of it!" Cher says in *Moonstruck* as she slaps Nicolas Cage.

All best,
Paul

Lagunitas, California
October 6, 2005

Dear Paul,

Please scrap last letter. It was probably impossible to read anyway. Plus I'll keep any of the more salient elements. This is the re-assessed, post-Katrina version. And now 10/19 the post post-Katrina, pre-Bush White House-collapse letter which wants a poem inserted from said *Working Title* manuscript; remember, all the titles from these poems come from the US Dept. of Labor's *Dictionary of Occupational Titles*, 2002. Politics is so tiresome and so necessary at the same time, (argg!! talk about the "Theater of the Absurd!!") Ok recent favorite poem as preamble to political:

ARMHOLE FELLER

I fall for absences, like most men fall for foreplay. My heart doubles as an empty CD case, goes grazing for vacancies in its spare time. Phantom limbs or a phantom heart, I chose the former. I'm the kid with no arms who holds his own handle-less hoe. Some people live in their heads, I live in a bottle of undaunted dark matter. I've been falling for armholes ever since the fifth grade, when sally tulip's armpits suckered me in. Things aren't things aren't things she said, nor damask lids of darling either. I believed her, the hull of her and the plumes. I didn't factor in falling fulltime in a factory. So I quit and threw phantom pitches for the New York Pigeons. Be a stump, buster, and average around one orange a month. As the fabric of my dreaming befalls me, I pucker up with my fallen arms in the shape of a big set of lips, and blow a kiss to the penny-less wind.

And now: blah blahh blahh blah blah blah ummm, uhhuh?? So, do you think there is a "The Human Condition" or simply human condition(s) plural in all their multitudes and complexities?? I mean, we're all suffering, right? perhaps it's just a question of degrees. In the wake of Katrina, in the wake of Iraq, in the wake of this perpetual nightmare called the Bush Administration with its crumbling facades of freedom and democracy, wealth and equality (words robbed blind of any real meaning). All such American ideals are clearly afforded to those with the means to buy them. Freedom for sale, democracy for sale, equality for sale, and now public safety for sale. The hypocritical and manipulative arc of this government feels so extreme. Seems like the winds of Katrina have lifted off the thin veil of "liberty & justice for all" to reveal the gross oppression and racism upon which this country was founded. And here in the suburbs of Northern California we poem on, padded by our "Home Equity." (Until the big one hits of course [economic downturn, earthquake, etc.].) Doesn't that term strike such an ironic chord in these times? So what is our song for America? Must we write yet another? I've found myself returning to Whitman, Rukeyser, Rexroth, Baraka, etc. in my grief to speak to and for the times, to lay forth the raw truth of things in human poetic terms. Framed against the thin buoyancy of privilege as white with means in America, framed further still beyond the limit of thinking, privilege a guilty balloon. It depends on what one does with one's means, yes? And then I turn deeper still, to Dickinson, to Rumi, to Dogen, to Lala, to Hildegard of Bingen, to St. John of the Cross, etc., the great mystics seeing beyond their temporary human experiences, beyond their circumstances amidst the fiery empires of their times embroiled within, or on the cusp of yet another revolution. These poets wrote straight to the core, with an "intimate contact "of heart, speaking to what's common to all sentient beings in all times. When I was at the Art Institute, Paul Kos, the great conceptual artist, used to talk about the timely vs. the timeless in art. I choose the timeless, even as the empire collapses around us, which isn't to say one doesn't respond to the times or take responsibility for their participation in the times, but that one goes forward with an understanding and strength of mind, with wisdom and insight, rather than virulent rage, resentment, and despair. And yet I wonder is there safety in that choice, is there privilege in that choice? Some don't get the opportunity to choose, or do they? Even in the face of extreme poverty and oppression, Mumia Abu Jamal, a political prisoner right here in America, condemned to death by the state for a crime he *might* not have committed, speaks with such courage and wisdom, such raw conviction. I think too, of Lorine Niedecker, the quiet white librarian up at her cabin on Black Hawk Lake in Wisconsin. I think of Everett Reuss wandering the canyons of Southern Utah, I think of Langston Hughes wandering the canyons of Harlem, the social canyons, the political canyons, the poetic canyons. They all eat equally of us, these canyons, blur blue into questions, questions being questions, questions being poems, poems driving us into being more fully embodied & awake in human form.

And now back to our regular scheduled programming. I had written in my last letter about the house being finished, a recent artist's grant I got and other poemy related things. It all seems so insignificant now, and then significant again in this now. Hard to keep track of the "nows" and their squirmy little ways, going from significant to insignificant depending on the whim of mood. How's bout we leave those judgments up to the reader, eh? As I was saying, back in May the "Van Gogh's Ear" crew was here from Paris. Mostly Ian & Eric though they seemed to have an entourage fluttering about, and they brought all their film equipment to film the readings and do interviews of Bay Area Poets. They were supposed to film and interview Diane di Prima, but she wasn't feeling well or was in a crabby mood or they couldn't find her place or something. So they settled on little ole me for the day. We had them up to the bus in Lagunitas a couple days after the reading at Diesel in which I gave a particularly nervy and bumbling reading. That night I read this piece called "Chaotic Torper of a Plowman" after Rilke's "Archaic Torso of Apollo." My poem was written as a homophonic translation (not to be confused with a homophobic translation) from the English. I thought it hilarious but I did notice a lot of perplexed head scratching in the audience. Needless to say, a homophonic translation, any translation for that matter, must be translated *from* something *into* something else. So this piece isn't a translation at all, really. I'm not sure what the fuck it is, but it sure rings well in my loose noodle! I guess I was just sounding off from the English and in turn from the original German, which I don't "know." I found myself reading the English as if it were a foreign language, sounding out each line in my head and then writing it forward in my newly discovered "tongue."

The next day Ian & Eric came out to Lagunitas to visit us in the bus to do some filming and interviewing. I figured if they want footage of an American poetry landmark they must go to Bolinas, so we called up Joanne, who was busy, and then Bob Grenier who it turned out needed help planting tomatoes anyway. After tomato planting at Bob's house in Bolinas, we looked at some of his recent scrawl poems which I adore. He's made these large prints on the computer which are no easier to read but all the more delicious to the eye. Soon enough Bob and Eric got in to discussing some French translations of Bob's works from "Sentences." After a couple glasses of orange juice and some somber reflections on Creeley, who Bob knew quite well, we headed down to the Coast Café for some sublime lamb shepherd's pie.

Wanting also to get back to your letter from March regarding recent poetry's lack of "intimate contact." I'm certain that's a core drive for poetry, but a difficult one to embrace as it seems to take such deep surrender to vulnerability and humility. I think a lot of us are scared shitless to reveal the more raw parts of ourselves if this is in fact what you mean by "intimate contact." We are tempted often to hide out in cliché, or the "overly familiars" or god forbid, we don't even have the language of intimate contact. And then there's the temptation to hide out in the obscurities (my personal favorite). But this "earth tone" & "bass note" you speak of is the antidote, the compliment I seek. Grounding the reader in a kind of primal sound and pattern rather than concept and logic. A sound that creates an intimate connection to heart and mind no matter however mysterious the "theme" of the poem, or the "plot." "Tone poems" or primarily sound- based poems meet you in the body and heart, not just the head, and so there's often a disconnect with "understanding." If the traditional logical sequenced events or narration of thought isn't there, then it must be incomprehensible and therefore "bad." Oh how scared we are of the unknown. A few years ago Joanne Kyger said to me after I read her a couple poems from *Letters to Early Street*, "Where's the plot?" And I was like, "the plot? A poem needs a plot?" I never really considered plot in poetry except of course in long sequences or epics. I very much appreciate it in Joanne's poems because her poems are a pieced or poemed narration in the great plot of her life chronicled daily. That sort of plot-driven narrative, though I appreciate it in others, simply doesn't fit my manner of thought or being. My plots seem to be tethered to speedy and random nuggets of instants, worded as sound. I like the idea of plot being sewn to this bass note you mention, one that grounds us to the ear and heart of earth. To the sounding off of water, for example, to the sounding off of "Says

Phoebe," to the sounding off of even empty sky as the ultimate "hymn to indirec-
tion," or hymn to emptiness. Over the last couple of years I've also been tinkering
with such "hymns" based on particular kooky quotes by Thirteenth Century Zen
master Dogen. One reads: "Secretly borrow the nostrils of your ancestors and take
up the hoof of a lone donkey." Try and glean *meaning* from that one, as if meaning
mattered more than Being. I think this too is an issue with contemporary American
poetry, its addiction to meaning. Or maybe not just the poetry world, but
American society in general seems to have this literalist sense of the world and a
bad case of "irony deficiency" as the visionary activist and astrologer Caroline
Casey would say. And metaphor, forgetaboutit! If you can't buy it or fuck it, it's
meaningless, right? And then of course the issues of the day are presented and then
taken as black and white. "Either you're with us or against us." Our tolerance for
complexity has so dwindled as our every fantasy and desire is met virtually and
instantaneously. Meaning as commodification— blah blah blah.

Being is the only antidote!! Goddamnit! You can sell oxygen and even lungs (I
know someone who has a new pair) but you can't sell breath. Another Dogen
quote reads: "There are mountains hidden in hiddenness." This really gets it for
me, the quest for an acceptance of mystery. How does that Iris DeMent song go?
"Just let the mystery be…" And in that Being, new poetic, and by extension,
human, possibilities arise! May it be so!

Over n' out,
Albert

Mill Valley, California
November 1, 2005

Dear Albert:

This is the last letter of the eight we have written. The occasion tempts me to
write to an ultimate purpose, but I can't think of one that wouldn't grind the con-
versation to a halt. I've been politically outraged also, but I hesitate to name the
moment: post-911, post-Katrina, post-Soviet, post-human. Today it was

announced that records have determined that the Gulf of Tonkin incident that provoked the Vietnam War was fraudulent or just plain false—there had been "translation errors," the newspaper reported. Hundreds of thousands of lives were lost over a translation error? Will we learn one day that the attack on the World Trade Center was also fraudulent?

I read today in *Smithsonian* magazine that the great flood of 1927, the most ruinous event in U.S. history before Katrina, led directly to the Great Depression, the election of Herbert Hoover (who was assigned by Coolidge to supervise the flood recovery and became a hero doing it), and to the massive shifting of black voting allegiance to the Democrats when mistreatment of blacks in the flood refugee camps came to light.

I'm glad you mentioned Lorine Niedecker, whom you place in the category of a "white woman" who lived on the economic margin. The "thin buoyancy of white privilege" is a great phrase. The imaginations of Niedecker and Joseph Cornell were driven by isolation and loss of estate. There had once been a thriving fishing camp. It fell toward despair and helped Niedecker see and feel the murky water more clearly. None of the Objectivists had "white privilege" that I can see, except for the Pulitzer Prize winning George Oppen, who had the advantages of family wealth. But the disadvantages of his leftist politics and Jewishness were so severe he had to flee to Mexico for eight years in the 1950s. The Objectivists were shadowy figures of the underground. If it weren't for figures of the Pound-Williams tradition like Creeley, Palmer, Bernstein, and Hejinian, they could have well disappeared altogether. Because of her status as a woman, Niedecker may enjoy more critical attention in the next twenty years than any of the others. We have to be grateful that the *Norton Anthology of Modern Poetry*, 3rd Edition, has restored the Objectivists, save Carl Rakosi, who deserves better, to the canon. Their restoration is due to the good services of the new editor, Jahan Ramazani, and I believe my own long letter recommending their inclusion, as well as the inclusion of a poetics section and the new two-volume structure, had an effect. The Second Edition had been destructively revisionist in removing Zukofsky, Schuyler, Corso, Berrigan, and others. Indeed, it was that false move and the outcry to follow that helped make possible my own anthology, *Postmodern American Poetry*.

Joanne Kyger's desire to locate the "plot" of your poem is surprising, given her own history as a member of the Spicer Circle. The Objectivists called for sincerity and objectification—that is, the intensity and precision of the authentic. Zukofsky's idea was not "plot" or "concept" but rather a series of discrete particulars that would "convey the totality of perfect rest." It was a sinuous and yet practical journey that demanded, more than beauty, realization—"rays of the object brought to a focus," as he wrote in "A" 6. Ultimately, "One will see / gravel in gravel." There are many ways to define this sense of coherence, balance, or discretion that Zukofsky calls "perfect rest." In "The Poem," Williams puts in balance "particulars, wasps, / a gentian—something / immediate, open / scissors, a lady's / eyes—waking / centrifugal, centripetal." The word "plot" is misleading with regard to the crossings and counter-forces of poetry. Marianne Moore preferred the terms humility, concentration, and gusto. Pound wrote, "Dichten=condensare," which prepared the way for Niedecker's "No layoff / from this / condensary." But I like even better her statement: "Beauty—impurities in the rock." In any event, there is a nexus, or compression, that has very little to do with the demands of story. Even good fiction is riddled with gaps. Joanne may have been asking the poem to surrender its locus, announce its system of weights and measures.

William Carlos Williams disdained simile and the sonnet, and there are many poetics with justifiable prohibitions. I favor having available all the tools of our sincerity, from hyperbole to Stein's "continuous present." Dogen's line, "There are mountains hidden in hiddenness," is consistent with Heidegger and mysticism, philosophies that thrive on tautology and paradox: "the thrownness of the thrown" and so on. Meister Eckhart wrote in his German sermons, "I shall say again what I never said before." I love that kind of thinking, because it understands that you can't go beyond the facts—the world as found, if you will. Stevens: "It was evening all afternoon. / It was snowing / And it was going to snow. / The blackbird sat / In the cedar limbs."

It's been a pleasure surveying the landscape together, Albert. In the process of writing these letters, you've completed building a house. It's cause for celebration.

All the best,
Paul

Notes and Permissions

INTRODUCTION

Rilke, Rainer Maria. *Letters to a Young Poet*. Trans. M.D. Herter Norton. New York: W.W. Norton & Company, Inc., 1934. 17.

O'Connor, Flannery. *The Habit of Being: Letters of Flannery O'Connor*. Ed. Sally Fitzgerald. New York: Farrar, Straus and Giroux, 1988.

Hoffman, Katherine. *Georgia O'Keeffe: A Celebration of Music and Dance*. New York: George Braziller, 1998.

Gordon, Ken. "What About Franz?" *Poets & Witers* Nov. 2006: 10-11.

Bourriaud, Nicolas. *Relational Aesthetics*. Dijon, France: Les Presse Du Reel, 1998.

Myles, Eileen. "Letters to Poets: Conversations about Poetics, Politics, and Community Panel." AWP, Hilton, NY. 31 Jan. 2008. In this panel Eileen first mentioned how the *Letters* project enacts a "relational aesthetics."

ANSELM BERRIGAN & JOHN YAU

John Yau, January 13, 2005

Brackhage, Stan. "Stan and Jane Brakhage Talking" with Hollis Frampton. *Artforum* Jan. 1973: 72-73.

BRENDA COULTAS & VICTOR HERNÁNDEZ CRUZ

Brenda Coultas, December 22, 2004

Cruz, Victor Hernández. "Writing Migrations." *Panoramas*. Minneapolis: Coffee House Press, 1997. 121.

Ginsberg, Allen. "After Lalon." *Cosmopolitan Greetings*. New York: Harper Perennial, 1995.

Coultas, Brenda. *The Marvelous Bones of Time: Excavations and Explanations*. Minneapolis: Coffee House Press, 2007.

Brenda Coultas, January 9, 2005

Coultas, Brenda. *A Handmade Museum*. Minneapolis: Coffee House Press, 2003.

Brenda Coultas, April 11, 2005

Brossard, Nicole. *Intimate Journal*. Toronto, Canada: The Mercury Press, 2003.

Sikelianos, Eleni. *The Book of Jon*. San Francisco: City Lights Press, 2004.

---. *The California Poem*. Minneapolis: Coffee House Press, 2004.

Sanders, Ed. *Tales of Beatnik Glory*. Cambridge, MA: Da Capo Press, 2004.

Dylan, Bob. *Chronicles Volume One*. New York: Simon & Schuster, 2004.

Victor Hernández Cruz, July 7, 2005

James, Henry. *Portrait of a Lady*. London: Macmillan and Co., 1881.

Flaubert, Gustav. "Madame Bovary. *La Revue de Paris*" 1 Oct. 1856-1 Dec. 1856.

Kerouac, Jack. *On the Road*. New York: Viking Press, 1957.

Williams, William Carlos. *In The American Grain*. New York: New Directions Books, 1956.

Hawthorne, Nathaniel. *The Scarlet Letter*. Boston: Ticknor, Reed & Fields, 1850.

Brenda Coultas, September 21, 2005

Cockrum, Col. Wiliam. *History of The Underground Railroad as it was Conducted by The Anti-Slavery League*. Oakland City, IN: J.W. Cockrum Printing Company, 1915.

Victor Hernández Cruz, December 7, 2005

Rushdie, Salman. *Satanic Verses*. New York: Viking Press, 1989.

Rushdie, Salman. *Midnight's Children*. New York: Vintage, 2006.

Plato. *The Republic*. Trans. Desmond Lee. New York: Penguin Classics, 2003.

TRUONG TRAN & WANDA COLEMAN

Wanda Coleman, January 19, 2005

Weinstein, Debra. "Prayer." *Rodent Angel*. New York: New York University Press, 1996. 60.

Wanda Coleman, January 23, 2005

Rilke, Rainer Maria. *Letters to a Young Poet*. Trans. M.D. Herter Norton. New York: W.W. Norton & Company, Inc., 1954. 39.

Wanda Coleman, February 22, 2005

Rilke, Rainer Maria. *Letters to a Young Poet*. Trans. M.D. Herter Norton. New York: W.W. Norton & Company, Inc., 1954. 35.

Wanda Coleman, May 2, 2005

Tran, Truong. *within the margin*. Berkeley: Apogee Press, 2004.

Jeffers, Robinson. T*he Double Axe and Other Poems*. New York: Random House, 1948.

Coleman, Wanda. *Mambo Hips and Make Believe*. Santa Rosa, CA: Black Sparrow Press, 1999.

Nettelbeck, F. A. *Bug Death*. Santa Cruz: Alcatraz Editions, 1979.

Schmidt, Arno. *School for Atheists*. Los Angeles: Green Integer, 2000.

The Doors. Dir. Oliver Stone. Perf. Val Kilmer and Kathleen Quinlan. Bill Graham Films, 1991.

Wanda Coleman, October 22, 2005

Rilke, Rainer Maria. *Letters to a Young Poet*. Trans. M.D. Herter Norton. New York: W. W. Norton & Company, Inc., 1954. 66.

PATRICK PRITCHETT & KATHLEEN FRASER

Patrick Pritchett, December 22, 2004

Kaplan, Aryeh, ed. *Sefer Yetzirah: The Book of Creation*. York Beach, ME: Samuel Weiser, Inc., 1990.

Marcuse, Herbert. *Eros and Civilization: A Philosophical Inquiry into Freud*. Boston: Beacon Press, 1966.

Fraser, Kathleen. *hi dde violeth i dde violet*. Vancouver, B.C.: Nomados Press, 2003.

Kathleen Fraser, February 22, 2005

Wolsak, Lisa. Photograph as described by author.

Patrick Pritchett, May 13, 2005

Stevens, Wallace. "Tea of the Palaz of Hoon." T*he Collected Poems of Wallace Stevens*. New York: Vintage, 1990. 65.

Benjamin, Walter. *Illuminations*. New York: Schocken, 1969. 188.

Shelley, Percy Bysshe. *Shelley's Poetry and Prose*. Ed. Donald Reiman. New York: W. W. Norton, 2002. 72-90.

Kathleen Fraser, June 25, 2005

Barthes, Roland. T*he Pleasure of the Text*. Trans. Richard Miller. New York: Hill and Wang, 1975. 7.

Wittgenstein, Ludwig. *Philosophical Investigations*. Trans. G.E.M. Anscombe. Oxford: Basil Blackwell Publishing, 1953.

Patrick Pritchett, October 23, 2005

Alighieri, Dante. *Dante: De Vulgari Eloquentia*. Ed. and Trans. Steven Botterill. Cambridge: Cambridge University Press, 1996.

Zukofsky, Louis. *Prepositions +: The Collected Critical Essays*. Middletown, CT: Wesleyan University Press, 2001. 12-17, 193-202.

Pound, Ezra. "A Retrospect." *The Literary Essays of Ezra Pound*. New York: New Directions, 1968.

Blake, William. "Jerusalem." *The Complete Poetry and Prose of William Blake*. Newly Revised Edition. Ed. David V. Erdman. New York: Anchor Press, Doubleday, 1988.

Donoghue, Denis. *Speaking of Beauty*. New Haven, CT: Yale University Press, 2003. 123.

Barthes, Roland. T*he Responsibility of Forms*. Berkeley: University of California Press, 1991.

Scarry, Elaine. *On Beauty and Being Just*. Princeton: Princeton University Press, 2001. 114-15.

Duncan, Robert. *Fictive Certainties*. New York: New Directions, 1998.

Beckett, Samuel. "Exorcising Beckett." Interview with Lawrence Shainberg. T*he Paris Review* 104 (Fall, 1987).

Shapiro, David. Public speech at Tucson Poetry Festival. Ocotillo Literary Endeavors, Inc., Tucson. October, 2005.

Kathleen Fraser, December 17, 2005

Alighieri, Dante. *Dante: De Vulgari Eloquentia*. Ed. and Trans. Steven Botterill. Cambridge: Cambridge University Press, 1996.

Gluck, Robert. E-mail to the author.

HAJERA GHORI & ALFRED ARTEAGA

Hajera Ghori, April 26, 2005

Ghori, Hajera. Poem that begins "At times / I see only . . ." is currently unpublished. Used by permission of the author.

JENNIFER FIRESTONE & EILEEN MYLES

Jennifer Firestone, December 22, 2004

Date My Mom. MTV. Dec. 2004.

Myles, Eileen. *Cool For You*. New York: Soft Skull Press, 2000.

---. "The Lesbian Poet." *School of Fish*. Santa Rosa, CA: Black Sparrow Press, 1997. 129-130.

---. "The Poet." *Maxfield Parrish: Early and New Poems*. Santa Rosa, CA: Black Sparrow Press, 1995. 110.

Mullins, Brighde. Introduction. "Readings in Contemporary Poetry." *Dia Art Foundation*. 22 Nov. 1996. 22 Dec. 2004. <http://www.diacenter.org/prg/poetry/96_97/ intrmyles.html>.

Myles, Eileen. "Holes." *Not Me*. New York: Semiotext(e), 1991. 32.

Rivers and Tides. Dir. Thomas Riedelsheimer. Perf. Andy Goldsworthy. Mediopolis Film- und Fernsehproduktion, 2002.

Eileen Myles, February 2, 2005

The George Burns and Gracie Allen Show. CBS Television. 1950.

Jennifer Firestone, April 15, 2005

Myles, Eileen. *Skies*. Santa Rosa, CA: Black Sparrow Press, 2001.

---. *Hell*. Libretto by Eileen Myles. Music By Michael Webster. 2004.

"Growing Pains—Female facial hair gets plucky." *Bitch Magazine: Feminist Response to Pop Culture* Spring 2005.

Sontag, Susan. *On Photography*. New York: Picador, 1973.

Firestone, Jennifer. *Flashes*. Currently unpublished.

---. *Holiday*. Exeter, England: Shearsman Books, 2008.

Eileen Myles, July 14, 2005

Being John Malkovich. Dir. Spike Jonze. Perf. John Cusack, Cameron Diaz, John Malkovich and Catherine Keener. Gramercy Pictures, 1999.

Jennifer Firestone, October 12, 2005

Peggy & Fred in Hell. Dir. Leslie Thornton. Perf. Janis Reading and Donald Reading. 1985- 1996.

Conrad, CA. "A Conversation with Eileen Myles." *Philly Sound: New Poetry*. 14 Mar. 2005. 12 Oct. 2005. <http://phillysound.blogspot.com/2005_03_01_ archive.html>.

Mullen, Harryette. *Muse & Drudge*. San Diego: Singing Horse Press, 1995.

Vallejo, Cesar. T*rilce*. Riverdale: Sheep Meadow Press, 1992. 7.

Harryman, Carla. "Fish Speech." *There Never was a Rose Without a Thorn*. San Francisco: City Lights Books, 1995. 41.

Rilke, Rainer Maria. *Letters to a Young Poet*. Trans. M.D. Herter Norton. New York: W.W. Norton & Company, Inc., 1934. 17.

KAREN WEISER & ANNE WALDMAN

Anne Waldman, December 30, 2004

Shikibu, Murasaki. T*ale of Genji*. Trans. Edward Seidensticker. New York: Alfred A. Knopf, 1976.

---. *Tale of Genji*. Trans. Royall Tyler. New York: Penguin, 2001.

Shonagon, Sei. *Makura no Soshi (The Pillow Book)*. Trans. Ivan Morris. Irvington, NY: Columbia University Press, 1967.

Michitsuna no Haha. *Kagero Nikki: The Gossamer Years: The Diary of a Noblewoman of Heian Japan*. Trans. Edward Seidensticker. Tokyo: Charles E. Tuttle Publishing, 1973.

Pound, Ezra, and Ernest Fenollosa. "Nishikigi." *The Classic Noh Theater of Japan*. Trans. Ezra Pound. New York: New Directions, 1959. 84-85.

Waldman, Anne. *In the Room of Never Grieve: New and Selected Poems, 1985-2003*. (Parts of Book III of the *Iovis* project published in this collection. Letters refer to published and new unpublished sections of this epic poem). Minneapolis: Coffee House Press, 2003.

Anne Waldman, January 2, 2005

Weiser, Karen. *Placefullness*. New York: Ugly Duckling Presse, 2004.

Waldman, Anne. *Structure of the World Compared to a Bubble*. New York: Penguin Poets, 2004.

Karen Weiser, January 10-February 6, 2005

Codrescu, Andrei. *Wakefield*. New York: Algonquin Books, 2004. 71.

Durand, Marcella. "Will Alexander Interview." *The Poetry Project Newsletter* Feb.-Mar. 2005.

Kestrel's Eye. Dir. Mikael Kristersson. Perf. Caisa Persson. First Run/Icarus Films, 1998.

Blakeslee, Sandra. "Minds of Their Own: Birds Gain Respect." *The New York Times*. 1 Feb. 2005.

Poe, Edgar Allan. *Poe: Poetry, Tales, and Selected Essays*. New York: The Library of America, 1996. 397-431, 1373-1385.

Reprinted from "'clack' the summer parallel's" by Karen Weiser, by permission of *Chicago Review*. Copyright Spring 2006. Vol. 51/52. Issue 4/1: 155.

Anne Waldman, April 25, 2005

Stein, Gertrude. *Useful Knowledge*. New York: Station Hill Press, 1989.

Cinévardaphoto: Ydessa, The Bears, and etc., Ulysses and Salut les Cubains. Dir. Agnès Varda. 2004.

Duncan, Robert. "My Mother Would Be A Falconress." *Bending the Bow*. New York: New Directions, 1968.

Arendt, Hannah. *Eichmann in Jerusalem: A Report on the Banality of Evil*. New York: Penguin Classics, 2006.

Waldman, Anne. "Without Stitching Closed the Eye of the Falcon." From the CD *The Eye of the Falcon*. With Ambrose Bye. Farfalla/McMillan & Parrish, 2006.

From *Manatee / Humanity*. New York: Penguin Poets, 2009. Used by permission of the author.

Bowes, Ed. Personal conversation with the author. Ed Bowes is a writer, filmmaker, husband of Anne Waldman.

Waldman, Anne. Poem that begins "to the contrary" is currently unpublished. Used by permission of the author.

Anne Waldman, May 2, 2005

Noh Theatre Production. Unpublished program notes. Tokyo. 2004.

Waldman, Anne. *In the Room of Never Grieve: New and Selected Poems, 1985-2003*. (Parts of Book III of the *Iovis* project published in this collection. Letters refer to published and new unpublished sections of this epic poem). Minneapolis: Coffee House Press, 2003.

Waldman, Anne. *Dark Arcana: Afterimage or Glow* (with photographs by Patti Smith). Chester, NY: Heaven Bone Press, 2003.

Karen Weiser, June 22, 2005

Audubon, John James. *John James Audubon Writings & Drawings*. Ed. Christopher Irmscher. New York: Library of America, 1999.

Reprinted from "Now Then" in *Pitching Woo*, by Karen Weiser, permission of Cy Press. Copyright 2006 by Cy Press.

de Toqueville, Alexis. *Democracy in America*. New York: A Bantam Classic, 2000.

Anne Waldman, July 3, 2005

Waldman, Anne. Poem that begins "Across from me is a crossing of leg . . . " (in progress) is currently unpublished. Used by permission of the author.

Ginsberg, Allen. "Memory Gardens." *Collected Poems 1947-1980*. New York: Harper and Row, 1984. 531-534.

Waldman, Anne. *Structure of the World Compared to a Bubble*. New York: Penguin Poets, 2004. 19-20.

Olson, Charles. T*he Maximus Poems*. Berkeley: University of California Press, 1985.

Sabina, Maria. *Selected Works*. Poets For the Millennium Ser., Vol. 2. Ed. Jerome Rothenberg. Berkeley: University of California Press, 2003.

Rothenberg, Jerome, ed. T*echnicians of the Sacred: A Range of Poetries from Africa, America, Asia, Europe and Oceania*. Berkeley: University of California Press, 1985.

Karen Weiser, February 3, 2006

Reprinted from "The plant must grow tired" in *Pitching Woo*, by Karen Weiser, permission of Cy Press. Copyright 2006 by Cy Press.

Weiser, Karen. "The plant must grow tired." *Boog City* 2006.

Anne Waldman, February 7, 2006

Waldman, Anne. Poem that begins "etiquette of all on stage . . . " (in progress) is currently unpublished. Used by permission of the author.

JILL MAGI & CECILIA VICUÑA

Jill Magi, December 4–29, 2004

Magi, Jill. *Threads*. New York: Futurepoem, 2007.

Vicuña, Cecilia. *Instan*. Berkeley: Kelsey Street Press, 2002.

Nisenson, Eric. *Ascension: John Coltrane and His Quest*. New York: Da Capo Press, 1995.

Vicuña, Cecilia. *quipoem / The Precarious*. Trans. Esther Allen. Middletown, CT: Wesleyan University Press, 1997. q. 23, q. 30.

Thomas, Lorenzo. *Extraordinary Measures: Afrocentric Modernism and Twentieth-Century American Poetry*. Tuscaloosa: The University of Alabama Press, 2000.

Martin, Agnes. *Writings*. Ed. Dieter Schwarz. Ostfildern, Germany: Hatje Cantz Publishers, 1998. 32, 17, 16.

Harjo, Joy. *The Woman Who Fell From the Sky*. New York: Norton, 1996. 3.

Jill Magi, April 12, 2005

Freire, Paulo. *Pedagogy of the Oppressed*. Trans. Myra Bergman Ramos. New York: Continuum Publishing Co., 2000. 69.

Kaplinski, Jaan. *The Wandering Border*. Trans. Jaan Kaplinski, Sam Hamill and Riina Tamm. Port Townsend, WA: Copper Canyon Press, 1987. 67.

Cecilia Vicuña, September 7, 2005

Vicuña, Cecilia. *Palabrarmas*. Santiago, Chile: RIL, 2005.

O'Gorman, Angie, ed. *The Universe Bends Towards Justice: A Reader on Christian Nonviolence in the U.S.* Philadelphia: New Society Publishers, 1990. 244.

Cecilia Vicuña, February 12, 2006

O'Hern, James. *Honoring the Stones*. Willimantic, CT: Curbstone Press, 2004.

de Zegher, Catherine, ed. *Inside the Visible: An Elliptical Traverse of 20th Century Art in, of, and from the Feminine*. Cambridge, MA: MIT Press, 1996.

Tzu, Lao. *Tao Te Ching*. Trans. David Hinton. Berkeley: Counterpoint Press, 2007.

King, Elizabeth is a visual artist. She is represented by Kent Gallery, New York.

ROSAMOND S. KING & JAYNE CORTEZ

Rosamond King, December 22, 2004

Organization of Women Writers of Africa. Yari Yari Pamberi: Black Women Writers Dissecting Globalization. Conf., 12-16 Oct. 2004, Institute Of African-American Affairs, New York: New York University.

Jayne Cortez, June 3, 2005

Cortez, Jayne. *Fragments: The sculpture of Melvin Edwards with poetry by Jayne Cortez*. New York: Bola Press, 1994.

---. "Collage for Romare Bearden." *Festivals and Funerals*. New York: Bola Press, 1971.

---. "Wilfredo Lam's Paintings" (from the Bob Blackburn Printmaking Workshop). *Coagulations: New and Selected Poems*. New York: Thunder's Mouth Press, 1984.

---. "In A Stream of Ink" (from the Bob Blackburn Printmaking Workshop). *Coagulations: New and Selected Poems*. New York: Thunder's Mouth Press, 1984.

JUDITH GOLDMAN & LESLIE SCALAPINO

Leslie Scalapino, December 7–December 11, 2004

Scalapino, Leslie. *way*. San Francisco: North Point Press, 1988.

---. *Zither & Autobiography*. Middletown, CT: Wesleyan Poetry Series, 2003. 37, 42.

Scalapino, Leslie. *The Tango*. New York: Granary Books, 2001.

Scalapino, Leslie. "A Sequence." *that they were at the beach--aeolotropic series*. San Francisco: North Point Press, 1985.

---. "Narrating." *Biting the Error: Writers Explore Narrative*. Eds. Gail Scott, Robert Gluck, Camille Roy. Toronto: Coach House Press, 2004.

Judith Goldman, March 17-22, 2005

Scalapino, Leslie. "hmmmm." *Considering how exaggerated music is*. San Francisco: North Point Press, 1982. 17.

---. "The Radical Nature of Experience" and "The Recovery of the Public World." *The Public World / Syntactically Impermanence*. Middletown, CT: Wesleyan University Press, 1999.

Browne, Laynie. "Anna Povlovna's Soiree." *War & Peace 2*. Berkeley: O Books, 2005.

Spahr, Juliana. "Paper for UCSC panel on Poetry and Crisis, April 2004." 17 Mar. 2005. <http://people.mills.edu/jspahr/crisis2.htm>.

Reprinted from "Tactic inside and out: Gregg Bordowitz on Critical Art Ensemble" by Gregg Bordowitz, by permission of *ArtForum* Sept. 2004. Vol. 43. Issue 1: 214. Copyright 2004 by *ArtForum*.

Kahn, Joseph. "May 5-11: Economy; Enron's Name Games." *The New York Times*. 12 May

2002. Section 4, Column 2: 2. ("FatBoy/Death/Star/Ricochet" are names found
    in Kahn's article.)

Epstein, Jack. "'Shock And Awe' Assault Pending: U.S. War Strategy Is To Intimidate Iraq
    into Surrender." *San Francisco Chronicle.* 21 Mar. 2003: W11.

Salladay, Robert. "Governor Prepares to Take Offensive In Pushing Agenda." *San Francisco
    Chronicle.* 2 Dec. 2003: A5.

Leslie Scalapino, April 16, 2005

Scalapino, Leslie. "The Forest is in the Euphrates River." *Day Ocean State of Stars' Night.
    Poems & Witings 1989 & 1999-2006.* Los Angeles: Green Integer Books, 2007.

---. from "Delay Rose." *EOAGH: Issue 2: In Remembrance of Jackson Mac Low.* Eds. Tim
    Peterson and John Mercuri Dooley. <http://www.chax.org/eoagh/issuetwo/
    scalapino.htm>.

Judith Goldman, August 1-4, 2005

Cheney, Dick. "Cheney's Views." Interview with Wolf Blitzer. *CNN.com.* 23 June 2005. 1
    Aug. 2005. <http://www.cnn.com/2005/US/06/23/cheney.interview/>.

Blair, Tony. "In Full: Blair on bomb blasts." *BBCNews.com.* 7 Jul. 2005. 1 Aug. 2005.
    <http://news.bbc.co.uk/1/hi/uk/4659953.stm>.

Nichols, John. "Enron: What Dick Cheney Knew." *The Nation.* 15 Apr. 2002. 21 April
    2005. <http://the nation.com/doc/20020415/nichols>.

Steiner, Konrad. Personal conversation with the author. July 2005.

O'Brien, Geoffrey G. Personal conversation with the author. July 2005.

Reprinted from "Without a Doubt" by Ron Suskind, by permission of *The New York Times.*
    17 Oct. 2004, Sunday. Section 6, Col. 1, Magazine Desk: 44. Copyright 2004 by
    The New York Times.

Esterhammer, Angela. *The Romantic Performative: Language and Action in British and
    German Romanticism.* Stanford: Standford University Press, 2001. 69.

Reprinted from "The Forest is in the Euphrates River" in *Day Ocean State of Stars' Night*
    by Leslie Scalapino, by permission of Green Integer Books. Copyright 2007 by
    Green Integer Books.

Brady, Taylor. E-mail to the author. 3-7 Mar. 2003.

Reprinted from *The Writing of the Disaster* by Maurice Blanchot, translated by Ann
    Smock, by permission of the University of Nebraska Press. Copyright 1986 by
    the University of Nebraska Press.

Nealon, Chris. "Camp Messianism, or, the Hopes of Poetry in Late-Late Capitalism."
    American Literature 76.3 (Sept. 2004): 579.

Goldman, Judith. "Prince Harry Considers Visiting Auschwitz." *DeathStar/rico-chet.*
    Berkeley: O Books, 2006.

Leslie Scalapino, August 12-15, 24, 2005

Reprinted "case senSitive" in *DeathStar / rico-chet* by Judith Goldman, by permission of O
Books. Copyright 2006 by O Books.

Scalapino, Leslie. "'Can't' is 'Night.'" *Day Ocean State of Stars' Night: Poems & Witings
1989 & 1999-2006*. Los Angeles: Green Integer, 2007.

Judith Goldman, March 25 -April 1, 2006

McGann, Jerome and Lisa Samuels. "Deformance and Interpretation." *New Literary History*
30.1 (1 Nov. 1999): 33.

Adorno, Theodor W. A*esthetic Theory*. Ed. and Trans. Robert Hullot-Kentor. Minneapolis:
University of Minnesota Press, 1998. 2, 3.

Der Derian, James. A*ntidiplomacy: Spies, Speed, Terror, and War*. Malden, MA: Blackwell
Publishing, Inc., 1992. <http://www.watsoninstitute.org/infopeace/vy2k/
derderian.cfm>.

"ACLU Sues Pentagon for Documents on Peace Groups." *ACLU Press Release*: 14 June
2006. ACLU. 25 Mar. 2006. <http://www.aclu.org/safefree/spyfiles/
25880prs20060614.html>.

Holland, Marge. "California National Guard investigated for domestic spying." *World
Socialist Web Site*. 27 Sept. 2005. 25 Mar. 2005. <http://www.wsws.org/
articles/2005/sep2005/cali-s27.shtml>.

Goldman, Judith. *Civilian Border Patrol*. Currently unpublished.

"Bush denies Iraq is in civil war." *BBCNews.com*. World News Summary. 21 Mar. 2006. 25
Mar. 2006.<http://news.bbc.co.uk/1/hi/world/4829786.stm>.

TRACI GOURDINE & QUINCY TROUPE

Traci Gourdine, January 15, 2005

Charles, Ray. *Famous Black Quotations and some not so famous*. Ed. Janet Cheatham Bell.
Chicago, IL: Sabayat Publications, 1986.

Harrison, Paul Carter. *Famous Black Quotations and some not so famous*. Ed. Janet
Cheatham Bell. Chicago, IL: Sabayat Publications, 1986.

Pleasure, King. "Moody's Mood for Love." *King Pleasure Sings / Annie Ross Sings*. Lyrics
Eddie Jefferson. Music James Moody. Prestige, 1952.

Davis, Miles. *Sketches of Spain*. Arr. Gil Evans. Colombia Records, 1960.

Quincy Troupe, February 23, 2005

Troupe, Quincy. T*he Pursuit of Happyness*. New York: Amistad, 2006.

---. "The Architecture of Language." *The Architecture of Language*. Minneapolis: Coffee
House Press, 2006. 83.

Morrison, Toni. Personal conversation with the author.

Quincy Troupe, August 24, 2005

Troupe, Quincy. "The Architecture of Language." *The Architecture of Language*. Minneapolis: Coffee House Press, 2006. 42.

---. *The Accordian Years*. This work is in progress and currently unpublished.

Troupe, Quincy, ed. *Black Renaissance/Renaissance Noire*. Bloomington: Indiana University Press, 2005.

Traci Gourdine, February 7, 2006

Emerson, Ralph Waldo. "The Poet." *Essays, Second Series*. 1844. Ralph Waldo Emerson Texts. 7 Feb. 2006. <http://www.emersoncentral.com/poet.htm>.

Quincy Troupe, April 26, 2006

Troupe, Quincy. *Miles and Me*. Berkeley: University of California Press, 2000.

---. *The Legacy of Charlie Footman*. This work is in progress and currently unpublished.

BRENDA IIJIMA & JOAN RETALLACK

Brenda Iijima, September 20, 2005

Retallack, Joan. "Essay as Wager." Introduction. *The Poethical Wager*. Berkeley: University of California Press, 2004. 19, 21-46.

---. *AFTERRIMAGES*. Middletown, CT: Wesleyan University Press, 1995.

---. *Mongrelisme*. Providence, RI: Paradigm Press, 1999. Unpaginated.

Winter Soldier. Dir. Fred Aronow, et. al. Milliarium Zero/Milestone Films, 1972.

Joan Retallack, October 17, 2005

Iijima, Brenda. From "Eco Quarry Bellwether." *Primary Writing* 37 (Oct. 2005).

---. "Eco Quarry Bellwether." *If Not Metamorphic*. Ahsahta Press, forthcoming.

Brenda Iijima, January 4, 2006

Mac Low, Jackson. *Doings: Assorted Performance Pieces 1955-2002*. New York: Granary Books, 2002.

Iijima, Brenda. *Remembering Animals*. Currently unpublished.

Brathwaite. Kamau. *Born to Slow Horses*. Middletown, CT: Wesleyan University Press, 2005.

---. *Middle Passages*. New York: New Directions, 1994.

Smith, Gerald S., ed. *Contemporary Russian Poetry: A Bilingual Anthology*. Bloomington: Indiana University Press, 1993. 270.

Howe, Susan. *My Emily Dickinson*. Berkeley: North Atlantic Books, 1985.

Joan Retallack, April 23, 2006

Mac Low, Jackson. *Doings: Assorted Performance Pieces 1955-2002*. New York: Granary Books, 2005. 59-63.

Iijima, Brenda. From "Eco Quarry Bellwether." *Primary Writing* 37 (Oct. 2005).

Bohr, Niels. T*he Philosophical Writings of Niels Bohr. Volume I: Atomic Theory and the Description of Nature.* Woodbridge, CT: Ox Bow Press, 1987. 102-19.

Retallack, Joan. *Memnoir*. Sausalito, CA: The Post-Apollo Press, 2004.

---. "The Reinvention of Truth." A poetic work-in-progress. Currently unpublished.

Brenda Iijima, June 20, 2006

Žižek, Slavoj. *Organs Without Bodies: On Deleuze and Consequences.* New York: Routledge, 2003. 35-36.

Reprinted from *A Theologico-political Treatise, and a Political Treatise* by Benedict de Spinoza, by permission of Dover Publications. Copyright 1951 by Dover publications. 387.

Reprinted from "Great African Queens" in *The Afrocentric Experience,* by permission of Everton Obi Elliott. Copyright 2000 by Everton Obi Elliott. <http://www.swagga.com/queen.htm>.

Reprinted from *Worldwide Guide to Women in Leadership*, by permission of Martin K.I. Christensen. Copyright 2001 by Martin K.I. Christensen. <http://www.guide2womenleaders.com/index.html>.

Wolf, Christa. T*he Author's Dimension: Selected Essays.* New York: The University of Chicago Press published by arrangement with Farrar, Straus & Giroux, 1993. 76.

Matossian, Mary Kilbourne. *Poisons of the Past: Molds, Epidemics, and History*. New Haven: Yale University Press, 1991.

Grosz, Elizabeth. T*ime Travels: Feminism, Nature, Power*. Durham, NC: Duke University Press, 2005. 47.

Flannery, Tim. T*he Weather Makers: How Man Is Changing the Climate and What It Means for Life on Earth*. New York: Atlantic Monthly Press, 2006.

Joan Retallack, December 10, 2006

Ortner, Sherry. "Is Female to Male as Nature is to Culture?" *Women, Culture, and Society*. Ed. Michelle Rosaldo and Louise Lamphere. Palo Alto, CA: Stanford University Press, 1974.

Newman, Cathy. "The Joy of Shoes." *National Geographic* Sept. 2006.

Cage, John. *Silence*. Middletown, CT: Wesleyan University Press, 1961. 67-75.

DANA TEEN LOMAX & CLAIRE BRAZ-VALENTINE

Dana Teen Lomax, December 22, 2004

Braz-Valentine, Claire. *This One Thing I Do*. New York: Samuel French, Inc. 1989.

---. "To Laura Bush." *The Web: A Global Anthology of Women's Political Poetry*. Ed.
    Jessica R. Newman. Boulder: Radical Poetry Collective, 2004. 96-97.

---. E-mail to the author. December, 2004.

Davis, Angela. "Masked Racism: Reflections on the Prison Industrial Complex." Fall,
    1998. *Color Lines*. 20 Dec. 2004. <http://www.colorlines.com/
    article.php?ID=114>.

Lomax, Dana Teen. *Currency*. Long Beach: Palm Press, 2006.

Crumpacker, Caroline. "Licked All Over by The English Tongue: An Interview with
    Harryette Mullen." *double change* #3. 22 Dec. 2004.
    <http://www.doublechange.com/issue3/mullensint-eng.htm>.

Desser, Chris. *Onthecommons.org* 20 Dec. 2004. <http://www.onthecommons.org/
    profile.php?id=1891>.

Dana Teen Lomax, May 1, 2005

Howe, Fanny. *The Wedding Dress*. Berkeley: University of California Press, 2003. 62.

Lomax, Dana Teen. "One." *Currency*. Long Beach: Palm Press, 2006. 1.

---. "One." 1 May 2005. <http://www.sonaweb.net/lomaxpoems.htm>.)

Claire Braz-Valentine, June 27, 2005

Braz-Valentine, Claire. "When Will I Dance." *The Best Stage Scenes of 1999*. Ed. Jocelyn A.
    Beard and Joanne Genadio. Lyme, NH: Smith & Kraus, 2001.

Holy Bible: New International Version. Grand Rapids, MI: Zondervan, 1996. Matthew 25:43.

Clifton, Lucille. "Miss Rosie." *No More Masks!* Ed. Florence Howe and Ellen Bass. New
    York: Anchor Books, 1973. 229.

Rilke, Rainer Maria. *Letters to a Young Poet*. Trans. Stephen Mitchell. New York: Vintage
    Books, 1986. 8-9.

Braz-Valentine, Claire. "Open Letter To John Ashcroft." *New Millenium Writings*. Ed. Don
    Williams. New Knoxville: Messenger Writing & Publishing, 2003. 164-166.

Somers, Janet. "Art from the Inside: San Quentin classes in painting and other arts give
    inmates a new perspective and a view of life beyond bars." 17 June 2005. *San
    Francisco Chronicle*. 27 June 2005. <http://www.sfgate.com/cgi-bin/
    article.cgi?f=/c/a/2005/06/17/NBGK6D82TU1.DTL>.

Dana Teen Lomax, October 16, 2005

O'Connor, Flannery. *A Good Man is Hard to Find and Other Stories*. Fort Washington, PA:
    Harvest Books, 1955.

Claire Braz-Valentine, December 15, 2005

Claire Braz-Valentine. *This One Thing I Do*. New York: Samuel French, Inc., 1989.

---. *This One Thing I Do*. *Competition Monologues II: 49 Contemporary Speeches for Young Actors from the Best Professionally Produced American Plays*. Ed. Roger Ellis. Lanham. MD: University Press of America, 1989. 30-31.

Masefield, John. "Sea-Fever." *Salt-Water Poems and Ballads*. New York: Macmillan Publishing Company, 1916. 55.

ALBERT FLYNN DESILVER & PAUL HOOVER

Albert Flynn DeSilver, November 28, 2004

Berrigan, Anselm. "Berrigan and Durand Interview Each Other." *Readme*. Summer 2000. 28 Nov. 2004. <http://home.jps.net/~nada/berrigan.htm>.

Nisargadatta, Sri. *I Am That: Talks with Sri Nisargadatta*. Ed. and Trans. Maurice Frydman. Bombay: Chetana Publishing, 1973.

DeSilver, Albert Flynn. *Letters To Early Street*. Albuquerque: La Alameda Press, 2007.

Albert Flynn DeSilver, December 2, 2004

Ackerman, Diane. A*n Alchemy of Mind: The Marvel and Mystery of the Brain*. New York: Scribner, 2004.

Serra, Richard. T*orqued Ellipses* sculptures at Dia Beacon, NY.

Paul Hoover, December 18, 2004

Welish, Marjorie. *Handwritten*. New York: Sun Press, 1979.

DeSilver, Albert Flynn. A *Pond*. Woodacre, CA: Owl Press, 2001. Used by permission of the author.

Ginsberg, Allen "To Aunt Rose." *Collected Poems: 1947-1980*. New York: Harper & Row, 1984. 184.

Crane, Hart. "My Grandmother's Love Letters." *Complete Poems of Hart Crane*. Ed. Marc Simon. New York: W.W. Norton & Co., 2001.

Paul Hoover, December 20, 2004

Williams, William Carlos. *Selected Essays of William Carlos Williams*. New York: New Directions, 1969. 256.

Vee, Bobby. "The Night Has a Thousand Eyes." Written by Benjamin Weisman, Dorothy Wayne, and Marilynn Garrett. Liberty Records, 1963.

Baurdillon, Francis William. "The Night Has a Thousand Eyes." *A Victorian Anthology, 1837-1895*, Ed. Edmund Clarence Stedman. New York: Houghton, Mifflin & Co., 1895.

Hoover, Paul. *Edge and Fold*. Berkeley: Apogee Press, 2006.

---. *At the Sound*. Chicago: Beard of Bees Press, 2007.

---. *Poems In Spanish*. Richmond, CA: Omnidawn, 2005.

Hoover, Paul and Nguyen Do, eds. *Black Dog, Black Night: Contemporary Vietnamese Poetry*. Minneapolis: Milkweed Editions, 2008.

Hoover, Paul and Maxine Chernoff, eds. and trans. *Selected Poems of Friedrich Hölderlin*. Richmond, CA: Omnidawn, 2008.

Gontard, Susette. *The Recalcitrant Art: Diotima's Letters to Hölderlin and Related Missives*. Ed. and Trans. Douglas F. Kenney and Sabine Menner-Bettscheid. Albany: State University of New York Press, 2000: Letter XV, 176.

Hoover, Paul. *Fables of Representation*. Ann Arbor: University of Michigan Press, 2004.

Albert Flynn DeSilver, December 22, 2004-February 8, 2005

U.S. Department of Labor. *Dictionary of Occupational Titles*. Indianapolis: JIST Works, 2002.

Terkle, Studs. *Working: People Talk About What They Do All Day and How They Feel About What They Do*. New York: The New Press, 1997.

Goswami, Amit. *The Self Aware Universe*. New York: Tarcher/Penguin, 1993.

What the Bleep Do We Know!? Dir. William Arntz. Perf. Marlee Matlin and Barry Newman. Lord of the Wind, 2004.

Bang, Mary Jo. *Louise in Love*. New York: Grove Press, 2001.

Paul Hoover, February 26, 2005

Duncan, Robert. "Poetry: A Natural Thing." *The Opening of The Field*. New York: New Directions, 1960. 50.

Mallarmé Stéphane. "Crisis in Poetry." *Mallarmé: Selected Prose Poems, Essays, & Letters*. Trans. Bradford Cook. Baltimore: The Johns Hopkins Press, 1956. 41.

Perloff, Marjorie. *The Poetics of Indeterminacy: Rimbaud to Cage*. Princeton: Princeton University Press, 1981.

Stevens, Wallace. "The Snow Man." *Wallace Stevens: The Collected Poems*. New York: Vintage Books, 1982. 9.

Moonstruck. Dir. Norman Jewison. Perf. Cher and Nicolas Cage. MGM, 1987.

Albert Flynn DeSilver, October 6, 2005

Flynn DeSilver, Albert. "Armhole Feller." *ISM Quarterly*. 6 Oct. 2005. <http://www.ismcommunity.org/magazine>.

Rilke, Rainer Maria. "Archaic Torso of Apollo." *The Selected Poetry of Rainer Maria Rilke*. Trans. Stephen Mitchell. New York: Vintage, 1980.

Dogen, Eihei. *Moon in a Dew Drop: Writings of Zen Master Dogen*. Ed. Kazuaki Tanahashi. San Francisco: North Point Press, 1985.

Casey, Caroline. <http://www.visionaryactivism.com>.

DeMent, Iris. "Let The Mystery Be." *Infamous Angel*. Rounder Records, 1993.

Paul Hoover, November 1, 2005

Barry, John M. "After the Deluge." *Smithsonian Magazine* Nov. 2005: 115-121.

Ramazani, Jahan, Richard Ellmann, and Robert O'Clair, eds. *The Norton Anthology of Modern and Contemporary Poetry*, 3rd Edition. New York: W.W. Norton & Company, Inc., 1994.

Hoover, Paul, ed. *Postmodern American Poetry: A Norton Anthology*. New York: W.W. Norton & Company, Inc., 1994.

"Perfect Rest." *Preposition 13*, quoted in David Wray's "'cool rare air': Zukofsky's Breathing with Catullus and Plautus." *Chicago Review* 50: 2/3/4 (Winter 2004/05).

Zukofsky, Louis. "A"-6. *"A."* Berkeley: University of California Press, 1978. 24, 27.

Williams, William Carlos. "The Poem." *Williams Carlos Williams: Selected Poems*. Ed. Charles Tomlinson. New York: New Directions, 1985. 151.

Pound, Ezra. A *BC of Reading*. New York: New Directions, 1934. 36.

Niedecker, Lorine. "Poet's Work." *The Granite Pail: The Selected Poems of Lorine Niedecker*. Ed. Cid Corman. Berekely: North Point Press, 1985. 54, 59.

Eckhart, Meister. *Meister Eckhart: Selected Writings*. New York: Penguin Books, 1994. 233.

Stevens, Wallace. *Wallace Stevens: The Collected Poems*. New York: Vintage Books, 1982. 92.

Also Available from **saturnalia books**:

Days of Unwilling
poetry by Cal Bedient

Famous Last Words by Catherine Pierce
Winner of the Saturnalia Books Poetry Prize 2007

Dummy Fire by Sarah Vap
Winner of the Saturnalia Books Poetry Prize 2006

Correspondence by Kathleen Graber
Winner of the Saturnalia Books Poetry Prize 2005

The Babies by Sabrina Orah Mark
Winner of the Saturnalia Books Poetry Prize 2004

Midnights
Poems by Jane Miller / Artwork by Beverly Pepper
Artist/Poet Collaboration Series Number Four

Stigmata Errata Etcetera
Poems by Bill Knott / Artwork by Star Black
Artist/Poet Collaboration Series Number Three

Ing Grish
Poems by John Yau / Artwork by Thomas Nozkowski
Artist/Poet Collaboration Series Number Two

Blackboards
Poems by Tomaž Šalamun / Artwork by Metka Krašovec
Artist/Poet Collaboration Series Number One

Letters to Poets was printed using the fonts Perpetua and Charlotte Sans.

www.saturnaliabooks.com
distributed by University Press of New England